Rigid Designation and Theoretical Identities

Rigid Designation and Theoretical Identities

Joseph LaPorte

UNIVERSITY PRESS

Great Clarendon Street, Oxford, OX2 6DP
United Kingdom

Oxford University Press is a department of the University of Oxford.
It furthers the University's objective of excellence in research, scholarship,
and education by publishing worldwide. Oxford is a registered trade mark of
Oxford University press in the UK and in certain other countries

© Joseph LaPorte 2013

The moral rights of the author have been asserted

First published in 2013

Impression: 1

All rights reserved. No part of this publication may be reproduced,
stored in a retrieval system, or transmitted, in any form or by any means,
without the prior permission in writing of Oxford University Press,
or as expressly permitted by law, or under terms agreed with the appropriate
reprographics rights organization. Enquiries concerning reproduction
outside the scope of the above should be sent to the Rights Department,
Oxford University Press, at the address above

You must not circulate this work in any other form
and you must impose this same condition on any acquirer

British Library Cataloguing in Publication Data
Data available

Library of Congress Cataloging in Publication Data
Data available

ISBN 978–0–19–960920–8

Printed in Great Britain by
MPG Books Group, Bodmin and King's Lynn

Links to third party websites are provided by Oxford in good faith and
for information only. Oxford disclaims any responsibility for the materials
contained in any third party website referenced in this work.

*for my parents, who first did philosophy with me
and who shared with me their appreciation of it*

Preface

I am grateful for help to many philosophers, some of whose personal communication I mention at various points in the book. A few philosophers whose correspondence I much value but do not later mention, or mention while leaving even more than the usual too much unsaid, are Bruce Aune, Alexander Bird, Michael Devitt, Bernard Linsky, Dan López de Sa, Chris Menzel, David Oderberg, Steve Schwartz, Kyle Stanford, Jason Stanley, and Arthur Sullivan. In some cases, considerable time has passed. Also, I am very grateful for anonymous comments from two referees for OUP. My debt to and respect for various workers in the discipline should be apparent from the sources I cite, whether I cite them in agreement or in order to frame a contrasting position.

Work on this book was generously supported by a grant from the National Endowment for the Humanities. Hope College provided time off from teaching and also further assistance, including help with the bibliography and proofreading. Worthy of special mention are Mike Bertrand, Rachel Brisbin, and Maggie Rohweder. Mike provided especially valuable assistance when time was at a premium. He also helped me gather literature and was a trusted resource for discussion of it.

Hope College helped not least of all by providing a good working atmosphere over the years. For this, I am especially grateful to my five colleagues in this congenial department.

My family has given much support. I enjoyed discussing a lot of the relevant science with my brother-in-law Chamindra, from whom I learned a lot. My brother Charles provided encouragement and assistance at many points, on the book and much else. His help and discernment, as well as that of his spouse Colette, is deeply appreciated. Carmelita's loving support was, as always, indispensable. My children too did much to accommodate.

Some of the material here is borrowed from published articles. Chapter 1 contains overlap with my entry "Rigid Designators," in the *Stanford Encyclopedia of Philosophy*, first published in 2006. Chapters 2 and 3 contain overlap with both (2006) "Rigid Designators for Properties," *Philosophical Studies* 130, pp. 321-36, © Springer 2006 and (2000) "Rigidity and Kind," *Philosophical Studies*, 97: 293-316, © 2000 Kluwer Academic Publishers.

Table of Contents

1. Rigid Designators for Concrete Objects and for Properties — 1
2. On the Coherence of the Distinction — 22
3. On Whether the Distinction Assigns to Rigidity the Right Role — 42
4. A Uniform Treatment of Property Designators as Singular Terms — 64
5. Rigid Appliers — 89
6. Rigidity – Associated Arguments in Support of Theoretical Identity Statements: on their Significance and the Cost of their Philosophical Resources — 124
7. The Skeptical Argument Impugning Psychophysical Identity Statements: on its Significance and the Cost of its Philosophical Resources — 148
8. The Skeptical Argument Further Examined: on Resources, Allegedly Overlooked, for Confirming Psychophysical Identities — 176

Detailed Table of Contents

1. Rigid Designators for Concrete Objects and for Properties	1
1. A Basic Characterization of Rigid Designators and Their Interest	2
1.1. Names, Ordinary Descriptions, and Identity Statements	2
1.2. Standard Clarifications from Kripke	3
1.3. Clarifications on Rigidity's Relationship to the Necessary A Posteriori	4
2. On the Significance of Rigidity for Identity Statements about Properties	7
2.1. Identity Statements with Just Names for Properties	8
2.2. Theoretical Identity Statements About Properties	9
3. Complications and Elaboration	11
3.1. What Stays the Same in the Rigid Designation of Properties?	11
3.2. The Agenda of Chapters to Come	13
2. On the Coherence of the Distinction	22
1. The Problem of Artificial-Property Designators	22
2. The Problem of Shadowing	25
2.1. A Parallel for Concrete-Object Designators	27
2.2. Responses to the Problem	28
2.2.1. Without Shadowing Candidates	29
2.2.2. The Irrelevance of Shadowing Candidates	32
2.2.2.1. Beyond *Shadowing*: a General Problem with a General Remedy	32
2.2.2.2. Context at Work to Relieve the Shadowing Problem	34
2.2.2.2.1. Context at Work for Shadow-Attended Property Designators	34
2.2.2.2.2. Context at Work for Shadow-Attended Concrete-Object Designators	35
3. A Confusion Between Rigidity and Meaning Constancy?	36
4. Conclusion	37
3. On Whether the Distinction Assigns to Rigidity the Right Role	42
1. Rigidity's Duty of Securing the Necessity that Characterizes Identity Statements Featuring Rigid Designators	42
2. Other Duties Attributed to Rigidity	46
2.1. Work Securing Essential-Property Attributions	46
2.2. Work Securing Externalism	49

2.3. Work Securing Aposteriority	51
2.4. Work Refuting Descriptivism	51
2.4.1. Are 'Bachelor' and 'Soda' Descriptive?	53
2.4.2. Why Refuting Descriptivism is Not What is Most Important About Rigidity	55
2.5. Work Securing Linguistic Stability	57
3. Conclusion	57
4. A Uniform Treatment of Property Designators as Singular Terms	**64**
1. Descriptions as Singular Terms	65
2. Avoiding Millian Dualism	68
2.1. Accommodating English Grammar: Uniform vs. Nonuniform Accounts	69
2.2. Patterns of Reasoning Formalized: Uniform vs. Nonuniform Accounts	71
2.2.1. A Millian Treatment of the Rigid – Nonrigid Distinction for Singular Property Designators	72
2.2.2. Uniformly Singular Treatments of the Rigid – Nonrigid Distinction for Property Designators	74
2.2.2.1. A Basic Second-Order Treatment	74
2.2.2.2. A Basic First-Order Treatment	75
2.2.2.3. Beyond Adjectives	76
2.2.2.4. Comparing the Treatments	77
2.2.2.4.1. Faithfully Representing the Copula	78
2.2.2.4.2. Theoretical Issues in the Background	79
3. Conclusion	81
5. Rigid Appliers	**89**
1. Rigidity for Mere Appliers	90
1.1. A Basic Account: Rigid and Nonrigid Designators for Predicables	91
1.1.1. The Account	91
1.1.2. The Lessons of Rigidity	92
1.1.2.1. How Necessity Follows from Rigidity with Designation Multiplied	92
1.1.2.2. Predicative Arguments Concerning A Posteriori Necessity, Essence, and Mind	95
1.1.2.3. Generalizing: How to Reformulate with Predicates Arguments with Singular Terms for Properties	97
1.1.2.4. Predicative Versions of the Familiar Arguments Appealing to the Rigidity of Concrete-Object Designators	98

	1.1.3. Objections	100
	1.1.3.1. Rigidity Performs the Modal Duties to Which I have Assigned it	100
	1.1.3.2. News of the Rigidity of Nonsingular Property Designators is Appropriately Surprising and Important	103
	1.2. Nominalist-Friendly Variations of the Basic Account	106
	1.2.1. "Properties" in Semantic Work	107
	1.2.2. Rigidity for Radical Nominalism	108
2.	A Rival Account	110
	2.1. Essential Application as Rigidity	111
	2.2. Essential Application as a Component of Rigidity	112
	2.3. Essential Application and Anti-Descriptivism	114
3.	Conclusion	116

6. Rigidity-Associated Arguments in Support of Theoretical Identity Statements: on their Significance and the Cost of their Philosophical Resources — 124

1.	Significance	125
	1.1. Are Theoretical Identity Statements Uninformative?	126
	1.2. Is What is Designated What Matters, Not Designation?	127
	1.3. Do Mechanisms that Secure Rigidity Draw from Rigidity's Significance?	128
2.	Costs	131
	2.1. Rigidity Without Cost and Controversy	131
	2.1.1. On the Rigidity of Name-Like Subject Terms	131
	2.1.2. On the Rigidity of Theoretical Expressions	132
	2.1.2.1. Doubts	132
	2.1.2.2. Facile Defenses of Rigidity to be Avoided	134
	2.1.2.2.1. Support from Essentialism	134
	2.1.2.2.2. Support from Stipulations that Come Too Easily	134
	2.1.2.3. A Defense of De Facto Rigidity	137
	2.1.2.4. A Defense of De Jure Rigidity	139
	2.2. Theoretical Identity Statements Without Hidden Essentialist Costs	141
3.	Conclusion	143

7. The Skeptical Argument Impugning Psychophysical Identity Statements: on its Significance and the Cost of its Philosophical Resources — 148

1.	Significance	148
	1.1. Against Specific Psychophysical Identities, Not Materialism	148

xii DETAILED TABLE OF CONTENTS

   1.1.1. Why Not Conclude that No Psychophysical Identity Statement is True?   149
   1.1.2. Psychophysical Identities: Is What Eludes us Just Conceptual or Explanatory?   152
  1.2. Is Type Identity Irrelevant?   154
   1.2.1. Type Identity Obtains if Multiple Realizability Does   155
   1.2.2. Why Type Identity Matters and Why Supervenience or Token Identity is No Substitute   157
   1.2.3. How to Redirect the Skeptical Argument to Address Supervenience and Token Identity Instead of Type Identity   161
 2. Costs   163
  2.1. The Privilege of an Insider's Perspective: a Cost Too High for Eliminative Materialists   164
  2.2. Two-Dimensionalism: No Commitment, No Cost   170
  2.3. Modal Rationalism and Apriority: No Commitment, No Cost   171
 3. Conclusion   173
8. The Skeptical Argument Further Examined: on Resources, Allegedly Overlooked, for Confirming Psychophysical Identities   176
 1. Psychophysical Identity Statements' Support is Undermined by Missing De Jure Connections to Physically Described Matter   177
 2. Why Not Dispense with De Jure Connections in Favor of Correlation and Scientific Induction?   179
  2.1. Why De Jure Connections Must Attend Correlation and Scientific Induction   180
   2.1.1. Problematic Theoretical Identity Statements and Correlation   181
   2.1.2. Problematic Theoretical Identity Statements and Broad Inductive Principles Testifying to Identity   186
  2.2. Are De Jure Connections Controversial?   190
   2.2.1. The Recognitional Theory of Reference   190
   2.2.2. The Theory of Direct Reference   192
 3. De Jure Connections Supplied by way of Scientific Necessitarianism?   193
  3.1. From Subject Terms to Properties to Law-Governed Behavior: the Missing De Jure Link?   196
  3.2. From Subject Terms to Constitution to Law-Governed Behavior: the Missing De Jure Link?   198
  3.3. From Subject Terms to Constitution to *Fundamental*-Law Governed Behavior   200
  3.4. From Fundamental Laws to Fatalism to Identity   204

3.5.	Dissolving the Problem with Scientific Development	207
	3.5.1. A New Sort of Theory	207
	3.5.2. Familiar Work on Familiar Sorts of Theories	208
3.6.	Where We Are Left: Scientific Empiricism	211
4. Concluding Remarks		213

References	219
Index	237

1

Rigid Designators for Concrete Objects and for Properties

Some terms for concrete objects, such as 'Hesperus' and 'Phosphorus', are rigid. The rigidity of these terms is important, because it helps to determine whether certain statements containing the terms, including identity statements like 'Hesperus = Phosphorus', are necessary or contingent.

The foregoing observations command broad agreement. They are, as one author suggests, "as close to uncontroversial as any interesting views in analytic philosophy" (Hughes 2004, p. vii).[1] There has been much *less* agreement about whether and how designators for *properties* are rigid: here I include (perhaps generously: see §2 below) terms like 'white', 'brontosaur', 'beautiful', 'c-fiber firings', 'hot', 'heat', 'molecular motion', 'H_2O', 'pain', 'courage', and so on.

In this book, I articulate and defend the position that terms for properties *are* rigid designators. Furthermore, I argue that property designators' rigidity is put to good use in important philosophical arguments supporting and impugning certain theoretical identity statements. The book as a whole constitutes a broad defense of a tradition or set of traditions originating largely in seminal work from Saul Kripke (see note 1), which has generated a wealth of thoughtful work from savvy detractors whose objections and challenges indicate where development and clarification is needed, as well as from sympathizers who have put forward important contributions toward the needed development and clarification.

In the present chapter, I introduce briefly the general topic of this book and lay out its basic plan. In section (1), I characterize the rigid – nonrigid distinction in its full generality, with no special regard to the specific case of property designators: I clarify the basic modal and epistemological interest of the distinction. In section (2), I offer an account of the rigid – nonrigid distinction for property designators specifically, and I discuss interesting work performed by rigidity in property designators. In section (3), I introduce various complications and objections. It is in the course of addressing these complications and objections, in chapters to come, that I will support and enrich my favored account of the rigidity of property designators. I end the present chapter with a chapter-by-chapter agenda for the rest of the book.

1. A Basic Characterization of Rigid Designators and Their Interest

My overview of rigidity proceeds as follows. In section (1.1), I offer a now-standard characterization of the rigid – nonrigid distinction in its full generality and the basic interest of the distinction. In section (1.2), I rehearse clarifications from Kripke. In section (1.3), I offer an important clarification that is less familiar than those clarifications, standard as they are, from section (1.2).

1.1. Names, Ordinary Descriptions, and Identity Statements

A rigid designator designates an object with respect to every possible world in which that object exists and never designates anything else instead. Kripke, who coined the word 'rigid designator', is not the first philosopher to discuss the idea behind the term he coined, but his illuminating discussions have made the importance of rigidity widely appreciated. Kripke argues famously that an identity statement must be necessarily true, even if the statement is not a priori, provided that the identity sign is flanked by two rigid designators for the same object: the classic example is 'Hesperus = Phosphorus' (see, e.g., Kripke 1971, p. 154; 1980, p. 102). 'Hesperus = Phosphorus' was discovered a posteriori to be true. 'Hesperus' is a name that was given to a heavenly body seen in the evening, and 'Phosphorus' is a name that was, unknown to the first users of the name, given to that same heavenly body seen in the morning. The heavenly body is Venus.

One might initially suppose that since the statement 'Hesperus = Phosphorus' was only discovered empirically to be true, it must be contingently true. But, says Kripke, it is necessarily true. The only respect in which it might have turned out false is not metaphysical but epistemic: thus, for all that speakers knew at one time, 'Hesperus = Phosphorus' could have failed to be true, just as for all that speakers knew at one time, 'the circle cannot be squared' could have failed to be true. But 'the circle cannot be squared' is, as it turns out, true with respect to all metaphysically possible worlds. Just so, 'Hesperus = Phosphorus' is true with respect to all metaphysically possible worlds: it is necessarily true. It is necessarily true because the proper names 'Hesperus' and 'Phosphorus' designate the same object and they designate it rigidly: each proper name designates the object that it *actually* designates with respect to all possible worlds in which that object exists and neither designates anything else instead of that object with respect to any possible world. The object that 'Hesperus' and 'Phosphorus' name with respect to all possible worlds is Venus. Since 'Hesperus' and 'Phosphorus' both name Venus with respect to all possible worlds, and since Venus = Venus in all possible worlds, 'Hesperus = Phosphorus' is true with respect to all possible worlds.

A description like 'the brightest non-lunar object in the evening sky', on the other hand, is *not* rigid. That explains why the identity statement

H. Hesperus = the brightest non-lunar object in the evening sky is true but not *necessarily* true. While Hesperus is in fact the brightest object in the evening sky apart from the moon, Hesperus might have been dimmer: had, say, Hesperus been obscured by cosmic dust, Mars might have been the object designated by 'the brightest non-lunar object in the evening sky' rather than Hesperus. In that case, the above identity statement (H) would have been false. So the reason that (H) could have been false is that 'the brightest non-lunar object in the evening sky' does not designate Hesperus rigidly. It designates Hesperus with respect to this world, which explains why (H) is true, but this description designates Mars with respect to some other worlds, which explains why (H) could have been false: (H) would have been false had some other such world been actual.

1.2. Standard Clarifications from Kripke

Some potential misunderstandings are well known.

First, a rigid designator designates the same object with respect to all possible worlds as it is used in the *actual world*, not as it is used in other possible worlds in which the object gets picked out: for although we identify objects in other worlds by our own names, natives of some of these worlds use other names (Kripke 1980, p. 77; for discussion, see Fitch 2004, pp. 103–4).

Second, although the statement (H) is not necessarily true, it is nevertheless Kripke's view and the standard view that the object that is in fact the brightest in the evening sky, Venus (Hesperus), *is* necessarily identical to Hesperus.

Third and finally, 'Hesperus' is rigid because it picks out Hesperus in all worlds that *contain* Hesperus and because the designator fails to pick out anything *other* than Hesperus in worlds that *fail* to contain Hesperus. There is more than one refined account of a rigid designator that conforms to that requirement. On one such refined account, a rigid designator designates its designatum in every possible world containing the designatum and in other possible worlds the designator *fails* to designate. In places, Kripke suggests that this is his idea:

when I use the notion of a rigid designator, I do not imply that the object referred to necessarily exists. All I mean is that in any possible world where the object in question *does* exist, in any situation where the object *would* exist, we use the designator in question to designate that object. In a situation where the object does not exist, then we should say that the designator has no referent and that the object in question so designated does not exist (Kripke 1971, p. 146; a disclaimer is reported in Kaplan 1989b, p. 570, note 8).

In other places, Kripke seems to have in mind another account of rigidity: one according to which a rigid designator designates its object in *every* possible world, *whether or not* the designatum exists in that world. Hence, he says, "If you say, 'suppose Hitler had never been born' then 'Hitler' refers here, still rigidly, to something that would not exist in the counterfactual situation described" (Kripke 1980, p. 78).

The foregoing quotation hints that in order for a statement containing a proper name to express, of the referent, that it *might not have existed*, the name must refer to the relevant object in all possible worlds, period. That might provide a substantive reason for saying that names are marked by the stronger type of rigidity, which Salmon has dubbed *obstinate rigidity* (1981, p. 34). On the other hand, it may be that no substantive issues ride on which conception of rigidity is acknowledged (Stanley 1997a, pp. 557, 566ff.; see also Brock 2004, p. 285, note 13). Kripke himself never *argues* on the foregoing grounds that names are obstinately rigid (though others have: see, e.g., Besson 2009, p. 10; Plantinga 1985, p. 84; particularities of Plantinga's characteristically interesting account are discussed in Menzel 2008, §5.1). Despite occasional slips, in which Kripke slides into an endorsement of one or another refined version of rigidity, he deliberately sidesteps these "delicate issues" when he gives them his full attention (1980, p. 21, note 21). Nor will there be a need to sort out these matters in this book. It is enough to recognize that the designators that I will be discussing are rigid in the noncommittal respect that the designators pick out the same designatum with respect to all possible worlds containing that designatum and the designators never pick out anything else instead.[2]

There are stronger and weaker brands of necessity that correspond more or less closely (see note 2) to the possible notions of rigidity. Kripke argues that a sentence like 'Hesperus = Phosphorus' is at least "weakly" necessary (1971, p. 137), which would require that the statement be true with respect to all those possible worlds with respect to which Venus exists, but which would not require that the statement be true with respect to possible worlds lacking Venus. The statement may enjoy a stronger necessity, too, which would render it true with respect to all worlds, period. In this work, when I say "necessity," I commit to nothing more than weak necessity.

1.3. Clarifications on Rigidity's Relationship to the Necessary A Posteriori

As I have indicated (in §1.1), rigid designation seems to play a crucial role in securing necessity with surprising epistemological significance. Since empirical work on the part of astronomers was required to determine that 'Hesperus = Phosphorus' is true, that statement seems to be a posteriori. Yet the statement is necessarily true, since both 'Hesperus' and 'Phosphorus' rigidly designate the same object. So we seem to have an illustration of necessary, a posteriori truth.

That it secures the necessary a posteriori is a major reason for much excitement over rigidity (see also Schwartz 2002 pp. 270ff.): for generations before the work of rigidity was appreciated, all necessity was generally thought to be a priori. The received tradition ran together the notions *necessary*, *a priori*, and some other notions like *analytic*: "usually they're not distinguished," as Kripke reported (1971, p. 149). Rigid designation indicates that necessity and apriority have to be distinguished: again, the reason is because the rigidity of designators like 'Hesperus' and 'Phosphorus' secures the necessary truth of 'Hesperus = Phosphorus', even though we do not know a priori that 'Hesperus = Phosphorus' is true.

One reason that many philosophers did not see the prospect of a posteriori necessity as they considered statements like 'Hesperus = Phosphorus' seems to be that they were under the influence of a tradition, associated chiefly with Russell and Frege, according to which names like 'Hesperus' and 'Phosphorus' are "abbreviated descriptions," as Russell (1919, p. 179) would put it, for descriptions that we see, in hindsight, to be rather unsophisticated: this tradition would take 'Hesperus' to be shorthand for a definite description like 'the brightest non-lunar object in the evening sky'.[3] If 'Hesperus' really *were* shorthand for a nonrigid description like 'the brightest non-lunar object in the evening sky', then 'Hesperus = Phosphorus' would *not* be necessarily true since, as I have indicated, 'the brightest non-lunar object in the evening sky = Phosphorus' is only *contingently* true: Phosphorus could have been dimmer. Accordingly, philosophers did not see 'Hesperus = Phosphorus' as an example of the necessary a posteriori: similar words apply to other examples they considered.

But Kripke convinced the philosophical community that 'Hesperus' and 'Phosphorus' are both rigid designators for Venus, rather than shorthand for descriptions like 'the brightest non-lunar object in the evening sky': accordingly, 'Hesperus = Phosphorus' is necessarily true, not contingently true. Since it took empirical investigation to determine that 'Hesperus = Phosphorus' is true and necessarily so, philosophers came to acknowledge the necessary a posteriori: hence, rigidity was seen to have "startling consequences for the theory of necessary truth," as Putnam observes (1975, p. 232).

But although much of the excitement about rigidity centers around its securing of the necessary a posteriori, developments in the philosophy of language since Kripke's work have complicated a proper evaluation of this evident coup. The theory of direct reference (named by Kaplan 1989a; see 1989b, p. 571), in particular, has complicated matters. According to that theory, the semantic content of a name like 'Hesperus' or 'Phosphorus' is nothing more than the referent Venus, which is the *same* for 'Hesperus' and 'Phosphorus'. 'Hesperus' and 'Phosphorus' express no descriptive information, like *appears in the evening* or *appears in the morning*, that might cause the content of one name to differ from the content of the other. Accordingly, if the theory of direct reference is correct, then to say *that Hesperus = Phosphorus* is to say no more and no less than to say *that Hesperus = Hesperus*. Since it is a priori that Hesperus = Hesperus, it is a priori that Hesperus = Phosphorus. For this reason, the theory of direct reference might give us grounds to dispute the claim that rigidity is associated with propositions that are necessarily true and a posteriori (Soames 2002, pp. 240, 243; 2003 pp. 444–5; Salmon 1986, pp. 133–42; Fitch 1976; for further discussion, see Fitch 2004, pp. 110–13; Hughes 2004, pp. 84–108).[4]

For purposes in this book, neutrality with respect to the theory of direct reference is desirable. Accordingly, I will not take any stand on whether the proposition *that Hesperus = Phosphorus* is a priori, as direct reference theorists claim, or whether it is a posteriori: here I follow Kripke's lead.[5] But while I will make no commitments with regard to whether the *proposition* that Hesperus = Phosphorus is a posteriori, I will maintain that the *sentence* or *statement* (interpreted sentence) 'Hesperus = Phosphorus' is necessarily true and a posteriori in an interesting way that lends substance to rigidity's claim to secure the necessary a posteriori (for similar claims, see Fitch 2004, pp. 110–13; Hughes 2004, pp. 106–7; cf. Kripke 1980, pp. 20–1). When I say that the *statement* 'Hesperus = Phosphorus' is a posteriori, though necessary, I mean to be understood to say something like this: a competent speaker of the language who can take for granted that she understands and can competently use the sentence 'Hesperus = Phosphorus' is nevertheless not in a position to know a priori whether the sentence, on its present interpretation, is true. It takes a posteriori investigation, astronomical investigation in this case, to determine that.

To say that the *statement* 'Hesperus = Phosphorus' is a posteriori, as I do, is consistent with the theory of direct reference. A direct reference theorist can concede that the relevant speaker is not in a position to know a priori whether 'Hesperus = Phosphorus', on its present interpretation, is true because a direct reference theorist can say that this speaker would need astronomical investigation to determine that the *sentence* 'Hesperus = Phosphorus' expresses the *proposition* that Hesperus = Phosphorus, which *proposition* is known a priori to be true.

By attending to the necessity of statements like 'Hesperus = Phosphorus' in the foregoing manner, then, rather than to the necessity of propositions like the proposition that Hesperus = Phosphorus, we can honor the claim that rigidity secures the necessary aposteriority of 'Hesperus = Phosphorus' and the like without committing ourselves against the theory of direct reference. So far so good. Even so, the reader might wonder whether the claim that *statements* like 'Hesperus = Phosphorus' are necessary and a posteriori, which claim happily escapes controversy about the theory of direct reference, is still a startling claim about a posteriori necessity with appropriate significance. It is. Thus, theorists under the influence of the so-called "Frege – Russell" tradition, according to which a name like 'Hesperus' is shorthand for a nonrigid description like 'the brightest non-lunar object in the evening sky', could not have anticipated the a posteriori necessity of statements like 'Hesperus = Phosphorus'. That is because, as I have indicated, 'Hesperus = Phosphorus' would be *contingently* true if 'Hesperus' were shorthand for such a description. So we can understand how it could have "seemed a platitude" to our forbears that 'Hesperus = Phosphorus' and similar statements of identity are contingent (Noonan 2008, §7; see also Gibbard 1975, pp. 187–8). But of course, if 'Hesperus' and 'Phosphorus' are rigid designators, then although perfectly competent speakers were unable to see, without astronomical observation, that the statement 'Hesperus = Phosphorus' is true, that statement is necessary, contrary to what seemed a platitude. The necessary aposteriority of various statements is appropriately *surprising*, then.[6]

More importantly, significant philosophical claims *depend* on the necessary aposteriority of statements. These would include various well-known claims about essence. So suppose that the essence of a physical object like a planet has to do with origins (cf. Kripke 1980, pp. 112–14). We might accordingly coin 'O' for certain token processes that include gravity's work at pulling together into a single body a massive cluster of dust and other matter that swirls around a center point in space, and gravity's work shaping the product gradually into a sphere. If we can accurately make essence-ascribing claims like, "concerning the item that is Hesperus: what it is to be *that item* is to be the planet with origin O," then we can affirm a statement that is necessary and a posteriori. We have to find out a posteriori whether the essence-ascribing statement is true or false, by learning whether the planets are indeed generated in the way that astronomers think that they are generated, by processes like O: so if there were something incoherent or wrong-headed about the necessary a posteriority of statements, then the incoherence or wrong-headedness would apparently have to spoil, in turn, essence ascriptions like the foregoing one, which is necessary and a posteriori. Something similar can be said for other claims about essence.[7]

So the necessary aposteriority of statements is surprising, or anyway would have been surprising for earlier generations, and such aposteriority is also interesting: important claims about essence demand it. Although surprising and interesting, this conception of aposteriority is inoffensive to all parties in the dispute over direct reference. Happily, then, without inviting controversy we can acknowledge that rigidity secures the necessary a posteriori, so long as we are careful to attend to the distinction between propositions and statements. As I appeal to the connection between rigidity and the necessary a posteriori throughout this book, it will be to the necessary aposteriority of statements.

2. On the Significance of Rigidity for Identity Statements about Properties

Kripke maintains that it is not just concrete-object designators like 'Hesperus' and 'Phosphorus' that are rigid. Designators like 'whiteness', 'heat', 'pain', 'water', 'Brontosaurus', and so on, are also supposed to be rigid. I will be calling all such terms "property designators," counting kinds of phenomena, kinds of substances, kinds of organisms, and so on, as "properties."[8]

To recognize rigidity in terms like the foregoing is natural, despite resistance from various quarters: on its face, 'whiteness', say, would seem to designate the same color, whiteness, from world to world. And designators like this would seem to feature in identity statements whose behavior relevantly resembles the behavior of identity statements featuring rigid concrete-object designators. Thus, property designators, like concrete-object designators, would seem to feature in identity statements whose necessary truth comes from there being one thing that both of the identity statement's designators track through all possible worlds. In the following two subsections (§2.1 and §2.2), I will say more about the rigidity-relevant correspondence that obtains between identity statements that contain property designators and those that contain concrete-object designators, respectively. The relevant division into subsections reflects a distinction between statements that contain only names or name-like designators, whose informativeness is accordingly limited, and statements that contain designators with content that allows them to expose, in theoretical terms, the *essential nature* of the designatum. This distinction between rigid-designator-containing statements seems to hold whether the statements concern properties or concrete objects.

Consider statements about concrete objects first. Compare 'Hesperus = Phosphorus', which contains just names, to 'Hesperus = the planet with origin O'. By virtue of its theoretical designator, 'the planet with origin O', the statement 'Hesperus = the planet with origin O' tells us just what it is about the subject that qualifies it to be or to count as that thing and not something else (assuming, as I have been, that origins *are* in this way tied to a thing's being Hesperus: see §1.3 above). Following the ancient formulation of one of the Church Fathers, we might say that the informative designator expresses what it is to be Hesperus "in itself" and "that thing only which it is." Or, borrowing from Locke, we could say that the theoretical designator expresses just that about Hesperus "whereby it is, what it is." By contrast, 'Hesperus = Phosphorus', which lacks such a theoretical designator, fails to provide such rich information about the essential nature of the object.[9]

Because 'the planet with origin O' informs us of just what it is to be Hesperus, I classify 'Hesperus = the planet with origin O' as a *theoretical identity statement*. Theoretical identity statements, as I will understand them, invariably expose the subject's essence. The subject term in a theoretical identity statement, in this case 'Hesperus', tracks from world to world the same object as the theoretical expression, which characterizes the object explicitly by its essence: both designators are therefore rigid. To be a little more precise, I will say that where t is a designator for some subject of investigation, which might be a property or a concrete object, ⌜t = r⌝ is a true theoretical identity statement just in case ⌜to be r⌝ expresses a proper answer to such essence-oriented questions as ⌜what is it to be t?⌝ and ⌜what is t's essence or nature?⌝[10]

'Hesperus = the planet with origin O' is a theoretical identity statement; 'Hesperus = Phosphorus' is not. I will discuss the corresponding distinction for statements about *properties* below. I will discuss, first, relatively simple statements containing just names or name-like terms for properties: this is the topic of section (2.1). Then I will discuss, in the lengthier section (2.2), theoretical identity statements.

2.1. Identity Statements with Just Names for Properties

Examples of statements about properties that seem to be necessarily true by virtue of rigid designation, even though they do not reveal theoretically interesting information about the designata, any more than 'Hesperus = Phosphorus' does, include 'whiteness = albescence', 'heat = hotness', 'pain = dolor', and 'water = aqua'. Both members of each pair of terms seem to designate the same item rigidly, at least on a reasonable use. But the designators are names, or at least they are very name-like, and so they do not disclose much.

The foregoing statements seem to be a priori. But there are similar identity statements containing just names or name-like terms that are not a priori: an example would be 'Brontosaurus = Apatosaurus'. 'Brontosaurus' was coined as a genus-term in

RIGID DESIGNATORS FOR CONCRETE OBJECTS AND FOR PROPERTIES 9

the nineteenth century by O. C. Marsh, who thought he had discovered a new genus of dinosaur in Wyoming. As it turns out, the fossils he discovered were fossils of a dinosaur genus that he himself had already discovered and named 'Apatosaurus'. Marsh supposed that the specimen he associated with the name 'Brontosaurus' must be from a different genus than the specimen he associated with the name 'Apatosaurus', because there was such a difference in size between the two specimens. He did not realize that the reason for the difference in size was only that one of his specimens was not fully grown. Later, another scientist, Elmer Riggs, straightened out the matter, determining that Marsh had applied two names to the one genus (see Gould 1991, pp. 79ff.).

It took empirical investigation on the part of scientists like Riggs to learn that 'Brontosaurus = Apatosaurus' is true. Accordingly, philosophers before Kripke, when apprised that both names designate the same genus, would have seen only that the statement is true; they would not have seen that the statement is necessarily true. But if 'Brontosaurus' and 'Apatosaurus' not only designate the same genus but *rigidly* designate the same genus, as they seem to do, then 'Brontosaurus = Apatosaurus' is not only true but necessarily true.

2.2. Theoretical Identity Statements About Properties

Statements like 'pain = dolor', 'whiteness = albescence', 'heat = hotness', 'water = aqua', and 'Brontosaurus = Apatosaurus', though they seem to be necessarily true by virtue of rigidity, are not those identity statements about properties that have commanded intense and sustained attention for decades now.[11] The identity statements about properties that have commanded such attention are theoretical identity statements, like 'pain = c-fiber firing', 'whiteness = the combination of all of the colors of the visible spectrum', 'heat = the motion of molecules', 'water = H_2O', and 'Brontosaurus = the evolutionary group including population G and its descendants' (where 'G' names a population). Theoretical identity statements can be about concrete objects, but the most salient examples of these statements are about properties (see note 11).

Kripke endorses some theoretical identity statements, like 'water = H_2O'. And he rejects other theoretical identity statements, like 'pain = c-fiber firing', which move has been especially controversial. So if a Kripkean line on these matters is right, as I will argue, then reflection on rigidity leads to important insights about essence, both affirmative and negative.

A Kripkean line regarding 'water = H_2O' and 'pain = c-fiber firing' may be motivated as follows. Both *'water = water'* and *'pain = pain'* are necessarily true because each contains two token designators that designate the same item and that designate that item with respect to *every possible world*, or rigidly: so if we replace one token of 'water' in 'water = water' or one token of 'pain' in 'pain = pain' with *another rigid designator for the same item*, the resulting statement will inherit the necessity of its parent. So again, 'pain = dolor' is necessarily true: 'dolor' rigidly designates the same item that pain rigidly designates. In the same way, 'water = aqua' is necessarily true.

Now, just as 'water = aqua' is necessarily true, so is 'water = H_2O': 'H_2O', like 'aqua', rigidly designates the very same item that 'water' rigidly designates. Because of 'H_2O's content, which expresses just what it is to be water (see chapter 6 §2), 'water = H_2O' is a true theoretical identity statement. But 'pain = c-fiber firing' is different from 'pain = dolor' and 'water = aqua', and it is different from its fellow theoretical identity statement 'water = H_2O'. We have no good reason to suppose that 'pain = c-fiber firing' is true at all, let alone necessarily true, since we have no good reason to suppose that what 'c-fiber firing' designates, and designates rigidly, is the same item that 'pain' designates, and designates rigidly.

There is, of course, an explanation to be offered as to how it is that we have solid reason to affirm that 'H_2O' and 'water', as we use them, designate the same item rigidly, while we have no such reason to think that 'pain' and 'c-fiber firing', as we use them, designate the same item rigidly. 'H_2O' was presumably coined or compositionally assembled to serve as a designator, with respect to all possible worlds or situations, for the chemical H_2O: i.e., the matter whose molecules have two atoms of hydrogen bonded in the right way to one atom of oxygen. 'Water' was coined to serve as a designator, with respect to all possible worlds or situations, for a then-unknown microstructural substance comprising samples called "water." Since, as later examination would reveal, the salient microstructural substance comprising the samples called "water" was the chemical H_2O, 'water' turned out to be a rigid designator for H_2O. 'Water' designates H_2O even with respect to worlds in which H_2O has different observable characteristics (Kripke 1980, pp. 128–9) and water fails to designate non-H_2O even with respect to worlds in which non-H_2O has those characteristics that we associate with the term, like clarity, potability, liquidity, and so on (see especially Putnam 1975). We coin 'water' as a rigid designator for the microstructural substance itself, not for any of the characteristics that the relevant microstructure happens, in fact, to generate in matter.

But even though 'water' was coined as a rigid designator for an underlying microstructural substance that was at the time of coining unknown to speakers, 'pain' was not coined for any corresponding underlying entity, such as a neurophysiological phenomenon or a functional phenomenon that was at the time of coining unknown to speakers. Speakers coined 'pain' in order to have a designator for the *sensation*, not in order to have a designator for any underlying phenomenon generating the sensation or endowing the sensation with a functional role. For that reason, even if we can confirm that some neurophysiological phenomenon n happens to be what in fact generates pain sensations from behind the scenes, so to speak, this would not give us grounds to conclude that 'pain' rigidly designates n; for 'pain' would still designate the sensation, and not n, with respect to worlds in which the sensation occurs without n and 'pain' would fail to designate n with respect to worlds in which n occurs without the sensation.

So while a mere understanding of our referential practices or our intent to rigidly designate a physical entity meeting certain conditions, plus a look at the empirical world to see what meets those conditions, suffices to show us that 'water' and 'H$_2$O' rigidly designate the same item, no analogous route can indicate that 'pain' and 'c-fiber firing' rigidly designate the same item. We cannot, then, confirm 'pain = c-fiber firing' in the same clear way that we can confirm 'water = H$_2$O'. And if there is any *other* way that we *can* confirm 'pain = c-fiber firing', it is not easy to see what that would be:[12] for all that we can tell by other means, it would seem that the sensation and the physical phenomenon could each be present without the other. And so it seems that we cannot confirm 'pain = c-fiber firing' at all.

3. Complications and Elaboration

I have articulated a broadly Kripkean line concerning the rigidity of property designators and concerning rigidity's role in important arguments concerning properties. But in doing so, I have set aside, as Kripke does, difficult and pressing issues concerning how property designators *could* in fact be rigid. I will address these issues in detail in the next four chapters of this book. After that, I will turn, in the final three chapters, to doubts and complications that various parties have voiced concerning rigidity's work in theoretical identity statements about properties, especially concerning rigidity's work in psychophysical identity statements: so I explain in an agenda of the book, which I provide in section (3.2) of this chapter. But before I provide an agenda of chapters to come, I set the stage, in section (3.1), with a provisional answer to a basic question toward which I have just gestured.

3.1. What Stays the Same in the Rigid Designation of Properties?

One of the first and most fundamental of questions to confront us, which was articulated early in the tradition of attempts to work through the issues sketched in the foregoing section (§2), concerns just how it is that the designatum of a property designator stays the same, from world to world. In the case of a singular concrete-object designator, the matter seems straightforward: what stays the same from possible world to possible world is the *extension* of the term, where 'extension' is understood rather liberally to be the item that a singular expression names or uniquely describes or the items to which a predicative expression applies. The extension of 'Hesperus' is Hesperus: and the extension of 'Hesperus' is Hesperus with respect to every possible world.

Kripke seems to take 'heat' or 'whiteness' to be rigid in the same straightforward way that 'Hesperus' is rigid (see note 15). But if a designator like 'heat' or 'whiteness' is rigid in the same straightforward way that 'Hesperus' is rigid, then 'heat' or 'whiteness' also has to have the *same extension* with respect to every possible world (as Schwartz, for one, stresses: 2002, pp. 265–6; 2006, p. 283). And if 'heat' or 'whiteness' does indeed have the same extension from world to world, then that extension can*not* be the *particulars* or the *set of particulars* that we might naturally, at least on a first glance, take to be the extension: after all, the particulars that instantiate heat or whiteness change from world to world. Our ovens might never have been heated in the way that they are, and other ovens that happen never to have been sold and used might have been heated instead. White doors and cupboards might have been some other color, while your dark trousers might have provided us with the finest of models for whiteness. So the term 'heat' or 'whiteness' has a different extension from one world to the next, if the extension is the set of particulars exhibiting the property.

Fortunately, the extension of 'heat' or 'whiteness' need not be understood as the set of particulars instantiating the property. Rather than to take 'heat' or 'whiteness' to be a term that *applies* (*merely* applies: see note 13) to this and that *particular* item, we might take 'heat' and 'whiteness' to be *singular* expressions, which may be understood roughly as expressions that purport to pick out just one item, in the way that a name like 'Hesperus' picks out Hesperus by naming it or in the way that a definite description like 'the brightest non-lunar object in the evening sky' picks out Hesperus by denoting it (but for a discussion of complications about descriptions, see chapter 4, §1). The one item that a singular designator names or denotes is the designator's extension: so 'Hesperus' and 'the brightest non-lunar object in the evening sky' share the same extension, Hesperus.

If 'heat' and 'whiteness' are *singular* in the way that Hesperus is, then each of these terms has a singular extension. The extension of 'heat' or 'whiteness' is presumably the *property* heat or whiteness, respectively, which is an abstract object or at least an entity that is only realized in, and not identical to, the particulars in which it is found. So understood, 'heat' and 'whiteness' can be taken to be *rigid* in just the way that 'Hesperus' is:[13] all of the foregoing terms, understood as singular, can be taken to have a single extension that remains the *same* from world to world, which extension is the property heat, the property whiteness, or the body Hesperus, as the case may be.

The foregoing is not the only way of understanding the semantics of what I will call "designators" for properties;[14] on the contrary, as chapters 4 and 5 will indicate, the proposal to treat these designators as singular, rather than as merely predicative, is not without controversy. But although there are other ways to understand the semantics of property designators, we seem to give the proposal that property designators are *rigid* the "best run for its money" by taking property designators to be singular, as Donnellan (1983, p. 90) suggested decades ago: to recognize property designators as singular is "the obvious route to an analogy" (Bird and Tobin 2009, §3.3) between property designators and concrete-object designators with respect to rigidity because it allows us to say that property designators, like concrete-object designators, are rigid in the familiar, straightforward way, and the only way that Kripke articulates. Kripke himself seems to treat property designators as singular, or at least he seems to treat as singular those property designators whose *grammar* typically *suggests* a singular treatment: e.g., 'heat' and 'whiteness'.[15] Accordingly, for the next three chapters, I will be treating property designators as singular.

I will be treating as singular not only terms like 'heat' and 'whiteness' but also terms like 'hot' and 'white'. The grammar of 'hot' and 'white' does *not* in general suggest a singular treatment. Still, if conformity with apparently proper grammar is important (for qualms about that, see chapter 4, §2.1), then I can appeal these terms' apparently grammatical use in certain *contexts* that suggest singularity: e.g., 'hot and cold are extremes of temperature', 'white is a color', 'rough and tough is what she is' (cf. Salmon 2003, p. 484), and so on. Count nouns, or at any rate words that normally function as such, similarly suggest a singular use sometimes, as in 'oak is a type of tree', 'oval is a shape', or 'tiger is unfortunately eaten in Asia'.

By treating property designators as singular, at least with regard to the right contexts, I am able to air, with relatively few complicating distractions, a great many of the main objections and clarifications to be addressed concerning the rigidity of property designators: these objections and clarifications cry out for attention even on this best-case scenario in which property designators *are* to be treated as singular. After I have defended and clarified the claim that property designators are rigid, at least provided that they may be given a singular treatment, I will consider the status of the relevant claims to rigidity *without* a best-case scenario, as I explain in the following agenda.

3.2. *The Agenda of Chapters to Come*

I have used the present chapter to lay out basic issues concerning the rigid – nonrigid distinction in general and its significance, as well as to introduce my position on whether the rigid – nonrigid distinction carries over to property designators specifically. In the chapters immediately ahead, I will offer a detailed articulation and defense of the position that I have introduced here concerning whether the rigid – nonrigid distinction carries over to property designators. Then I will defend the use to which I have put the distinction, to support substantive claims about theoretical identity statements, including psychophysical identity statements. I will now go chapter by chapter to provide a little more detail.

One worry that confronts the favored account of rigidity for property designators (from §3.1) is that the account cannot vindicate a rigid – nonrigid *distinction*. I have offered no examples of *non*rigid designators for properties: Kripke does not explicitly offer any either. Such examples were slow to arise in the wake of Kripke's famous work,[16] and there are worries about the authenticity of those examples that have somewhat belatedly surfaced in the literature. Some philosophers have worried that there *are no* nonrigid designators for properties, in which case rigidity for property designators is trivialized. I address this threat in chapter 2.

Even if the favored account of rigidity can honor a *distinction* between property designators that it would count as rigid and property designators that it would count as nonrigid, the distinction may not be a rigid – nonrigid distinction. To be a rigid – nonrigid distinction, the distinction would have to classify designators according to whether they fill the right role. The role would include those duties so fundamental that if they were not performed, we would fail to have rigidity (or nonrigidity) at all: such work could be specified in a job description of rigidity. To be sure, an account of rigidity should not necessarily have to secure *all* of the work to which rigidity has been assigned in classic sources: e.g., work in traditional arguments associated with rigidity, which support some theoretical identity statements like 'water = H_2O' and impugn other theoretical identity statements like 'pain = c-fiber firing'. One could maintain that there is a genuine rigid – nonrigid distinction without endorsing these traditional arguments. Still, if a distinction fails to assign to rigidity certain central work belonging to rigidity's role, then the distinction fails to qualify as a rigid – nonrigid distinction. I address whether the distinction that I recognize as a rigid – nonrigid distinction for property designators assigns to rigidity the work belonging to rigidity's role, in chapter 3.

Throughout chapters 2 and 3, I operate under the assumption, as I have indicated, that the expressions for properties at issue are singular designators: given the best-case scenario that this assumption affords, I argue, the most straightforward understanding of the rigidity of property designators is tenable. But the assumption to which I have helped myself in order to work with a best-case scenario is an unfortunately *strong* assumption. In chapters 4 and 5, I discuss the plausibility of the assumption and I examine the case for rigidity without it. In chapter 4, I offer conditional arguments in support of the claim that *all* expressions for properties are singular, as well as clarification of this claim. In chapter 5, I set aside singularity and the best-case scenario that it affords: I examine prospects for a rigid – nonrigid distinction for *non*singular expressions. A veritable industry devoted to articulating a rigid – nonrigid distinction for property designators has generated widespread pessimism concerning whether the distinction carries over to nonsingular expressions. Since I urge, contrary to the received wisdom, that the rigid – nonrigid distinction *does* carry over to merely predicative expressions, I am obliged to articulate and defend an account of the rigid – nonrigid distinction for mere appliers that is sufficiently detailed to do justice to the usual resistance: that is the work of this especially long chapter.

Chapter 5 concludes my discussion over the course of four chapters about whether there *is* a rigid – nonrigid distinction for property designators and, if there is one, how it is to be characterized and how widely it is to be understood to apply to the diversity of property designators. In the final three chapters of the book, I defend the philosophical power of the distinction, which is manifested in its use in familiar arguments supporting or impugning various theoretical identity statements that would reveal the essences of interesting properties. These chapters address those who would accept the distinction but who would nevertheless object to these familiar rigidity-centered arguments.

Skeptical arguments impugning psychophysical identity statements have generated a vast amount of discussion in a tradition that is rather narrowly focused on mind. In deference to this tradition, I gather my defense of the skeptical argument concerning psychophysical identities more or less together into the final two chapters. In chapter 6, by contrast, I defend constructive arguments supporting theoretical identity statements expressing the essences of water, whiteness, etc. In these final chapters, considerations about how readers might readily approach the issues have been more influential than the goal of reflecting a division of topics according to their nature.

The arguments making use of rigidity face objections according to which they are unconvincing and also objections according to which they are insignificant even if they are convincing. In chapter 6, I will argue that constructive arguments making use of rigidity are significant if convincing and that they are convincing. The objections according to which the constructive arguments making use of rigidity are not convincing would hold that they appeal to philosophical resources that are controversial or worse and hence that they come at too high a cost; but I will maintain that the arguments make modest appeal to plausible resources. Hence, the arguments enjoy considerable interest for little cost.

In chapter 7, I will argue, in similar fashion, that the skeptical argument impugning psychophysical identities is significant if convincing. I will also argue that the significant impact of the argument comes at little cost, in terms of controversial philosophical resources. That the skeptical argument comes at little cost heads off one sort of objection according to which the argument is unconvincing. The argument is also vulnerable, as a skeptical argument, to another salient variety of objection according to which the argument is unconvincing: the argument might be unconvincing not because it appeals to unreasonable, costly philosophical tools or doctrines but because it overlooks philosophical tools or doctrines that are established or plausible and that are capable of putting an end to skepticism, establishing psychophysical identities. I argue in chapter 8 that no such resources are available. This will complete my discussion of whether skeptical arguments impugning psychophysical identities are convincing.

The book as a whole offers, then, a detailed articulation and a sustained defense of property designators' rigidity and of the work that this rigidity is supposed, in a broadly Kripkean tradition, to perform. I turn to the project.

Notes

1. Ubiquitous appeals to the rigidity of ordinary names testify that names are indeed rigid and that this matters. There has been surprisingly little resistance to the appeals. "Disagreement is endemic in philosophy," Frank Jackson says, but the thesis "that names are rigid designators" seems to escape the controversy: here "there is very substantial agreement" (2007, p. 17). Dan López de Sa similarly writes that "There is a considerable consensus" over the rigidity of various singular terms and the nonrigidity of others (2001, pp. 613–14). The *locus classici* of the relevant claims about rigidity are of course to be found in the work of Kripke (1971; 1980).

    In this monograph, I do not call into question the usual line with respect to the rigidity of proper names, or address maverick dissent (for a discussion of which, see LaPorte 2011). What is at issue in the present work is not whether rigidity characterizes ordinary proper names like 'Hesperus' and 'Phosphorus', but rather whether rigidity characterizes designators for *properties* in a way that carries comparable philosophical significance. Kripke famously gives an affirmative answer but he seems to anticipate the discord that has followed, apologizing after his lectures that "thoroughness had to be sacrificed" in his discussion of these matters specifically (1980, p. 22, note 1).

2. If properties exist in all possible worlds (at least those properties that I will be discussing), then rigid designators for them are obstinately rigid by default, even if proper names for contingently existing objects like Venus are only rigid on the weaker refined understanding: in that event, terms for properties will be "strongly rigid," in the vocabulary of Kripke: this is a special case of obstinate rigidity reserved for designators that designate a necessarily existing object (1980, pp. 48–9).

   In view of Kripke's use of 'strongly rigid', the neat connection that one might expect to see between "strong rigidity" and "strong necessity" is lost (strong necessity is discussed in the paragraph of the text that starts after this note's marker). 'Hesperus = Phosphorus', or perhaps 'if Hesperus exists then Hesperus = Phosphorus', is strongly necessary provided the designators are obstinately rigid, even though they are not strongly rigid. The connection between the weak form of rigidity and weak necessity is also less tidy than one might have supposed: for Kripke, an identity statement is weakly necessary "if whenever the objects mentioned therein exist, the statement would be true" (1971, p. 137). So according to one plausible construal, a statement like 'Hesperus = Phosphorus' is weakly necessary if, for any possible world w with respect to which there is an existing designatum for 'Hesperus' and 'Phosphorus' (as we use 'Hesperus' and 'Phosphorus'), 'Hesperus = Phosphorus' is true with respect to w. But on this construal, designators need not even rise to being *weakly* rigid, in order to yield weak necessity: even if 'Hesperus = Phosphorus' contains just *non*rigid designators, it can be weakly necessary (as I explain in chapter 3, note 1). "Weak necessity" stands in need of further clarification and there are other possible construals or refinements (again, see chapter 3, note 1): I will presuppose as weak an understanding as needed, in any context.
3. For similar examples of nonrigid descriptions that are supposed to be shorthand for ordinary proper names, see Russell 1912, pp. 55, 59; 1919, pp. 178–9; see also Frege 1952b, pp. 57, 58n. For further discussion of descriptivism about names, see chapter 3, §2.4.
4. Other examples of the necessary a posteriori made famous by Kripke may be accepted by direct reference theorists, though whether these examples owe anything to rigidity may be contested: thus, Soames (2002, pp. 264ff.; see also 2004, pp. 87, 94–7; 2006a, p. 651) accepts the necessary aposteriority of 'anything is water if and only if it is H_2O' but denies that the necessity owes anything to rigidity.
5. Kripke initially suggests that even a *proposition* like Hesperus = Phosphorus is a posteriori. He writes, in "Identity and Necessity," "You certainly *can*, in the case of ordinary proper names, make quite empirical discoveries that, let's say, Hesperus is Phosphorus, though we thought otherwise. We can be in doubt as to whether Gaurisanker is Everest or Cicero is in fact Tully" (1971, p. 143). Similarly, in *Naming and Necessity*, Kripke says, "We do not know a priori that Hesperus is Phosphorus, and are in no position to find out the answer except empirically" (p. 104). The connection to propositions is acknowledged quite explicitly by Kripke: "I hold that propositions that contemporary philosophers would properly count as 'empirical' can be necessary and known to be such" (1980, p. 160). But Kripke later professes agnosticism about whether propositions like the foregoing are a posteriori (1979, pp. 269f. and 281, note 44; 1980, p. 21). While I follow the later Kripke's lead by avoiding commitment to the theory of direct reference or its rivals, I do not commit with him to the rather unpopular view that the best response, all things considered, is agnosticism about the theory. Perhaps our considered opinion ought to be that the theory of direct reference is decidedly successful or that it is

decidedly unsuccessful: the reason that I do not commit one way or the other is because it does not matter for my purposes *what* the wisest reception is, to the theory of direct reference, not because I am convinced that the wisest reception is agnosticism.

6. This case for surprise from the text is enough, but much more could be said. Even to say that there should be surprise associated with the necessary aposteriority of statements as opposed to that of propositions, as I do for simplicity, might by presupposing the relevant distinctions obscure some of the surprise that has attended conceptual development concerning the necessary a posteriori. The necessary aposteriority of statements should surprise anyone who maintains that there is no necessary a posteriori without being *clear* about whether it is propositions or whether it is statements that are at issue: and before rigidity became appreciated, the urgency of becoming clear about the distinction had not dawned. Kripke himself evidently failed to distinguish carefully until there had been sufficient development in his reflections (see note 5). Also observe that although I focus on the so-called "Frege – Russell" tradition of seeing names as shorthand for garden-variety definite descriptions (see Kripke 1980, pp. 27ff., 58ff.; see also the foregoing note 3), the prejudice against the necessary a posteriori is not limited to that tradition: indeed, the prejudice predates that tradition (as Kripke notes after his famous lectures: 1980, pp. 158–9; see also Putnam 1975, p. 233).

7. Without the necessary aposteriority of statements, it is impossible to say what it is to be something like Hesperus even *uninformatively* (uninformative with respect to the issue at hand: see note 9), or even to coin a rigid designator for Hesperus if we were to try. Suppose, e.g., we were to say, in a dubbing ceremony, "'Hesperus' may be an abbreviated description that is shorthand for 'the brightest non-lunar object in the evening sky', but I am looking for a *name* for the individual, a rigid designator that refers to that individual even with respect to situations in which the individual is dim and so fails to satisfy the description: therefore, I use 'Schesperus' as a rigid designator to name the individual. I use 'Schesperushood' for the relevant individual's essence and I apply 'Schesperizer' to what has that essence." If this *were* possible, then presumably we could do the *same* with respect to 'Phosphorus'. Then 'Schesperus = Schphosphorus' would be an a posteriori but necessarily true statement. So would the essence-expressing statements 'concerning the x that is Hesperus: what it is to be x is to be the Schphosphorizer' and 'concerning the x that is Phosphorus: the essence of x is to be what instantiates Schesperushood'. So without necessary aposteriority for statements, we could not specify the essence of Hesperus even uninformatively, by means of terms like 'Schesperushood', or coin rigid designators for Hesperus (cf. Russell, who would apparently receive the prospect of being limited to nonrigid, accidental descriptions with equanimity: 1912, pp. 57, 59).

8. Here I follow various workers, including Boër (1985, p. 134), Linsky (1984, p. 262), Phillip Bricker (p.c.), Soames (2006b, p. 711), and others (see also Swoyer 2008, §7.12), who understand kinds to be a type of property. Other workers would reject this categorization and in fact deny that any kinds at all are properties (e.g., Lowe 1997, pp. 35–6); but I would affirm the relevant claims in the text about rigid designation, with respect to the terms in my litany and other terms like them, regardless of whether all of the relevant terms are counted as terms for "properties" or not. So there is no need for me to try to resolve the issue of whether all of the terms in the litany should be counted as terms for "properties." Those who would distinguish between "properties" and "kinds," or terms for these respective entities, typically do so on the basis of what sort of *instances* the relevant entities have, whether particularized properties or tropes or modes like the white patch covering the top of Everest, on the one

hand, or individuals like Everest, on the other hand. My central claims about a rigid – nonrigid distinction would pertain to terms that designate entities with either sort of instances, so again, there is no need to come to a resolution regarding the designata in question; the reader can make the obvious adjustments to my examples where necessary in order to assign the designata that she would recognize if I assume different ones (on rare occasion more caution will be necessary: see chapter 5, note 26).

9. The first quotations are borrowed from St. Gregory of Nyssa's "On the Soul and the Resurrection." Locke's frequently quoted passage is from *An Essay Concerning Human Understanding* III.3.15, p. 417. On anyone's account, a statement that contains ordinary names, like 'Hesperus = Phosphorus', fails to inform much about the entity's nature, even if that statement is necessarily true and even if it expresses, as some would grant, nontrivial information. To say in detail just how identity statements containing only names are limited in their informativeness would require a theory of names (which, again, is unnecessary here: see §1.3). But to see how name-limited identity statements are informationally impoverished, in the relevant respect, even on a descriptivist view, consider a particularly strong version of descriptivism, like that of Plantinga, who suggests that 'Hesperus' and 'Phosphorus' express the same as the "world-indexed" descriptions 'the evening star in α' and 'the morning star in α', respectively, in which 'α' serves as a name for the actual world (Plantinga 2003, p.133; I discuss descriptivism further in chapter 3, §2.4). Certainly 'Hesperus = Phosphorus' could, in view of such content, enlighten us astronomically with the information that the star appearing in the evening is the same as the one appearing in the morning. But 'Hesperus = Phosphorus' would still not compare to 'Hesperus = the planet with origin O' in regard to information about the essential nature of the entity (Plantinga would acknowledge as much: see 2003, p. 141).

10. The last and most precise of these explications does not explicitly require rigidity, but what the explication does explicitly require can be met only provided both designators are rigid. *Any* satisfying explication of 'theoretical identity statement' will require rigidity (on this head, see first note 6 of chapter 6, which gathers threads from the relevant discussions that begin at chapter 3, §1), as I will explain later after I say more about *non*rigidity. I will argue, further, that the requirement of rigidity *is met* by the usual examples of theoretical identity statements, in chapter 6 (§2.1).

The expression ⌜to be t⌝ and kindred expressions like ⌜being t⌝, ⌜having t⌝, and so on, may perhaps sometimes call for disambiguation (for discussion, see Lewis 1983a, p. 87; 1999c, p. 307; López de Sa 2008a, p. 9; Schnieder 2005; 2008, especially pp. 207–8; see also Salmon 2005, p. 132, note 22). If so, the intended reading is that according to which ⌜to be t⌝ designates rigidly the salient property that belongs, with respect to any possible world w, to: what is t in w. Other alleged readings are less natural and hence give rise to controversy and doubt (besides the foregoing references, see Tye 1981, pp. 24–5).

Although it is handy for me to appeal to the foregoing understanding of a *true* theoretical identity statement, there could be natural adjustments in the direction of generality. So we might say, in general, that a theoretical identity statement is an identity statement in which a theoretical expression is somehow *supposed* to designate the subject by way of expressing the nature or essence of the subject.

11. Statements like 'whiteness = albescence', 'heat = hotness', 'pain = dolor', and 'Brontosaurus = Apatosaurus', have received relatively little attention in the philosophical literature, and

this attention has been late in coming. The neglect marks a lost opportunity, since these statements, which contain just names or name-like terms, are simpler than theoretical identity statements, like 'whiteness = the combination of all of the colors of the visible spectrum' or 'heat = the motion of molecules', which illuminate theoretically interesting essences. The simpler statements demonstrate the effects of rigidity on property designators more clearly, as they raise fewer distracting objections (one of the first to call to attention to such statements in order to illuminate them in isolation is Bolton 1996, p. 157; Kripke offers no examples of non-theoretical identity statements about properties; for further discussion of these points, see LaPorte 2004, chapter 2, and Beebee and Sabbarton-Leary 2010, §2.2). In the same way, the effects of rigidity can be seen more clearly in 'Hesperus = Phosphorus' than in a theoretical identity statement like 'Hesperus = the planet with origin O', whose necessary truth can be obscured by distracting objections to essentialism (I address objections to theoretical identity statements about properties in chapter 6 and in chapter 7, §1.2).

There are good reasons for the neglect that has attended statements like 'whiteness = albescence' or 'heat = hotness' in those discussions that have taken place, even if additional discussions to compensate for this neglect would have been welcome: a chief reason that Kripke and others commonly appeal to name-limited statements about concrete objects like 'Hesperus = Phosphorus' is to illustrate the necessity and even a posteriori necessity of statements that contain only rigid designators. Philosophers *could* appeal to statements about properties like 'whiteness = albescence' or 'water = aqua', to illustrate basic lessons about necessity and the necessary a posteriori; but they are wise to select examples concerning concrete objects, like 'Hesperus = Phosphorus', as these face fewer complications (for related observations, see Ahmed 2009, pp. 127–8, note 4). What is most obviously special about the rigidity of property designators *specifically* has to do with *essentialism*, not necessity or the necessary a posteriori. Scientists appear to enlighten us about the essential nature of familiar properties as they affirm theoretical identity statements like those I will discuss in the text. This enlightenment is especially striking and plausible when properties, rather than concrete objects, are at issue: indeed, it is hard to find an example of a theoretical identity statement about a concrete object in the literature, though I have proposed 'Hesperus = the planet with origin O' as a respectable candidate.

12. See chapter 8, note 2. There are, of course, other possible routes to showing that two designators designate the same property than the route (discussed further, and with greater caution, in chapter 6, §2.2) by which it is shown that 'water' and 'H_2O' designate the same property. We know that 'triangularity' and 'trilaterality' are rigid designators for the same property (assuming a coarse conception of properties, anyway: see chapter 8, §3); but it is not because one term has been coined to designate an underlying entity that is, as we learn from empirical research, picked out openly by the other, in the way that 'water' has been coined to designate an underlying entity that is, as we learn from empirical research, picked out openly by 'H_2O'. Rather, we know a priori that 'triangularity = trilaterality' is necessarily true; for all that we know a priori, 'water = H_2O' could be false.

It seems clear that 'pain = c-fiber firing' is not known to be true in the way that 'triangularity = trilaterality' is known to be true, any more than 'pain = c-fiber firing' is known to be true in the way that 'water = H_2O' is known to be true; indeed, 'water = H_2O' is surely less unpromising as a potential analogue for 'pain = c-fiber firing' than is 'triangularity = trilaterality'. Accordingly, materialists of various stripes have continued to resist, in some fashion or other, Kripkean efforts to drive apart the apparently distinct cases of 'water = H_2O' and 'pain = c-fiber firing'. The final chapter of this book, chapter 8, is devoted to such resistance: there, I address *responses*, on the part of identity theorists, to the effect that 'water = H_2O' and 'pain = c-fiber firing' are somehow analogous after all, with respect to some means for confirming their necessary truth.

13. This understanding of the rigidity of property designators like 'heat' and 'whiteness' was favored by a variety of workers early in the discussion over rigidity. Boër (1985, pp. 129–35), Donnellan (1983, pp. 90f.), and Mondadori (1978) have all taken terms like 'heat' and 'whiteness' to be "abstract nouns," as Donnellan puts it, following Mill (Donnellan 1983, p. 90): such terms are supposed to name an abstract object. Early treatments are typically inchoate and there is some tendency to backslide: thus, Donnellan construes terms for species as *names*, and so as rigid singular terms: therefore, he says, such a term "is not to be thought of as designating its extension" (1983, p. 90), which he thinks would include different organisms in different worlds. This seems confused, since a rigid singular term *does* designate an "extension," according to a common understanding of "extension" that Donnellan himself evidently adopts, citing with apparent deference philosophers who "talk about the *extension* of a term and usually apply this notion both to singular terms, such as names, and general terms" (1983, p. 90). Accordingly, a singular species term that is rigid should after all be thought of as designating its extension, the *species*; it is just that it could not be thought of as designating the extension of any corresponding *general* term whose extension includes the organisms *belonging* to the species. More precisely, a property designator cannot be thought to rigidly designate the extension of a *merely* general term: there are important subtleties in the vicinity. Some authors take a term for a property to *apply* to particulars in one capacity, as a first-order general term, and to *refer to* or denote a single property in *another* capacity, as a second-order singular term (see chapter 4, §2.2.2.1). Given such an understanding, a property designator could be said to have a single property for a *second-order* extension, in its capacity as a singular designator, even though the property designator has many particulars or a set of particulars that instantiate the property for a *first-order extension*, in its capacity as a general designator. Of course, in this case, we are free to think of a rigid term for a property "as designating its extension," or rather one of its extensions, with respect to all possible worlds: that would be the property designated by the expression in its capacity as a singular term.

14. Such terminology is intended to be neutral with respect to the issue of singularity: so we may construe what it is to be a "designator" quite broadly (see chapter 5, §1.1.1), in order to include as "designators" not only singular expressions, which *name* or *denote* a property (or other entity), but also merely predicative expressions, if there are any, which might be said to "*express*" (see chapter 4, note 8) a property. And we could understand what it is to "designate" a property or other entity accordingly.

15. Kripke evidently *uses* 'heat' as a singular designator for an object, rather than as a mere applier, as when he affirms the *identity* statement "heat = molecular motion" (1980, p. 154; see also p. 136). And Kripke would apparently think of the "referent" (1980, p. 132) of such a term, in the way that I have, as an abstract object that is contingently *instantiated* by particular items (see 1980, pp. 135–6). Kripke discusses 'yellowness' rather than 'whiteness' (1980, p. 140, note 71): he seems to be talking about 'yellowness' as the designator when he says that a property "is picked out and rigidly designated" (1980, p. 128, note 66).

Kripke's position with respect to terms like 'hot' or 'yellow', which in typical contexts are *not* grammatically singular, is less clear. He explicitly addresses 'hot' in a frequently cited passage where he suggests that its similarity to 'heat' will have to be "suitably elaborated" (1980, p. 134). This might be taken to indicate that he thinks of 'hot' and 'yellow' as nonsingular terms that are rigid in some special respect that pertains to *predicative*, as opposed to singular, designators; yet it seems more likely that Kripke is not even addressing rigidity in the foregoing passage, but rather the causal theory of reference (a distinct topic: see chapter 2, note 4; chapter 3, §2.2–§2.4; see also Fitch 2004, p. 124). Even so, it may be that Kripke does indeed take terms like 'hot' and 'yellow' to enjoy some special form of rigidity for nonsingular designators, as some authors have supposed him to do (Soames 2002, pp. 245ff.). Kripke does not use terms like 'hot' and 'yellow' in any simple identity statement of the form $x = y$ and there is a hint that the "identification" statements that Kripke has in mind for terms like these are biconditionals instead (Kripke 1980, p. 138; see also Soames 2002, pp. 256, 267): so perhaps he thinks of such terms as genuinely nonsingular and thereby unfit to flank the '=' sign. Still, he would take them to be rigid (see, e.g., 1980, p. 149).

16. Kripke does suggest some examples of reference-fixing descriptions for property designators that he would evidently be committed to seeing as nonrigid (1980, p. 136; 140, note 71; see pp. 55ff. for an explanation of reference fixing): these would be nonrigid according to the account that I defend, as well (see chapter 2). Even so, Kripke's commitments are not obvious with respect to nonrigidity: hence, none of the early sources cited in note 13 offers any example of a nonrigid property designator and such sources indicate collectively a general uncertainty about what the contrast to rigid property designators is supposed to be. Despite this general uncertainty (to which Linsky also testifies: 1984, p. 267; see also below, chapter 2) over the intended contrast, various workers have come to my attention since I have articulated a contrast (including Linsky), who anticipated basically the same contrast, with regard to singular designators (Bealer 1987, p. 315; Jackson, Pargetter, and Prior 1982, p. 218; Peterson 1986, p. 297; Tye 1981).

2

On the Coherence of the Distinction

The distinction that I recognize between those property designators that I take to be rigid and those that I take to be nonrigid is a distinction that has been criticized as incoherent, by some critics, and as coherent but without much relevance to *rigidity*, by other critics. In the present chapter, I address worries that the distinction is incoherent: typically, the worry is that an account like mine is not entitled to recognize any *non*rigid designators for properties. Without nonrigid property designators, *all* property designators become rigid so that the rigid – nonrigid distinction is lost or trivialized.

Each of sections (1) and (2) focuses on some specific group of designators that my favored account of a rigid – nonrigid distinction for property designators is alleged to categorize erroneously as rigid: so, according to the objection that is discussed in each section, my account cannot help but categorize *all* property designators as rigid and the rigid – nonrigid distinction is lost. In section (3), I discuss a proposed diagnosis of the supposed illusion that there is a distinction at hand.

1. The Problem of Artificial-Property Designators

Provided that 'Brontosaurus' is singular, as I presuppose in this chapter, it is rigid in the same straightforward way that many other singular designators are rigid (see chapter 1, §3.1). 'Brontosaurus' designates its extension, which is the brontosaur *genus*. The extension of 'Brontosaurus' is the *same* genus of dinosaur with respect to every possible world, even though the concrete organisms belonging to Brontosaurus vary from world to world. So the term's extension should not be thought to be those concrete individuals actually instantiating Brontosaurus or the set of those concrete individuals: if that were the extension, then the extension would vary from world to world, thereby spoiling 'Brontosaurus'' claim to rigidity.

On the foregoing account, designators for *natural* properties (or kinds: see note 3), like 'Brontosaurus' or 'white', are not *unique* among designators for properties in their rigidity: contrary to what might be expected, even terms for *artificial* properties are rigid. Just as 'Brontosaurus' designates the same abstract property in all possible worlds, so 'bachelor', 'lawyer', 'soda pop', 'funny', 'expensive', 'grue', and so on, also designate the same respective property in all possible worlds. 'Lawyer', for example, designates lawyerhood in every possible world. To be sure, what we might call the "metaphysical extension" of lawyerhood differs from one world to the next[1]: Johnny Cochran is a member of the metaphysical extension of lawyerhood as things are, but he might have become a mail carrier instead. Still, 'lawyer' designates lawyerhood with respect to all possible worlds.

On my proposal, then, designators for artificial properties are rigid. Some philosophers think that this dooms the proposal. The worry about counting artificial-property designators as rigid (or one such worry)[2] is that this would trivialize rigidity by counting *every* property designator rigid. Hence, Schwartz says that if we appeal to "the semantics of rigidity to explain the necessity of 'soda = pop' or 'bachelors are unmarried males'" (2002, p. 271), then we eviscerate the distinction that we recognize. "Rigidity has lost its exclusivity, like a club of which all are automatically members," he writes, "and thereby its interest" (p. 266). The thought goes back some decades: Cook urges that "the contrast between 'cat' and 'bachelor'" is supposed to be what "shows the significance of the fact that 'cat' is a rigid designator" (1980, p. 64). Many others would concur.[3]

But the foregoing worry is not in fact directed at a genuine "glaring problem" (as Schwartz would call it: 1980, p. 190; see also 1977, pp. 37ff.; 2002; 2006, p. 283). My preferred account does *not* trivialize rigidity. It is simply not the case that every property designator rigidly designates its property on my preferred account. 'Brontosaurus', which names a type of dinosaur, seems to pick out Brontosaurus rigidly. But other designators pick out this dinosaur by way of its fitting a particular accidental description. 'The largest dinosaur on a 1989 U.S. postage stamp' is an example: this expression designates Brontosaurus, since Brontosaurus happens to have been the largest dinosaur on a 1989 U.S. postage stamp. But the expression does not designate, with respect to every *other* possible world, the *same* dinosaur type as the one that it actually designates. The U.S. postal service might have had only two dinosaurs on its stamps of 1989, rather than three: without Brontosaurus, there would have been only Tyrannosaurus and Stegosaurus. Had that been so, 'the largest dinosaur on a 1989 U.S. postage stamp' would have designated Tyrannosaurus, not Brontosaurus. 'The largest dinosaur on a 1989 U.S. postage stamp' happens to designate Brontosaurus, but it does not *rigidly* designate Brontosaurus.

The rigidity of 'Brontosaurus' would seem, then, to find a contrast in certain *descriptions*, just as the rigidity of names like 'Hesperus' and 'Ben Franklin' do. It would not seem to be a "trivial" matter at all that expressions like 'Brontosaurus' are rigid; on the contrary, it is significant that such expressions are rigid, and that others, such as 'the largest dinosaur on a 1989 U.S. postage stamp', are not. It is significant for the very reason that the differences between expressions like 'Hesperus' and 'the brightest non-lunar object in the evening sky' are significant. Consider the salient modal parallels: 'Brontosaurus' and 'Apatosaurus' rigidly designate the same genus of dinosaur so there could be no world for which 'Brontosaurus = Apatosaurus' is false, because as a rigid designator each of the terms 'Brontosaurus' and 'Apatosaurus' designates the very same thing in every other world as it does in the actual world, where both 'Brontosaurus' and 'Apatosaurus' designate the same thing. No similar argument from rigidity can support the necessity of a statement like 'Brontosaurus = the largest dinosaur on a 1989 U.S. postage stamp', any more than a similar argument could support the necessity of 'Hesperus = the brightest non-lunar object in the evening sky'. This is fortunate, since, just as the familiar latter statement about concrete objects is true but only contingently so, the statement 'Brontosaurus = the largest dinosaur on a 1989 U.S. postage stamp' is true but contingently so. With respect to those worlds in which Tyrannosaurus is the largest dinosaur on a 1989 U.S. postage stamp, the sentence 'Brontosaurus = the largest dinosaur on a 1989 U.S. postage stamp' is false: for in those worlds, the largest dinosaur on a 1989 U.S. postage stamp is Tyrannosaurus, and obviously Brontosaurus is not identical to *that*. The reason that no argument from rigidity parallel to that supporting the necessity of 'Brontosaurus = Apatosaurus' can support the necessity of a statement like 'Brontosaurus = the largest dinosaur on a 1989 U.S. postage stamp' is, as I have indicated, that the second designator in the latter statement does not pick out Brontosaurus in every possible world, but rather picks it out in some worlds and not in others, so it is not rigid. Since one of the designators in the identity statement does not rigidly designate its designatum, there is no reason to take the statement to be necessary, even if it is true.

The foregoing contrast between statements with different modal profiles is of course manifested in any number of similar statements with terms for natural designata like species, colors, and so on. 'The honeybee = Apis mellifera' is necessarily true by virtue of containing two rigid designators for the honeybee; 'the honeybee = the biological species typically farmed for honey' is contingently true by virtue of containing one rigid designator and one nonrigid designator for the honeybee. 'White = albescent' is necessarily true by virtue of containing two rigid designators for the color; 'white = the color of Antarctica' is contingently true by virtue of containing one rigid designator and one nonrigid designator for the color.

Significantly, the rigid − nonrigid distinction found in the foregoing designators, which stand for *natural* entities, also seems readily applicable to designators of *artificial* entities. Bachelorhood is apparently *rigidly* picked out by 'bachelor' but *non*rigidly picked out by the expression 'the marital status most commonly broached in discussions about analyticity'. Bachelorhood could not have failed to be bachelorhood. But bachelorhood could have failed to be the marital status most commonly broached in discussions about analyticity. Philosophers might have preferred to appeal to spinsterhood in illustrating analyticity. If philosophers had done so, 'the marital status most commonly broached in discussions about analyticity' would *not* have designated bachelorhood, though it happens to do so as things are. There are worlds, then, with respect to which 'the marital status most commonly broached in discussions about analyticity' designates bachelorhood and others, such as the spinsterhood-preferring world, in which the expression designates some other marital status. Thus, that expression does not rigidly designate bachelorhood. 'Bachelor', by contrast, does.

Similarly, 'soda pop', 'soda', and 'pop' all rigidly designate the beverage soda pop; but 'the beverage Uncle Bill requested at our Super Bowl party' only contingently designates that beverage.

The connection to necessity is straightforward. 'Soda = the beverage Uncle Bill requested at our Super Bowl party' is true but not necessarily true, since the second designator is not rigid; it refers to milk, or juice in some worlds, and in those worlds, the sentence is false. 'Soda = pop' is, on the other hand, necessarily true, since it is true and both designators rigidly designate soda pop.

It seems mistaken then, to suppose that designators for artificial properties stand in contrast to designators for natural properties over rigidity, as if that contrast relevantly resembled the contrast between descriptions like 'the brightest non-lunar object in the evening sky' and names like 'Hesperus'.[4] The foregoing considerations indicate that both natural properties and artificial properties have their own respective rigid and nonrigid designators corresponding to 'Hesperus' and 'the brightest non-lunar object in the evening sky'.

My account of rigidity, which extends that status to designators of artificial properties, does not, then, seem to be troubled on that score. To the contrary, it would be troublesome were the account *not* to count artificial-property designators as rigid, given the foregoing parallels between designators for concrete objects on the one hand and designators for properties, whether natural or artificial, on the other hand. It seems right to extend the status of rigidity to artificial-property designators.

2. The Problem of Shadowing

I have argued that the account of rigidity that I favor is not trivialized even though terms for artificial properties, and not just natural properties, can be rigid: this trivialization threat does not materialize. But there is yet a *second* alleged trivialization problem, according to which rigidity as I understand it cannot be kept to the right designators: again, the worry is that all property designators come out rigid. The second accusation of trivialization addresses those designators that I have said are *non*rigid: the objection charges that these are rigid after all. According to the objection, each of the supposedly nonrigid property designators that I have recognized is characterized by *two* potential designata, between which no principled selection can be made. One potential designatum is the familiar candidate for nonrigid designation, which I recognize as the true designatum. The other potential designatum, a candidate for *rigid* designation, appears to be equally good as a candidate for designation, whatever the world of evaluation: so the candidate for rigid designation *shadows* or follows the designator's lead from world to world, so to speak, presenting itself as a rival to what would otherwise be the clear designatum with respect to that world. Since it is unclear which property is the relevant designatum, the host candidate, which is a different property from world to world, or the shadowing candidate, which is the same property from world to world, it is unclear whether the designator is nonrigid or rigid, or whether perhaps no sense can be made of the claim that the designator is either nonrigid or rigid. Illustrations will help to clarify.

I have said that 'the color of Antarctica' and 'the biological species typically farmed for honey' are nonrigid designators. 'The color of Antarctica' designates whiteness since Antarctica is white: that is its color. But 'the color of Antarctica' designates some other color with respect to possible worlds in which Antarctica is a dark, lush jungle: its designatum changes from world to world. In the same way, 'the biological species typically farmed for honey' designates the honeybee, Apis mellifera, but there are other possible worlds with respect to which it designates one or another species of honeyguide birds of the family Indicatoridae, instead: honeyguide birds lead people to bees' nests, and there are possible worlds in which these birds, rather than honeybees, are farmed for the sake of obtaining honey.

The relevant *worry* is that 'the color of Antarctica' designates *not* white with respect to this world and other shades with respect to other worlds, but rather that it designates, with respect to all possible worlds, the property of *being the color of Antarctica*, and that 'the biological species typically farmed for honey' designates *not* Apis mellifera with respect to this world and a species of bird with respect to other worlds, but rather that it designates, with respect to all possible worlds, the property of *being the biological species typically farmed for honey*.

The property of *being the color of Antarctica* is of course distinct from white and the property of *being the biological species typically farmed for honey* is distinct from Apis mellifera. The metaphysical extension of white contains just white items, as usual, even with respect to possible worlds in which Antarctica teems with dark jungles; but the metaphysical extension of the property of *being the color of Antarctica* does not contain white items, with respect to those other possible worlds, since in those worlds the color of Antarctica is not white (any reader who supposes that 'being the color of Antarctica' could be used for white or anything besides the relational property for which I am using it should of course attend to the intended reading: see chapter 1, note 10). Similar words apply to Apis mellifera and the property of *being the biological species typically farmed for honey*.

What I call the "shadowing problem" is the problem of saying how a denoting expression like 'the color of Antarctica' or 'the biological species typically farmed for honey' can be said to nonrigidly designate white or Apis mellifera rather than rigidly designate the shadowing property *being the color of Antarctica*, or *being the biological species typically farmed for honey*.[5] In response, I observe below first that the shadowing problem, which appears to some theorists to threaten any account of a rigid – nonrigid distinction for property designators like the one I favor, is not really unique to designators for *properties*: it generalizes to designators for concrete objects, as well. So if it scotches any principled distinction between rigid and nonrigid designators, then what it precludes is not only the application of rigidity to designators for properties specifically, but the application of rigidity to designators in general. That is all work for section (2.1). In section (2.2), I address whether the shadowing problem scotches any principled distinction between rigid and nonrigid designators in general. My conclusion will be that it does not.

2.1. A Parallel for Concrete-Object Designators

The shadowing problem might initially appear to afflict only designators for properties, not designators for concrete objects. After all, with respect to a designator like 'the president of the USA', "there is an object that we can see and touch," as Schwartz urges (2002, p. 270). This object that we can see and touch is the item that we designate, it might seem. No shadowing candidates seriously rival the designatum's claim to be the real designatum, because concrete objects like the president are "constituents of the actual world that may be studied and checked for identity" with the designatum (Collins 1988, p. 202; for related citations and discussion, see chapter 8, §2.1.2). So it might seem.

But contrary to initial appearances, the trouble of shadowing does afflict 'the president of the USA'. The familiar, favored candidate for designation can be seen and touched, but so can competing, shadowing candidates for designation. Thus, my application of rigidity and nonrigidity to property designators does not introduce any special problems about shadowing that are not faced by the widely accepted application of rigidity and nonrigidity to concrete-object designators.

One shadowing candidate vying to be the designatum of 'the president of the USA' is the *persisting officer* Prez, discussed by Alan Sidelle (1992b; see also 1995). A persisting officer like Prez is an individual who is *constituted* at any given time by the man or woman in a given office, like the U.S. presidency, just as a river is constituted by the water particles in it. Just as there is regular change in the water molecules that constitute a river, so also there is regular change in the men or women who constitute Prez. And just as a river might have been constituted by different particles instead of the ones in it, had the sky rained different water molecules to the earth, so also Prez might have been constituted by different persons, had election results sent different persons into office. Prez is not *identical* to any man or woman in the White House any more than a river is identical to the water particles in it. A person like George Washington or Barack Obama is each essentially such that he issues from the union of particular cells from his natural parents, we may suppose. Prez, on the other hand, is essentially such that he issues from the first presidential inauguration in the United States. So Prez came into existence the moment George Washington was sworn into office. Although Prez was constituted in 1790 by George Washington, he later came to be constituted by other men, including Bush and Obama. The moment before Bush left office, Prez was constituted by Bush, but in 2009, with the swearing in of Obama, Prez ceased to be constituted by Bush and became constituted by Obama. Had Hillary Rodham Clinton or John McCain won, Prez would have become constituted by Clinton or McCain, not Obama, in 2009.

In every possible world featuring Prez, Prez is evidently the president of the USA: 'the president of the USA' would accordingly seem to designate Prez with respect to every possible world or rigidly. So 'the president of the USA' seems to be just as well suited to be used as a rigid designator for Prez as it is suited to be a nonrigid designator for Obama (as Sidelle suggests: 1992b, pp. 417, 419). Hence, the shadowing problem afflicts nonrigid concrete-object designators like 'the president of the USA' as well as nonrigid designators for properties.

It does not matter that the president can be seen and touched. Prez, like Obama, can be seen and touched: so there are no grounds here for discrimination against Prez or his candidacy for designation. Many people have seen and touched Prez, just as many people have seen and touched Obama. Some people have seen and touched both Prez and Obama at the same time, like Joe Biden, when he has shaken the president's hand. So even though the designatum of a concrete-object designator like 'the president of the USA' can be seen and touched, shadowing remains a problem because Prez remains a candidate for rigid designation.

When I say that Prez is a candidate for designation, I take for granted that Prez exists. This might be denied, of course: a philosopher could refuse to recognize "unusual" objects like persisting officers in one's ontology. I am doubtful that any such stance in metaphysics provides a satisfying resolution to problems about designation like those under discussion (in part for reasons suggested in note 1); but even if one *could* dodge problems concerning the designation of concrete-object designators, like the shadowing problem, by thinning out one's ontology and declining to recognize "unusual" objects like persisting officers, one could also dodge issues about the designation of *property* designators, like the shadowing problem, by thinning out one's ontology and declining to recognize "unusual" properties like the property of *being the biological species typically farmed for honey* (this move is suggested in Bird and Tobin 2009, §3.3). So again, there is no special trouble here for property designators.

My application of rigidity and nonrigidity to property designators does not, then, introduce any *special* problem of shadowing that is not faced by the widely accepted application of rigidity and nonrigidity to concrete-object designators. This is not, of course, to say that there is no *general* problem of shadowing candidates for designation. For all that I have said so far, some fundamental flaw in ascriptions of rigidity and nonrigidity to terms for properties and concrete objects *both* has been uncovered. My aim in this book is not to defend the rigid – nonrigid distinction in *general*; rather, my aim is to defend a rigid – nonrigid distinction as it applies to property designators specifically.[6] So a problem, or alleged problem, for rigidity in general, as shadowing turns out to be, could be set aside. However, *this* general problem for rigidity has frequently raised suspicions concerning the rigidity of property designators *specifically*: so I will try to address it.

2.2. Responses to the Problem

If an expression like 'the biological species typically farmed for honey' nonrigidly designates Apis mellifera, as I claim, then a proper understanding of the problem of shadowing seems to require an understanding of *how* it does so. "*In virtue of what*," as

Devitt would ask (2005, p. 154; see also 2009, p. 240), does such an expression "nonrigidly designate that," i.e., Apis mellifera, rather than an artificial candidate for designation that shadows the right one? In the following two sections, (2.2.1) and (2.2.2), I will provide answers. In section (2.2.1), I answer that 'the biological species typically farmed for honey' designates Apis mellifera because Apis mellifera is the one and only item satisfying the predicate '... is a biological species typically farmed for honey'. So no unusual, shadowing property is even a *proper candidate* for designation, on any reasonable English use of 'the biological species typically farmed for honey'. In the section following that discussion (§2.2.2), I will argue, further, that even if the relevant shadowing property *were* a proper candidate for designation, the designator would still nonrigidly designate Apis mellifera in certain contexts, rather than rigidly designate any shadowing property.

2.2.1. Without Shadowing Candidates 'The biological species typically farmed for honey' designates a *biological species*. Compare the property of *being the biological species typically farmed for honey* or, more precisely, *being identical to the biological species typically farmed for honey*: this is instantiated, in any possible world, by *whatever* sole biological species is typically farmed for honey *at that world*. This property, which is suspected of *shadowing* from world to world whatever would otherwise be nonrigidly designated by 'the biological species typically farmed for honey', is *not a species*, unlike the true designatum of 'the biological species typically farmed for honey'. The property of *being identical to the biological species typically farmed for honey* is not a species because it is a higher-order entity: it is a property *of* species, rather than a *species*, just as the property of *being identical to the person who farms the most honey* is a property *of* persons, rather than a *person*. Since the property of *being identical to the biological species typically farmed for honey* is a property of species, and is not itself a species, it is not a candidate to be the designatum of 'the biological species typically farmed for honey'. It does not shadow, from world to world, whatever the real designatum is at that world, impugning that real designatum's status as the designatum.

It might be protested that the relevant shadowing property is *not*, after all, the higher-order property of *being* identical to *the biological species typically farmed for honey* but rather the lower-order property of *being* in *the biological species typically farmed for honey*: *this* is not a property of species, but rather a property of honeybees. Since honeybees instantiate both Apis mellifera and the property of *being in the biological species typically farmed for honey*, we might be tempted to say, with respect to any possible world in which 'the biological species typically farmed for honey' might appear at a glance to designate the species Apis mellifera or some species of birds nonrigidly, that in reality the property of *being in the biological species typically farmed for honey* has as much claim to be the designatum. Again, however, it would be a mistake to say this: and again, the reason is that the supposed shadowing entity is not a species but the true designatum is. The following considerations show this: and since they apply as well to the higher-order property just rejected as a candidate for designation, they provide further testimony against its candidacy.

The property of *being in the biological species typically farmed for honey* cannot be a species because whether an organism instantiates the property of *being in the biological species typically farmed for honey* is something that humans can easily alter by deciding what to farm; an organism's *species* is not so easily subject to human fancy. A decision to outlaw bee-farming could hardly change whether a particular bee instantiates its *species*; but such a decision *could* change whether a particular bee instantiates the property of *being in the biological species typically farmed for honey*. Accordingly, the property of *being in the biological species typically farmed for honey* is a property of little *biological* interest. Any *species*, by contrast, is of considerable biological interest: so the designatum of 'the biological species typically farmed for honey', a species, cannot be the property *being in the biological species typically farmed for honey*, which is something other than a species.

It is hard to see, then, how 'the biological species typically farmed for honey' could be plagued by a shadowing problem. Initially promising candidates for shadowing properties fail to amount to anything. There is nothing special about this example, which concerns biology. Consider another designator that I have said is nonrigid: 'the color of Antarctica'. As it happens, Antarctica is white, so white is the designatum of 'the color of Antarctica'. 'The color of Antarctica' would have designated a dark shade had the planet been warmer. There is a higher-order relational property, that of *being identical to the color of Antarctica*. This is a property of colors and is instantiated by white if Antarctica is white, by green if Antarctica is green, and so on: but it is hard to believe that this higher-order relational property is *itself* a color, as the designatum of 'the color of Antarctica' is a color. The property of *being identical to the color of Antarctica* is rather a property *of* some color rather than a color, again in the same way that the property of *being identical to the highest mountain on Antarctica* is a property *of* some mountain rather than a mountain. We might consider another candidate for the position of being the relevant shadowing property: the lower-order relational property of *being something with the color of Antarctica*. But similar reflection indicates that this property is also not a color. The shade that something like K2 or George Washington would need to have in order to be endowed with the relevant relational property would vary depending on weather patterns in Antarctica. Take by contrast some specific *color*, like the one that happens to characterize Antarctica: the shade that K2 or Washington would need to have in order to be endowed with that *non*relational property would *not* vary depending on weather patterns in Antarctica. This indicates that the property of *being something with the color of Antarctica* is not a color[7]: so it is not the designatum of 'the color of Antarctica'. Again, it is hard to find candidates for shadowing apart from those just discussed that would seem even on first glance to follow the intended designatum of 'the color of Antarctica' from world to world: so the shadowing problem fails, for want of shadowing entities qualifying for designation, to ruin this designator's status as a nonrigid property designator.

Something similar can be said for expressions for *artificial* entities like professions or brands: e.g., 'the brand of soda endorsed by Ray Charles'. *Pepsi* is that brand, not a gruesome, shadowing entity that happens to be Pepsi but that would have been Coca

Cola or Canada Dry had one of these companies made Charles a better offer than Pepsi did. The relevant gruesome property is not a *brand* at all, so it cannot be the brand endorsed by Charles; the extension of the alleged shadowing entity changes from world to world from Pepsi to Coke to Canada Dry to other brands. But there is no *brand*, whether Pepsi or Coke or Canada Dry or anything else, that happens to be Pepsi but that would have been Coke or Canada Dry had Charles endorsed Coke or Canada Dry: no one would register a trademark for anything like *that*. Since the relevant abstract entity that is instantiated by Pepsi in our world but Coke in others and so on, is not a brand of anything, it is not in the right category to be the designatum. Further, it seems clear that Charles has never *endorsed* any such gruesome shadowing entity. He has never made any professions about it at all; he has never heard of it or given it a thought. If the above considerations are correct, then no shadowing problem afflicts 'the brand of soda endorsed by Ray Charles' any more than such a problem afflicts 'the biological species typically farmed for honey' or 'the color of Antarctica'.

I have been arguing that descriptions that I have claimed to be nonrigid really are. No shadowing problem attends them, because none of these property designators is endowed with more than one potential designatum, one of which shadows others from world to world in the relevant respect. Still, it would be inaccurate to say that *all* singular property designators are free from any shadowing problem for this reason. Unlike the property designators I have been putting forward as models of nonrigidity, some other property designators *do* seem to be endowed with more than one candidate for designation, one of which shadows the designator from world to world in something like the relevant respect so that no one of the candidates seems without further qualification to earn genuine designation. Property designators with more than one potential designatum of the relevant sort include general descriptions that fail to inform us much about the designatum, like 'the *property* that is instantiated by all and only items that are the color of Antarctica' or 'the *entity* that is instantiated by all and only quantities of the brand of soda endorsed by Ray Charles'. Without a restricting context, I can say, accurately, "there is no *one* property that is instantiated by all and only items that are the color of Antarctica, since *both* the color white and *also* the relational property of *being something with the color of Antarctica* are instantiated by all and only items that are the color of Antarctica." So for all I have said yet, an abundance of potential designata spoils *some* designators' claim to a single nonrigid use, as proponents of the shadowing problem would have it.

I will argue in section (2.2.2) that even where shadowing presents an abundance of potential designata, as for the examples in the foregoing paragraph, context can select just the right potential designatum, thus redeeming a designator's claim to nonrigidity. But even were I to stop here, without putting forward those considerations of section (2.2.2), the rigid – nonrigid distinction would seem secure: I have just argued that *some* property designators, like those garden-variety property designators that I have been citing as models of nonrigidity, do not suffer from the shadowing problem, and they are enough to secure a distinction.

2.2.2. The Irrelevance of Shadowing Candidates Supposed shadowing entities are not in the right category to be described by those nonrigid property designators that I have been citing, such as 'the biological species typically farmed for honey' and 'the color of Antarctica': the alleged shadowing entities can be ruled out as potential designata on basic semantic grounds. So I have argued (in §2.2.1). But suppose that, contrary to the lesson of section (2.2.1), the descriptive content of designators like 'the biological species typically farmed for honey' or 'the color of Antarctica' *were* applicable to shadowing properties. In that case, for any designator like 'the biological species typically farmed for honey' or 'the color of Antarctica', there would be not one but *two* potential candidates for designation, so the worry that shadowing spoils their nonrigidity would still be with us, for all that I have yet said. And the general attending worry that shadowing spoils any rigid – nonrigid *distinction* for property designators would also still be with us. Nevertheless, in the present section (2.2.2), I point out that shadowing would *still* not present any intractable problems for a rigid – nonrigid distinction.

A variety of different designators suffer from the condition of having more than one proper candidate for designation; but there is a well-known resolution. That resolution seems applicable to the special case of shadowing. In section (2.2.2.1), I discuss the general problem and the well-known resolution, which is that a single designatum can emerge from a pool of proper candidates by virtue of being favored by the context. Of course, conditions have to be right for context to do its work selecting a designatum. So in section (2.2.2.2), I argue that conditions *are* indeed right, in familiar situations, for context to do its work selecting the real designatum instead of *shadowing* rivals where that is an issue. So context redeems the rigid – nonrigid distinction, in view of the shadowing problem.

2.2.2.1. Beyond *Shadowing*: a General Problem with a General Remedy Definite descriptions have long been known, for reasons quite independent of shadowing, to give rise to problems concerning how an *apparent* designatum could qualify as the *genuine* designatum in view of a rich field of alternative candidates that likewise meet the relevant descriptive requirements. I will suggest that shadowing is a special case of these general problems for definite descriptions, where shadowing is an issue at all.

Consider your announcement to someone in a neighboring room, as you admire some flowers in your kitchen: "the kitchen table has a bouquet on it." Here 'the kitchen table' seems to designate your table. But there is a problem for explaining how this could be: there are *other* bona fide kitchen tables, like your neighbor's table, which threaten your table's entitlement to *unique* designation and hence to designation *at all*. Presumably, your statement 'the kitchen table has a bouquet on it' is true or assertible by virtue of the bouquet on your table, regardless of how many of the other tables in the universe are without bouquets: so the threat to designation fails to materialize, in some important respect. Still, the task remains of articulating *how*.

How could it be that, even though more than one object satisfies the predicate '... is a kitchen table', the rich field of candidates for designation fails to spoil the description's claim to designate your table? As I have indicated, context would appear to provide the explanation. The context indicates that tables outside of your home are irrelevant. They are ignored or disqualified as potential designata: context seems to limit the domain of discourse to your home or your kitchen or some other approximate local vicinity.[8] A *shift* of context could make your table irrelevant, in the same way. Thus, suppose that the neighbor who gave you the flowers pays a visit and says that her own table is similarly adorned. In your response, "you mean the kitchen table has a bouquet on it?," the designator is used for her table, not yours.

Suppose that a shadowing property, *being something with the color of Antarctica*, were a proper designatum for 'the color of Antarctica' because contrary to what I have argued, the shadowing property satisfies the predicate '... is a color of Antarctica'. Since white, too, satisfies the predicate, the description would then illustrate the problem of uniqueness faced by definite descriptions in general. The remedy that I have been discussing would seem as applicable here as anywhere: context could still, in principle at least, select white as the proper designatum. Or consider 'the property that is instantiated by all and only items that are the color of Antarctica'. I have argued that both white and *being something with the color of Antarctica* do seem equally qualified to satisfy the predicate '... is a property that is instantiated by all and only items that are the color of Antarctica'. So some property designators like 'the property that is instantiated by all and only items that are the color of Antarctica' *do* apply properly to shadowing candidates: neither white nor its rival uniquely satisfies the predicate, in a general context. Still, a selective context could distinguish white, or its rival, as the designatum. Since white would be nonrigidly designated in the relevant contexts and its rival rigidly designated in the relevant contexts, a principled rigid – nonrigid distinction is thereby honored. Accordingly, I regard the shadowing problem, where shadowing is even an issue at all, as a special case of a well-known problem of uniqueness for definite descriptions.

Ambiguity presents problems similar to the foregoing problems for definite descriptions, and admits a similar resolution. Shadowing is typically taken to arise on account of ambiguity (Linsky 2006, pp. 659–61; 2011, p. 40; Martí 2004, pp. 138 and 140, note 17), contrary to my diagnosis. In any event, if the shadowing problem *were* to arise by way of ambiguity, it might arise by way of semantic ambiguity or by way of structural, or syntactic, ambiguity. Suppose that 'the color of Antarctica' is *semantically* ambiguous, in the way that 'seal' is ambiguous: then the rich field of potential designata could again, in principle at least, be narrowed straightforwardly in the right contexts. Different uses of 'seal' do not nullify the reading on which 'seal' is used for the animal, say: context sometimes assures the relevant designatum, as in 'seal is the great white shark's favorite prey', even if other contexts call for some other designatum.

A more plausible form of ambiguity for 'the color of Antarctica' would be syntactic ambiguity, which attends an expression like 'visiting relatives': the sentence 'Kim enjoys visiting relatives', say, might be true on one reading, according to which Kim likes to visit, but false on another reading, according to which Kim likes relatives who are visiting. But again, context can clarify the right reading. Similar words would apply to 'the color of Antarctica' if it were syntactically ambiguous. Ambiguity in general therefore seems to pose no threat in principle to the distinction between rigidity and nonrigidity.

I have urged that context can *in principle* secure the right designatum for 'the color of Antarctica', just as it could for 'the kitchen table', 'seal', and so on. Whether context *does* in practice secure a designatum depends on whether speakers do in practice communicate in the proper contexts. And they do: the job of the following section (2.2.2.2) is to demonstrate this.

2.2.2.2. Context at Work to Relieve the Shadowing Problem After illustrating how context selects the right designatum for nonrigid property designators instead of a shadowing rival, I will put closure on my discussion of shadowing by revisiting briefly concrete-object designators. The harmlessness of shadowing, for rigidity in general, will become clear in view of a broadly applicable resolution.

2.2.2.2.1. CONTEXT AT WORK FOR SHADOW-ATTENDED PROPERTY DESIGNATORS That speakers naturally use some property designators nonrigidly is indicated when speakers affirm statements like 'Blanche's favorite color = the color of Antarctica'. Let us suppose, for simplicity, that Antarctica is indeed white and that this is Blanche's favorite color. In that case, a speaker would presumably tell the truth by uttering "Blanche's favorite color = the color of Antarctica."

Clearly the speaker could, and in typical contexts would, avoid using 'Blanche's favorite color' to designate the relational property of *being identical to Blanche's favorite color* or to designate *being something with Blanche's favorite color* (even if, contrary to what I have suggested in the foregoing section, §2.2.1, such a reading or use could issue in successful designation in English). Otherwise, the speaker would utter something false by 'Blanche's favorite color = the color of Antarctica'. The reason that the speaker would utter something false by 'Blanche's favorite color = the color of Antarctica', if she were to use 'Blanche's favorite color' to designate the relational property of *being identical to Blanche's favorite color*, is that the relational property of *being identical to Blanche's favorite color* is not the same property as the one designated by 'the color of Antarctica', whether the designatum of 'the color of Antarctica' is white, on the one hand, or the relational property of *being identical to the color of Antarctica*, on the other hand. The relational property of *being identical to Blanche's favorite color* would have been instantiated by turquoise had Blanche's tastes differed, but white would *not* have been instantiated by turquoise; and neither would the relational property of *being identical to the color of Antarctica* have been instantiated by turquoise, since Antarctica would hardly have been turquoise had Blanche's tastes differed.

It is correct to say, "Blanche's favorite color = the color of Antarctica," in a typical context in which such a statement might be uttered, only because in a typical context 'Blanche's favorite color' would be used to designate white. Hence, 'Blanche's favorite color' serves at least sometimes to designate white, not a shadowing entity. The same holds for 'the color of Antarctica'.

Again, there might be *other* possible uses of 'Blanche's favorite color' and therefore other possible readings of 'Blanche's favorite color = the color of Antarctica', which other readings might come into play in *a*typical contexts; but that is irrelevant.[9] For all I will contest here (but cf. §2.2.1), there *could* be bizarre contexts in which someone would assert a *false* and indeed *necessarily* false proposition by 'Blanche's favorite color = the color of Antarctica' by using 'Blanche's favorite color' to designate rigidly the relational property of *being identical to Blanche's favorite color*. Such an unlikely use of 'Blanche's favorite color' to express a necessary falsehood by the utterance of 'Blanche's favorite color = the color of Antarctica' would not cause paradox for my position that 'Blanche's favorite color = the color of Antarctica' could be used in other contexts and indeed typically *would* be used to say something true.

2.2.2.2.2. CONTEXT AT WORK FOR SHADOW-ATTENDED CONCRETE-OBJECT DESIGNATORS
I have suggested that the concrete-object designator 'the president of the USA' has a second potential designatum besides Obama, and this second potential designatum is the persisting officer Prez. Prez, like Obama, would seem to satisfy the descriptive content of the designator by virtue of swearing into office, vetoing legislation, nominating candidates for the Supreme Court, and so on. If indeed Prez is as qualified a candidate for designation as Obama then 'the president of the United States' is unlike 'the color of Antarctica', say, or 'the biological species typically farmed for honey', insofar as 'the president of the USA' really *is* attended by a candidate for designation that satisfies the relevant predicate and that follows the designator's lead from world to world, rivaling for the position of designatum what would ordinarily be thought to be designated, non-rigidly, in the respective world. In any event, we can consider whether shadowing *would* be amenable to resolution with the help of context, in the manner just indicated for property designators (in §2.2.2.2.1), *were* Prez to serve as a genuine shadowing entity for the concrete-object designator 'the president of the USA'. The answer would seem to be that yes, shadowing would indeed be amenable to the resolution.

If Prez serves as a shadowing entity, we might say, truthfully, "there is no such item as *the* president of the USA: Prez and Obama are both presidents of the USA." There is a uniqueness problem like that attending expressions like 'the kitchen table' (see § 2.2.2.1). But again, the problem is resolved by context, which limits the universe of discourse in the same way that it limits the universe of discourse for 'the kitchen table': if I say, "persisting officers might begin their lives with gray hair but still they sometimes endure for centuries after that: hence, with the first inaugural ceremony, the president of the USA began life as a wise, experienced, gray-haired general," then I say something true of Prez, not Obama, so you could gather from the context, if you were informed about Prez, that I am using the description for Prez rather than for Obama. Other contexts could assure that Obama is the designatum. If I say, "the president of the USA would still have had an African father even had he never been president," or "the president of the United States can keep his job only for two terms," then I say something true of Obama but not Prez, so you would gather from the context that I am using the description for Obama. Generally, speakers are more interested in talking about Obama than Prez, so generally they use the description 'the president of the USA' for Obama: this is a nonrigid reading or use of the designator. So despite shadowing entities like Prez, concrete-object designators like 'the president of the USA' can be nonrigid designators, at least on the right readings or uses.

The foregoing resolution to the problem of shadowing can be applied more broadly, as I have already suggested, to secure nonrigid designation for 'the president of the USA', despite other potentially confounding candidates for designation besides Prez. It is sometimes suggested that 'the president of the USA' might rigidly designate the office of the presidency, say (Sullivan 2007, p. 14). The office would be distinct from the shadowing office-person Prez, who is a concrete individual. Suppose that indeed 'the president of the USA' designates the office rigidly in a context in which someone utters, 'the president of the USA is the commander in chief': still, 'the president of the USA' designates Obama nonrigidly in other contexts, like that in which someone utters, 'the president of the USA just exercised his authority'. Again, the problem of shadowing manifests a problem that is wider than shadowing and whose remedy is more general.

Shadowing does not show that there is no rigid – nonrigid distinction for concrete-object designators any more than it shows that there is no rigid – nonrigid distinction for property designators.

3. A Confusion Between Rigidity and Meaning Constancy?

I have discussed two objections to the coherence of my favored rigid – nonrigid distinction for property designators. Both of those objections urge that designators that are supposed to be nonrigid seem to come out rigid on my view. In the present section (§3), I address a final objection to the coherence of the rigid – nonrigid distinction that I favor. This objection offers something like a diagnosis of the supposed illusion of a distinction. According to the diagnosis, it is only by "confusing rigidity with consistency of meaning" (Schwartz 2002, p. 272) that we can maintain that any property designators are rigid. The alleged rigidity of an expression like 'white' reflects, according to this objection, only "the obvious and rather uninteresting fact that words have the same meaning when talking about other possible worlds as they do when talking about the actual world" (p. 272). *Any* term for a property "names the same property in every possible world because trivially words keep the same meanings" no matter what possible world we are talking about (p. 273): and hence, there is no real distinction between rigid and allegedly nonrigid property designators.

The foregoing objection is a natural one, and has it right that we must distinguish sameness of meaning across possible worlds from sameness of designation, or rigid designation: to say that an expression is rigid just because it keeps the same meaning from world to world would indeed be confused. But my own account does not fall into this confusion. In my view 'white' is rigid, while 'the color of Antarctica' is not. But *both* 'white' and 'the color of Antarctica' *keep the same meaning* when we talk about counterfactual situations. 'The color of Antarctica' is nonrigid because it *designates* white with respect to this world, but not with respect to some other worlds, where Antarctica is some dark color characteristic of jungles, instead; with respect to those worlds, 'the color of Antarctica' designates a dark shade. But 'the color of Antarctica' designates white *or* some dark shade, depending on the world, precisely because white or the dark shade satisfies the description *on its present meaning*. So 'the color of Antarctica' has the same *meaning* whether it *designates* white or the dark shade. In this way, I would distinguish constancy of designation, or lack thereof, with constancy of meaning.

One might take the *meaning* of each of the foregoing designators to be a function taking possible worlds as arguments and yielding abstract objects, properties, for values.[10] In that case, a rigid designator for a property would be a designator whose meaning is a constant function, yielding the same abstract object, the property that is the relevant term's designatum, for every possible world. A nonrigid designator for a property, by contrast, would yield different abstract objects, or designata, at different worlds. The meaning of 'white' is a constant function: 'white' designates white in any possible world and hence is rigid. The meaning of 'the color of Antarctica' is a function that yields a different value depending on the possible world: white in this possible world but darker shades in others. Since the designatum varies from world to world, 'the color of Antarctica' is nonrigid. But the designatum is the *value* of the relevant function for any possible world, *not* that function itself. Although the designatum, or the value of the relevant function, varies from world to world, the function *itself*, which is the *meaning* of the expression, does not. 'The color of Antarctica' has just one meaning as it denotes different colors at different worlds: the meaning is a non-constant function that remains the same non-constant function regardless of the value of the function at a world.

4. Conclusion

The distinction that I recognize between different sorts of designators, some of which I take to be rigid and some of which I take to be nonrigid, is a distinction that various capable philosophers have taken to be spurious. But a close look at the distinction in view of initially plausible objections indicates that the distinction is genuine. If my reasoning in this chapter is correct, singular designators for properties can be divided into two camps, one for those expressions that designate just what they designate with respect to every possible world, and the other for those expressions that change designata from world to world.

Still, there remain objections according to which the distinction to which I have called attention fails to perform work proper to a *rigid – nonrigid* distinction, even if it is a genuine distinction. It is the business of the next chapter to argue, in response to such objections, that the distinction that I have secured is a rigid – nonrigid distinction because it performs the duties constituting the role of the rigid – nonrigid distinction.

Notes

1. Following Salmon (1981, p. 46), I call the set of a property's instances, or perhaps those instances themselves, the property's "metaphysical extension." The *semantic* extension of a singular *designator* for a property, by contrast, is the property itself. In chapters 4 (§2.2.1) and 5 (note 6) I discuss the connection between the metaphysical extension of a property and the semantic extension of any merely *general* term that there might be for that property. In the present chapter, as I have indicated (in chapter 1, §3.1), I ignore general terms, treating property designators as singular, although such a treatment is compatible with a treatment of the same designators as general terms or predicates, if, say, singular terms of one order are taken to be general terms of another order.

    The foregoing artificial properties might fuel more ontological skepticism than a natural property would. Some qualms might be alleviated by different examples of artificial properties, which the reader is free to substitute; but in any case, we may presuppose realism here, in order to indulge the objection: I would certainly want my favored rigid – nonrigid distinction to hold up on the assumption of realism about artificial properties anyway. I would generalize this practice, in the hope of being able to articulate a theory about language that is available to philosophers of different metaphysical persuasions with regard to the nature and existence of properties (see also my treatment of nominalism in chapter 5; for a contrasting approach, see, e.g., Bird and Tobin 2009, §3 or Linsky 1984, pp. 259–60, who are happy to push ontological commitments against the sort of problems that I address in this chapter and chapter 5).

2. Some of the common objections to counting artificial-property designators as rigid do not threaten the very distinction that I would draw between designators that I would count as rigid and designators that I would count as nonrigid: I save discussion of those objections for the next chapter (chapter 3, §2.2).

3. Thus, Macbeth argues that an account of rigidity that extends the honor to artificial-property designators fails to honor the rigidity of the relevant terms "except in a trivial sense in which all predicates are rigid" (Macbeth 1995, p. 263; see also pp. 266, 268–71, 276–7). Macbeth specifically addresses predicates and general terms, but these might be construed as singular as well, in a fashion (see note 1): and in any event, Macbeth apparently intends to discuss *all* designators for properties (or kinds, which I treat as properties: again, see chapter 1, §2, especially at note 8), not just *nonsingular* designators for properties (Macbeth pp. 270–1; 276–7; 279, note 7). Schwartz sometimes directs his attention, too, specifically to general terms (see the following note 4), but he too would apparently extend his observations to singular property designators: indeed, in places he is explicit about addressing singular property designators (see the paragraph corresponding to this note for a quotation). Soames, or time-slices of Soames, joins Macbeth and Schwartz in rejecting the rigidity of artificial

general terms and predicates. If general terms and predicates for artificial properties are rigid, Soames says, then all general terms and predicates "turn out, trivially, to be rigid" (2003, p. 427; see also 2002, pp. 260–1; Soames has more recently had second thoughts with respect to general terms, though perhaps not with respect to predicates: see 2004, pp. 95–6; 2006b, p. 712). Gómez-Torrente also focuses on general terms in his criticisms: if we grant that even "'bachelor' designates *being a bachelor* in all possible worlds and is therefore rigid," a crucial contrast between rigid and nonrigid designators is lost, says Gómez-Torrente. "The notion is thus trivialized" (Gómez-Torrente 2006, p. 229). I would resist the basic triviality objection at issue for essentially the same reason, whether the focus is on singular terms or on general terms and predicates (even supposing that general terms and predicates are not also singular, as they might be construed: again, see the foregoing note 1): in all cases, the essential modal work of rigidity finds a parallel in expressions for artificial properties on the one side and natural properties on the other (I elaborate on the generality of my response, which for the sake of exposition I frame here by reference just to singular terms, in chapter 5, especially at note 11). Cf. my response to the shadowing problem, where the differences between terms of different grammatical categories will take on more importance than it does in my response to worries about artificial-property designators (see below, note 5).

4. Various workers say explicitly, to the contrary, that just as "there is a contrast between proper names and definite descriptions, in that the former are rigid whereas the latter are non-rigid," there ought to be a corresponding contrast between terms that are "natural kind terms and those that are not" (Schwartz 1980, p. 196; 2006, pp. 277, 283; see also Gómez-Torrente 2006, p. 228 and Putnam 1975, p. 265). There may be some parallel between descriptions and designators for artificial properties, on the one hand, and proper names and designators for natural properties on the other, inasmuch as the *causal theory of reference* might, or might typically, apply to both members of the latter pair yet to neither member of the former pair; but these parallels have little to do with rigidity (see chapter 3, §2.2–§2.4).

5. Shadowing has apparently been independently considered by a few philosophers, before a recent explosion of published discussion. Linsky (1984, p. 268) anticipates the phenomenon of shadowing as a potential objection to his account of rigidity, in a publication that has only relatively recently seen much of an audience (see chapter 4, §2.2.2.1). Michael Devitt has apparently independently anticipated the phenomenon of shadowing, appealing to it in then-anonymous refereeing comments to LaPorte 2000; in response, I included discussion that I had unwisely earlier set aside as distracting. A number of workers have since addressed the problem in print, taking a variety of perspectives: Cordry 2004, pp. 247–9; Devitt 2005, pp. 140ff., 153f.; Haukioja 2006, pp. 157ff.; Inan 2008 pp. 222f.; Linsky 2006; López de Sa 2001, pp. 614ff.; 2006; 2007; 2008a; Martí 2004, pp. 136ff.; Martí and Martínez-Fernández 2010; Schwartz 2002, pp. 268f., 273; Sullivan 2007, pp. 14–15). Soames raises essentially the same problem for general terms and predicates specifically (2002, pp. 259–62; Soames later distinguishes between general terms and predicates, clearing general terms but not predicates from the criticism: Soames 2004, pp. 94–7; 2006b, pp. 712–14). In the present chapter, I address just singular terms, as I have emphasized, although again, that would *include* general terms on the supposition that they can *also* serve as singular terms (see note 1). A different response to the phenomenon of shadowing is needed in the case of absolutely nonsingular expressions (for two presentations of the *problem*, see Inan 2008, p. 222 and Soames's

aforementioned works): I provide such a response in chapter 5 (§1.1.2.1 and §1.1.2.3). The responses below (in §2.2 of this chapter), which effectively address the phenomenon of shadowing as it attends singular expressions, fail to apply to that phenomenon as it attends nonsingular expressions.

6. See chapter 1, note 1, and accompanying text for an account of my aims in the book. Not surprisingly, discretion will be needed periodically throughout the book for the reason it is needed here, with regard to the selection of material.

7. At the very least, we may observe that no such lower-order property, and for that matter no higher-order property like being identical to the color of Antarctica either, is a *natural* property, in this case a natural color. So no such lower-order or higher-order property could be the designatum of 'the *natural* color of Antarctica', which is accordingly not shadowed by the relevant lower-order or higher-order property even if 'the color of Antarctica' *is* shadowed, contrary to what I have argued, by the relevant lower-order or higher-order property since somehow that property is after all a color, though an artificial or gruesome one.

8. See Stanley and Szabo (2000) for a development of the idea that context restricts the domain of discourse. Perhaps, as some workers would maintain, context has other related work instead; the effect is likely to be similar for purposes here. For example, context might help to discriminate between items *within* the universe of discourse, rather than just help to limit the universe of discourse. Thus, on Lewis' (1983d, pp. 240–3) account, "'the F' denotes x if and only if x is the most salient F in the domain of discourse, according to some contextually determined salience ranking" (p. 241): this might allow for 'the kitchen table' to designate even when there are two tables in the domain, as when you say, comparing two tables in the kitchen "the kitchen table will make a sturdier vase holder than the other table beside it." Context might also help *communication* without assuring proper *semantic designation*, as it would if I were to use a metaphor to call attention to "the diamond in the rough that is holding up your vase," as I nodded in the direction of your table: so some workers favor a Gricean resolution to the problem of uniqueness (see Ludlow 2009, §7; Ludlow provides a useful survey of the problem in § 4.3). Even if, for all that context can do to help, the problem of uniqueness causes an expression like 'the kitchen table' to be without a *semantic* designatum, that problem still does not rob the expression of a "designatum" in another, perhaps derivative respect: following Kripke (1977), we could in this event call the relevant table the "speaker's designatum." Something similar would presumably hold for 'the color of Antarctica'. Even if your statement 'the color of Antarctica is white' is not literally true because competing candidates for designation rob 'the color of Antarctica' of any semantic designatum, the statement still *conveys information* about the speaker's designatum, white, without being literally true: and since the speaker's designatum would be some dark shade with respect to other worlds, the designation achieved with the designator seems nonrigid. Claims about rigid and nonrigid designation need not be bound to semantic designation (for other thoughts that would push further in this direction, see Neale 2008). So where I speak of "designation," readers might take different positions concerning whether what is achieved is genuine semantic designation: readers inclined to adopt a Gricean construal will construe accordingly or make adjustments where I speak of what a term expresses, its content, and so on.

9. The challenge to nonrigidity that is presented by shadowing constrains the range of possible readings for expressions like 'Blanche's favorite color' that I consider in the text: the challenge is that supposedly nonrigid property designators like this rigidly designate shadowing entities. But at least some philosophers would say that 'Blanche's favorite color' is rigid for quite different reasons: that 'Blanche's favorite color' rigidly designates not a shadowing entity like *being Blanche's favorite color* but rather *white*. Swinburne would appeal to such a rigid reading instead of a nonrigid one: so for Swinburne, the true reading of 'Blanche's favorite color = the color of Antarctica' is *necessarily* true: see Swinburne 2007, pp. 150–1. Kripke considers whether definite descriptions in general have, along *with* their typical nonrigid use, a rigid use of the sort that Swinburne recognizes for property designators specifically: Kripke doubts it (1980, pp. 59–60, note 22). There is no need for me to commit one way or the other on this matter; it is enough to say that even if there *is* a necessarily true reading, there is a contingently true reading too, as is indicated by the naturalness of a statement like, 'Blanche's favorite color = white: but *that need not have been the case*, since Blanche would have preferred some other color had documentaries never drawn her attention to Antarctica'. For other compelling considerations to the effect that property designators are at least sometimes used nonrigidly, even if there is a rigid reading, see Martí and Martínez-Fernández 2010, §2.

10. Kripke suggests that this is how he would account for 'sense' or 'meaning' (1980, p. 59, note 22). To be sure, 'meaning' is often used for something more or something else. Thus, the present account will not allow for a difference in meaning between necessarily co-designative expressions like 'white' and 'white such that the successor of 2 is 3' (similar issues arise for distinguishing between the properties designated: see chapter 5, note 18). This barebones account of meaning could certainly be supplemented: for example, we might wish to take into account not only possible worlds but also *im*possible worlds so that, with respect impossible worlds in which the successor of two is not three, the value of the function would not be the same for 'white' and 'white such that the successor of 2 is 3' (for a sympathetic treatment of uses like this for impossible worlds, see Vander Laan 1997, pp. 610ff.). Or we might like to take into account structure, computation procedures, and so on (for discussion and references, see Fitting 2011, §3.6), to reflect a difference in what we call the "meaning" of the foregoing designators. But though one might hope to see the simple account of meaning at hand replaced by something richer, the simple account will suffice for present purposes.

3

On Whether the Distinction Assigns to Rigidity the Right Role

I have just defended, in chapter 2, a distinction between property designators. But even if the distinction that I recognize is indeed a *genuine* distinction, it might or might not be a *rigid – nonrigid* distinction because it might or might not classify designators according to whether they fill the right role: i.e., according to whether they perform those duties so central to rigid or nonrigid designation that no phenomenon could count as being rigid or nonrigid designation if it were not to honor those duties. I address these worries in the present chapter. In section (1), I address the worry that what I call "rigidity" fails to accomplish duties that make up rigidity's role, according to my own account of which duties make up rigidity's role. In section (2), I address worries according to which what I call "rigidity" fails to accomplish other work that I have overlooked but that allegedly belongs to rigidity's role.

1. Rigidity's Duty of Securing the Necessity that Characterizes Identity Statements Featuring Rigid Designators

I have argued, in chapter 2, that rigidity as I understand it for property designators features in identity statements that are necessarily true. But does rigidity, as I understand it, perform any work *securing* the necessity with which it is associated in identity statements about properties? Perhaps instead rigidity merely happens to attend necessity in these statements, in which case the distinction that I have articulated for property designators is questionably a rigid – nonrigid distinction. The duty of securing necessity or contingency in identity statements seems central to the role of rigidity and nonrigidity (as I suggest in chapter 1, §1).

Schwartz for one would endorse something like an argument from explanatory parsimony to the effect that "rigidity," as I would understand it, is idle. In particular, he would say, such rigidity fails to perform work securing the necessity of necessarily true identity statements featuring rigid designators. "We do not need the semantics of rigidity to explain the necessity of 'soda = pop'," Schwartz observes (2002, p. 271), and we do not need rigidity to explain the necessity behind "*a posteriori* truths involving natural kind terms," like 'water = H$_2$O', either; all of this necessity "can be explained by other features" that might obtain without rigidity (Schwartz 2002, p. 274; Devitt and Soames offer related arguments: see chapter 6, §1.3). The natural conclusion to draw, suggests Schwartz, is that "rigidity does *no work at all*" when it is applied to terms for properties (p. 273), and hence that there is something wrong with applying a rigid – nonrigid distinction to property designators.

The foregoing charge is not right. To be sure, Schwartz *is* right to suggest that the necessity of statements like 'soda = pop' and 'water = H$_2$O' follows from general features or conditions that could perform the work of securing necessity even in the absence of rigidity. Other capable workers have gone astray here, supposing on the contrary that any identity statement is necessarily true *only* if both designators are rigid. Bolton, for example, mistakenly affirms the general claim that "'$x = y$' is necessarily true only when 'x' and 'y' are rigid designators" (in an otherwise enlightening paper: Bolton 1996, p. 147; Carruthers 2000, p. 42 makes the same mistake). For a counter-example, consider 'the color of Henry Morton Stanley's cap = the color of John Rowlands' cap'. Since Stanley is Rowlands, the designators together designate the same color or together fail to designate any color, with respect to any possible world. So the statement is necessarily true.[1] But the designators are not rigid: the designators co-designate a different color with respect to other possible worlds in which Stanley has different sartorial habits. Something similar holds, of course, for statements about concrete individuals: 'Stanley's cap = Rowlands' cap' is necessarily true even though hat owners might have owned different hats instead of the ones that they own, so the designators are not rigid.

Because an identity statement without rigid designators can be necessarily true, Schwartz is right to say that no appeal to rigidity or even to any conditions that necessarily secure rigidity is *needed* in order to account for the necessity of any identity statement about properties. An appeal to a general principle like the following could account for the necessity of any identity statement about properties, or indeed about concrete objects.

A General Principle on the Necessity of an Identity Statement: An identity statement is necessarily true if and only if each designator designates any entity x, with respect to any possible world w, just in case the other designator designates x with respect to w.

An appeal to this principle could account for the necessity of any identity statement without prejudging the issue of rigidity. But even though an appeal to the foregoing principle could account for the necessity of any identity statement without prejudging the issue of rigidity, rigidity might, for all that, be performing work securing the necessity. Rigidity secures necessity when both designators in an identity statement rigidly designate the same item, which is a *special case* of the satisfaction of the more *general* conditions for the necessary truth of an identity statement that are stated in the General Principle. When both of the designators in a true identity statement are *rigid* designators of the same entity, then each designator stays with the *actual* designatum from world to world, never designating anything else. This assures that the identity sign is flanked by designators each of which designates any entity x, with respect to any possible world w, just in case the other designates x with respect to w: so rigid co-designation assures necessity.

It may be easier to see that rigidity's work securing necessity is not called into question by the presence of more general accounts of the same necessity if we transfer our attention from the rigid designation of properties, which is in dispute, to the rigid designation of *concrete objects*. Virtually no one disputes that *if* 'Hesperus' and 'Phosphorus' are both rigid designators for Venus, *then* rigidity is responsible for the necessity of 'Hesperus = Phosphorus'.[2] So given the familiar view that 'Hesperus' and 'Phosphorus' *are* both rigid designators for Venus, we are free to attribute to *rigidity* this work securing necessity; but we are also free to offer more general accounts of the necessity that do not appeal to rigidity or even so much as commit to rigidity.

A *general* rigidity-blind account of 'Hesperus = Phosphorus''s necessity might maintain that 'Hesperus' and 'Phosphorus' both designate, with respect to any possible world w, *the planet in w that originates in the process O*, O being the token process that involves gravity's work at pulling together into a single body a massive cluster of dust and other matter that swirls around a center point in space and gravity's work shaping the product gradually into a sphere (see chapter 1, §1.3). In the same way, a *general* account of 'Stanley = Rowlands''s necessity might maintain that 'Stanley' and 'Rowlands' both designate, with respect to any possible world w, *the product of S and E* (a particular sperm and egg: see Kripke 1980, pp. 112–14). In each case, that of 'Hesperus = Phosphorus' and that of 'Stanley = Rowlands', there would then be no possible world for which the relevant two designators designate different individuals rather than the same one, whether that individual is a planet or a person or whatnot.

Provided that popular accounts of the *essentiality of origins* are true and provided that the designators behave as indicated, so that both 'Hesperus' and 'Phosphorus' designate, with respect to any possible world w, *the planet in w that originates in the process O* and both 'Stanley' and 'Rowlands' designate, with respect to any possible world w, *the product of S and E*, we can specify in greater detail the *reason* that there is no possible world for which 'Hesperus' and 'Phosphorus' or 'Stanley' and 'Rowlands' designate different individuals. The reason is that both terms in each pair are *rigid*, so there is some *one* individual that both members of the relevant pair of designators designate, without any change, with respect to all possible worlds: in general, as I have indicated, if both members of a pair of terms t and t' rigidly designate the same thing, then the foregoing General Principle obliges us to acknowledge that ⌜t = t'⌝ is necessarily true.

Still, an account of the necessity of 'Hesperus = Phosphorus' or 'Stanley = Rowlands' that appeals merely to the General Principle plus the claim that the designators in the respective pairs both designate, with respect to any possible world, *the planet in w that originates in the process O* or *the product of S and E*, is not an account that *presupposes* the rigidity of the designators. For all that the account says, 'the planet with origin O' designates one planet with respect to some worlds and another planet with respect to other worlds, a planet's *origins* being *accidental* rather than essential to it: and something similar may be said of Stanley's origins in the uniting of a particular sperm and egg, which origins might be thought accidental to Stanley rather than essential to him (see, e.g., Lewis 1986, pp. 251–3; for discussion, see Sainsbury 1991, p. 271; other accounts according to which proper names are not rigid are discussed by Girle 2003, pp. 87–91 and Sosa 2001).

Necessary co-designation would account for the necessity of 'Hesperus = Phosphorus' even if it were to turn out that 'Hesperus', 'Phosphorus', and 'the planet with origin O' are all *non*rigid designators sharing, with respect to any given possible world, the same designatum.[3] We can account for the necessity of 'Hesperus = Phosphorus' by appeal to rigidity or by appeal to a general, rigidity-blind argument. But the availability of different accounts does not show, by anyone's lights, that 'Hesperus' and 'Phosphorus' fail to be rigid designators of Venus nor that their rigidity fails to secure the necessity of 'Hesperus = Phosphorus'.

Considerations similar to the foregoing can be applied to statements about abstract objects, rather than concrete ones. Thus, a statement like 'soda = pop' or 'white = albescent' is necessary if and only if, with respect to any possible world w, both designators designate the same item with respect to w. They could do this without being rigid, but that does not show that 'soda' and 'pop' or 'white' and 'albescent' fail to be rigid, nor that their rigidity fails to secure the necessity of 'soda = pop' or 'white = albescent'.

That no appeal to rigidity is *necessary* for establishing certain interesting results about, say, 'soda = pop', fails to indicate rigidity's absence or idleness. Rigidity is sufficient for establishing the relevant results even if it is not necessary for achieving them: and rigidity is sufficient because, provided that 'soda' and 'pop' are rigid, as I have argued, rigidity is doing the relevant work.

So far (starting with chapter 1) as I have elaborated on the important work carried out by rigidity, I have followed a tradition of focusing on what rigidity is sufficient for establishing: and in effect, I have just defended in the present chapter what I have had to say on that score. But I would also maintain that rigidity is *necessary* for establishing certain interesting results. In part because I have been challenged to defend such a position,[4] but more importantly because the significance of the rigid – nonrigid distinction might be better appreciated by an illumination of what rigidity's work is necessary for establishing (see also on this head chapter 6, note 6), I will end the present section of this chapter (§1) with a brief discussion of rigidity's work in this regard.

To see that rigidity is necessary for establishing significant results consider, for example, theoretical identity statements, which expose essence. If it were *not* the case that both designators are rigid in an identity statement, then one or both designators would fail to track the subject matter, so to speak, by its essence. So the statement would not answer what it is in essence to be the subject matter, in the straightforward way that it would have to do in order to qualify as a theoretical identity statement (by my characterization: chapter 1, §2). Ordinarily, nonrigidity would issue in contingency, as in 'white = the color of Stanley's cap' or 'heat = what Stanley's cap is designed primarily to combat', but a statement containing only nonrigid designators could also be *necessary*, as I have indicated: indeed, a statement containing only nonrigid designators could even illustrate the necessary a posteriori. Consider 'what Stanley's cap is designed primarily to combat = what Rowlands's cap is designed primarily to combat', which contains two nonrigid designators: such a statement, though necessary and even a posteriori (for someone introduced to the man on two different occasions), does not indicate the relevant nature or essence, what it *is* to *be* heat, as a genuine theoretical identity statement would.

The impoverishment of nonrigid-designator-containing statements, by comparison with genuine theoretical identity statements, comes out in a variety of contexts. It would be absurd for a scientist or philosopher looking into the fundamental nature or the essence of heat to settle upon a statement like 'heat = what Stanley's cap is designed primarily to combat', rather than 'heat = the motion of molecules'. In the same way, no moral philosopher investigating the essence of what is right or permissible would seriously propose anything like 'rightness = the moral status of Karen's agony-ridden decision on Tuesday'. Again, more extensive nonrigidity fails to help, even when it secures necessity. Despite the attending necessity, statements like 'the unpleasant phenomenon that specialists in anesthesiology are trained to relieve = the unpleasant phenomenon that anesthesiologists are trained to relieve' or 'the disease spread by mosquitoes = the disease spread by insects of the family Culicidae' do not expose essence in the way that investigators after theoretical identity statements hope to do. Such statements might sometimes be useful for, say, providing an audience with a grasp of the topic; but they do not bring essences to light.

2. Other Duties Attributed to Rigidity

In the foregoing section (1), I have addressed concerns about how well the rigidity of property designators, as I understand it, is able to perform duties that I regard as integral to rigidity's role or function: a correct account of the rigid – nonrigid distinction must assign to rigidity these duties, which concern rigidity's work securing the necessity of various identity statements. In the present section (2), I address other alleged duties. Each of sections (2.1) – (2.5) addresses some alleged duty that rigidity, as I understand it, fails to perform or at least that rigidity as I understand it fails to perform very well. I argue in each case that it is not rigidity's duty to perform the work in question any better than rigidity as I understand it does.

2.1. *Work Securing Essential-Property Attributions*

Theoretical identity statements are not the only statements that are necessarily true by virtue of the subject matter's having theoretically interesting essential properties. Unlike 'heat = the motion of molecules', 'heat is a physical phenomenon' is plausibly taken to be necessarily true but it is not an identity statement. Other such statements include 'white is a color', 'Brontosaurus is a dinosaur', and so on. I will call such statements "essential-property attributing," on the assumption that the statements are indeed necessarily true in virtue of the subject matter's essential properties.

A number of workers indicate that the rigidity of property designators is supposed to secure the necessity of essential-property attributing statements like the foregoing in the same straightforward way that it is supposed to secure the necessity of identity statements like 'white = the combination of all of the colors of the visible spectrum'. Thus, for a number of authors, rigidity is supposed to underwrite arguments showing that, since essential-property attributing statements about properties are true, they are also necessarily true (Gómez-Torrente 2006, p. 228; Haukioja 2010, p. 2; Soames 2002, pp. 244, 257; 2003, pp. 431–2; 2004, pp. 87, 93–4; 2006a, pp. 650–1; see also Cordry 2004, pp. 252–3; Glüer and Pagin 2011, p. 6). But the rigidity of property designators guarantees no such thing, as I understand that rigidity. This failure is indicated by a look at statements with a relevantly similar form that attribute *non*-essential properties: e.g., 'white is popular' or 'cocaine is white'. 'White', 'popular', and 'cocaine' are all rigid, by my account, and the statements 'white is popular' and 'cocaine is white' are true; but these statements fail to be necessarily true since there is nothing to prevent white from becoming unfashionable or cocaine from taking on another color.

The failure of rigidity to underwrite the necessity of *essential-property attributing* statements like 'white is a color' in the same, straightforward way that rigidity underwrites the necessity of *identity* statements is problematic *if* it is rigidity's duty to underwrite the necessity of essential-property attributing statements in the relevant way: in that case, the failure presents a "challenge," as Soames (2006b, p. 715; cf. Soames 2006a, pp. 650f.) thinks it does, for an account like mine of the rigidity of property designators. But if it is *not* rigidity's duty to underwrite the necessity of statements like 'white is a color' in the relevant straightforward way, then the failure of rigidity to do the underwriting does *not* present much of a challenge to any account of property designators' rigidity. I will argue that it is not rigidity's duty to underwrite the necessity of statements like 'white is a color' in the relevant straightforward way.

If an account of property designators' rigidity were really faced with a challenge here, then an account of *concrete-object* designators' rigidity would also be faced with a similar challenge: yet no one, to my knowledge, recognizes any such challenge to concrete-object designators' rigidity.

Identity statements about concrete objects are supposed to be necessarily true if true at all, provided they contain rigid designators: this would include statements like 'Stanley = Rowlands' and 'Stanley = the product of sperm S and egg E'. And again, I have argued that the same should be said for identity statements about properties: this would include statements like 'white = albescent' and 'white = the combination of all of the colors of the visible spectrum'. But essential-property attributing statements about white are *not* identity statements, so there is no reason to suppose that rigidity should guarantee the necessity of 'white is a color' in the same way, unless rigidity also guarantees in the same way the necessity of analogous essential-property attributing non-identity statements about *concrete objects*, like 'Stanley is a mammal', 'Stanley is descended from an egg and a sperm', or 'Stanley is descended from Elizabeth Parry', all of which are plausibly held to be necessarily true in virtue of the essence of the subject matter, but none of which is an identity statement. *These* statements about Stanley, *not* identity statements like 'Stanley = Rowlands', are the appropriate essence-attributing analogues, concerning concrete objects, for statements like 'white is a color': so, contrary to Gómez-Torrente, a statement like 'Stanley = Rowlands' is by no means "strictly analogous" in rigidity-relevant respects to a statement like 'white is a color' (Gómez-Torrente 2006, p. 228; see also pp. 227, 230).[5]

Rigidity does *not* secure the necessity of statements like 'Stanley is descended from Elizabeth Parry' in the same simple manner that rigidity secures the necessity of 'Stanley = Rowlands'. So it is hard to see how it could be fair to expect rigidity to secure necessity for 'white is a color' in the same simple manner that rigidity secures the necessity of 'white = albescent'. That rigidity does not secure the necessity of statements like 'Stanley is descended from Elizabeth Parry' in the same simple manner that rigidity secures the necessity of 'Stanley = Rowlands' can be seen as follows: 'Stanley = Rowlands' is necessarily true because the statement is true and because both designators are rigid. Not so for 'Stanley is descended from Elizabeth Parry'; on the contrary, for all that the truth of this statement and the rigidity of its designators guarantees, the statement might still be contingent. 'Stanley' and 'Elizabeth Parry' might each designate its designatum with respect to all possible worlds in which that designatum exists, and never designate another item, even if nothing *essential* to Stanley has anything to do with his descent from his mother Parry. For all that rigidity requires, Stanley might be essentially a nonmaterial soul created directly by God and without any essential ties to his ancestors, as Plantinga (1974, pp. 65–6), for one, suggests. Such a position raises no trouble for Plantinga's longstanding (and perhaps insufficiently celebrated: Davidson 2003, pp. 4, 15) recognition of the foregoing terms' rigidity.

A further indication that rigidity is not *supposed* to underwrite the necessity of 'Stanley is descended from Elizabeth Parry' in the way that it underwrites the necessity of 'Stanley = Rowlands' is the following. There is a familiar version of the argument from rigidity that differs a little from the version discussed in the foregoing paragraph: according to that other familiar version, 'Stanley = Rowlands' is necessarily true *since both designators rigidly designate the same object* (cf. Kripke 1971, p. 154; 1980, pp. 102, 104). Clearly there is no plausible parallel argument concerning 'Stanley is descended from Elizabeth Parry', which fails to contain two designators for the same object.

None of the foregoing should suggest that rigidity is *irrelevant* to the necessity of essence-attributing statements that are not identity statements; on the contrary, rigidity is certainly relevant (as Mackie, for one, sees: 2006, pp. 6–10). Even if 'white is a color' is necessarily true by virtue of white's essential character, 'the property most often mentioned in chapter 4 is a color' is not necessarily true; the difference is of course in the rigidity or nonrigidity of each statement's designator for white. 'Brontosaurus is a dinosaur' seems necessarily true; but 'the most famous genus named by Marsh is a dinosaur' is not necessarily true. Before the significance of rigidity was appreciated, people might naturally have supposed that some expression like 'the most famous genus named by Marsh' is a *synonym* for 'Brontosaurus' (see chapter 1, §2.1), in which case they would have denied the necessity of 'Brontosaurus is a dinosaur'; but a proper appreciation of rigidity belies this error. Rigidity *does*, then, underwrite in *some* capacity the necessity of essential-property attributing statements that are not identity statements. Still, rigidity should not be expected to do this underwriting in the *same straightforward way* that it underwrites the necessity of identity statements.

2.2. Work Securing Externalism

I have argued (in chapter 2, §1) that the extension of rigidity to artificial-kind terms does not threaten to make all property designators rigid, thereby obliterating a distinction between property designators that I regard as rigid and property designators that I regard as nonrigid. Further, this extension of rigidity is *needed* if rigidity is to be able to account, as I suggest that it should do, for the necessity of statements like 'soda = pop' and the contingency of statements like 'soda = the beverage Uncle Bill requests at Super Bowl parties'. Still, for all that I have said the extension of rigidity to artificial-kind terms may be problematic for the reason that it would *prevent* rigidity from performing *other* work that is integral to rigidity's role. Thus, rigidity is often thought to be the mechanism that does the work of putting meanings "out of the head," to use Putnam's phrase. Rigidity cannot do this work, on my proposed account, so if this work is part of rigidity's role, then I have mischaracterized the distinction that I erroneously take for a rigid – nonrigid distinction between property designators.

Consider a term like 'whale'. What makes a thing belong to the designated taxon is not its possession of properties like *having a fish-like appearance* or *exhaling a large, visible spout of vapor* that a speaker associates with 'whale', but rather its possession of *underlying* properties or the right relations to paradigm whales. Just what 'whale' refers to is knowable only by empirical investigation of sample whales. Something similar holds, famously, for 'water': what qualifies something to count as belonging to the designated substance is not a superficial appearance known a priori by speakers but an underlying structure discovered empirically. Compare, by contrast, 'bachelor': what qualifies something to belong to the relevant kind has nothing to do with possession of underlying properties that sample bachelors like the Supreme Court justice David Souter have. The reference of 'bachelor' is determined a priori.[6]

Rigidity is often supposed to be what makes 'water' different in this way from terms like 'bachelor'. Rigidity causes our terms to designate a property marked by some unknown underlying essence, on this view, rather than a property marked by descriptive conditions associated by speakers with a term. Thus, Putnam writes, "We picture 'water' as acquiring a 'rigid' use: as being used to denote whatever is substance-identical with [most of] the paradigms in our actual environment" (1992, p. 435). Gampel is similarly explicit about sharing this common impression of rigidity's work: for him, rigidity "ties reference to actual samples of the kind, to whatever in this world has played the relevant causal role" (1997, p. 157; see also p. 161). Carney agrees: a term's "extension, if it is a rigid designator, is initially determined by a similarity relation pegged to paradigms" (1982, p. 155; for similar suggestions see Carruthers 2000, pp. 42–3; Ereshefsky 2002, p. S315; 2007, pp. 298ff.; Garcia 2007, p. 263; Haukioja 2006, pp. 157, 163; Johnson 1990, p. 65; Alex Levine 2001, p. 328; McKenna 2009, p. 10; Putnam 1975, p. 234, discussed below; de Sousa 1984, p. 566; van Brakel 2005, p. 59; see also Donnellan 1973, p. 712; 1983, p. 91; those who would resist include Boër 1985, pp. 134–5; López de Sa 2008b; Martí and Martínez-Fernández 2010, §3; Salmon 2005, pp. 120ff.).

If rigidity were a mechanism to distinguish terms like 'whale' from terms like 'bachelor', then my proposed account of the rigid – nonrigid distinction for property designators would be in trouble (Schwartz 1977, pp. 37ff.; 1980, pp. 196f.; 2006, p. 283; Macbeth 1995, esp. pp. 265–6). But rigidity is not a mechanism to distinguish terms like 'whale' from terms like 'bachelor'. I am, in giving this answer, obliged to answer the question: If rigidity is not what secures a natural-property term or a natural-kind term's reference to a kind with an unknown underlying real essence, what does? The answer is not far to seek. 'Whale' was given a *causal baptism* rather than an old-fashioned analytic definition; 'bachelor' was not. *That* is the relevant difference between terms like 'whale' and terms like 'bachelor'. This difference holds even though both terms refer to the same property or kind across all possible worlds: so we need not and should not say that designating the same property or kind across all possible worlds, which is rigidity, is the same as having a causal baptism, which distinguishes terms like 'whale' from terms like 'bachelor'.

It seems to be a running together of different elements of a broad Kripke – Putnam theory of reference, in particular the running together of rigidity with causal grounding, that has led to the belief that rigidity is what distinguishes terms like 'whale' from terms like 'bachelor'. Putnam himself, as I have suggested, confuses these elements of the Kripke – Putnam theory of reference. In some places, Putnam seems to have compounded the confusion by supposing that causally grounded terms are indexical. Putnam calls causally grounded terms "indexical," because they designate whatever has the underlying essence of samples *around the speaker*. 'Water' and 'whale' are supposed to be indexical; 'hunter' and 'bachelor' are not, since they have analytic definitions. According to Putnam, "Kripke's doctrine that natural-kind words are rigid designators and our doctrine that they are indexical are but two ways of making the same point" (1975, p. 234).[7] Putnam is wrong: these are *not* two ways of making the same point. Rigidity has nothing to do with how a term gets hooked up to its referent, whether this is by way of samples around the speaker, as with causally grounded, or "indexical," terms like 'whale', or by description, as with terms like 'bachelor'. Rather, rigidity has to do with whether the term refers to the same entity with respect to all possible worlds. "Non-indexical" kind terms, such as 'hunter' and 'bachelor', can refer to the same thing with respect to all possible worlds just as well as "indexical" ones, like 'water' and 'whale'.

2.3. Work Securing Aposteriority

Closely related to the mistaken claim that rigidity is a mechanism that pulls meanings "outside the head" is the mistaken claim that the necessity associated with rigidity is invariably a posteriori. I have argued (in chapter 2, §1) that 'the honeybee = Apis mellifera' is necessarily true if true at all, by virtue of the rigid designation of both designators flanking the '=' sign. For Schwartz, this overlooks the requirement that identities underwritten by rigidity are a posteriori (2002, p. 270): if my point about the claim 'the honeybee = Apis mellifera' is "to be effective this claim must be not only necessarily true but *a posteriori*—a discovery. But I cannot see that it is." Others have expressed similar sentiments, including Putnam. "When terms are used rigidly," Putnam claims, the modal status of statements "becomes dependent upon empirical facts" (Putnam 1992, p. 437; see also Gert 2009, p. 225; Haukioja 2006, pp. 155, 167–8 notes 6 and 12). If rigidity is invariably tied to aposteriority in the way that workers like the foregoing suggest, then the a priori status of 'the honeybee = Apis mellifera' presents problems for my account of the statement's necessity in terms of rigidity, assuming as I will that this statement *is* a priori.

My account of 'the honeybee = Apis mellifera''s necessity in terms of rigidity is not problematic: not every identity statement whose necessity is guaranteed by its containing only rigid designators is a posteriori. Kripke discusses identity statements that are not a posteriori yet that contain two uncontroversially rigid designators for *concrete objects*. None of the above writers sees any problem with the application of rigidity to terms like 'Stanley' and 'Rowlands' or the consequent necessity of 'Stanley = Rowlands'. The truth of this statement might be a posteriori for some people, such as people who initially use each name without realizing that the same individual answers to both. But it could also be *a priori* and presumably it *would* be *a priori* for Stanley, who bestowed on himself the name 'Stanley' because he preferred it to the name by which he had formerly been known, 'Rowlands'. Hence, the necessity associated with rigidity need not be a posteriori. There are other statements that are known a priori to be necessarily true but that are commonly regarded as containing just rigid designators: e.g., 'the successor of 2 = 3', which contains one designator that is commonly taken to be rigid de facto. This statement's necessity in case of truth is assured by the rigidity of the designators: but the statement is apparently a priori if any statement is.[8]

2.4. Work Refuting Descriptivism

The foregoing material (especially from §2.2 and §2.3) contains hints of a widespread impression that what is important or most important about rigidity is that it undermines descriptive accounts for various expressions. As Jason Stanley would say, "the central reason" for the perceived importance of the rigidity of proper names is that the rigidity "threatens a certain picture, the descriptive picture, of the content of names" (Stanley 1997a, p. 555). Various other writers suggest the same.[9]

If rigidity's most important work is to testify against descriptivism, then presumably any articulation of the rigid – nonrigid distinction for property designators must honor that work if it is to qualify as a concept of rigidity: this work would be central to rigidity's role. In that case, my defense of my preferred rigid – nonrigid distinction for property designators would be misdirected, since I have done little to indicate how my account honors this work. Further, it might be suspected that no defense of my preferred account will be satisfactory, especially in view of competition: it might be thought that there are probably phenomena vying for the title 'rigidity' that do a better job of refuting descriptivism than what my account calls "rigidity" does, since for my account terms like 'bachelor' and 'soda' qualify as rigid, even though these expressions are usually thought to have analytically associated conditions of application and hence to be accounted for best by descriptivism (see Devitt 2009, pp. 241, 245). If refuting descriptivism is the gold standard by which any account of rigidity is to be judged, "the main theoretical purpose that such a concept must serve," as Orlando holds (2009, p. 215) following Devitt, then a good deal rides on how well my account can hold its own, by comparison with rivals, according to this measure. If rivals outdo my account with terms like 'bachelor' and 'soda', that is arguably a strike against my account.

An argument from rigidity's alleged role to undermine descriptivism, destructively aimed at my account while constructively aimed at rival accounts, gains power when offered in conjunction with an argument to the effect that supposedly descriptive terms like 'bachelor' and 'soda' have always been paradigmatic *non*rigid designators that were originally grouped together at least partly by the intuition that they are importantly similar and importantly different from names. If the supposed intuitive baptism of *rigidity* by means of paradigmatic instances and foils, in classic work introducing rigidity, could receive theoretical support from an account of rigidity's role that would explain *why* alleged foils like 'bachelor' and 'soda' fail to count as rigid, unable as they are to carry out the proposed role, then there would be a manifold case from coherence on behalf of the account of rigidity that could tie all of this support together.

The argument from paradigms, which could be coupled with the argument from rigidity's role in opposing descriptivism, finds a voice in a number of authors including Gómez-Torrente (2006). He says that "terms for natural kinds, stuffs and phenomena—such as 'cat', 'water' and 'lightning'—are intuitively rigid" for Kripke (Gómez-Torrente 2006, p. 228), while terms for artificial properties are "are not rigid for Kripke" (p. 230); indeed, they are paradigmatic foils. Schwartz agrees: terms like 'bachelor' are, by his reading of the classic texts, "terms that Kripke and Putnam do not want to be rigid designators" (2006, p. 283).

I find the textual argument from paradigms unpersuasive, for reasons at which I have hinted in scattered places. Let me gather the relevant points, in the present paragraph, before returning to descriptivism. There is no strong evidence that Kripke regards terms like 'bachelor' and 'soda' as nonrigid. The best case available appeals to a frequently cited passage in which Kripke lists several terms like 'cat', 'water', and 'lightning', in order to say of them that they have "a greater kinship with proper names than is generally realized"; notably missing in this passage is any term for an artificial property, like 'bachelor' or 'soda' (1980, p. 134). But this is little testimony that Kripke regards terms like 'bachelor' or 'soda' as nonrigid. As I have already observed (in chapter 1, note 15), Kripke appears to be addressing not rigidity but rather the causal theory of reference (a distinct topic: see the foregoing sections of this chapter), in the foregoing passage. Putnam is a different story than Kripke. For Putnam, terms like 'bachelor' and 'soda' really are supposed to be nonrigid; but that is because, although Putnam means to defer to Kripke in his use of 'rigid', Putnam confuses Kripke's notion of rigidity with other salient elements in the so-called "Kripke-Putnam theory of reference" (see §2.2 and §2.3, including note 7).

It is not clear that terms like 'bachelor' and 'soda' are presented as intuitively or paradigmatically nonrigid, in the classic introduction of the notion of rigidity (Kripke's introduction to which Putnam defers). So that is not a reason to count these expressions as nonrigid. So I have just argued. I will now go on to argue that it will not do to group these expressions as nonrigid on the basis of their allegedly descriptive status, either. The reason is two-fold. First, I will argue (in §2.4.1) that it is hardly clear that a descriptivist understanding of these expressions is tenable. And second, I will argue (in § 2.4.2) that it is not part of rigidity's role to refute descriptivism, or at least it is not part of rigidity's role to do a better job of refuting descriptivism than rigidity as I understand it does: so even if, contrary to what I think, a descriptivist understanding of the relevant expressions *is* tenable, that provides no reason to count these expressions as nonrigid.

2.4.1. Are 'Bachelor' and 'Soda' Descriptive? It is not obvious that terms like 'bachelor' and 'soda' are descriptive. There is nothing wrong, in principle, with having a name for bachelorhood or sodahood: if these properties exist, as I have been presupposing in this chapter, and if properties can be designated with singular terms, as I have also been presupposing, then we should be able to name these properties. Unless descriptivism is a true account of all names, in which case there would be no special worries about the descriptive status of 'bachelor' and 'soda', it is plausible to suppose that 'bachelor' and 'soda' name without the help of an associated description (Salmon's view is that they do: 2005, p. 133, note 23). One way, at least, that this could be the case is if 'bachelor' and 'soda' are not shorthand for any expression with more structure: they simply name bachelorhood and sodahood, respectively, so that a competent user might have little idea of what the referent is like. If that is the semantics of 'bachelor' and 'soda', then their semantics puts no pressure on my account even if opposing descriptivism is rigidity's primary task.

Perhaps, to consider another possibility, 'bachelor' is shorthand for a phrase such as 'eligible unmarried male' and 'soda' is shorthand for 'sweet, carbonated beverage'. In that case, a competent user would have to be able to describe the designatum in the relevant ways, at least if a competent user would have to know what the expression is shorthand for and be competent with the words in the abbreviated expression. Even if 'bachelor' is shorthand for a phrase such as 'eligible unmarried male' and 'soda' is shorthand for 'sweet, carbonated beverage', my account of the rigid – nonrigid distinction would still count 'bachelor' and 'soda', as well as the expressions they abbreviate, as rigid. So someone who sees the primary function of rigidity as that of opposing descriptivism might find here a reason to balk at my account.

But here again, it is not at all clear that the apparent descriptive status of the relevant expressions is genuine. To see this, consider that 'sweet', 'carbonated', and 'beverage' are not obviously descriptive. Suppose they are not: 'sweet' is not shorthand for any definite description with a form like, 'the property P such that: necessarily, P characterizes x if and only if x is A and x is B and x is C'. Instead, 'sweet' just refers to sweetness without describing sweetness as a property or the like (if you doubt that 'sweet' is nondescriptive, you can pick different examples: you might prefer the examples 'female' and 'fox', which together define 'vixen'). 'Carbonated' and 'beverage' simply refer nondescriptively in the same manner to their respective properties. In that case, it is odd to suppose that by stringing the three words together into 'sweet, carbonated beverage', we produce a definite description denoting sweet-carbonated-beveragehood, of say the form 'the property P such that: necessarily, P characterizes x if and only if x is sweet and x is carbonated and x is a beverage'. Instead, it seems more plausible to say that 'sweet, carbonated beverage' designates sweet-carbonated-beveragehood in something very close to the way that 'sweet' refers to sweetness and so on. 'Sweet, carbonated beverage' is compositional, to be sure; but I would distinguish compositionality from descriptivism (see chapter 6, §2.1.2.4).

Perhaps we could adapt a characterization of Mark Richard's, by saying that 'sweet, carbonated beverage' or 'unmarried, eligible male' provide us with something "like a *picture* of what's named," in a way that 'soda' and 'bachelor' do not, even though none of these expressions denotes the property designated by describing it (Richard 1993, p. 207). If all of this is so, and if we may characterize *descriptivism* about a term as a theory according to which that "term is semantically equivalent to (that is, synonymous with) a definite description," as Teresa Robertson (2009, p. 132) for one sensibly maintains, then even if 'soda' is synonymous with 'sweet, carbonated beverage', 'soda' does not conform to a descriptivist understanding and neither does 'sweet, carbonated beverage' nor the one-word components.

To be sure, there *are* some decidedly *descriptive* expressions for bachelorhood or sodahood or closely related properties that my account of the rigid – nonrigid distinction for property designators would count as rigid: my account would qualify as rigid 'the property P such that: necessarily P characterizes x if and only if x is eligible to be married & x is unmarried & x is male'. Some other competing accounts of the rigid – nonrigid distinction for property designators, by contrast, would *not* qualify this description as rigid.[10] There is not much independent textual pressure to count definite descriptions like this as *paradigmatically* nonrigid, by anyone's reckoning; in this respect, 'the property P such that: necessarily P characterizes x if and only if x is eligible to be married & x is unmarried & x is male' differs from 'bachelor', which as I have said raises textual controversy concerning whether it serves as something like a paradigm grounding 'nonrigid'. Still, if opposing descriptivism can somehow be shown to be the primary function of rigidity and hence the primary measure by which an account of rigidity should be judged, then we might find it to be a strike against my account that my account would not pit rigidity against descriptivism by counting descriptions like the foregoing as nonrigid.

But I will argue now that opposing descriptivism is *not* the primary function of rigidity or the primary measure by which an account of rigidity should be judged. Along with various others, I find there to be "ample and clear" reason to take rigidity's primary role instead to be that of supporting the modal status of various statements, and especially identity statements (here I echo Glüer and Pagin: 2011, p. 35, note 13; see also Haukioja 2010, §2.2; Sosa 2006, p. 488). Since I have already motivated that alternative understanding of rigidity's role (in chapter 1, §1.1), it will be enough here (in §2.4.2) to belie descriptivism's opposing claim to command the center of rigidity's role.

2.4.2. Why Refuting Descriptivism is Not What is Most Important About Rigidity Any account of rigidity should allow that rigidity has a *limited* use for opposing certain *forms* of descriptivism. My account of rigidity allows for that. Still, we should not suppose that refuting descriptivism is what is most important about rigidity nor that the ability to undermine descriptivism is the primary measure by which an account of rigidity should be judged.

There is, as I have just mentioned, a kernel of truth behind the common supposition that refuting descriptivism is rigidity's main work: rigidity does create trouble for primitive descriptivist views. According to the descriptivist tradition associated with Frege and Russell, for example, names are "abbreviated" garden-variety definite descriptions (Russell 1919, p. 179; for further references, see the foregoing chapter 1, note 3): thus, Henry Morton Stanley's name, as most speakers use it anyway, might be shorthand, on the relevant descriptivist view, for 'the most famous explorer of the Congo'. Rigid designation creates problems for such a view. 'The most famous explorer of the Congo' is not rigid: even if it designates Stanley, there are other possible worlds with respect to which 'the most famous explorer of the Congo' designates Samuel Clemens, who might have been fonder of outdoor expeditions. On the other hand, 'Stanley' is rigid. 'Stanley' designates Stanley with respect to all possible worlds containing Stanley, and there are no possible worlds with respect to which 'Stanley' designates something else: thus, with respect to possible worlds in which Stanley stays at home and with respect to which Clemens is the designatum of 'the most famous explorer of the Congo', Stanley, not Clemens, is still the designatum of 'Stanley'. In view of this discrepancy between the name 'Stanley' and the description 'the most famous explorer of the Congo', it is hard to see how the name could be mere shorthand for the description. Similar words apply to property designators, according to my characterization of their rigidity. Therefore, my characterization of rigidity for property designators performs as expected by this standard. 'White' is not shorthand for 'the color of Antarctica', 'heat' is not shorthand for 'the phenomenon we sense most acutely when we approach fire', and so on; rigidity tells otherwise.

Rigidity creates problems for some primitive descriptivist views: so I acknowledge. But while that achievement of rigidity is interesting (as I have suggested: chapter 1, §1.3), its importance should be kept in perspective. Rigidity does little to get at the *roots* of descriptivism. Rigidity refutes only *naïve versions* of descriptivism; there are more sophisticated varieties. Now that the philosophical community has absorbed the lessons of rigidity, descriptivism remains an attractive theory to many philosophers for essentially the same reasons that motivated ill-fated early formulations of the basic theory.[11] Hence, it is hard to see how rigidity's importance could lie with the task of refuting descriptivism.

In explaining rigidity's unsuitability for refuting descriptivism, I will continue to appeal to concrete-object designators, whose claim to rigidity is not in question. The basic problem with tying rigidity's importance too closely to rigidity is that one could *not* conclude that 'Stanley', say, is nondescriptive on the grounds that it is rigid; for all that its rigidity assures, 'Stanley' might be synonymous with 'the most famous explorer of the Congo *in* α', say, where 'α' is a name for the actual world. Such "world-indexed" descriptions (see note 12) support one of many varieties of descriptivist proposals according to which names are descriptive despite their rigidity. Rigidity is no help in refuting these proposals: a little ingenuity, then, permits descriptivists to circumvent troubles posed by rigidity.

Not only are arguments from rigidity not well suited to the task of refuting descriptivism, but more promising arguments for the purpose of refuting descriptivism are well known: "the strongest and most persuasive" arguments against descriptivism, as Salmon (1979, p. 446) characterizes them, are arguments from error and ignorance. I have indicated that 'Stanley' might be synonymous with a *rigid* description like 'the most famous explorer of the Congo *in* α' even if this term is not synonymous with a *non*rigid description like 'the most famous explorer of the Congo': so rigidity fails to tell against a suitably refined descriptivism. Arguments from error and ignorance, on the other hand, weigh against even refined descriptivisms like the foregoing. Could not someone refer to Stanley with 'Stanley' even if she associates with 'Stanley' only the description 'the namesake of Stanley Falls' or the thought "that famous guy from way back—oh, now who was just telling me about him?"? If so, the broad tradition of arguments from error and ignorance indicates, then the content of 'Stanley' cannot be the same as that of 'the most famous explorer of the Congo' *nor* 'the most famous explorer of the Congo *in* α'. In general, arguments from *rigidity* against descriptivism, according to which some description d cannot share the content of a name or other rigid designator because d is not rigid, may be parried without much trouble by appeal to a "rigidified" description, e.g., a world-indexed variant of d. But arguments from error and ignorance remain to be addressed. Accordingly, arguments from error and ignorance seem to present a more serious threat to descriptivism than arguments from rigidity.[12]

It would appear, then, that the task of refuting descriptivism is not one that rigidity is well suited to accomplish. And there are more promising resources for this task:

arguments from error and ignorance. So if rigidity has real importance, as tradition maintains, then I suggest that that importance would have to rest with other work.

2.5. Work Securing Linguistic Stability

A final job that I will discuss because it has been attributed to rigidity and because, if it were fairly so attributed, it would create some trouble for the account of rigidity defended here, is the job of securing stability for the meaning or reference of terms. Various authors attribute this job to rigidity. Thus, Michael Ghiselin urges that we

> do not attach a name to a class, then discover the defining properties which are its essence, but rather redefine our terms as knowledge advances. Therefore the view of Kripke ... that natural kind terms are, like proper names, "rigid designators," should be dismissed as nugatory, and with it the accompanying essentialism (Ghiselin 1987, p. 135).

Read and Sharrock agree: for them, our property designators are not properly called "rigid" if we cannot count on "the permanency of what they are used to depict" (2002, p. 156; see also Wolf 2007, p. 219). But words that are *rigid*, as I understand that notion, could fail to keep the same meaning or reference as they are used by different communities at different times, just as any *other* expression could fail to keep the same meaning or reference as it is used by different communities at different times. So rigidity as I understand it cannot perform the job of securing linguistic stability.

Fortunately, it is not rigidity's *duty* to secure linguistic stability: that job would be quite independent from the modal work that rigidity is responsible for performing. Thus, suppose that indeed our natural-property terms or natural-kind terms are constantly being redefined, so that the precise entity a term refers to continues to change as the term's meaning continually changes: an example might be 'lunacy', which began as a word for madness *caused by the moon* but which is now simply a word for madness (Bruce Aune's example, p.c.). We should not expect such a word to designate rigidly the *same* condition now as it did in earlier times. But *at any given time* it could still rigidly designate a single condition: that is, at any given time in the history of the English language, such a word might designate, with respect to each possible world, the same condition c, though the term may at other times fail to designate c since its meaning varies from time to time. Thomas Kuhn develops just this position in his (1990). So the mere evolution of meaning (which I discuss at length elsewhere: 2004) does not destroy the rigidity thesis. A term need not keep its meaning over time in order to be rigid at a time.

3. Conclusion

In the present chapter, I have defended the account of rigidity for property designators proposed in chapter 1 against objections that the account fails to assign to rigidity the duties integral to rigidity's role: those duties that any phenomenon would have to perform in order to count as *being* rigidity. I have granted that rigidity as I understand it does not perform all of the alleged duties that workers in the tradition have come to associate with rigidity; but that is no fault of the account. Some of the duties that have come to be associated with rigidity are not really rigidity's duties, as I have observed in section (2). Rigidity as I understand it does perform its *proper* duties, which are substantial: so I have argued in section (1).

These are the conclusions of the present chapter. A brief survey of surrounding chapters is now in order, for context. In chapter 1, I have articulated a basic account of rigidity for property designators and explained why it matters. In chapter 2, I have defended the relevant account against worries that it fails to honor a genuine *distinction* between rigid and nonrigid designators. In the present chapter, as I have just said, I urge that the genuine distinction that my account honors is a distinction that reflects *rigidity's* role, which I articulate in chapter 1.

In these foregoing chapters, I have been treating property designators as singular terms (see chapter 1, §3.1). This is especially plausible for *grammatically* singular terms like 'Apatosaurus', 'heat', and 'whiteness'. Taking a cue from grammar and following Kripke's lead (see chapter 1, note 15), I have treated these as *genuinely* singular terms, and not just grammatically singular terms. I have taken the terms to be capable of flanking the '=' sign. This has seemed natural for the terms in statements like 'Brontosaurus = Apatosaurus'. But it may have seemed less natural for the terms in statements like 'white = albescent'. Grammar does *not* typically suggest a singular treatment of terms like 'white' and 'albescent' or for 'apatosaur', 'hot', and so on: grammar typically suggests a *non*-singular treatment, which would tell *against* the use of such terms in an identity statement. If such terms are nonsingular, then the account of rigidity for property designators that I have defended in the foregoing chapters, which treats property designators as *singular* terms, cannot be *complete*: at best, the account could provide a *start* at illuminating the rigidity of property designators by illuminating the rigidity just of those property designators that are singular. And this is *at best*: matters might be much worse. Some philosophers would deny that the account of rigidity for property designators that I have defended in the foregoing chapters represents even a good *start* at illuminating the rigidity of property designators. They maintain, instead, that *no* property designators are genuinely singular terms, not even those terms whose grammar recommends a singular treatment. I address these worries in the following two chapters.

Notes

1. It is *weakly* necessary (see chapter 1, §1.2), on one sharpened understanding of 'weak necessity', whose need of refinement is exposed by cases like this. 'The color of Henry Morton Stanley's cap = the color of John Rowlands' cap is true in all possible worlds in which either of the designators designates anything (and is never false): let us say, then, that it has "designator-relative" weak necessity. Of course, the statement is not true in all possible worlds in which the *actual* designatum *white* exists: so let us say that it does not enjoy "designatum-relative" weak necessity (for more on the distinction, see note 3).

2. The rigidity of proper names like the foregoing is generally accepted (see chapter 1, note 1 and accompanying text): that is why rigidity is generally thought to *be* responsible for the necessity of statements like 'Hesperus = Phosphorus'. However, the non-conditional claim that rigidity *is* responsible for the necessity because the relevant names *are* rigid invites more dispute than the merely conditional claim that rigidity *would be* responsible if the names *were* rigid: it is the virtually undisputed, merely *conditional* claim that is needed to make my point in this section that rigidity's work securing necessity is not impugned by rigidity-blind, alternative accounts of the necessity. Below in the text, I discuss minority voices concerning the claim that names are in fact rigid, which as I have indicated is occasionally disputed.
3. If Venus' names are shorthand for the description 'the planet with origin O', then 'Hesperus = Phosphorus''s necessity is *weak* necessity, at least on familiar accounts of the semantics of definite descriptions (see chapter 4, §1). If anti-essentialists about origins are right, then 'Hesperus = Phosphorus' can claim only weak necessity of the *designator-relative* variety (see the foregoing note 1). If, on the other hand, *essentialists* about origins are right, then 'Hesperus = Phosphorus' can claim also the *designatum*-relative variety of weak necessity.
4. I thank Steve Schwartz for applying pressure on just this matter. In my answer, I address *identity* statements; but similar points could be made with respect to statements that do not assert identity, which statements I ignore here for simplicity: see §2.1 below. I also ignore here the possible separation of the two criteria met by a rigid designator: first, that it designates the same item x with respect to all possible worlds in which x exists, and second, that it never designates anything other than x instead. Some of the interest of rigidity would naturally be preserved with the satisfaction of one or the other condition of rigidity alone. I ignore this complication, focusing on ordinary rigidity and nonrigidity.

For a closely related discussion concerning what the *aposteriority of statements* is necessary for, as opposed to what *rigidity* is necessary for, see chapter 1, §1.3, including note 7.
5. Because Kripke regards statements like 'white is a color' as necessary, it might be easy to suppose that it is rigidity's duty to secure the necessity of such statements; but Kripke's arguments for the necessity of statements like the foregoing make no mention of rigidity (1980, pp. 112–13; 123–7). Kripke appeals to rigidity only to argue for the necessity of *identity* statements, including those about properties (e.g., 1980, pp. 144ff., 148ff.). Or rather, in his *primary* arguments, which are in the main body of the text, and in the arguments Kripke *continues to stand behind*, he appeals to rigidity only to argue for the necessity of *identity* statements; admittedly, Kripke does broach rigidity in a footnote on essential properties (1980, p. 114, note 56), but he later retracts the relevant argument (1980, p. 1). It is unclear, then, on what grounds one should support the claim that it is rigidity's duty to perform the work in question.

It might be suggested that Kripke *regards* statements like 'white is a color' or 'water is a compound' *as* "identity statements" in some broad sense that includes statements whose form is not to be expressed with the '=' sign (Soames 2002, pp. 244, 254–7; 2003, pp. 425, 431–3). But such a reading seems strained. To include 'white is a color' with "identity statements" would falsify, as I have indicated, Kripke's claim that "Theoretical identities, according to the conception I advocate, are generally identities involving two rigid designators and therefore are examples of the necessary *a posteriori*" (1980, p. 140; see also 109). So it is more natural to understand Kripke as more restrictive in his use of 'identity statement' (as the usual interpretation would have it: see, e.g., Berger 2002, pp. 57–69; Donnellan 1983, pp. 92–3; Gendler and Hawthorne 2002, p. 31; Hughes 2004, p. 89; Jackson 2003, p. 329; Levin 1987, p. 285; Mackie 2006, pp. 169–70, 196ff.; Okasha 2002, p. 52; Schwartz 2002, p. 274; Shoemaker 1998, p. 60; Sidelle 1992a, p. 269; Steward 1990, p. 389; Zalta 2006, p. 598; see also Kripke's revealing clarifications about what "identity statements" amount to: 1980, pp. 98, 107).

6. Perhaps, as tradition would have it, 'bachelor' is shorthand for something like 'unmarried, eligible male'. Or perhaps some such phrase is used to fix the reference of 'bachelor', even though what 'bachelor' expresses is not structurally complex (on reference fixing, see Kripke 1980, pp. 55ff.). Either way, the term is not causally grounded. 'Bachelor''s tie to the foregoing conditions has occasionally been disputed, but for the sake of sparing the popular foil we can assume that tradition is right about this tie.

7. Though the identification of causal grounding with indexicality seems confused (see, for a lengthy discussion, Burge 1982, pp. 102–7), there is no need to straighten out that confusion here. I mention talk of indexicality only to point out that the confusion of causal grounding with rigidity, which is the confusion at issue here, can also take the form of a confusion of "indexicality" with rigidity. Others follow Putnam in this confusion. Schwartz discusses the new theory according to which "natural kind terms like 'gold', 'tiger', and 'water', are indexical or rigid. This means that contrary to traditional theories, the meaning of such a term is not given by a conjunction or cluster of properties semantically associated with the term" (1978, p. 566; for similar thoughts, see Maitra 2003, p. 26, note 7; but cf. Schwartz 2002 for second thoughts).

A further confusion in the vicinity that is implicated with the foregoing confusions, as Jason Stanley has emphasized (in personal communication), is a confusion between metasemantic issues and semantic issues. The topic of causal grounding is a *meta*semantic one: it pertains to how a term comes to *have* its referent. The topic of rigidity, by contrast, is a *semantic* one: it pertains to what the referent *is*. I elaborate on this distinction in chapter 8, §2.2.2.

Perhaps it should be noted, to quell any doubts about the matter, that Putnam intends to apply 'rigid', following Kripke, to any term that "refers to the same individual in every possible world" (1975, p. 231); he is not introducing a novel use for the term. Simple confusion about the relation between rigidity and the causal theory seems to explain why he believes that terms whose meaning is "in the head," like 'hunter', are not rigid, while terms that are causally grounded, like 'water', are rigid (see, besides the references immediately above, 1975, p. 265). A careful reading of Kripke indicates that he, unlike Putnam, does *not* confuse rigidity with causal grounding. For Kripke, the extension of '*pain*' with respect to other possible worlds is *not* determined by the underlying nature of actual sample pains (1971, p. 163, note 18), so to identify rigidity with causal grounding would rule out the rigidity of 'pain'; but Kripke maintains that 'pain' is rigid and 'pain''s rigidity does important work for Kripke.

8. Dan López de Sa has offered the example 'the successor of 2 = 3' (in p.c. and then in 2008b). Another example of an a priori identity statement in which both designators are rigid, if Kripke (1971, p. 163, note 18) is right anyway, is 'pain = sensation S', where 'S' is an appropriate name. So for Kripke rigidity cannot be closely tied to aposteriority. Since an expression like 'the successor of 2' seems to attach to its designatum in any possible world by way of the designatum's satisfying a description, rather than by way of the designatum's being a specimen cited in a causal baptism, it testifies not only against the tight association some writers recognize between aposteriority and rigidity but also against the tight association some writers recognize between causal grounding and rigidity.

9. Many writers testify to the perception that rigidity is important because it is responsible for undermining descriptivism (see also Cartwright 1998, pp. 71–2; Devitt 2005, p. 145; Gómez-Torrente 2009, pp. 135f, 138, 146; Maier 2009, pp. 253, 256; Schwartz 2006, p. 277; Sosa 2006, pp. 478–80). Some of the foregoing authors distance themselves from the perception to which they testify (including Cartwright and also Stanley: 1997b, p. 156).

Sometimes philosophers suggest that *all* rigid expressions resist a descriptivist account or indeed that the rigidity of an expression just *is* its lack of any associated descriptive information: thus, Alex Levine says that rigid designators "are terms that refer independently of the truth of any descriptions associated with them" (2001, p. 328). Carney says that "rigid designators have no sense" (1982, p. 154). Hull says that rigid designators "denote what they denote, and that is it" (1988, p. 497). Others express or discuss similar views (see, e.g., Ereshefsky 2007, p. 298; Leonhard, Michel, and Prien, 2008; Mueller 1995, §2). The general mistake of thinking that all rigid expressions are nondescriptive is belied by de facto rigid designation: 'the successor of 2' is rigid but clearly descriptive. A suggestion that is more plausible than the suggestion that *all* types of rigid expressions resist a descriptivist account is the suggestion that *some special* types of rigid expressions, such as proper names or other expressions whose rigidity is de jure, resist a descriptivist account. Kripke seems open to this possibility, though he does *not* seem open to the suggestion that the importance of rigidity is tied to the refutation of descriptivism even about just names or expressions that are rigid de jure (see note 11; I discuss the de facto – de jure distinction further in chapter 6, §2.1.2).

10. I argue later for the rigidity of expressions like 'the property P such that: necessarily P characterizes x if and only if x is eligible to be married & x is unmarried & x is male' (see chapter 6, §2.1.2.3). And I offer an analysis of certain theoretical expressions (broadly construed to include expressions from the social sciences like 'unmarried, eligible male') according to which they are synonymous with such rigid descriptions. In view of the present discussion (chapter 3, §2.4.1), this type of analysis of theoretical expressions, which construes them as definite descriptions, might be better replaced with an analysis according to which theoretical expressions are compositional phrases but not ones that describe the designatum (such an analysis would differ from any offered in chapter 6, but would develop a hint from LaPorte 2000, p. 313, note 12, written before I knew of forbears; for criticisms, cf. Devitt 2005, pp. 143, 154). But while I doubt that the analyses that I offer for theoretical expressions in chapter 6 are the best representations possible for all English theoretical expressions, there is no reason to augment or pare, and for two reasons. First, some theoretical expressions are more plausibly held to be descriptive than others: 'the element with atomic number 79' is a better candidate than 'H_2O', 'molecular motion', or 'sweet, carbonated beverage' and might plausibly be analyzed along the lines indicated in chapter 6. Second, as for the rest of the foregoing theoretical expressions, they can be interpreted likewise for purposes of chapter 6, since my primary concern in chapter 6 is not with representing natural language, as I explain there; it is instead with identifying *an* interpretation of theoretical expressions that comes close enough to the English expressions to do the rigidity-relevant work that we might reasonably suppose the English reading to support. That is the work of supporting the necessity of theoretical identity statements.

While I would count 'the property P such that: necessarily P characterizes x if and only if x is eligible to be married & x is unmarried & x is male' as rigid, Devitt apparently would not, at least if that expression is understood as an applier (which it might be even if it is also a singular expression: see chapter 4, §2.2.2). This is not necessarily to say (as I explain in chapter 5, §2.3) that Devitt's account of rigidity would be superior to mine even were superiority to be figured – unwisely, as I will argue in the following section (§2.4.2) – by how well that which the account passes as "rigidity" plays the role of helping to refute descriptivism.

11. For descriptivist accounts that respect recent observations about the rigidity of names and similar expressions, see Jackson 2007, p. 25; Justice 2003; Lewis 1999e, pp. 353, note 22, 356–7; Plantinga 1985, pp. 82–7; 2003, chapter 6; Sidelle 1992b; 1995. These more sophisticated descriptivist accounts are motivated by the same worries that inspired earlier, more primitive descriptivist accounts: descriptivism is supposed to illuminate puzzles about how speakers can tell whether a word applies to an object (Jackson 2004, pp. 273–5; 2007, p. 25), about how negative existential statements could be true, about how identity statements like 'Stanley = Rowlands' could be informative and a posteriori, and so on (Davidson 2003, pp. 13–16; Plantinga 2003, chapter 6; some of these puzzles are suggested in chapter 1, §1.2 and §1.3). Accordingly, while it might be suggested that rigidity's importance has to do with its ruling out of descriptivist help with these issues (Sosa indicates that the suggestion is common: 2006, pp. 478–80), that suggestion seems unlikely since rigidity does little work of this sort, leaving untouched as it does moderately sophisticated, updated versions of descriptivism like the foregoing, which versions of descriptivism are carefully formulated in order both to shed light on the relevant issues and also to honor rigidity. Kripke would seem to agree: if the real importance of rigidity is tied to the refutation of descriptivism about names or expressions that are rigid de jure, then Kripke curiously seems to miss the point of rigidity. Although Kripke insists that names are never synonymous with *non*rigid descriptions (1977, p. 272, note 9), he does *not* endorse the "Millian" claim that names are never synonymous with *rigid* descriptions and he apparently wishes to be read as leaving the question of descriptivism open: his conclusions are reserved. "The spirit of my earlier views," he says, "suggests that a Millian line should be maintained as far as is feasible" (Kripke 1979, p. 248; see also 1979, p. 273, note 10; Almog interprets Kripke differently than I do, but Kripke has rejected the alternative interpretation: see Almog 1986, pp. 223–5; Kripke 2005, p. 1007, note 7; and in talks Kripke has continued to emphasize that "he does not consider himself a Direct Reference theorist": Baumann 2010, p. 338, note 8).

12. For further discussion of arguments from error and ignorance, see Devitt and Sterelny 1999, pp. 54ff.; Salmon 1981, pp. 27–9; Soames 2010, p. 82. Whether there are names or name-like expressions that are descriptive despite arguments from error and ignorance or other arguments brought against them is not a matter that must be resolved for purposes here. Some names in natural language are more naturally regarded as descriptive than others: Dummett takes 'St. Joachim' to have been "introduced as denoting the father of the Blessed Virgin, whoever that may have been" (1991, p. 48). So 'St. Joachim' may be shorthand for a rigidified description like 'the father of Mary in α'. Kripke adduces a similar example, 'Jack the Ripper', which he takes to have been introduced for the murderer of so and so (1980, pp. 79–80): this name, too, might be shorthand for a rigidified description. But it is unlikely that there are many proper names that are descriptive in this way in natural language. Subtler accounts of descriptivism may apply to more names: for discussion, see, in addition to the foregoing references of the present section, chapter 8, §2.2. Just as there are different

descriptivisms, there are different methods of rigidification. Plantinga discusses world indexing, to which I have appealed, in 1974 (pp. 62–5). Instead of naming a world, one might use an operator @ for "actually" in which case the rigidified description becomes 'the @(evening star)'. Kaplan's operator 'dthat' also rigidifies: 'dthat(the evening star)' designates the object that is actually the evening star with respect to all possible worlds in which it exists; however, Kaplan's operator is supposed to produce a directly referring, nondescriptive designator (see, e.g., Kaplan 1989a, pp. 521–2; for qualms, see Almog 1986, p. 224n.; Kaplan 1989b, pp. 579ff.).

4

A Uniform Treatment of Property Designators as Singular Terms

If the case from the foregoing chapters is cogent, then the rigid – nonrigid distinction carries over more or less straightforwardly from concrete-object designators to property designators, provided that property designators are all singular terms. I have been assuming for simplicity that property designators *are* all singular terms; but this is no small assumption.

Some property designators are more plausible candidates for singularity than others: 'whiteness' and 'courage' are better candidates than 'white' and 'courageous'. In counting terms like 'white' and 'courageous' as singular, I have appealed to favorable contexts of use: e.g., contexts in which a speaker might say, 'white is a color' or 'courageous is what she is' (see chapter 1, §3.1). Still, even if contexts like these suggest a singular treatment of 'white' and 'courageous', other contexts do not: e.g., contexts in which a speaker might say, 'K2 is white' or 'she is courageous'. In contexts like these, as Mill (1843) long ago pointed out, the relevant property designators appear to *classify* or *characterize* particular objects *having* the relevant property rather than to *name* or describe that property itself, as a singular term would (see also Ariansen 2001 at the section "Semantics"; Martí 2004, p. 143; ter Meulen 1981, p. 106 and passim; Wright 1998, pp. 258–9).

It would appear on face value, then, that some but only some property designators submit to a rigid – nonrigid distinction of the sort that I have defended in the foregoing chapters, because the favored account fails to apply in the case of "some expressions that are not singular terms," as Soames, for one, urges (Soames 2002, p. 246; for similar views, see Boër 1985, p. 129; Donnellan 1973, p. 712; Fitch 2004, p. 124; Gómez-Torrente 2004, p. 38; 2006, p. 237; May 2003, §10; Martí and Martínez 2007, p. 104, note 3; Soames 2003, p. 430; cf. Soames 2004, pp. 94–7; 2006b, pp. 713–14). Familiar property designators resist the account, as they are used in familiar contexts.

The dualist position suggested in the foregoing paragraphs, according to which some but only some property designators are singular, might well be regarded as something like a natural default position. This natural default position is of course to be distinguished from the more radical position that *no* property designators are singular, so that *none* would be subject to the relevant account of the rigid – nonrigid distinction: I save until the following chapter discussion of the more radical position. Here in the present chapter, I do not call into question the default claim that *some* terms, like 'whiteness' and 'courage', are or can be treated as bona fide singular terms: I embrace that part of the default position. What I will challenge is the default claim that terms like 'white' and 'courageous' have to be treated differently. I will argue that they do not. Considered reflection indicates that a *uniform* treatment of property designators as singular is plausible and indeed preferable to the initially more plausible dualist alternative, which treats some property designators but not others as merely predicative. Dualism fails, if I am right, to indicate any need to muster a second account of the rigid – nonrigid distinction for those property designators that are *non*singular; my preferred account, which treats property designators as singular, would seem fit to accommodate the rigidity or nonrigidity of property designators in general.

Before I address the foregoing dualist challenge to the comprehensiveness of my favored rigid – nonrigid distinction for property designators, I address a second, related challenge. The second challenge shares with the foregoing challenge the conviction that some but not all property designators are singular terms, but goes further, maintaining also that some but not all *concrete-object* designators are singular terms. According to this second challenge, definite descriptions are not singular, whether for properties or concrete objects. This second challenge threatens to undermine any rigid – nonrigid distinction at all, as I will explain in the following section (§1); but I will go on to argue in that section that the challenge cannot in the end upset the distinction.

1. Descriptions as Singular Terms

I have been treating definite descriptions, like 'the substance with atomic number 79', or 'the brightest nonlunar body in the evening sky', more or less as singular terms. Given such a treatment, it is natural to take, say, the statement 'Hesperus = the brightest nonlunar body in the evening sky' to share the same logical form as 'Hesperus = Phosphorus': $x = y$. But a salient and popular tradition from Russell (1905, 1919) maintains that the description in a statement like 'Hesperus = the brightest nonlunar body in the evening sky' is really a quantifier phrase, not a *term* (not even a *complex* term: see chapter 6, note 9): accordingly, the statement has a different and more complicated underlying logical form than $x = y$. We might well worry, then, that definite descriptions are not after all characterized properly as rigid or nonrigid: as I have emphasized, the original account of the distinction applies just to singular terms.

If definite descriptions are *not* characterized properly as rigid or nonrigid, then some or all of the valuable lessons supposedly to be learned from rigidity might after all fail to materialize. Accordingly, rigidity's significance might stand or fall depending on the success of Russell's theory of descriptions. One consideration in this connection is this: definite descriptions like 'the successor of eight' and 'the substance with atomic number 79' serve as the classic examples (maybe the only examples: see chapter 6, note 9) of designators that are rigid *de facto* (see chapter 6, §2.1.2): such expressions are supposed to be rigid just as names are, even though they are rigid for a different reason.

Accordingly, definite descriptions play a crucial role in the articulation of a distinction between *de facto* and *de jure* rigidity.

More important is the following consideration: the tradition honoring a rigid – nonrigid distinction appeals to definite descriptions along the lines of 'the brightest nonlunar body in the evening sky' as the classic examples (some would say the only examples: see chapter 6, §1.3) of designators that are *non*rigid. Accordingly, definite descriptions play a crucial role in the articulation of any distinction between *rigid* and *nonrigid* designators. And they are responsible for certain identity statements' being contingently true.

In view of the foregoing considerations, if statements containing definite descriptions are not after all simple identity statements since the definite descriptions are not singular terms, we might well suspect, at least, that there is something wrong with how the rigid – nonrigid distinction and its significance have been conceived. Indeed, one well-known philosopher of language goes beyond merely suspecting trouble: Martí (2004) positively *recognizes* trouble for rigidity's significance along something like the foregoing lines.

In view of the Russellian insight or apparent insight that sentences like 'gold is the substance with atomic number 79' and 'Hesperus is the brightest nonlunar body in the evening sky', "are not real statements of identity: their logical form, the propositions they express, are not of the form '$x = y$'" (2004, p. 144), Martí claims that it is "not surprising" that rigidity fails to perform the work that it is supposed to perform for the relevant statements. Thus, for example, Martí resists the position that 'gold is the substance with atomic number 79' is a theoretical identity statement whose necessity follows from truth plus rigidity. For Martí, if such statements are indeed necessary, this necessity "does not follow from their truth plus the rigidity of the terms involved" (p. 144).

I have maintained, contrary to Martí, that rigidity *does* perform the work that it is supposed to perform for 'gold is the substance with atomic number 79': in particular, the necessity of 'gold is the substance with atomic number 79' *does* follow from truth plus the rigidity of the terms (chapter 1, §2 and §3). A defense of my position therefore seems appropriate here.[1]

Even given a Russellian understanding of definite descriptions, I will argue, rigidity performs the right work for the relevant statements. I do not dispute the Russellian claim that statements like 'gold is the substance with atomic number 79' or 'Hesperus is the brightest nonlunar body in the evening sky' have an underlying logical form that is more complicated than $x = y$. But this concession about form is not so damaging to familiar claims concerning rigidity as appearances might initially suggest. Even on a Russellian view, statements like 'gold is the substance with atomic number 79' and 'Hesperus is the brightest nonlunar body in the evening sky' remain "identity statements" in some broad, meaningful respect that involves the identity relation, though they are not simple identity statements.[2] 'Hesperus is the brightest nonlunar body in the evening sky' expresses, for Russell, the following, where 'Bx' is used for 'x is a brightest nonlunar body in the evening sky':

(∃x)(Bx & (y)(By → y = x) & x = h).

This says that there is some unique x that is a brightest nonlunar body in the evening sky, and that x is identical to Hesperus: so the statement remains an "identity statement" on some substantial use of 'identity statement'.

    Just as a Russellian analysis of definite descriptions does not threaten the claim that statements like 'Hesperus is the brightest nonlunar body in the evening sky' are "identity statements" in a broad, substantial sense, it does not threaten the basic lessons of rigidity: thus, 'Hesperus is the brightest nonlunar body in the evening sky' is *necessarily* true *provided* that it is true and provided that 'Hesperus' and 'the brightest nonlunar body in the evening sky' are "rigid designators" in *one or the other* of *two* respects, *either* of which can give 'rigid designator' the interest that it is supposed to have. The two respects are as follows.

    The *first* respect in which an expression can reasonably be counted a "rigid designator" is the more straightforward: this respect is met just in case the expression *refers* to the same object from world to world in the way that a genuine name does. 'Hesperus' is a good candidate for being a rigid designator in this simple respect. The *second* respect in which an expression can reasonably be counted a "rigid designator" permits the rigidity of descriptions: an expression is to be counted rigid if it is a definite description, like 'the brightest nonlunar body in the evening sky', whose attending predicate to be exposed on analysis, here 'B', is *uniquely satisfied* by the same entity from world to world.[3]

    As it happens, 'the brightest nonlunar body in the evening sky' is nonrigid, and 'Hesperus' is rigid: as a result, 'Hesperus is the brightest nonlunar body in the evening sky' is contingently true, whether the statement has the form that Russell would ascribe to it or the simple form $x = y$. The status of 'gold is the substance with atomic number 79' similarly depends on rigidity. On a Russellian treatment of definite descriptions, we should understand 'the substance with atomic number 79' to be a rigid designator for the substance *gold* just in case the predicate ' . . . is a substance with atomic number 79' is uniquely satisfied by the substance *gold*, which is here taken to be an abstract object, from world to world. If 'the substance with atomic number 79' is a rigid designator for the substance *gold*, and if 'gold' is also a rigid singular designator for that same substance, then 'gold is the substance with atomic number 79' is necessarily true. Again, it does not matter whether the statement has, ultimately, a more complicated form than $x = y$, which more complicated form renders it synonymous with a statement like, 'there is some unique x that is a substance with atomic number 79 and x = gold'. The lessons of rigidity apply regardless.

    I will continue, then, to treat definite descriptions as singular terms. For purposes here, they are best treated that way, since they serve to describe just one entity when they designate at all.[4] My claims about the role of singular terms in identity statements can be sustained, in essence, because the relevant expressions take their place in the right way in identity statements, suitably understood. Still, in calling definite descriptions "singular," I do not issue any judgment about whether they are ultimately referring terms or whether they are instead denoting expressions that must be defined in a way that eliminates the surface appearance of simple reference.

2. Avoiding Millian Dualism

I have addressed one tradition that threatens the uniform status of property designators, and indeed the uniform status of concrete-object designators as well, as singular terms that are subject to a rigid – nonrigid distinction. In the sections that remain, I address a different tradition that threatens, for different reasons, the uniform status of property designators as singular terms that are subject to the original rigid – nonrigid distinction: this time property designators specifically are targeted as terms that are sometimes nonsingular.

Following Mill, the tradition in question takes at face value both the apparent singularity of terms like 'whiteness' in a statement like 'whiteness is a property', and also the apparent nonsingularity of terms like 'white', in a statement like 'K2 is white', as I have indicated. If such a dualism is correct, then we cannot say that each property designator (according to some suitably broad understanding of "designator" that includes appliers: see chapter 5, §1.1.1) is rigid or nonrigid in the *same* straightforward *way* that a *concrete-object* designator is: as a device that names or denotes its object, in this case a specific property, either with respect to some worlds but not others or else with respect to all worlds. Accordingly, as I have indicated, there has been pessimism from some informed quarters about whether property designators are uniformly rigid or nonrigid in the same way that concrete-object designators are. Gómez-Torrente, for example, writes: "given that many terms that interest Kripke (e.g., 'cat', 'animal', etc.) are not singular terms, this way of proceeding is not available to the Kripkean" (2004, p. 38). Soames likewise urges that such an extension of rigidity to property designators in general "has no plausibility," in view of "count nouns, such as *human*, *tiger*, and *mammal*, as well as adjectives such as *loud* and *hot*" (2002, p. 246; see also pp. 245, 248).

If the case for Millian dualism is persuasive, then that puts pressure on me to produce a second account of rigidity for *non*singular property designators, in order to show that rigidity applies to property designators in general. But the case for Millian dualism is not persuasive: so I will argue in the sections that remain in the present chapter. By contrast, a uniformly singular treatment of property designators fares much better, in terms of plausibility, than the dualist rival: so even if I can *produce* (as I will argue: see note 5) the predicative account of rigidity that would be needed, along with the singular one, to achieve a dualistic compromise, the compromise should be rejected. Considerations in favor of dualism fail, then, to indicate any need for a nonsingular account of the rigid – nonrigid distinction, or even to indicate that a nonsingular account might be *desirable* for purposes of presenting an attractive alternative to a uniformly singular construal.[5]

2.1. *Accommodating English Grammar: Uniform vs. Nonuniform Accounts*

Mill (1843) articulates as well as anyone the dualistic alternative to a uniform treatment of property designators as singular terms. For Mill the "*concrete* name" (p. 29) 'white', say, "denotes" not the property whiteness itself, but only concrete "individuals, collectively and severally," that have that property: "of them alone can it properly be said to be a name" (p. 31).[6] 'Whiteness', by contrast, names the attribute that is *possessed* by concrete objects. 'Whiteness' is an "*abstract* name," which is to say that it is "the name of an attribute" (p. 29).

The Millian dualistic tradition, which remains strong,[7] enjoys the advantage of reflecting surface grammar more smoothly than monistic competitors, on first blush anyway. 'Snow is white' is grammatical, but 'snow is whiteness' or 'snow is the property of being white', where the 'is' marks the *is* of predication, is apparently not grammatical. The suggestion here is that names cannot sensibly or correctly appear in predicative position: as Wright says, "the copula cannot grammatically link a pair of singular terms" (1998, p. 253). In the same way, while '*P. tigris* is a species' and 'bachelorhood is a state characterizing Supreme Court Justice David Souter' are grammatical, 'tiger is a species' or 'bachelor is a state characterizing Supreme Court Justice David Souter' are apparently not grammatical. The suggestion is that general terms cannot sensibly or correctly appear as names for a property in the subject position of a sentence.

According to the Millian position, the *syntactical* difference between adjectives and count nouns, on the one hand, and singular-term variants, on the other, reflects an underlying *semantic* difference: that is, on the Millian view, there is a semantic relationship, that of naming, that '*P. tigris*' bears to the relevant property, and that 'tiger' does not. So 'tiger is a species' would fail to amount to a genuine statement in a language permitting it, or it would fail to state any proposition, or it would fail to express a possible truth, or it would suffer from some other such crippling defect, since 'tiger' does not name anything but rather is true of each, severally, of the tigers in the world. Something similar can be said for the other ungrammatical sentences above.

A count noun like 'tiger' or an adjective like 'white' does have a semantic relationship to the relevant property, according to Millian dualism, but the relationship is not one of naming. So while 'white' cannot be used to talk *directly* about whiteness as a subject of discourse, as it would if it could be used in, say, the identity statement 'white = the color of Antarctica', whiteness does *constrain* the use of 'white' by semantic design since 'white' is correctly applied just to objects like Antarctica that instantiate whiteness.[8] The *semantic* extension of 'white' is the same as the *metaphysical* extension of the property whiteness, from possible world to possible world (see chapter 2, note 1).

The ungrammaticality of statements like 'tiger is a species' or 'snow is whiteness' seems *initially* to give strong grounds to favor the Millian position (Wright 1998, pp. 240, 245, 258–9; Wiggins 1984, p. 320). However, further reflection indicates that we would be unwise to infer much about the semantics of designation from the ungrammaticality of these statements. Syntax does not always mirror semantics.[9] The pronouns 'me' and 'I' are distinct syntactically. 'I am fond of anyone fond of me' is grammatical; 'me am fond of anyone fond of I' is not. But we are not tempted here to suggest that the two terms for the subject name different entities or otherwise bear a different semantic relationship to the subject (for a variety of related examples, see Oliver 2005; Schnieder 2006, pp. 124–5, 129; Swoyer 2008, §1.2; Wolterstorff 1970, p. 71). Thus, the usual first-order formalization for 'I am fond of anyone fond of me', '(x)(Fx,i → Fi,x)', uses just one constant, 'i', which shares a single semantic relationship to the designatum of both of the English terms 'me' and 'I'.

Surface grammar does not seem to reflect the semantic content of 'I' and 'me'. So it is hard to see any *substantive* objection to the position that 'me' and 'I' are rigid designators of me and that 'me am identical to I' is accordingly necessarily true. To be sure, rigidity's lessons for 'me am identical to I' obtain only for a language *containing* the statement. *English* seems to lack the statement; but if English forbids as ungrammatical 'me am identical to I', that is a limitation of English, not rigidity, a limitation resulting in our inability to formulate statements whose necessity would otherwise be underwritten by rigidity in a straightforward and familiar manner. Rigidity's lessons for 'me am identical to I' apply just as they should, with respect to any language containing the statement: that would include a language otherwise just like English except that it recognizes as grammatical the interchangeability of 'I' and 'me'.

So the limits of English's grammar presents only a minor inconvenience, not a real substantive barrier, to theorists trying to illustrate rigidity and its consequences. This lesson carries over straightforwardly from the case of 'I' and 'me' to the case of 'whiteness' and 'white'. Grammar is not much indication that there is any substantial problem with statements like 'white = albescent'.[10] If 'white = albescent' is ungrammatical, let us appeal to a slightly amended or refined English (something I would recommend for independent reasons anyway: see chapter 6, §2.2).

Of course, even though a language otherwise like English could permit the interchangeability of 'I' and 'me' without altering the designation of either term, such a change in grammar *would* interfere with the effortlessness with which English-speaking audiences can discern the proper subject of a complex statement. The utility of a grammatical distinction between 'I' and 'me', in the absence of a semantic distinction, suggests that there might be similar advantages in distinguishing between terms like 'white' and 'whiteness', even if the semantic relationship that each bears to the relevant property is the same. And there would seem to be such advantages: the grammatical distinction between 'white' and 'whiteness' affords one efficient way, although not the only possible way, for speakers to indicate whether or not they are using the property-designator-cum-copula in a typical predicative fashion to say something about objects with the property. Typically, as Mill says, "When we say snow is white, milk is white, linen is white, we do not mean it to be understood that snow, or linen, or milk, is a colour. We mean that they are things having the colour. The reverse is the case with the word whiteness" (1843, p. 30). The choice of the word form 'white' provides a natural syntactic signal that the copula in '... is white' serves as the 'is' of predication rather than identity. If 'whiteness' were substituted for 'white', the resulting statement would say something different, at least on its most natural reading: 'milk is whiteness' is correctly or most naturally read as an identity statement. The grammar involving different forms of the property term thus has a natural explanation that leaves untouched any recognition of codesignation with regard to *semantics*.

The foregoing paragraphs indicate that it is hardly clear that Millian semantic dualism's accordance with surface grammar, so far as it goes, is much testimony on dualism's behalf. I have not yet *questioned* dualism's accordance with surface grammar. But it is not clear that, in the final analysis, dualism's accordance is so impressive as it appears on a first glance to be: indeed, it is not even clear that Millian dualism does better on this score than an opposing uniformist position. Dualism has trouble accommodating the grammar of certain sentences: in particular, the way we use anaphora seems to recommend the anti-Millian interpretation of adjectives as *names* or name-like devices ("abstract names," in Millian terminology). 'K2 is white and that is a bright color' is apparently grammatical. But 'that' cannot refer back to the proposition *that K2 is white*, since *that K2 is white* is not a color but a proposition. Instead, 'that' in 'that is a bright color' evidently refers back to that which 'white' *names*. A Millian cannot tolerate such an interpretation, since 'white' does not name anything on her account: it serves behind the predicative *is*. Here grammar departs from Millian semantics, by allowing for the formulation of a sentence that should apparently fail, in virtue of its composition, to express anything.

There are corresponding considerations about *non*rigid designators for properties. Dualists cannot give a straightforward reading of 'K2 is *the color of Antarctica* and *that* is a bright color', which appears to feature, in predicative position, a nonrigid definite description for the color that 'that' refers to rigidly. I discuss these matters further below.[11]

2.2. *Patterns of Reasoning Formalized: Uniform vs. Nonuniform Accounts*

A lesson suggested by the foregoing section (§2.1) is that while patterns of reasoning featuring the range and power of the rigid – nonrigid distinction are reflected in some measure in the semantics of English, such patterns should even so not be thought to be reflected in too thorough-going a way in this natural language: hence, as I have indicated, the different grammatical constraints upon 'I' and 'me', as illuminating they might be for other purposes, seem to forbid the expression of certain lines of reasoning that would be honored by the rigid – nonrigid distinction. Differences between a Millian treatment of the rigid – nonrigid distinction and uniformist alternatives seem, therefore, to be best resolved by appeal to how *naturally* each treatment can reflect, in a *refined* language that approximates English, salient patterns of reasoning that English honors in a more or less satisfactory way and as consistently as we might expect for a natural language. In the present section (2.2) I look at the relevant options for representing the rigid – nonrigid distinction in a refined formal language. I will favor a uniformist treatment over its Millian rival.

2.2.1. *A Millian Treatment of the Rigid – Nonrigid Distinction for Singular Property Designators* Not only does an initial look at English grammar suggest a Millian treatment of property designators, but so do familiar formalizations of English property designators in first-order logic (see the opening paragraphs of chapter 5). In a typical first-order language, a general term like 'white' is absorbed into the predicate '...is white', or 'W', which forms a sentence when followed by a singular term like 'k' for 'K2': hence, 'Wk', for 'K2 is white'. A variable such as 'x' may be substituted for a name: it must be bound by a quantifier to obtain a closed sentence, which has truth value, as in '(x)Wx' for 'everything is white'. Since 'white' has only a predicative role, it fails to name a property that is in the domain of quantification or that can itself be a subject of predication. Nor can 'white' flank the '=' in an identity statement.

A language like this readily accommodates a Millian understanding of property designators. Although 'white' is formalized with a predicate rather than a name (but see note 7), we could represent 'whiteness', which Millians construe as a *name* for the intended property, with a term like 'w', which accordingly would have no *predicative* role: 'w' could not *apply* to objects with the property. Connections between the predicate '...is white' and the singular term 'whiteness' would have to be honored or established by appeal to some philosophical principle or meaning postulate like,

M. Necessarily, (x)(Wx ≡ x exemplifies w).

No such statement relating the predicate '...is white' and the singular term 'whiteness' would rise above the status of a philosophical principle or postulate, to take up the status of a *logical truth* instead (as understood by, say, Quine 1961, pp. 22–3). Compare by contrast '(x)(Wx ≡ Wx)': this statement is a logical truth because regardless of the interpretation of the nonlogical vocabulary 'W', the statement remains true. '(x)(Wx ≡ x exemplifies w)' falls short of this standard: replacement of 'W' and 'w' sometimes issues in falsehood, as in '(x)(x is winsome ≡ x exemplifies whiteness)'. 'W' and 'w''s different semantic properties preclude us from substituting an occurrence of either with the other or alternatively resorting to semantically neutral vocabulary, in order to have the same property designator on both sides of a biconditional that would accordingly remain true regardless of the interpretation of that property designator.

In the first two or three decades after the introduction of the term 'rigid designator', dualistic treatments of property designators were generally presupposed in discussions about how to apply to property designators the rigid – nonrigid distinction. Accordingly, the focus of these discussions tended to be on those property designators that are singular, like 'whiteness', or 'w'.[12] The name 'w' is naturally taken to be rigid, according to the original conception of rigidity. The *predicate* 'W' cannot be handled along these lines, of course, which is unfortunate. A similar disparity arises for corresponding *non*rigid designators for the same property, or promising candidates.

'The color of Antarctica' can be interchanged with the singular term 'w' when used as a *definite description*, in which case it can be counted a nonrigid designator for more or less the reason that singular concrete-object designators like 'the brightest nonlunar body in the evening sky' can be counted nonrigid designators. But 'the color of Antarctica''s use in *predicative* position cannot be handled along these lines (see note 11 and the accompanying text).

The foregoing dualist account seems to present an unnecessarily busy reconstruction of salient patterns of reasoning that appear with at least some frequency in English and that we might hope to capture in a refined language featuring the rigid – nonrigid distinction. Consider the apparently well-formulated English argument

K2 is white and that is the color of Antarctica
so K2 is the color of Antarctica.

The reasoning cannot be simply rendered. Part of the problem is, as I have already indicated (in §2.1), that 'that' has no explicit referent: any attempt to bring out the logical form must provide a referent for 'that'. Since a Millian needs to introduce a distinct name for the property that is the referent, like the singular 'whiteness', important connections must be secured by appeal to suppressed premises, including a philosophical principle or a meaning postulate something like the foregoing (M), to the effect that, as a dualist would put it, "whatever is white exemplifies whiteness." So the terse reasoning in English with which we began has become:

K2 is white,
[whatever is white exemplifies whiteness]
[so K2 exemplifies whiteness]
and that [namely, whiteness] = the color of Antarctica
...
so K2 is the color of Antarctica.

As the ellipses indicate, we are still not finished laying bare the valid form of the reasoning with which we began. The problems centering on anaphora have been resolved; but there remains an ambiguity arising from the distinct semantic relations to a property that the corresponding singular and predicative property designators bear: 'the color of Antarctica' appears both as a predicative expression, in the conclusion, and also as a singular term, in the premises. Since the singular and predicative uses of 'the color of Antarctica' have different semantic values, for the Millian dualist, we will have to fill in the gap of reasoning with still more by way of premises, including some philosophical principle or meaning postulate to the effect that whatever "exemplifies the color of Antarctica" (on a singular reading) "is the color of Antarctica" (on a predicative reading).

A Millian reconstruction of a valid pattern of reasoning like the foregoing is strangely complicated, then: unnecessarily so. More straightforward alternatives are available, which make do with a single rendering of 'white' and 'the color of Antarctica'. Such alternatives would seem better to mirror the apparently simpler reasoning in English.[13]

2.2.2. Uniformly Singular Treatments of the Rigid – Nonrigid Distinction for Property Designators One *alternative* to a dualistic reconstruction of the rigid – nonrigid distinction construes all instances of the English 'white' as *singular*. Another alternative that treats property designators uniformly construes all instances of 'white' as *non*singular. Of course, the uniformly nonsingular alternative presents special challenges to the task of explaining how the rigid – nonrigid distinction could transfer from concrete-object designators, which are singular, to property designators, which would be nonsingular: so the rival, uniformly singular construal of property designators would seem to be a good first resort, if it is tenable, as an alternative to Millian dualism. And a uniformly singular construal *does* seem to be tenable, at least for all that Millianism-inspired considerations of the present chapter indicate; more radical resistance to a uniformly singular treatment of property designators might present trouble, but that is a problem for later (see note 5). The business here is to present an attractive, uniformly singular alternative to Millian *dualism*, in view of the considerations that have inspired *it*.

In the early years of discussion, the rigid – nonrigid distinction for property designators was generally represented in a first-order language that reflects Millian dualism, as I have observed (see note 12). Relatively recently, Salmon's (2003; 2005) endorsement of a formerly overlooked paper by Linsky (1984) has given celebrity to one rival to the Millian treatment, which I will survey briefly in section (2.2.2.1): this rival treats property designators uniformly as higher-order singular terms. Another rival to Millian dualism treats property designators as first-order singular terms, as dualism does: I discuss this uniformly singular first-order option in section (2.2.2.2). Either uniform treatment would seem to be superior to a dualistic, Millian treatment because it is better, and indeed good, for representing a wide range of typical patterns of reasoning turning on the rigid – nonrigid distinction for property designators. I will not select between the uniform treatments. Perhaps neither displaces the other: either might suffice in general or each might have its claim to superiority for representing certain patterns of reasoning. I will leave that issue unresolved, but I will broach some general considerations that might come down in favor of one treatment or the other.

2.2.2.1. A Basic Second-Order Treatment Different variants of a typed, second-order treatment of property designators have been endorsed in several works published over just the last few years (Linsky 2006; Salmon 2003; 2005; Soames 2004, pp. 94–7; 2006b, pp. 713–14). Here I follow Linsky's seminal exposition (Linsky 1984). The second-order treatment is framed in a language that is richer than the familiar first-order language sufficient for a Millian treatment. Second-order predicate letters supplement familiar first-order predicate letters like 'W', thus allowing 'W' to serve *also* as a *name* that can appear in the position of an argument, as any ordinary name like 'k' does in a statement like 'Wk'. So we may introduce the second-order predicate letter

'B²' for '... is abstract', in order to express 'white is abstract': 'B²W'.[14] The second-order vocabulary also introduces variables like 'F' that take the place of predicate letters and are bound in the expected fashion to obtain closed sentences. Thus, if we take white to be abstract then we will also take black, oval, hot, and so on to be abstract. All are abstract: '$(F)(B^2F)$'.

The second-order language seems fairly straightforwardly to allow 'white' to serve as a rigid designator even though it has a predicative role: after all, the (first-order) predicate 'W' serves also as a (second-order) *name* for something that is the subject of predication or quantification, and the rigidity of names is familiar. What is needed, for a contrast, is a *nonrigid* expression for a property that similarly serves a predicative as well as a singular role. Here Linsky turns, naturally enough, to definite descriptions.

Linsky would render 'the color of Antarctica', '$(\imath F)C^2(\text{Antarctica},F)$' (1984, p. 272), using the inverted iota operator $\imath$ (read as 'the') to form the definite description. So the contingently true identity statement 'white is the color of Antarctica', which contains a rigid and a nonrigid designator for whiteness, would be formalized, 'W $=^2$ $(\imath F)$ $C^2(\text{Antarctica},F)$'. Here the definite description appears as a singular term. But, like 'W', the definite description is a first-order *applier* as well as a second-order singular term. So just as we can say 'K2 is white', or 'Wk', we can say, 'K2 is the color of Antarctica', or '$(\imath F)C^2(\text{Antarctica},F)k$': here we read the copula as the *is* of predication, not identity. Both 'Wk' and '$(\imath F)C^2(\text{Antarctica},F)k$' are true, with respect to the actual world, just in case K2 is white, although the truth value of the respective statements diverges with respect to other possible worlds: with respect to a world in which Antarctica is lush green, either '$(\imath F)C^2(\text{Antarctica},F)k$' is false, since K2 is not green, or else 'Wk' is false because K2 is, like Antarctica, green.

The impressive second-order treatment of the rigid – nonrigid distinction for property designators that I have just limned is not the only natural alternative to a Millian treatment available. I present a first-order alternative in the following section.

2.2.2.2. A Basic First-Order Treatment The second-order treatment of the foregoing section (2.2.2.1) handles all property designators as singular terms for properties, without giving up their role in predicates like '... is white', which applies to concrete white things. 'White' is represented by a second-order singular term 'W', which also serves as a first-order predicate letter.

A first-order formalization that treats all property designators as singular assigns 'white' a *first*-order singular term, 'w'. But a first-order language needs predicates like '... is white', too. Unfortunately, in a typical first-order language at least, 'w' would amount to a *mere* singular term, and not a predicate. Accordingly, 'w' could not supplant a first-order predicate letter like 'W' in a sentence like 'Wk' because the substitution would not issue in a sentence. The content of 'wk' would be no more than *whiteness K2*, which is not a proposition, or a thought, as Frege would say, because in some important respect the parts fail to "hold together" (Frege 1952a, p. 54). So the non-predicate 'w' cannot supplant 'W'. Nor can 'W' be retained in the language along with 'w', as a second formal rendering of 'white'; that would of course frustrate the current aim of presenting a uniformly singular first-order rendering of property designators, since 'W' is not singular in a first-order language.

What is needed is a formal language that treats property designators like 'white' and 'whiteness' as first-order singular terms but that allows for these terms to be employed in predicates like '... is white'. A language with a special two-place predicate for the *is* of predication could meet this demand. I will sketch how a language with such a predicate might be formulated: the basic approach permits variation, of course (just as the foregoing second-order approach does: see note 20).

Let us render predication by means of the predicate letter 'Δ', with a nod to Bealer (1982, pp. 82; 258, note 2), an influential figure who favors a first-order language for treating properties. Because the symbol 'Δ' renders formally the copula in English (or, again, slightly modified English: see note 10), 'white' is prized away from the copula in '... is white': the term 'white' is thereby distinguished from the predicate '... is white', which contains both the term and the copula. Thus, 'K2 is white' is rendered '$\Delta k,w$': this expresses that K2 is white or that K2 exemplifies the relevant property.[15] Both K2 and the property whiteness receive a singular term.

The name 'w', as a first-order singular term, seems fairly straightforwardly to qualify as a rigid designator. A *non*rigid designator for the same property would accordingly be a first-order definite description. The foregoing definite description 'the color of Antarctica' may be formalized: '$(\imath x)(\Delta x,c \ \& \ \Delta \text{Antarctica},x)$'.[16] Accordingly, we can render the true but contingently true identity statement 'white = the color of Antarctica' as 'w = $(\imath x)(\Delta x,c \ \& \ \Delta \text{Antarctica},x)$'. Like 'w', a definite description can be put after the copula in a predicative statement, for which the 'is' is to be interpreted as the *is* of predication, rather than the *is* of identity: thus, 'K2 is the color of Antarctica' is formalized naturally as '$\Delta(\imath x)(\Delta x,c \ \& \ \Delta \text{Antarctica},x),k$'.

2.2.2.3. Beyond Adjectives I have focused on adjectives. Having dealt with the basic treatment of property designators as singular terms, I will indicate briefly, in this section (§2.2.2.3), how the treatment from the foregoing section (§2.2.2.2) might be extended to apply to count nouns and verbs, too. The basic second-order treatment from section (2.2.2.1) would seem to admit a similar extension, but for definiteness I focus just on the first-order treatment.

'White' is generally used as an adjective, but sometimes it is used as a count noun, as in 'there are nine whites on the soccer field but only eight greens'. We might opt to render the count-noun containing sentence 'x is a white' as an (open) identity statement, broadly construed (cf. Salmon 2005, pp. 123–4, note 13), that says that there is something white and that that is x: $(\exists y)(\Delta y,w \ \& \ x = y)$. Alternatively, we might treat 'x is a white' the same as 'x is white': '$\Delta x,w$'. In that case the 'Δ' absorbs the article 'a' as well as the copula 'is', in '... is a white'. On either rendering, the count noun 'white', like the adjective 'white', is treated as a name for whiteness.

Kripke does not suggest that verbs function as rigid designators, but they might be treated similarly, as others observe (e.g., López de Sa 2001, p. 618). On one natural treatment of verbs, the so-called "auxiliary" 'does' or 'do' is understood to perform the function that the copula 'is' or 'are' performs for adjectives: this allows, in a manner similar to that described in the foregoing material with respect to adjectives, for the predicate containing the verb to be distinguished from the verb itself, which verb may be a rigid or nonrigid singular term. Thus, 'x does stick' receives the formalization, 'Δx, s', in which the predicate '... does stick' is parsed: 's' is a rigid singular term and the special predicate letter 'Δ' represents 'does'. Nonrigid designation could be accommodated in the expected fashion: it is manifested in definite descriptions like 'the action that annoys Kim' or, more briefly, 'what annoys Kim'. Again, such definite descriptions may appear not only in subject position but also in predicates, as in, 'x does the action that annoys Kim' or 'x does what annoys Kim'. As we would expect, given that verbs are to be treated along the lines of adjectives and count nouns with respect to semantics, if not grammar, action types are identified with properties: hence, 'stickiness = what annoys Kim' or 'stickiness = the action that annoys Kim' may be true, on this account. If this treatment of action types as properties strikes you initially as awkward, the impression may be mitigated as you consider that stickiness is the property of sticking, which is a property of acting in a certain way. Of course, any *token* action of an object's sticking is not the same as the property of sticking; the token would presumably be treated, on this line of thinking, as a particular event involving the relevant object's *possession* of the property.

A complication arises with respect to an expression like 'x sticks', which presents, on the face of it, no copula or 'does' to be distinguished from the verb or property designator. How are we to avoid concluding that '... sticks' is a predicate that is after all incapable of decomposition into 'Δ ..., s', which contains 's' for *stick* and 'Δ' for *does*? Without such decomposition, a first-order formalization would seem to call for the predicate letter 'S', and that would be a problem for an account according to which property designators including verbs are treated uniformly as first-order names. So in order to handle the copula-lacking '... sticks', we might read the 'does' as implicit in the predicate. Hence, 'x sticks' may be analyzed as having the same logical form as 'x does stick' or 'x is sticky'. Accordingly, 'sticks' may be understood as a name of the property, and the 'does' may be understood to precede it tacitly in the sentence.[17]

2.2.2.4. Comparing the Treatments In the present section (§2.2.2.4) I compare the foregoing formal treatments of the rigid – nonrigid distinction for property designators. Both treatments seem naturally to represent the rigid – nonrigid distinction. One salient worry for the singular treatment calls for attention: its handling of the copula, which figures in definite descriptions like those I have been discussing,[18] might seem inadequate. I argue otherwise in section (2.2.2.4.1). Hence, both treatments seem able to represent the distinction formally, at least for typical discourse of the sort I have been discussing. In section (2.2.2.4.2), I gesture toward broader considerations, which have little to do with the distinction at hand: these broader issues, which certainly cannot be resolved here and which may be incapable of resolution, might ultimately favor the language of one treatment or another.

2.2.2.4.1. FAITHFULLY REPRESENTING THE COPULA Some property theorists, though not all,[19] recognize an important semantic difference between 'x exemplifies F' and 'x is F'. Neutrality over this matter is desirable here. If we are not to distinguish, then 'x exemplifies whiteness' and 'x is white' share the same formal representation(s). But if we are to distinguish, then each of 'x is white' and 'x exemplifies whiteness' must enjoy its own formal representation, at least assuming that both items are to be countenanced at all. A second-order treatment of property designators can distinguish: 'x is white' is rendered 'Wx', while 'x exemplifies whiteness' can be rendered in some other fashion: say, 'x $\in$ W', where '$\in$' is the predicate for exemplification. A dualistic Millian treatment, though it is undesirable for other reasons, does not lack formal resources here: it can draw upon 'Wx' and 'x $\in$ w'. But we might have questions about a uniform first-order treatment outlined in the foregoing material. Since 'w' is a name, we might on first blush construe 'Δx,w' as saying that *x exemplifies whiteness*, in which case, it would not be clear how to represent the predicative statement 'x is white'.

If a first-order language that treats property designators uniformly, as the foregoing language does, cannot accommodate the *is* of predication, in the event that this is distinct from exemplification, then this is a problem. But the first-order language at issue *can* accommodate the *is* of predication, in the event that this is distinct from exemplification. Here I outline one method of doing so. In the foregoing paragraph, I observe that we might construe the 'Δ' as a predicate for exemplification; but we might not, too. We might use the 'Δ' to represent the *is* of predication instead, assuming that that is different.

A typical way of characterizing the *is* of predication, on the part of those who would distinguish this from anything that they might call "exemplification," would be to take the *is* of predication to be nonrelational or quasi-relational, and to take 'exemplifies', again on the assumption that it is to be recognized, to be a relational predicate that takes names for arguments. Thus, Armstrong suggests the 'is' in '... is white' is not to be conceived as a "real relation" that attaches a property to a particular (1997, p. 30); instead, the copula might better be called a "non-relational tie," as strange as that sounds, or something else short of a real relation (Armstrong 1997, p. 30; see also Linsky 1984, p. 263; Wiggins 1984, pp. 318, 327–8; for animadversions, see Wright 1998, pp. 252–4; Gaskin discusses motives in helpful detail: 2008, chapters 5 and 6). Let us suppose that something along the foregoing lines is right. This way of seeing the relevant *is* as some sort of "tie" that is distinct from a genuine relation seems to be respected by the representation 'Wx' for 'x is white', which representation gives no appearance of expressing that x is standing in some relation to the property. But there is evidently no reason that 'Δx,w' cannot also be interpreted in a way that is friendly to this way of seeing matters, at least so long as properties exist and can be named at all (an assumption for the present chapter: see the opening paragraphs) and so long as we are correct in preferring over Millian dualism one or another uniform treatment of property designators, according to which the same property designator serves as a name as well as an applier. Given these assumptions, we may agree that 'white' names a *way that some things are*, and interpret 'Δx,w' as saying *that x is that way*. We need not say that the 'Δ' represents a "real relation," but only that it represents formally the copula, whether this is a real relation or something short of that. A real relation would merit a name, which can serve in the argument place of a statement, but the first-order treatment is no more committed to representing the copula with a name than is the second-order treatment discussed in section (2.2.2.1), which does not represent the copula with a name of any order.[20]

So 'Δx,w' may be taken to say that x is white, not that x exemplifies white. How, then, to treat exemplification, assuming that we acknowledge it at all? Here we would naturally recognize a robust, genuine relation between a property and its instances, which is of course distinct, on the assumption in question, from the *is* of predication: we would accordingly recognize it with a *name*, perhaps introducing 'r' for that distinct relation that we recognize to be in the domain of quantification.[21]

2.2.2.4.2. THEORETICAL ISSUES IN THE BACKGROUND I have just examined a salient consideration to the effect that one of the uniformly singular languages that I have canvassed (in §2.2.2.1 and §2.2.2.2, respectively) might represent rigid and nonrigid property designators from English more naturally or faithfully than the other. I found the consideration uncompelling and know of no better.[22] So I turn briefly to other sorts of considerations: we might do well to favor one representation or another on the basis of how satisfactorily the relevant languages perform with respect to challenges having little to do with the specifics of the rigid – nonrigid distinction and the property terms that are supposed to be subject to that distinction. These other challenges concern theoretical issues that lie in the background of a search for a formal language in which to represent the rigid – nonrigid distinction: here issues surrounding the semantic paradoxes come to the fore. One formal language might be preferable to the other because it provides better resources for handling paradoxes.

We see how paradoxes become relevant to the choice between languages when we reflect that in, say, the first-order language discussed in section (2.2.2.2), some definite descriptions do not designate any property, on pain of paradox: this is the case for, say, '($\imath$x)((y)(Δy,x $\equiv$ ~ Δy,y))' which would, if it designated, designate the property x that is properly predicated of anything y if and only if y is not properly predicated of itself (for simplicity, limit the universe of discourse to properties). Such a property, if it existed, would give rise to a property-theoretic version of Russell's Paradox. If '($\imath$x)((y) (Δy,x $\equiv$ ~ Δy,y))' designates, then the property that it designates either is or is not properly predicated of itself. But we get a familiar contradiction either way. If, on the one hand, description's designatum *is* properly predicated of itself, then it could *not* be properly predicated of itself: by virtue of satisfying the description, the designatum can be predicated of anything y, which in this case would include itself, only if y is *not* properly predicated of itself. If, on the other hand, the designatum x is *not* properly predicated of itself, then x would have to *be* properly predicated of itself, since the designatum is properly predicated of *every* y such that y is *not* properly predicated of itself. Hence, if '$(\imath x)((y)(\Delta y,x \equiv \sim \Delta y,y))$' designates, then the designated property is properly predicated of itself if and only if it is not properly predicated of itself; but there could be no such property.

The possibility of expressing definite descriptions for paradoxical properties is not by itself harmful: definite descriptions can fail to designate, as the classic example 'the king of France' illustrates. But although a language with definite descriptions for paradoxical properties is not thereby saddled with paradox, since definite descriptions for paradoxical properties can fail to designate, such an expressive language does bring with it a burden: it suggests the desirability of producing an intuitive account concerning which of its formulas really do designate properties, a comprehension principle.

Take an open formula like 'y is white' or '$\Delta y,w$': intuitively you might expect that there is some corresponding property P such that anything y has P (or is P, where the predicative *is* is the one in question) if and only if y is white. That property corresponding to 'y is white' would be the property white. Unfortunately, it is hard to generalize the foregoing correspondence to similar formulas and properties. The open formula '$\sim \Delta y,y$', unlike '$\Delta y,w$', has no corresponding property: we cannot affirm 'there is some property P such that anything y has P if and only if $\sim \Delta y,y$'. So we must be circumspect in formulating a comprehension principle to say which formulas have corresponding properties, to avoid paradox.

The same caution is not needed for avoiding paradox in saying which formulas have corresponding properties, if formulas leading to paradox cannot even be formed in the language, as for a typed language of the sort presented above (in §2.2.2.1). In such a typed language, a formula cannot predicate of a property, which has to belong to some order or other, a property of the same order. Thus, 'WW' is not permitted, and the same goes for the open formula '$\sim F'F'$'. So there is no worry that a principle would force us unwittingly to affirm that there is any property corresponding to open formulas that would include the ill-formed '$\sim F'F'$'. '$(\exists F)(F')(FF' \equiv \sim F'F')$' could not be forced upon us or again even formed.

Since type theory represents one approach for evading semantic paradoxes, we might find the restrictions of a typed language, like those of the second-order language discussed in section (2.2.2.1), to be attractive. But type theory represents *only* one approach for evading semantic paradoxes (Bealer 1982, pp. 94ff.; Menzel 1993, pp. 65; Swoyer 2008, §7.3; Wright 1998, p. 263), and type theory raises its own problems. One problem is the awkward introduction of "typical ambiguity" (Bealer and Mönnich 1989, pp. 186ff.; Menzel 1993, pp. 64–6): consider, for example, 'K2 and courage are not both white'. A typed representation recognizes an ambiguity in 'white', since a first-order predicate like 'W' can combine with a name for an individual like K2 to form 'Wk'; but 'courage', like 'white', is a first-order predicate, not a name for an individual, so the symbol string 'WC' is not a sentence of the language. We need a higher-order predicate letter 'W^2', in order to say that courage is or is not white. Since nothing like '~(Wk & WC)' is well formed, we cannot express 'K2 and courage are not both white', on any straightforward interpretation on which what is conveyed is that one and the same white belongs at most to one of K2 and courage. We can only express that K2 is not white[1] and courage is not some distinct white[2], by appealing to a hierarchy of words for 'white' and corresponding properties: this well-known but unwelcome feature of type theory could be avoided with a language like that from section (2.2.2.2) that avoids typing. A related problem, or alleged problem, is indicated by a charge according to which type theory's expressive constraints are so severe that the theory itself is inexpressible: after all, type theory has type-specific variables, so it is hard to see how we could say in a type-neutral way that *every* property, as opposed to every property *of a given type*, belongs to some type or other (Bealer 1994, pp. 164–5; Menzel 1993, p. 66).

One's favorite resolutions to paradoxes like the above might, then, determine a preference for a typed, second-order language like the one discussed in section (2.2.2.1), for representing properties, or instead might determine a preference for a first-order language like that from section (2.2.2.2): the outcome would favor one formalization of the rigid – nonrigid distinction for property designators over another. These wider, theoretical issues hovering in the background, which might weigh in favor of one language or another, are certainly not issues that have to be settled here. Indeed these issues may be unsettleable: thus, Bealer (1994, p. 162) stresses that no one has an ideal resolution to the semantic paradoxes, so that philosophers are not presently in a position, and may never be in a position, to settle differences between proponents of various languages who cope in different ways with the paradoxes. Such a dismal cognitive position need not detain the present pursuit, though: what takes center stage here, in an investigation of the rigid – nonrigid distinction for property designators, is a look at how naturally the relevant formal languages are able to render reasoning about properties as it occurs in the English language (or again, slight variants of the English language: see note 10 and accompanying text). These concerns from center stage leave neither of the foregoing treatments from sections (2.2.2.1) and (2.2.2.2) at a loss, even if the status of the relevant languages with respect to wider, theoretical issues in the background must be left unsettled.[23]

3. Conclusion

I have addressed two distinct dualisms in sections (1) and (2), according to which *some* terms like 'white', 'whiteness', and 'the color of Antarctica' are rigid or nonrigid singular terms, but according to which *others* are not. I have resisted the foregoing dualisms.

I have addressed the apparent problem, for a uniform treatment of property designators, that definite descriptions are not singular if they are to be treated along Russellian lines; only names and name-like terms for properties are singular. I have urged, on the contrary, that definite descriptions may be considered singular for purposes here.

I have also addressed the apparent problem, for a uniform treatment of property designators, that an initial look at English grammar favors Millian dualism according to which 'white' should be treated as nonsingular even though 'whiteness' is singular. I have urged that in the final analysis, the Millian case is not impressive. I have canvassed basic versions of salient options for a uniform treatment of property designators as singular. Such a treatment is preferable to a dualist treatment.

So far, in arguing throughout this book that property designators are subject to a rigid – nonrigid distinction, I have not had to turn to any account of the rigid – nonrigid distinction besides the original singular account. This account is sufficient for property designators that are singular, I have argued (in chapters 2 and 3). And it seems reasonable to suppose that this would include *all* property designators if it includes any, as I have also argued (in this chapter). So if we may take for granted, with Millians and with Kripke, that some property designators at least are singular, then it would seem we may treat all property designators as subject to the rigid – nonrigid distinction to which concrete-object designators are subject. But there are well-known reasons, which I will discuss in the following chapter, for denying that *any* property designators at all are singular. Philosophers moved by these reasons will reject from the start Kripke's treatment of property designators like 'whiteness' as rigid singular terms that can appear in identity statements. I have yet to address the foregoing philosophers, in arguing that property designators are subject to a rigid – nonrigid distinction.

I will argue in the next chapter that philosophers who do not recognize singular property designators *can* still countenance a rigid – nonrigid distinction for property designators: I will argue that if property designators are not singular, they may even so be called "rigid" in a new respect that remains to be articulated. This new respect, distinctive of nonsingular terms, is worthy of the rubric 'rigid': it carries the same substantial philosophical significance as that which is enjoyed by the original rigid – nonrigid distinction for singular terms.

Notes

1. The basic worry that Russell's theory of descriptions belies some confusion at the root of the rigid – nonrigid distinction extends beyond statements like 'gold is the substance with atomic number 79' to the most familiar statements cited in connection with rigidity, which address concrete objects: e.g., 'Hesperus = Phosphorus' and 'Hesperus = the brightest nonlunar body in the evening sky'. So my defense here (in §1) will amount to a defense of the rigid – nonrigid distinction in general, not a defense of that distinction as it applies to property

designators specifically. Since my aims in this book concern property designators specifically (see chapter 1, note 1 and accompanying text), it is not obvious that the foregoing worry merits a response here; but I would argue that the worry does merit a response. Martí raises the objection specifically in connection with property designators and the theoretical identity statements containing them: so property designators seem to motivate the objection, even though the objection generalizes. And even if the objection were not, as it seems to be, inspired by a look at property designators specifically, it provides the occasion for a clarification of the rigid – nonrigid distinction that fits helpfully beside other salient clarifications that I offer, in order to forestall misunderstanding, at the opening of this book (in chapter 1, §1.2, §1.3).

2. Russell says as much: citing his favorite example, 'Scott is the author of *Waverly*', he writes, "The meaning of such propositions cannot be stated without the notion of identity, although they are not simply statements that Scott is identical with another term, the author of *Waverly*" (1905, p. 492). Russell does not see his theory as rendering identity somehow otiose but rather as explaining how identity statements can be interesting: "The usefulness of identity is explained by the above theory" (p. 492).

3. The conditions are exhaustive, provided descriptions are to be handled along the foregoing lines, in that if a name or definite description is not rigid in one of the above respects, it is not rigid at all. Essentially this understanding of a "rigid designator" is entertained also by Neale (1990, p. 53, note 18). The foregoing conditions are somewhat roughly stated: e.g., I have ignored complications concerning worlds in which a designatum like Hesperus fails to exist (as usual: see chapter 1, §1.2). The approximation is close enough to indicate the core idea.

4. To be sure, on a Russellian treatment, a definite description like 'the substance with atomic number 79' has affinities to a *predicate* that can only be satisfied by one item: in this case, the single substance gold. Still, because a Russellian definite description *uniquely* describes or "denotes" an object (Russell 1905, p. 488; see also Neale 2005, p. 818f.), even if it does not *refer* to that object as a name would, Russellian definite descriptions are best counted singular, for my purposes, along with names, and for the reasons provided in the text. In chapter 5, I discuss, by contrast, accounts of "designation" that are so *thoroughly* nonsingular in spirit that for my purposes it will be necessary to abandon a singular treatment: the accounts from that chapter accommodate theorists who deny that any expressions like 'gold' or 'the substance with atomic number 79' either name *or* uniquely describe any entity (see the following note 5).

5. In chapter 5, I will produce a purely predicative account of the rigid – nonrigid distinction, not or at least not primarily in order to accommodate dualism, which I will impugn in this chapter, but rather in order to accommodate a *uniform* treatment of property designators as *non*singular. Although I am not convinced that a uniformly predicative treatment of property designators is *needed* to accommodate property designators, the claim otherwise turns on ontological disputes whose resolution would go beyond the scope of this work (for related observations, see chapter 2, note 1; chapter 5, note 1): so I will accommodate by offering a second account of the rigid – nonrigid distinction for merely predicative property designators. After developing a predicative account of the rigid – nonrigid distinction, I will go on to suggest that the designation of *both* properties *and* concrete objects *might* be reconstrued to conform to a simple, uniformly *predicative* treatment of designation (see chapter 5, §1.1.2.4). But a uniformly predicative account of designation in general is more than what I need for the purposes of this book, so it is not part of my agenda to evaluate the merits of such a radical construal of designation in general; I start this book with the advantage of assuming the

familiar rigid – nonrigid distinction for singular designators like 'Hesperus' and I proceed from that starting point to address property designators. There is no need to supplant or supplement this original treatment of '*Hesperus*' and the like with an alternative treatment, so I broach a predicative treatment of concrete-object designators primarily with another purpose in mind: to further illuminate the connection between singular and predicative treatments of the distinction at hand.

6. A more common expression for conveying the point today would be to say that 'white' *applies* to concrete objects or *is true of* them: see, e.g., Quine 1960, pp. 90–1. Where Mill's terminology has become obsolete, I avoid it except where I quote Mill: so Mill's "concrete names" would not count as names or naming devices in my terminology. Only singular terms *name*.

7. It is now common practice in this broadly Millian tradition to treat 'white' as ambiguous (see, e.g., May 2003; Peterson 1986, pp. 296, 310, note 16; Soames 2002), with a singular use on which it reads as does Mill's 'whiteness', in addition to the general use that Mill recognizes: in earlier chapters, I myself have fallen back upon a singular *use* of 'white', if necessary, in order to presuppose singularity, at least for some contexts (see chapter 1, §3.1).

8. Mill says that 'white' "connotes" or "implies" the property, so that in applying 'white' to snowballs and the like, "we convey the meaning that the attribute whiteness belongs to them" (p. 31). A common way of putting the position now is that 'white' "*expresses*" the property instead of naming it (Gómez-Torrente 2006, p. 234; Jubien 1989, p. 163; Swoyer 2008, §1.2; for further variants of expression, see, e.g., Quine 1961, p. 10; Sidelle 1989, p. 63; Wright 1998, p. 258).

9. Accordingly, claims like Mill's about the semantics of designation should be clearly distinguished from corresponding claims about syntax. Kaplan, for one, is clear about "the distinctive *syntactical* role played by expressions of differing syntactical categories" (1973, p. 518, note 31) but he suggests that terms like 'red', 'penguin', and "almost all single words other than particles" behave *semantically* as names do: they are, for Kaplan, rigid designators (the same position, or something close to it, is defended by Besson 2009, pp. 6–7; see also Swoyer 2008, who provides a fine overview of much of the literature on these topics). The basic position that general terms or apparent general terms function semantically as names predates discussions of rigidity, as one might expect: Everett Hall (1952, p. 22, note 1), for example, who maintains that general terms "name in precisely the same sense as a proper name," clearly distinguishes matters of syntax from semantics. What is at issue is general terms' "capacity of designating only, that is, as abstracted from any syntactical features such symbols may also have."

10. I am not alarmed, then, by Heintz's (1973, p. 25) worry that unless syntax mirrors semantics, we are somehow unable, awkwardly enough, to express certain *true* statements: e.g., 'piety is identical to pious'. Let us grant that we cannot express 'piety is identical to pious' in English; still, we can express it in a language *English'* that is superficially different from English in that it relaxes grammatical constraints a little, while remaining *semantically* identical with English. If necessary we may, when remarking on the relevance of rigidity to the relevant expressions, speak English'. This also addresses a worry raised by a referee, to the effect that because statements like 'piety is identical to pious' seem so odd, we are unable to consult our intuitions to determine whether the use is problematic. Again, I would argue that the use in question receives *some* support even from common English: consider 'pious is what Aeneas shows himself to be, in his descent into the underworld'. Further, as I will argue (in §2.2), ordinary reasoning patterns suggest support for such use in natural language. But

finally, unless there is some incoherence in such a use, as I indicate there is not (in the text corresponding to this note), the use can be recommended as good English' if, as we might expect, a cleaner alternative to English is desirable because English's endorsement is unclear, inconsistent, or otherwise short of complete.

11. I return to awkward Millian reconstruals in §2.2.1, where I discuss how well Millianism reflects patterns of reasoning sensitive to rigidity; here, my concern is rather with the related issue of the surface grammar of English. Linsky emphasizes that definite-description-like expressions such as 'the color of Antarctica', and not just name-like expressions such as 'white', appear to feature grammatically in predicative position (Linsky 1984, p. 263ff.; see also 2006, p. 664). This feature of English indicates powerfully that in the natural language, property designators in predicative position are subject to a rigid – nonrigid distinction: either the original rigid – nonrigid distinction for singular terms or a corresponding distinction for nonsingular terms (options I entertain in the present chapter and in the following chapter, respectively: chapters 4 and 5). If English does not *always* allow for definite descriptions to serve in predicative position in the way that a count noun or adjective can, we still should not conclude on that basis that we have anything more than a superficial limitation of grammar, as opposed to a substantial limitation for the rigid – nonrigid distinction (see note 10; for similar thoughts, see Salmon 2005, p. 124, note 14).

Heintz (1973), who is cited by Linsky as a forbear (Linsky 1984, p. 263; 2006, p. 664), also anticipates that definite-description-like expressions serve in predicative position in English, though he does not construe the expressions as singular terms (of any order: see §2.2.2.1 below), in the way that Linsky does. For Heintz, properties cannot be named or uniquely described: so apparent definite descriptions in predicative position are not really definite descriptions. He calls them "definite *ascriptions*," instead (pp. 83–4; 94). Geach, who shares the position that properties cannot be named or uniquely described, anticipates still earlier that what would at first glance appear to be definite descriptions for properties serve in predicative position (Geach, Ayer, and Quine 1951, pp. 133–4; Anscombe and Geach 1961, p. 156; see also Dummett 1981, pp. 212ff.). I will be discussing further, in chapter 5, the position that properties cannot be named or uniquely described.

12. As you would expect, early discussions tend to be inchoate, so dualism is often suggested but not made explicit. For some discussions that suggest that a rigid – nonrigid distinction for property designators might or should appeal to dualism, not all of which discussions are necessarily sympathetic to the distinction, see Boër 1985, pp. 129–35; Donnellan 1973, p. 712; 1983, pp. 90–1; Forbes 1981, pp. 32, 35; Hirsch 1993, p. 230; Lewis 1983a, pp. 86–7; 1983b, p. 101, note 6; May 2003; Mondadori 1978, pp. 35–8; Peterson 1986, pp. 296–8, 304, 310, note 16; Schnieder 2005, p. 237; 2006, p. 128; Soames 2002; Tye 1981; for criticisms of a dualistic treatment, see Linsky 1984, p. 263; Salmon 2003; 2005, pp. 125–6, 131.

13. The foregoing argument is broadly Salmonesque (see, e.g., Salmon 2005, pp. 125f.; Linsky has expressed similar sentiments in personal communication: see also Linsky 1984, p. 263). This argument (and Salmon's: personal communication; see also 2007, p. 87) is not directed against meaning postulates per se but only unnecessary ones: here meaning postulates seem to complicate needlessly speech that apparently takes recourse, simply enough, to one and the same 'white'. Semantic dualism appears in general to suffer from the *prima facie* drawback of multiplying beyond necessity semantic relations that would hold between property designators and their properties (see also Salmon 2003; 2005, pp. 125–6, 131; Swoyer 2008, §1.2).

14. The superscript here indicates the predicate's status as second order, not its degree, or number of places.
15. See §2.2.2.4.1 on the possibility of differentiating between the readings *K2 is white* and *K2 exemplifies white*.

    The distinction between a property designator and a predicate containing that designator, which is recognized formally here, has frequently been blurred in the tradition. Thus, Kripke (1980, p. 127) counts 'cow' and 'tiger' predicates; Loar calls count nouns and adjectives "predicates," parenthetically setting aside the copula in " '(is) gold', '(is a) tiger', '(is) hot' " (1995, p. 474); Quine speaks of "general terms, for example, predicates" (1961, p. 12) and accordingly counts as predicates both 'red' and 'is-red' (p. 11; see also pp. 30–1); Soames 2002, p. 245 counts 'tiger', and 'chunk of gold' predicates; Ariansen (2001) counts predicates like 'is a student' as "general terms." The suggestion here is that, as Dummett would say, recognizing Frege as a forbear, "the copula is a mere grammatical device" of no semantic significance (Dummett 1981, p. 214; see also Wald 1979, p. 288; Gómez-Torrente 2006, especially pp. 243–4, note 21). Although it has been blurred frequently, the distinction between property designators and predicates containing them is honored by Kaplan (1989b, pp. 580–1, note 30), Linsky (1984, p. 260; but see this chapter, note 20), Salmon (2003, e.g., at p. 486, note 22; see also the present chapter, note 20), Soames (2004, pp. 94–7; 2006b, p. 712; but cf. 2002 and 2006b, p. 737, note 1), and, in effect, by Wiggins (1984, p. 318). The distinction has importance if property designators are construed as singular (even if second order); otherwise, it loses importance (see chapter 5, note 3).
16. The term 'c' in '$(\imath x)(\Delta x,c \ \& \ \Delta\text{Antarctica},x)$' is a name not for the property of being colored, of course, but for the property of being a color. This definite description need not be taken as primitive and something similar may be said of the second-order '$(\imath F)C^2(\text{Antarctica},F)$' (as Linsky indicates: Linsky 1984, pp. 272–3), for which 'C^2' stands for '...is a color of...'.
17. By taking 'sticks' as a name positioned behind the tacit 'does', I have adapted a tip from Soames, who recognizes the copula as tacit in related contexts: 2006b, note 1. On a related alternative reading, the English verb 'sticks' is not simply a name but rather a complex *predicate* that on analysis would be resolved into a formula that contains a name, which is rigid or nonrigid, and the auxiliary 'does'. Whether the whole predicate 'sticks' would also be rigid or nonrigid, like the name it contains, would depend on whether the rigid – nonrigid distinction applies to predicates, as opposed to property designators: I discuss that matter in the foregoing note 15 and in the following chapter.
18. I take the copula to be implicit in 'the color of Antarctica': it is brought out explicitly in 'the color that Antarctica is' or perhaps 'the color that Antarctica exemplifies'.
19. Theorists who distinguish between the semantics of 'x exemplifies F' and 'x is F' include Menzel (1993, pp. 73, 76–7) and Salmon (2003, p. 483; 2005, p. 131; see also 1981, p. 74). Theorists who identify the relevant phenomena, rather than distinguish between them, include Levinson (1978, pp. 3–4); Mondadori (1978, p. 36), and Soames (2004, pp. 96–7; 2006b, pp. 712–13), among others.
20. For Linsky's treatment, which I discuss in §2.2.2.1, the copula for the *is* of predication never becomes expressed explicitly: Linsky, as we have seen, uses 'W' as a second-order singular term and a first-order predicate letter. When 'W' serves as a singular term for 'white', as in the true identity statement 'white = white', there is no copula for the *is* of predication to be represented, so its absence in 'W = W' is to be expected. But when 'W' serves as a first-

order predicate letter, as when it serves to represent the English 'x is white', there is a copula for the *is* of predication to be represented: this copula is not explicit in the representation, but is apparently instead implicit in the 'W', the formalization being 'Wx'. Salmon, by contrast, brings out the copula explicitly, but again, not as a self-standing predicate, so evidently we cannot take the copula to be a nameable relation: he introduces '*is*-{ }' as a predicate-*forming* operator on designators like 'white', thus permitting '*is*-{white}(x)' for 'x is white' (2005, pp. 123–4; Kaplan endorses a similar idea: 1989b, pp. 580–1, note 30; Salmon discusses Kaplan helpfully in 2005, p. 132, note 22). The foregoing operator makes perspicuous the distinction between a *name* for a property like 'white', on the one hand, and the 'white'-containing *predicate* '*is*-{white} . . .', on the other hand (see also note 15). The distinction is obscured on a treatment according to which 'W', which represents 'white', serves the dual function of being a name for the property, on the one hand, and also a full predicate, on the other hand.

21. In order to deal with exemplification and other genuine relations, the first-order language in question has to have a series of 'Δ' predicates, none of which would be a true relation: not just the dyadic 'Δ', on which I have focused, which allows for the formation of 'Δx,w', but also a triadic 'Δ', which allows for the formation of 'Δr,x,w', and so on.

    If the 'Δ' represents the *is* of predication, then does the term 'w' serve not only as a singular term but also as a *general* term? The answer is clearly an affirmative one, provided that we understand a general term to be a term that combines with the *is* of predication to form a predicate like '. . . is white', and we understand a singular term to be a term that has the semantic function of designating a single object and that fills the argument place of a predicate (this is, as Schnieder observes, the "standard" understanding of a general term: Schnieder 2005, p. 238, note 1; Salmon agrees: 2005, p. 123). Just as a second-order treatment of property designators like that of §2.2.2.1 maintains that a designator like 'W' is both singular *and* general, in the above respects, the first-order language in question maintains that a designator like 'w' is both singular and general, in the above respects. The difference is that a second-order treatment distinguishes by types: one and the same term 'W' is a *first-order* general term, as in 'Wk', for 'K2 is white', but a *second-order* singular term, as in 'B^2W', for 'whiteness is abstract'. The first-order treatment at issue is not committed to a hierarchy of types (it appeals to tools other than typing to handle the threat of paradox: see §2.2.2.4.2), so 'w' serves as a singular term and a general term of the same type or order. 'w' is a first-order singular term, by virtue of designating its property and filling the position of an argument in first-order predicates, as in 'Δw,b', for 'whiteness is abstract'. 'w' is also a first-order general term, by virtue of combining with a copula representing the *is* of predication in order to form a first-order predicate, as in 'Δk,w', for 'K2 is white'.

22. Frequently proponents of a second-order treatment might *appear* to present considerations to favor a second-order treatment over a first-order treatment on the basis of how naturally it can represent the rigid – nonrigid distinction. But a closer look indicates that these considerations generally compare the second-order treatment with a *dualistic* first-order treatment, rather than a first-order treatment like the one presented here (in §2.2.2.2). As I have suggested, dualistic treatments have historically been presented in first-order languages (see note 12 and accompanying text). Further, I do not know of any treatment of the rigid – nonrigid distinction for property designators in the literature that presents a *non*-dualistic first-order *rival* to dualistic treatments. So it is clear why Linsky or Salmon should associate first-order treatments with dualistic treatments, suggesting, say, that a first-order rendering of

English rigid and nonrigid property designators comes "at a considerable cost of naturalness" for the way that it has to relate naming property designators with the predicative property designators that are supposed to correspond to the naming ones (Linsky 1984, p. 263; see also Salmon's criticisms: e.g., 2005, p. 131). Such a criticism does not apply, of course, to a first-order treatment like the one presented here, according to which the same property designator can serve in both naming and predicative positions.

23. Section (2.2.2.4.2) is much indebted to helpful conversation with Christopher Menzel.

5

Rigid Appliers

I have argued that rigidity has significance for singular property designators, provided that there are any, in much the same way that it has significance for concrete-object designators. Hence, 'whiteness', 'courage', and 'heat' are rigid in the same way that 'Hesperus' is rigid, provided that they are singular (see chapters 1–3).

I have also argued that it is plausible to say that *all* property designators are singular, at least provided that it is plausible to say (as Kripke would: see chapter 1, note 15) that *some* property designators are singular. More specifically, I have argued that we should not be misled by striking grammatical appearances to recognize a division between what seem initially to be singular property designators like 'whiteness' or 'courage' or 'heat', and what seem initially to be nonsingular property designators like 'white' or 'courageous' or 'hot': grammatical appearances are not to be trusted in this matter. Terms like the foregoing may all be treated as singular, grammatical differences notwithstanding (see chapter 4).

Despite all that I have said, it is desirable to be able to show that a property designator's subjection to a rigid – nonrigid distinction does not depend on its singularity: that is what I set out to show in this chapter. The target audience is not so much hold-outs who, despite the arguments in chapter 4, might continue to entertain with more or less sympathy the dualist position that 'white' does not name even though 'whiteness' does. Granted, it is good to be able to accommodate such readers with another argument to reinforce my claim that the rigid – nonrigid distinction holds for all property designators, not just those property designators that these readers would recognize as genuinely singular. But there is another well-known audience whose demand for attention is more urgent. I have yet to provide this audience with even the start of a response to its reservations. In claiming that a uniform account of property designators as singular is plausible, I assume, as I have just conceded, that a grammatically singular term like 'whiteness' is indeed a name or name-like term and I have urged that 'white' follows suit: still, for all that I have said, neither 'white' nor 'whiteness' is a name because *no* property designator is a name. Such a position has a distinguished tradition: indeed, it has more than one distinguished tradition.

According to a tradition associated with Frege (see e.g., Frege 1979, pp. 119–20, 122), properties exist as "predicables" that cannot be designated with a singular term (Heintz 1973, p. 94). According to another well-known tradition, nominalism, there are no properties to designate with a singular term: accordingly, some highly capable workers have lodged the complaint that the account of rigidity that I defend can be defended adequately only provided that it is accompanied by a refutation of nominalism, which again I do not provide.[1] There are still further reasons sometimes offered for rejecting the singularity of property designators: for example, Martí observes that there is just an intuitively sharp distinction between concrete-object designators, say, which seem singular, and terms for properties, which do not (for elaboration, see Martí 2004, pp. 144ff.). Typical first-order languages formalize this intuition, regimenting as they do property designators as a whole into predicates: and deference to these familiar formal languages is itself a reason that some would incline toward a predicative treatment of property designators (Stamos 2003, p. 8 note 2; see also Berger's observations on this: 2005, pp. 86, 88). Authors who deny that property designators are singular often infer that they cannot be rigid, either (Martí and Martínez 2007, p. 104, note 3; Coleman and Wiley 2001, p. 502; Crane 2004, pp. 171–2; Schwartz 2002, p. 276, note 2; see also Haukioja 2010, §2.2).

If property terms are not singular terms (even higher-order singular terms: see chapter 4, §2.2.2.1), then either they are not subject to a rigid – nonrigid distinction after all or else the rigid – nonrigid distinction can be extended to nonsingular terms: mere appliers. So far, there has not been much enthusiasm on the part of authorities for the prospects of extending the rigid – nonrigid distinction to mere appliers. The primary reason that various workers cite for maintaining that the rigid – nonrigid distinction fails to characterize mere appliers is that *all* mere appliers would be rigid if any were.[2] A distinguished minority of workers recognizes a rigid – nonrigid distinction for mere appliers by tying "rigid application" to individuals' essential instantiation of certain properties.

In the present chapter, section (1), I take a minority position according to which the rigid – nonrigid distinction can be extended to mere appliers, but not the minority position that I mention in the foregoing paragraph, which associates rigidity with individuals' essential instantiation of certain properties: that account fails, I argue in section (2). I articulate another version of the rigid – nonrigid distinction for mere appliers, which I argue enjoys the appropriate philosophical significance. I close with a brief concluding section, (3).

1. Rigidity for Mere Appliers

In the present section, (§1), I show how the rigid – nonrigid distinction can be extended to mere appliers, whether general terms or predicates.[3] I begin by proposing, in section (1.1), a basic account of the rigid – nonrigid distinction for mere appliers that accommodates theorists who recognize the *existence* of properties. Variations on this basic account can accommodate theorists who deny the existence of properties, as I show in section (1.2).

1.1. A Basic Account: Rigid and Nonrigid Designators for Predicables

As I have just indicated, I offer in the present section (§1.1) an account of the rigid – nonrigid distinction for mere appliers that accommodates theorists who recognize the existence of properties. It will simplify the exposition if I use singular terms for properties in order to talk about the rigidity of mere appliers whose use is constrained by the property picked out by the appropriate singular term: so I will do that. The appeal to singular terms is a luxury that I will later drop when framing rigidity for nominalists (in §1.2).[4] I articulate the basic account of rigidity for mere appliers that is at issue in section (1.1.1), and I defend its philosophical significance in section (1.1.2).

1.1.1. The Account The nonrigid contrast for 'white', construed as a mere applier, is a merely *ascriptive use* of 'the color of Antarctica': often this expression, like 'white', enjoys a natural construal as a *general* term. Just as we can say "K2 is white," we can say "K2 is the color of Antarctica". Following Heintz (1973), I will call 'the color of Antarctica' a "definite ascription" rather than a "definite description" when it serves *only* as a general term that applies to objects like K2 (for further discussion, see chapter 4, note 11).

Even though mere appliers are not singular terms, we might continue to call them "*designators.*" In calling them so, we would follow precedent set by Carnap, for example, whose broad use of "the term '*designator*' for all those expressions to which a semantical analysis of meaning is applied" renders mere appliers "designators" (Carnap 1956, p. 6).[5] Further, if properties exist, even if only as "non-individual entities," as Sellars (1963, p. 248) would put it, we might still speak, in some meaningful respect, of predicates' designating *them*. If on the other hand properties fail to exist, as Sellars himself maintains, then they could hardly be what predicative designators designate; designating general terms would have other work to do than designating properties. Again, I save discussion of nominalism for a later section (§1.2).

According to a natural first attempt to specify in more detail a suitable use of 'designate' for nonsingular expressions, 'white' or 'the color of Antarctica' might be said to "designate" the property constraining the use of 'white' just in case 'white' or 'the color of Antarctica' shares the extension of that property with respect to every possible world, by virtue of applying, with respect to every possible world, to white objects.[6] But if that is the use of 'designate', then *non*rigid "designation" for merely predicative expressions would seem to be lost, as many have observed (Devitt 2005, pp. 140ff.; Salmon 1981, pp. 70–2; Schwartz 2002, pp. 268f.; 272f.; Soames 2002, pp. 250–1): 'the color of Antarctica', which is supposed to be a nonrigid designator, could not be said to designate at all the property constraining the use of 'white', since it fails to apply to white objects in worlds with respect to which Antarctica is a dark, lush jungle.

Here is a more favorable construal of "designation" for mere appliers:

A predicate F designates a property P just in case the metaphysical extension of P is identical to the semantic extension of F.[7]

On this use of 'designate', 'the color of Antarctica' designates the property constraining the use of 'white', as it is supposed to do. 'The color of Antarctica' designates the relevant property since this definite ascription applies to all and only white objects, which are just the objects in the metaphysical extension of the relevant property.

Although 'the color of Antarctica' is supposed to designate the property constraining the use of 'white', 'the color of Antarctica' is supposed to *fail* to designate that property *rigidly*. After all, 'the color of Antarctica' fails to apply to white objects with respect to worlds in which Antarctica is dark. Hence, a natural use of '*rigid* designation' for mere appliers is as follows:

A predicate F *rigidly* designates a property P just in case, *for every possible world* w, the metaphysical extension of P with respect to w is identical to the semantic extension of F with respect to w.

Such "rigid designation" for adjectives, common nouns, definite ascriptions, and the like, is significant for much the same reason that the originally articulated rigid designation for names and definite descriptions is significant, as I explain in the following section (§1.1.2). There are, to be sure, salient differences in the way that singular terms for properties, on the one hand, and merely predicative expressions, on the other, relate, or would relate, to their respective *designata*: these differences affect in interesting ways the specifics of how *rigid* or *nonrigid* designation, of the respective varieties, manifests its important effects. Still, the important philosophical lessons of rigidity for singular terms are closely analogous to the important philosophical lessons of rigidity for mere appliers. Indeed, the predicative version of rigidity enjoys more or less the full significance of its singular correlate, at least insofar as the justly famous applications are concerned: the spectrum of familiar arguments from rigidity, which concern a posteriori necessity, essences, mind, and so on (see chapter 1, especially §2), can all be reformulated according to the predicative account of rigidity.

1.1.2. The Lessons of Rigidity There is a striking difference between predicate designation, as I have articulated it, and singular-term designation for properties: a predicate is able to designate more than one property on a given use, but a singular term is not. In section (1.1.2.1) below, I explain this phenomenon and how it affects the manner in which necessity follows from rigidity for predicates. Then in sections (1.1.2.2)–(1.1.2.4), I argue that the philosophical significance of rigidity remains.

1.1.2.1. How Necessity Follows from Rigidity with Designation Multiplied 'The color of Antarctica' designates the property constraining the use of 'white'. The definite ascription designates that property by virtue of sharing that property's extension, which contains all and only white objects.

But 'the color of Antarctica' also designates other properties, like the property constraining the use of 'Antarctica-colored': i.e., the relational property of *being whatever color Antarctica is*, which property is possessed just by white objects but which property could have been possessed by dark objects instead, since Antarctica could have been dark.[8] 'The color of Antarctica' designates *both* the property constraining the use of 'white' *and* the property constraining the use of 'Antarctica-colored'. 'The color of Antarctica' apparently designates the one property rigidly and the other nonrigidly. 'White' also designates more than one property, since it nonrigidly designates the property constraining the use of 'Antarctica-colored' and it rigidly designates the property constraining the use of 'white'.

There can, of course, be more than two properties designated by a predicate: 'human' and 'the first species to the moon' both designate, one rigidly and the other nonrigidly, the property constraining the use of 'human'. But tradition would have it that 'featherless biped' shares the extension of 'human'. If so, 'human' and 'the first species to the moon' both nonrigidly designate the property constraining the use of 'featherless biped'. So the definite ascription 'the first species to the moon', say, is a nonrigid designator for the properties constraining the use of both 'human' and 'featherless biped', while it is a rigid designator for a third property, which is relational.

Since I maintain that the lessons of rigidity apply to predicates, I owe an account of how the lessons of rigidity *could* so apply, given that a predicate, unlike a singular term, can designate more than one property. An account of how the lessons of rigidity could apply with comparable significance to predicates is all the more pressing since *every* predicate is rigid for something or other on an account like the one in question: thus, 'the color of Antarctica', the paradigm of a nonrigid property designator, *rigidly* designates the property constraining the use of 'Antarctica-colored', as I have noted. Any account on which all designators are rigid is threatened, as a great many theorists indicate, with triviality or other debilitating afflictions.[9] Accordingly, I turn to the task of showing how the lessons of rigidity retain their force.

The basic work of rigid designation for singular terms is manifested in identity statements (see chapter 1, §1): significantly, if both singular terms in an identity statement rigidly designate the same object, i.e., if both terms rigidly designate and the identity statement is true, then the statement is not only true but necessarily true. Hence, so long as we agree that 'Hesperus' and 'Phosphorus' are rigid designators for the same planet, as most philosophers do, we cannot claim that 'Hesperus = Phosphorus' is contingent on the grounds that it was an a posteriori discovery that the two names designate the same planet (see, e.g., Kripke 1971, p. 154; 1980, p. 101–4). We must acknowledge that the statement is not only true by virtue of containing designators for the same object, but necessarily true by virtue of those designators' rigidity.

If 'white' and 'the color of Antarctica' serve as mere appliers, then the lessons of rigidity for 'white is the color of Antarctica' are manifested *not* in the identity statement 'white = the color of Antarctica', which contains singular terms, but rather in a corresponding "identification statement" like '(x)(x is white $\equiv$ x is the color of Antarctica)': this identification statement says that anything is white if and only if it is the color of Antarctica, so the statement can be said to "identify" each item that is white with an item that is the color of Antarctica and vice versa.[10]

If rigidity is to retain its significance as a phenomenon that characterizes mere appliers, then the necessity or contingency of identification statements like the foregoing must follow in the right way from the rigid or nonrigid designation of the relevant terms.

Fortunately, the necessity or contingency of identification statements does indeed follow in the right way from the rigid or nonrigid designation of the relevant terms. Consider, first, necessity. For biconditionals, which we may take to contain merely predicative general terms, just as for identity statements, which contain singular terms, if both designators rigidly designate the same property, then the statement is not only true but necessarily true: hence, the necessity of both the identity statement 'white = albescent', which features two singular terms for whiteness (at least on a reasonable use) and the corresponding identification statement '(x)(x is white ≡ x is albescent)', which features two predicative designators for the same property.

Just as necessity follows in the right way from rigid designation on the part of predicates, contingency follows in the right way, as well. If one designator rigidly designates a property but the other nonrigidly designates that same property, then the relevant statement is contingently true, as it is supposed to be. Hence, not only is the singular-term containing statement 'white = the color of Antarctica' contingent, but so is the corresponding predicate-containing statement '(x)(x is white ≡ x is the color of Antarctica)'.

With respect to identification statements, the lessons of rigidity do not follow from the designators' mere rigid designation of *something or other* and the relevant statement's truth: here identification statements differ from identity statements. It is fine to say, "if both singular terms in an identity statement rigidly designate the same object, *i.e.*, if both terms rigidly designate and the statement is true, then the statement is not only true but necessarily true." But in the corresponding claim about identification statements, the clause 'i.e., if both terms rigidly designate and the statement is true' must be dropped. The reason that the 'i.e.' clause may be added with respect to the claim about identity statements is that if both *singular* designators in an identity statement rigidly designate *some object or other* and the identity statement is *true*, then both singular designators rigidly designate the *same* object. Both terms (i) *designate* the same object o, since the statement is *true* by virtue of codesignation, and both terms (ii) *rigidly* designate the same object o as well, since both terms rigidly designate *some* object or other, and that object has to be *o* in each case, not any other object, since each term has only *one* designatum, o, to designate in any manner at all: a singular term cannot designate more than one object.

With respect to predicates, which can designate *more than one entity*, matters are different: both terms of an identification statement can rigidly designate some object or other, as 'white' and 'the color of Antarctica' do, and the relevant biconditional can be true, as '(x)(x is white ≡ x is the color of Antarctica)' is, even though the designators fail to designate *rigidly* the *same* object. So if '(x)(x is white ≡ x is the color of Antarctica)' is true by virtue of nonsingular designation on the part of the property designators, then it follows that there is some property that both 'white' and 'the color of Antarctica' *jointly designate*: as it happens, they codesignate the property that constrains the use of 'white'. But if '(x)(x is white ≡ x is the color of Antarctica)' is *true*, because there is some property that 'white' and 'the color of Antarctica' codesignate, and if moreover each designator rigidly designates some property or other but *different* ones, so that there is no property that both designators *jointly* designate *rigidly*, then it clearly does *not* follow that '(x)(x is white ≡ x is the color of Antarctica)' is necessarily true. So with respect to merely predicative designation, our appeal to a familiar principle should be to a simple version (itself familiar: see e.g., Kripke 1971, p. 154; 1980, pp. 102, 104), which applies more generally to all designation: the appropriate version of the principle is that if both terms in an identity statement rigidly designate the same object, then the statement is not only true but necessarily true.

The famous arguments from rigidity concerning a posteriori necessity, essences, and so on, have predicative versions. I show that in the following sections (1.1.2.2)–(1.1.2.4).

1.1.2.2. Predicative Arguments Concerning A Posteriori Necessity, Essence, and Mind Recall (from chapter 1, §2.1) the lessons of rigidity for the necessary a posteriori, illustrated most straightforwardly in a simple *identity* statement like 'Brontosaurus = Apatosaurus': Riggs discovered empirically that 'Brontosaurus = Apatosaurus' is true. Before the importance of rigidity became appreciated, philosophers would have supposed that 'Brontosaurus = Apatosaurus' is only contingently true, on the grounds that it was discovered empirically to be true; but if 'Brontosaurus' and 'Apatosaurus' rigidly designate the same genus, as they seem to do, then 'Brontosaurus = Apatosaurus' is not only true, but necessarily true. 'Brontosaurus = the herbivorous dinosaur genus with chevron bones that resemble those of carnivorous marine reptiles', by contrast, is *not* necessarily true, but is instead contingently true; still, that is irrelevant to the evaluation of 'Brontosaurus = Apatosaurus', since it is a mistake to think that 'Apatosaurus' is shorthand for anything like 'the herbivorous dinosaur genus with chevron bones that resemble those of carnivorous marine reptiles'.

Much the same can be said for '(x)(x is a brontosaur ≡ x is an apatosaur)', an identification statement corresponding to 'Brontosaurus = Apatosaurus': again, we must acknowledge that the statement is not only *true* by virtue of the relevant terms' designation of the same property, but *necessarily* true by virtue of those terms' *rigid* designation of the same property. We cannot claim that '(x)(x is a brontosaur ≡ x is an apatosaur)' is contingent, in the way that earlier generations of philosophers would have thought, on the grounds that it was an a posteriori discovery that the two predicates designate the same genus; '(x)(x is a brontosaur ≡ x is the herbivorous dinosaur genus with chevron bones that resemble those of carnivorous marine reptiles)', by contrast, *is* contingent, but that is irrelevant since it is a mistake to think that 'apatosaur' is shorthand for 'the herbivorous dinosaur genus with chevron bones that resemble those of carnivorous marine reptiles'.

'Brontosaurus = Apatosaurus' and '(x)(x is a brontosaur ≡ x is an apatosaur)' contain only names or name-like designators; but the foregoing observations carry over to identity statements with theoretically descriptive expressions. If 'water' and 'H$_2$O' rigidly designate the same property as singular terms, then 'water = H$_2$O' is necessarily true. In the same way, if 'water' and 'H$_2$O' rigidly designate the same property as predicates, then the corresponding biconditional, '(x)(x is water ≡ x is H$_2$O)', is necessarily true. Accordingly, in both cases, singular and predicative, rigidity allows for the statement to reveal in the right way an essential, rather than accidental, tie between H$_2$O and water.

The well-known attending troubles, or alleged troubles, for proposed theoretical identity statements like 'pain = c-fiber firing' again have analogues, on the alternative treatment of property designators as predicates. Here of course I only outline the arguments: I provide development in later chapters, especially chapters 7 and 8.

According to identity theorists, 'pain = c-fiber firing' is a genuine theoretical identity statement exposing the essence of pain. If so, 'pain' and 'c-fiber firing' are both rigid designators for the same phenomenon. If 'pain' and 'c-fiber firing' were not both rigid designators for the same phenomenon, then 'pain = c-fiber firing' would fail to expose the essence of that phenomenon in the way that a theoretical identity statement would (see chapter 1, §2 and chapter 3, §1). Rather, 'pain = c-fiber firing' would resemble 'pain = the phenomenon that Jones is trained to relieve' or 'water = the chemical usually served as a beverage', both of which feature one rigid designator and one nonrigid designator for the relevant subject and hence neither of which is a theoretical identity statement; or else 'pain = c-fiber firing' would resemble statements like 'the phenomenon that Jones, an anesthesiologist, is trained to relieve = the phenomenon that Jones, a specialist in anesthesiology, is trained to relieve' or 'what fills the Mississippi River = the chemical usually served as a beverage', both of which feature two nonrigid designators and hence neither of which is a theoretical identity statement, though one is necessarily true.

In order, then, for 'pain = c-fiber firing' to be a genuine theoretical identity statement, both 'pain' and 'c-fiber firing' must be rigid designators for the same phenomenon. But it would seem that we have no good reason to suppose that 'pain' and 'c-fiber firing' are rigid designators for the same phenomenon: for all that we know, there could be events of c-fiber firing that are present without pain, say. That seems, again on first blush, to be a problem for the identity thesis.

Something similar can be said for the predicative '(x)(x is pain ≡ x is c-fiber firing)'. Identity theorists who put their position in terms of predicates rather than singular terms would hold '(x)(x is pain ≡ x is c-fiber firing)' to be a genuine "theoretical identification statement," which may be understood as the predicative correlate of a theoretical *identity* statement. If '(x)(x is pain ≡ x is c-fiber firing)' is a genuine theoretical identification statement, then 'pain' and 'c-fiber firing' are both rigid designators for the same phenomenon. If 'pain' and 'c-fiber firing' were *not* both rigid designators for the same phenomenon, then '(x)(x is pain ≡ x is c-fiber firing)' would fail to expose the essence of that phenomenon, as a theoretical identification statement would do. Rather '(x)(x is pain ≡ x is c-fiber firing)' would resemble '(x)(x is pain ≡ x is the phenomenon that Jones, an anesthesiologist, is trained to relieve)' or '(x)(x is water ≡ x is the chemical usually served as a beverage)', both of which feature one rigid designator and one nonrigid designator for the relevant subject and hence neither of which is a theoretical identification statement; or else '(x)(x is pain ≡ x is c-fiber firing)' would resemble statements like '(x)(x is the phenomenon that Jones, an anesthesiologist, is trained to relieve ≡ x is the phenomenon that Jones, a specialist in anesthesiology, is trained to relieve)' or '(x)(x is what fills the Mississippi River ≡ x is the chemical usually served as a beverage)', both of which feature two nonrigid designators and hence neither of which is a theoretical identity statement, though one is necessarily true.

In order, then, for '(x)(x is pain ≡ x is c-fiber firing)' to be a genuine theoretical identification statement, both 'pain' and 'c-fiber firing' must be rigid designators for the same phenomenon. But it would seem that we have no good reason to suppose that 'pain' and 'c-fiber firing' are rigid designators for the same phenomenon: for all that we know, there could be events of c-fiber firing that are present without pain, say. That seems, at least on first blush, to be a problem for the identification thesis.

1.1.2.3. Generalizing: How to Reformulate with Predicates Arguments with Singular Terms for Properties

Section (1.1.2.2) suggests that the salient and familiar arguments from rigidity that appeal to singular terms for properties may be reformulated in a way that dispenses with singular terms. Here in section (1.1.2.3), I articulate a general strategy for such reformulation. If the strategy is a good one, then the salient arguments about properties that appeal to the original account of rigidity, which is formulated for singular terms (see chapter 1, especially §3.1), may be accepted by theorists who balk at the prospect of assigning singular terms to properties.

As they are formulated in classic texts, the arguments from rigidity concern identity statements. For singular terms t_1 and t_2, rigidity assures that ⌜$t_1 = t_2$⌝ is necessarily true provided that t_1 and t_2 are rigid designators for the same item (Kripke 1971, p. 154; 1980, pp. 102, 104). The interest of rigidity centers around this necessity (see chapter 1 and the present chapter, §1.1.2.2).

We may reformulate with predicates arguments from rigidity that concern identity statements by finding or introducing, for each singular term, a *predicate* whose *semantic* extension, with respect to each possible world w, is identical to the *metaphysical* extension, with respect to w, of the *property* that the singular term designates with respect to w. Thus, for a singular name like 'Brontosaurus' or 'white' on a singular construal, we may find a count noun or adjective like 'brontosaur' or 'white' on a nonsingular construal. With respect to a definite description like 'the herbivorous dinosaur genus with chevron bones that resemble those of carnivorous marine reptiles' or 'the color of Antarctica', we may recognize a nonsingular construal: a definite ascription written and pronounced in the same way. In general, where F_{t1} is a predicate corresponding in this manner to t_1 and F_{t2} is a predicate corresponding in this manner to t_2, claims to the effect that t_1 and t_2's joint rigid designation of a property P brings about necessity can be replaced by corresponding claims to the effect that F_{t1} and F_{t2}'s joint rigid designation of P brings about necessity[11]: necessity follows in an analogous fashion for $\ulcorner t_1 = t_2 \urcorner$ and $\ulcorner (x)(x \text{ is } F_{t1} \equiv x \text{ is } F_{t2}) \urcorner$. Claims about contingency also carry over. If $\ulcorner t_1 = t_2 \urcorner$ is contingently true because one of t_1 and t_2 rigidly designates a property P while the other nonrigidly designates P, then $\ulcorner (x)(x \text{ is } F_{t1} \equiv x \text{ is } F_{t2}) \urcorner$ is also contingently true because one of F_{t1} and F_{t2} rigidly designates P while the other nonrigidly designates P.

As examples in section (1.1.2.2) indicate, the necessity by way of rigid co-designation has analogous interest whether for singular terms or for mere predicates: so just as the necessity of 'Brontosaurus = Apatosaurus' would have surprised earlier speakers, in view of the statement's aposteriority, so would the necessity of '(x)(x is a brontosaur $\equiv$ x is an apatosaur)' have surprised earlier speakers, in view of the statement's aposteriority. Related observations hold for identity statements with theoretically descriptive expressions. Just as 'water = H_2O' or 'pain = c-fiber firing' is necessarily true, provided that the relevant expressions both rigidly designate the same entity, so '(x)(x is water $\equiv$ x is H_2O)' or '(x)(x is pain $\equiv$ x is c-fiber firing)' is necessarily true, provided that the relevant expressions both rigidly designate the same entity. And just as 'water = H_2O' or 'pain = c-fiber firing' exposes essence in the way that a true theoretical identity statement would have to do *only* if both designators in the respective statement rigidly designate the same entity, so too for '(x)(x is water $\equiv$ x is H_2O)' and '(x)(x is pain $\equiv$ x is c-fiber firing)'. Attending complications for establishing the required joint rigid designation for theoretical identity statements like 'pain = c-fiber firing' carry over to predicative versions.

1.1.2.4. Predicative Versions of the Familiar Arguments Appealing to the Rigidity of Concrete-Object Designators

The rigid – nonrigid distinction for singular terms does salient work in identity statements about properties, and I have urged that the rigid – nonrigid distinction for predicates does relevantly similar work in corresponding identification statements. This point holds not only with respect to identity statements about properties, but even with respect to identity statements about *concrete objects*, like 'Hesperus = Phosphorus'. So the familiar lessons of rigidity, even with respect to those statements on which rigidity's work was originally demonstrated, are mirrored in predicative statements: the foregoing predicative account of the rigid – nonrigid distinction thus seems to capture the significance of the rigid – nonrigid distinction as it pertains to singular terms *in general* and not just as it pertains to singular terms for properties. I address these matters briefly in the present section (§1.1.2.4), where I show that Kripke's familiar arguments concerning the rigidity of terms like 'Hesperus' and 'Phosphorus', which arguments establish the necessary a posteriori, have predicative versions.

Consider a *singular term* for a planet, like 'Earth': this may be attended by a *predicate* like 'earth' which applies to bits of Earth. Thus, we may speak of a handful of earth: you may lift earth in your hand without lifting Earth in your hand. Perhaps this use of 'earth' involves a bit of refinement in the ordinary use of the predicate 'earth', but that matters little: let us refine if that is needed, or use 'earth stuff' instead of 'earth'. Let us recognize or coin similar corresponding predicates for Venus, Hesperus, and Phosphorus: 'venus', 'hesperus', and 'phosphorus', respectively. The interesting modal and epistemological phenomena assured for 'Hesperus = Phosphorus' and 'Hesperus = the brightest non-lunar object in the evening sky' by the rigid – nonrigid distinction are mirrored in biconditionals containing corresponding predicates: the philosophical significance of the rigid – nonrigid distinction is honored in both varieties of statement.

The lessons for 'Hesperus = Phosphorus' are familiar: when scientists learned that 'Hesperus' and 'Phosphorus' designate the same thing, they recognized that 'Hesperus = Phosphorus' is true. After this discovery, philosophers would still deny that 'Hesperus = Phosphorus' is *necessarily* true, until they came to appreciate the significance of rigidity. Then they would be able to see that, since 'Hesperus' and 'Phosphorus' not only designate but *rigidly* designate the same thing, the statement is necessarily true (see, e.g., Kripke 1971, p. 154; 1980, pp. 102, 104).

Something similar holds for '(x)(x is a handful of hesperus ≡ x is a handful of phosphorus)' or, more simply, '(x)(x is hesperus ≡ x is phosphorus)'. When scientists could see that 'hesperus' and 'phosphorus' both apply to venus, i.e., to bits of Venus, people were bound to recognize that '(x)(x is hesperus ≡ x is phosphorus)' is true. After this discovery, philosophers would still have denied that '(x)(x is hesperus ≡ x is phosphorus)' is *necessarily* true, until they came to appreciate the significance of rigidity. Then they would be able to see that, since 'hesperus' and 'phosphorus' not only designate but *rigidly* designate the same thing (the property constraining the use of 'venus', which is the property of *being a bit of Venus*), the statement is *necessarily* true although a posteriori.

The reasons that the necessity of 'Hesperus = Phosphorus' was hard to see would seem to find a parallel for the case of '(x)(x is hesperus ≡ x is phosphorus)'. Much of the problem, as I have suggested, is that both statements are a posteriori, and earlier generations of philosophers supposed that any a posteriori statement must also be contingent. Also, earlier speakers in the descriptivist tradition of Frege and Russell would naturally have supposed that 'Hesperus' is shorthand for a definite description like 'the brightest non-lunar object in the evening sky' and that 'Phosphorus' is shorthand for a definite description like 'the brightest non-lunar object in the morning sky' (see chapter 1, §1.3). So earlier speakers in the descriptivist tradition of Frege and Russell should also naturally have supposed that a predicate corresponding to 'Hesperus', such as 'hesperus', would be shorthand for a definite *ascription*, which we may take (perhaps artificially but no matter: see chapter 4, note 11) to be written and pronounced in just the same way as the corresponding definite description. Had 'Hesperus' and 'Phosphorus', as well as 'hesperus' and 'phosphorus', been shorthand for the relevant descriptions or ascriptions in this way, then 'Hesperus = Phosphorus' and '(x)(x is hesperus ≡ x is phosphorus)' would not be necessarily true, as they are, since 'the brightest non-lunar object in the evening sky = the brightest non-lunar object in the morning sky' and '(x)(x is the brightest non-lunar object in the evening sky ≡ x is the brightest non-lunar object in the morning sky)' are not necessarily true: there are worlds in which the brightest body in the evening is one planet and the brightest body in the morning is another planet, since the relevant expressions are not *rigid* designators for the same entity. And of course the failure to distinguish between nonrigid designators, on the one hand, and rigid designators like 'Hesperus' or 'hesperus', on the other hand, could explain how our forebears might have failed to see the necessity.

The lessons of rigidity, with their modal and epistemological significance and surprise, seem to carry over, then, from 'Hesperus = Phosphorus' to '(x)(x is hesperus ≡ x is phosphorus)'. Accordingly, it would seem that the lessons from rigidity, not only for singular property designators but even for singular concrete-object designators, carry over to rigidity for corresponding predicates. I have discussed only one example, the most famous one available, of an interesting identity statement containing singular designators. But it seems clear that similar observations could be made for singular-term containing statements in general.[12] I have also proposed only one example of a predicative substitute for the likes of 'Hesperus' and 'Phosphorus': there are other plausible proposals and similar lessons obtain with respect to those proposals. A striking alternative to the foregoing proposal appeals to something like the Quinean use of predicates such as 'Hesperizer' (Quine 1961, pp. 8ff.), not for a bit of the planet, as I have used 'hesperus', but rather for any object that is the planet itself: we *could* work such predicates into definite descriptions, with a view to applying the original rigid – nonrigid distinction for singular terms (see chapter 4, §1); but we could also work with these predicates without appealing to any definite descriptions or singular terms, appealing just to the foregoing predicative account of the rigid – nonrigid distinction. I leave for other occasions discussion of various options for a unified predicative treatment of rigid and nonrigid designation for entities as diverse as the property white and the planet Hesperus: but it would seem that such an account could perform substantially the same work as the original account of the rigid – nonrigid distinction for singular terms.

1.1.3. Objections Two salient objections confront the account of the nonsingular rigid – nonrigid distinction that I have articulated. According to the first objection, nonsingular rigidity as I understand it fails to perform key modal duties whose neglect threatens nonsingular designators' claim to a rigid – nonrigid distinction and worse. According to the second objection, nonsingular rigidity as I understand it performs the right duties but for obvious and unremarkable reasons: so, the objection continues, if *this* is rigidity for nonsingular designators, then the discovery of rigidity for nonsingular designators is no interesting breakthrough after all.

1.1.3.1. Rigidity Performs the Modal Duties to Which I have Assigned it The pleasing correlation that I have observed between singular terms and predicates, with respect to the distinction between rigidity and nonrigidity, has been challenged, in effect, by Soames (2002). I claim that if 'water = H$_2$O' is necessarily true by virtue of the singular terms' rigid co-designation of the same property, then the biconditional '(x)(x is water ≡ x is H$_2$O)' is also necessarily true by virtue of the corresponding predicates' respective rigid co-designation of the same property. If instead, 'water = H$_2$O' is contingently true, by virtue of rigid designation on the part of one singular term but not the other, then the corresponding biconditional '(x)(x is water ≡ x is H$_2$O)' is also contingently true by virtue of rigid designation on the part of one predicate but not the other. So if 'water = H$_2$O' is true, it might yet be either necessarily true or contingently true, depending on the rigidity of the relevant designators, and so might be the corresponding biconditional.

According to Soames (2002, p. 310; see also p. 266), by contrast, the mere *truth* of a singular-term bearing statement like 'water = H$_2$O' guarantees the *necessity* of the corresponding biconditional '(x)(x is water ≡ x is H$_2$O)'. If Soames is correct about this, then something has gone badly wrong with the foregoing work. *Rigid* designation or its absence is irrelevant to the question of whether 'water = H$_2$O' is *true* (though Soames has no objections to taking 'water' and 'H$_2$O' to be rigid singular designators of the same kind: p. 309): the *mere co-designation* of 'water' and 'H$_2$O', with any combination of rigidity or nonrigidity, is all that is needed to secure the truth of 'water = H$_2$O'. If, then, Soames is right that the *necessity* of '(x)(x is water ≡ x is H$_2$O)' follows from the *truth* of 'water = H$_2$O', regardless of whether the property terms in 'water = H$_2$O' are rigid, nonrigid, or a mix, then it cannot be that the work that the rigid – nonrigid distinction performs in securing the modal status of an identity statement like 'water = H$_2$O' is also performed by a corresponding rigid – nonrigid distinction for the corresponding predicates, securing the modal status of an identification statement like '(x)(x is water ≡ x is H$_2$O)', in the analogous fashion that I have recognized.

The destructive effects of Soames' discovery, if that is what it is, would be felt throughout this book, not just in the present chapter, even though other chapters treat rigidity primarily as a feature of singular terms. If the necessity of '(x)(x is water ≡ x is H$_2$O)' follows from the mere *truth* of 'water = H$_2$O', then it would seem reasonable to say that the importance of rigidity for singular terms like 'water' and 'H$_2$O' has been overestimated by the philosophical community (as Soames suggests: see, e.g., pp. 264, 266, 310–11) because in that case, much of what is supposed to follow, significantly, from the truth of a statement like 'water = H$_2$O' *and* the rigidity of its designators, could be established from that statement's truth alone: from that truth alone would follow, for example, the surprising result that even though it took *empirical investigation* to determine that '(x)(x is water ≡ x is H$_2$O)' is true, it is necessarily true. So plenty is at stake for rigidity, with the assessment of Soames' claim.

Soames is moved to accept the relevant claim by the following line of reasoning. Terms like 'water' and 'H$_2$O' designate intensions, at least on one reasonable construal (p. 309), when used as singular terms. As it happens, 'water' and 'H$_2$O' both designate the same intension, which is a function from possible worlds w to the set of all and only bits of water at w (p. 308). Accordingly, Soames claims that the statement 'water = H_2O' correctly

says that a certain kind (i.e., intension) w_i is identical with a certain kind (i.e., intension) h_i. Since this is a statement about intensions, the claim that it is true is equivalent to the claim that ['(x)(x is water $\equiv$ x is H_2O)'] is necessary (Soames 2002, p. 310).

This is not right: it is a rare technical error in Soames' generally skillful work.

Let us suppose, plausibly enough, that 'water = H_2O' says that the intension w_i is identical to the intension h_i: it may still be that 'water' rigidly designates the relevant intension w_i but that 'H_2O' *non*rigidly designates h_i (w_i). The possibility of nonrigid designation is easily overlooked when attention is directed to the foregoing designators. But other expressions for the same intension bring the possibility of nonrigid designation into clearer view: e.g., 'the chemical usually served as a beverage'.

Let us suppose, again plausibly enough, that 'water = the chemical usually served as a beverage' says that a certain kind (i.e., intension) w_i is identical with a certain kind (i.e., intension) u_i: it is not the case that since this is a statement about intensions, the claim that it is true is equivalent to the claim that '(x)(x is water $\equiv$ x is the chemical usually served as a beverage)' is necessary. 'Water = the chemical usually served as a beverage' is true. But '(x)(x is water $\equiv$ x is the chemical usually served as a beverage)' is *not* necessary; it could easily have been that quantities of water failed to be quantities of the chemical usually served as a beverage.

Let us return to the plausible supposition that 'water = H_2O' says that a certain kind (i.e., intension) w_i is identical with a certain kind (i.e., intension) h_i. Whether '(x)(x is water $\equiv$ x is H_2O)' is necessary depends on whether 'H_2O' in 'water = H_2O' *rigidly* designates what 'water' rigidly designates. If the singular term 'H_2O' is shorthand for 'the chemical comprised of two hydrogen atoms bonded to one oxygen atom', and if that very chemical might have been comprised of something else or if there might have been some different chemical instead of the familiar one that were comprised of two hydrogen atoms bonded to one oxygen atom, then 'H_2O' is not a rigid designator for the intension h_i (which is identical to w_i and u_i).[13] Instead, 'H_2O' denotes h_i (and also w_i and u_i, since $h_i = w_i = u_i$) *non*rigidly, just as 'the chemical usually served as a beverage' denotes that intension nonrigidly.

It is important, with respect to the matter at hand, to distinguish between the *semantic* intension of a term like 'water', 'H_2O', or 'the chemical usually served as a beverage' and the kind or intension that such an expression *designates*. The semantic intension of 'water', 'H_2O', or 'the chemical usually served as a beverage', when it is used as a singular term, would be a function mapping possible worlds to kinds or properties that have or, as I will suppose for simplicity, that are themselves metaphysical *intensions*: functions, like w_i, from possible worlds to bits of matter. If the singular terms 'water', 'H_2O', and 'the chemical usually served as a beverage' have the same *semantic* intension, then they must also have, with respect to any possible world, the same *designatum*: that would be, with respect to the actual world at least, the metaphysical intension w_i (i.e., h_i; u_i). Since, if the *semantic* intensions of 'water', 'H$_2$O', and 'the chemical usually served as a beverage' are identical, then *for any possible world w*, the designatum of the singular terms 'water', 'H$_2$O', and 'the chemical usually served as a beverage', with respect to w, is the same metaphysical intension m serving as the designatum of each of the other terms too, and since m's value or metaphysical extension is the same as m's value or metaphysical extension regardless of the world – the same actual bits of water or whatnot – it follows that a claim that the *semantic* intensions of the singular terms 'water', 'H$_2$O', and 'the chemical usually served as a beverage' are identical *is* equivalent to the claim that '(x)(x is water ≡ x is H$_2$O ≡ x is the chemical usually served as a beverage)', which contains corresponding predicative terms, is necessary.

Of course, the semantic intension w^s_i of the singular term 'water' is *not* identical to the semantic intension of the singular term 'the chemical usually served as a beverage', since the expressions have a different value with respect to worlds in which the beverage served is usually vodka rather than water, so '(x)(x is water ≡ x is H$_2$O ≡ x is the chemical usually served as a beverage)', which contains corresponding predicative terms, is not necessary. Whether w^s_i is identical to h^s_i, the semantic intension of the singular term 'H$_2$O', depends on whether h_i, which is w_i and which is the designatum, as opposed to the semantic intension, of the singular terms 'H$_2$O' and 'water', is rigidly or nonrigidly designated: provided that 'water' rigidly designates h_i (w_i), then $w^s_i = h^s_i$ if and only if 'H$_2$O' also rigidly designates h_i (w_i). But since 'H$_2$O' might designate h_i (w_i) nonrigidly, while 'water' designates h_i (w_i) rigidly, it might be that '$w_i = h_i$' is true, even though '(x)(x is water ≡ x is H$_2$O)' is *not* necessarily true because $w^s_i \neq h^s_i$.

The mere truth of 'water = H$_2$O' is not, then, enough to secure the necessary truth of '(x)(x is water ≡ x is H$_2$O)'. If the two singular terms in 'water = H$_2$O' rigidly designate the same property, that *is* enough to secure the necessary truth of '(x)(x is water ≡ x is H$_2$O)', as well as the necessary truth of 'water = H$_2$O'; but if one singular term in 'water = H$_2$O' rigidly designates the relevant property and the other singular term designates this property nonrigidly, that secures the *contingent* truth of '(x)(x is water ≡ x is H$_2$O)', as well as the contingent truth of 'water = H$_2$O'.

1.1.3.2. News of the Rigidity of Nonsingular Property Designators is Appropriately Surprising and Important

I have argued that nonsingular rigidity performs the right modal duties. But it might be argued that the problem with my understanding of rigidity is not that it fails to perform the right modal duties; the problem is rather that it performs those duties for obvious and unremarkable reasons. According to this objection,[14] to say that F and G rigidly codesignate a property P that they actually codesignate is to say no more or less than that F and G are necessarily coextensive. But in that case, in my articulation of rigidity's main work supporting the necessity of biconditionals, I seem to have been saying only that given the necessary truth of ⌜(x)(Fx ≡ Gx)⌝ – i.e., given that F and G rigidly codesignate whatever they actually codesignate – it follows that ⌜(x)(Fx ≡ Gx)⌝ is necessary. This trivial observation could hardly support the interesting breakthrough that the discovery and articulation of a rigid – nonrigid distinction for mere appliers was supposed to represent. So goes the objection.

But the objection fails to account for all that it is for F and G to rigidly codesignate P. This is not merely for F and G to be necessarily coextensive. There are more requirements, as I will explain. It remains true that rigid codesignation of P rather obviously carries with it necessary coextensiveness. But I will urge that something similar can be said for the rigid codesignation of a concrete object o: the rigid codesignation of o obviously carries with it necessary coextensiveness.

I argue first that for F and G rigidly to codesignate P is more than for F and G to be necessarily coextensive. In this matter, predicative designators parallel singular designators. 'Hesperus' and 'Phosphorus' could be necessarily coextensive without rigidly codesignating Venus (as I have observed in chapter 3, §1). If both designators are shorthand for 'the planet associated with Aphrodite', then they are necessarily coextensive since necessarily, the planet associated with Aphrodite is the planet associated with Aphrodite; but both nonrigidly designate Venus. The same holds for two nonsingular designators like 'brontosaur' and 'apatosaur'. If both designators are shorthand for 'the most famous sauropod', then they are necessarily coextensive since necessarily, the most famous sauropod is the most famous sauropod; but both nonrigidly designate Elosaurus. To say that 'Hesperus' and 'Phosphorus' rigidly designate Venus or that 'brontosaur' and 'apatosaur' rigidly designate Elosaurus is to say much more than that 'Hesperus' and 'Phosphorus' or 'brontosaur' and 'apatosaur' are necessarily coextensive.

Even so, it might be charged that the necessity of ⌜(x)(x is a brontosaur ≡ x is an apatosaur)⌝ follows *obviously* from rigid codesignation as I understand it and hence that the modal duties performed by rigidity as I understand it are too unenlightening to deserve the title 'rigidity'. Again, the proper response to the charge is to observe that there is a parallel in singular rigid designation, whose modal duties are suitably enlightening to deserve the label 'rigidity' by all accounts. If necessary coextensiveness and the attending necessity of '(x)(x is a brontosaur ≡ x is an apatosaur)' follows obviously from 'brontosaur' and 'apatosaur''s rigidly codesignating Elosaurus, then so too does necessary coextensiveness and the attending necessity of 'Hesperus = Phosphorus' likewise follow obviously from 'Hesperus' and 'Phosphorus''s rigidly codesignating Venus (see chapter 3, §1). Necessity *given* rigid codesignation is clear, in either case. But that does not show that rigidity's work is unremarkable, in either case.

Since necessity given rigid codesignation is clear, we might ask how it is that rigidity's work is supposed to be remarkable. That is: if the surprising results associated with rigidity do not issue from a conditional claim like the claim that *if* two designators rigidly codesignate their designatum, *then* the relevant necessity follows,[15] then what do the surprising results associated with rigidity issue from? The answer to this question is that the surprising results associated with rigidity issue from *affirmations* of rigidity and of the attending necessity.

Let me follow Kripke as I articulate how the rigidity of our designators and the attending necessity was hard to see, and how it is therefore surprising and interesting, in order to show that parallel considerations arise whether we are talking about the rigidity of singular concrete-object designators, on the one hand, or we are talking about the rigidity of mere appliers, on the other hand. It was hard to see how the designators in 'Hesperus = Phosphorus' could be rigid and how the statement could accordingly be necessary, as Kripke explains,

because in advance, we are inclined to say, the answer to the question whether Hesperus is Phosphorus might have turned out either way. So aren't there really two possible worlds—one in which Hesperus was Phosphorus, the other in which Hesperus wasn't Phosphorus—in advance of our discovering that these were the same? (1980, p. 103)

The very same considerations apply to the biconditional '(x)(x is a brontosaur $\equiv$ x is an apatosaur)'. It was hard to see how the designators in '(x)(x is a brontosaur $\equiv$ x is an apatosaur)' could be rigid and how the statement could accordingly be necessary, to rework the foregoing quotation,

because in advance, we are inclined to say, the answer to the question whether brontosaurs are apatosaurs might have turned out either way. So aren't there really two possible worlds—one in which brontosaurs were apatosaurs, the other in which brontosaurs weren't apatosaurs—in advance of our discovering that these were the same?

The way to clarify and vindicate the necessity associated with rigidity, in view of the puzzlement, is similar in the two cases. Grant that "it is only a contingent truth (not true in every other possible world) that the star seen over there in the evening is the star seen over there in the morning" (Kripke 1980, p. 105). That is contingent because there could have been one star in the evening and another star in the morning, instead of Venus both times. Nevertheless, "that contingent truth" about how different stars might have been present instead of Venus "shouldn't be identified with the statement that Hesperus is Phosphorus" (Kripke 1980, p. 105). On the contrary, Hesperus would still have been Phosphorus even if some other similar planet had been present where Venus is in fact present.

In the same way, grant that it is only a contingent truth (not true in every other possible world) that the dinosaur genus found in this quarry is the genus found in that other quarry. Again, that is contingent because there could have been one genus at the one quarry and a different genus at the other quarry, instead of elosaurs both times. Nevertheless, that contingent truth about how different genera might have been present instead of elosaurs shouldn't be identified with the statement that something is a brontosaur if and only if it is an apatosaur. On the contrary, brontosaurs would still have been apatosaurs even if fossils from a different genus had been present where elosaur fossils are in fact present; that would not be a world in which brontosaurs fail to be apatosaurs. 'Hesperus = Phosphorus' and '(x)(x is a brontosaur $\equiv$ x is an apatosaur)' are necessary after all, because rigidity obtains after all.

Were the surprise and interest associated with rigidity to attend the *conditional* claim that if terms are rigid then necessity follows, then my account of rigidity for mere appliers might fail to capture that surprise and interest. But this is not where the surprise and interest associated with rigidity lie. The surprise and interest associated with rigidity lie in the realization that rigidity and the attending necessity *obtain*, despite certain puzzles: so I have been arguing. This surprise and interest is captured by my rigid – nonrigid distinction for mere appliers, offered here in section (1.1.1).

1.2. Nominalist-Friendly Variations of the Basic Account

I have articulated an account of rigidity for appliers in section (1.1). That account of rigidity accommodates theorists who recognize the existence of properties but who do not recognize singular terms for properties. But the account may not appear to accommodate nominalists, who deny not only that properties can be designated with a singular term but also that properties exist at all. From a nominalist's viewpoint, rigid designation of properties may still seem, on first blush, to be out of the question from the start.

In the same way that the account of rigidity for appliers in section (1.1) may appear, at least on first blush, to run into troubles with nominalism, it may appear to run into troubles with selective realism. Unlike nominalists, selective realists recognize some properties, but they are chary about recognizing too many.[16] Some selective realists think that few of our property terms correspond to real properties: for them, expressions like 'white' or 'the color of Antarctica' probably fail to designate any real property (see, e.g., Mellor 1991b, pp. 179–80; Lowe 2006, p. 467). If expressions like 'white' or 'the color of Antarctica' fail to designate any real property, then there must be something fundamentally wrong with arguments from rigidity, which purport to establish, by appeal to *designation*, the modal status of statements like 'white = the color of Antarctica' or '(x)(x is white ≡ x is the color of Antarctica)'; or so it might seem.

A closer look indicates, however, that nominalism and selective realism are not as recalcitrant for purposes of rigidity as we might have feared. There are two reasons for this. First, most nominalists (or selective realists, who are to be included tacitly in what follows) do not deny the existence of "properties" on an understanding that will suffice for purposes of supplying more or less the designata for property designators that I have been discussing to this point in the book. Second, although some radical nominalists do deny the existence of the relevant attenuated "properties" and so cannot acknowledge the rigid designation of properties of *any* sort, even these radical nominalists can acknowledge a suitably *amended* version of "rigid designation" for terms that apply rather than name, which further version of "rigid designation" bears the appropriate significance. The rigid – nonrigid distinction for property designators is not fundamentally about issues that divide nominalists from Platonists or other competitors.[17]

1.2.1. "Properties" in Semantic Work Most of those who put properties to work in semantics construe them as functions from possible worlds to individuals (e.g., Lewis 1986, pp. 50ff.; Martí 2004, pp. 137ff.; Mondadori 1978, pp. 37f.; Thomason 1969, p. 100).[18] On such an understanding, whiteness or the property constraining 'white' is a function that assigns, for each possible world, the set of all and only white objects. The property and the function can also be understood to be a set of ordered pairs, each pair consisting of a world and a set of objects possessing the relevant property with respect to that world. Most self-avowed nominalists, and in particular traditional nominalists about properties, should not be offended by such "properties." Whether there are functions from possible worlds to white objects is not what is at the heart of the traditional realist – nominalist debate. Differences lie deeper.

What nominalists have traditionally denied and what realists have traditionally affirmed is that there is something that white objects *share in common*, which is *over and above* white objects. Platonists (e.g., Plantinga 2003, p. 110) recognize an abstract object that white objects exemplify or in which they participate; Aristotelians (e.g., Armstrong 1978) recognize whiteness as something like a nonspatial part of white things. Nominalists agree with Platonists and Aristotelians that there are white objects like snowballs, but they deny that there is any need to account for the fact that snowballs are white by appeal to anything that snowballs share in common.[19]

While nominalists reject the notion that there is any abstract entity or part that snowballs share in common, they need not deny the existence of functions from possible worlds to individuals. They are free to adopt a reductive approach to properties according to which the relevant functions provide all that we need from properties: on this view, "whiteness," say, is crafted from white objects and the worlds containing them. Such an approach might indeed be said to represent "the most prominent form of nominalism in the contemporary arena," as Loux maintains (1998, p. 22).

Whether functions from possible worlds to individuals provide us with the same benefits that traditional properties could confer, as nominalists of the foregoing stripe hold, is a matter of controversy that need not be resolved for purposes here. It may be, on the one hand, that traditional properties perform real philosophical work that functions or similar entities could not perform: in that case, possible world semantics could at best *model* properties (Menzel 1993, p. 66) even though properties could not possibly be *reduced* to the objects to which possible worlds semantics appeals (Bealer 1982, pp. 15, 90; 1989, p. 199; Bealer and Mönnich 1989, p. 181; Jubien 1989, p. 160; Menzel 1993, pp. 62–4; Plantinga 2003, pp. 108f.; Swoyer 2008, §4.2). If this is right, then properties are more than the relevant functions and the relevant nominalists are wrong. But it may be, on the other hand, that functions from possible worlds to individuals provide us with all that we need from properties, so that there is no "one over many" that white objects share. Again, it does not matter here whether the relevant nominalist position is tenable; what matters here is that this nominalist position would still leave us with an abstract object, namely the relevant function, for property designators like 'white' and 'the color of Antarctica' to designate, either rigidly or nonrigidly. So the relevant nominalism does not undermine the position that there is a genuine rigid – nonrigid distinction of the sort that I have been discussing, which might apply to singular, so-called "property terms" that designate functions.

1.2.2. Rigidity for Radical Nominalism There are radical nominalists who reject even semantic surrogates for traditional properties of the sort discussed in the foregoing section (§1.2.1), because they reject abstract objects altogether: they do not recognize functions, sets, possibilia, and so on. On Sellars' view (1967), for example, whether properties are to be construed as functions or sets or some similar item, they are objectionable: there are no such entities, since there are no abstract entities of any sort. Accordingly, 'white' is not a singular term for a property; nor is it a general term whose use is constrained by a property.[20]

For all that radical nominalists deny with respect to our talk about properties, or apparent talk about properties, I will urge that they recognize enough to honor the important insights behind rigidity. Of special importance here is this: a radical nominalist does not reject the use of appliers but rather interprets sentences with appliers safely, without appealing to the existence of properties. Accordingly, a radical nominalist is free to recognize the use not only of an ordinary adjective like 'white' but *also* the use of a *definite ascription* like 'the color of Antarctica', which applies, as any other adjective, to individuals. Thus, Sellars (who takes aim at Geach and the Fregean tradition for recognizing properties at all, unnameable though they are supposed to be: Sellars 1963, pp. 247–8) is free to join Geach in saying that a proper answer to the English question "what is *the color of Antarctica*?" is, "clouds, snow, etc.," or that an English statement like the following is unobjectionable: "Hondas are *the kind of car that performed well on the test*." In sentences like the foregoing, apparent talk about an abstract entity, such as a "color" or a "kind of car," should be interpreted by Sellars, as for Geach, as talk about *concrete objects* instead: colored items and cars (see, e.g., Anscombe and Geach 1961, pp. 155–6).

Let us suppose, for the sake of argument, that abstracta are just irrelevant to the designation of expressions like 'the color of Antarctica': still, the *contrast* between a typical one-word predicate like 'white' and the foregoing definite ascription remains of interest for its bearing on the modal and epistemological status of biconditionals, in the ways relevant to rigidity. Accordingly, I will offer an account of rigidity with the expected interest that does not presuppose that any of our so-called "property-designators" really designates an abstract entity, whether a full-blown traditional property or a less offensive substitute such as a function.

Given that, for radical nominalists, there are no properties to designate, we cannot of course appeal to the account of predicates' designation from the foregoing section (1.1): that account would have predicates designate properties or anyway abstracta that amount to properties for present purposes. Instead of that account, I propose the following:

A predicate F designates Hs just in case F applies to all and only Hs.
A predicate F *rigidly* designates Hs just in case, *for every possible world* w, F applies to all and only Hs with respect to w.[21]

The modal status of a biconditional containing appliers F and G depends, according to the foregoing account, upon whether F and G rigidly or nonrigidly designate Hs, for any predicate H, in more or less the same way that the modal status of such a biconditional depends, according to the accounts of rigidity that I favor for realists, on whether F and G rigidly or nonrigidly designate H-hood. So we may formulate variations on the familiar arguments from rigidity for the necessary a posteriori, for claims concerning essence, for complications concerning the identity theory of mind, and so on.

Although a nominalist can*not* say that '(x)(x is a brontosaur $\equiv$ x is an apatosaur)' or, to return to the singular-term bearing comparative statement, 'Brontosaurus = Apatosaurus' is necessarily true on account of the designators' both rigidly designating the abstract entity Elosaurus, a nominalist *can* say that '(x)(x is a brontosaur $\equiv$ x is an apatosaur)' is necessarily true on account of 'brontosaur''s and 'apatosaur''s both rigidly designating *elosaurs*. Again, this modal status is surprising in view of the epistemological status of the statement as a posteriori. The scientist who minted 'brontosaur' and 'apatosaur' could not have known without empirical investigation that 'brontosaur' and 'apatosaur' designate the same dinosaurs; but just as we cannot infer from that, with earlier generations, that 'Brontosaurus = Apatosaurus' is contingent, we also cannot infer that '(x)(x is a brontosaur $\equiv$ x is an apatosaur)' is contingent. It is *not* contingent, since 'brontosaur' and 'apatosaur' both *rigidly* designate elosaurs. Of course, if 'apatosaur' were shorthand for 'the herbivorous dinosaur genus with chevron bones that resemble those of carnivorous marine reptiles', which does not rigidly designate elosaurs, then '(x)(x is a brontosaur $\equiv$ x is an apatosaur)' *would* be contingent; but 'apatosaur' is not shorthand for that.

Rigidity's work for theoretical identity statements, which invariably expose their subject's *essence*, similarly carries on in nominalist-friendly territory. 'Brontosaurus = Apatosaurus' does not expose essence, so let us revisit 'water = H_2O'. Unless both designators rigidly designate water, the statement will not expose essence as a theoretical identity statement would, even if the statement is necessarily true, as it might be if both of its designators, as opposed to just one, designate the subject nonrigidly: hence, 'the predominant chemical in Mark Twain's favorite river = the predominant chemical in Samuel Clemens' favorite river', though necessarily true, fails to expose the essence of water (again, for further discussion, see chapter 3, §1). So again, rigidity is needed for a singular statement to expose essence in the familiar manner that a theoretical identity statement does.

Similar words apply to predicative statements, as I have already indicated by appeal to a predicative variety of rigidity that presupposes the existence of abstracta (§1.1.2.2). Of course, nominalism complicates the issue of essentialism by eliminating abstracta:

for nominalists, a statement like '(x)(x is water ≡ x is H$_2$O)' does not reveal the essence of any abstract entity. Still, '(x)(x is water ≡ x is H$_2$O)' should perform analogous revelatory work concerning the subject matter that nominalists *do* recognize, which in this case would be water *quantities*: a theoretical identity statement accordingly understood invariably exposes *what qualifies something to be* water or whatever the subject may be, or *what it is to be* the relevant subject. As a proper parallel with 'water = H$_2$O' requires, '(x)(x is water ≡ x is H$_2$O)' performs the right revelatory work concerning the subject matter only on condition that 'water' and 'H$_2$O' both rigidly designate water (quantities). Otherwise, even if the statement is necessarily true, as it might be if both of its designators, as opposed to just one, nonrigidly designate the subject, the statement will no more expose in the manner that a theoretical identity statement would what qualifies something to be water or what it is to be water than '(x)(x is the predominant chemical in Mark Twain's favorite river ≡ x is the predominant chemical in Samuel Clemens' favorite river)', though it is necessarily true, does that.

The well-known attending troubles, or alleged troubles, raised by rigidity for proposed theoretical identity statements like 'pain = c-fiber firing' again have nominalist-friendly analogues. Identity theorists who put their position in terms of predicates rather than singular terms would maintain that '(x)(x is pain ≡ x is c-fiber firing)' is a true theoretical identification statement. If this is a true theoretical identification statement, then 'pain' and 'c-fiber firing' are both rigid designators for *pain* (events), according to the account of rigidity from the present section (1.2.2). If 'pain' and 'c-fiber firing' were not both rigid designators for pain, then '(x)(x is pain ≡ x is c-fiber firing)' would fail to reveal as a true theoretical identity statement would how its subject matter, pain, qualifies to *be* pain, as the discussion about essences from the foregoing paragraph indicates. But it would seem that we have no good reason to suppose that 'pain' and 'c-fiber firing' are both rigid designators for pain events: for all that we know, there could be events of c-fiber firing that are present without pain, say. That seems, at least on first blush, to be a problem for the proposal that '(x)(x is pain ≡ x is c-fiber firing)' is a true theoretical identification statement.

So we can honor the lessons of rigidity even if we embrace radical nominalism. A general account of how to recast traditional arguments from rigidity concerning identity statements, by appeal to the nominalism-friendly account of rigidity from the present section (1.2.2), may be found in section (1.1.2.3) above: the lessons apply with minor adjustments.

2. A Rival Account

I have endorsed, in the foregoing section (1), a broad account of rigidity for mere appliers. This account finds competition in another, markedly different account of rigidity for mere appliers that is already on the market: an investigation of this rival is in order. I will argue in the present section, (§2), that the rival is unsuccessful. In sections (2.1) and (2.2), I will argue that the rival fails to perform as it should the duties proper to rigidity's role: i.e., the duties the rival would have to perform in order to qualify as rigidity. In section (2.3), I will argue that the rival also fails to perform other work advertised for it.

2.1. Essential Application as Rigidity

According to the rival account of rigidity that is on the market, a general term like 'tiger' is rigid if and only if it is what we might call an "essential applier": i.e., the term is such that any item x to which the term applies, in any possible world, is part of the extension of that term in all worlds in which x exists (Cook 1980; Devitt 2005; Devitt and Sterelny 1999, pp. 85–6; Gómez-Torrente 2004; 2006). A striking feature of essential application, as an account of rigidity, is that it would seem to honor the rigidity of terms for natural kinds but not terms for artificial kinds and properties. Thus, 'tiger' is an essential applier because any particular tiger is essentially a tiger and could not have been something else like a dragonfly or a fir tree instead; but 'lawyer' does not apply essentially. This is supposed to be a point in favor of essential application's bid to serve as an account of rigidity (Cook 1980, p. 64; Devitt 2005, pp. 146f.; Gómez-Torrente 2006, p. 236; see also pp. 227f.). I do not recognize this as a point in favor. Rigidity's work does not include distinguishing between terms for artificial properties or kinds, on the one hand, and natural properties or kinds, on the other; and terms for artificial properties or kinds, like 'bachelor', are naturally counted rigid (see note 11 and discussion cited there).

I have argued that the basic duties of rigidity are elsewhere. These duties are manifested most clearly in identity statements or identification statements. If both terms in an identity or identification statement rigidly designate the same item, then the statement is not only true but necessarily true and this necessity supports various important arguments. Upholding this necessity is rigidity's primary responsibility.[22] But essential application seems not to honor these basic duties of rigidity (for similar observations, see Boër 1985, pp. 131ff.; Soames 2002, pp. 250–9; 2006a, pp. 650–1; Devitt 2005, p. 152). Both members of a pair of terms like 'water' and 'H$_2$O' might essentially apply, with respect to the actual world, to the same stuff even if the relevant identification statement fails to be necessarily true. Thus, suppose that '(x)(x is water $\equiv$ x is H$_2$O)' is true. Suppose, further, that anything that is water is essentially water and anything that is H$_2$O is essentially H$_2$O, so that 'water' and 'H$_2$O' are rigid appliers for the same bits of matter.[23] For all that, '(x)(x is water $\equiv$ x is H$_2$O)' may be only contingently true: there might be non-actual possible worlds containing quantities of bona fide water that have a chemical structure XYZ rather than H$_2$O, as some anti-essentialists maintain (see chapter 6, §2.2).

If essentialist intuitions make the foregoing point hard to see, a change of examples may help: consider '(x)(x is a tuatara $\equiv$ x is a rhynchocephalian)'. 'Tuatara' and 'rhynchocephalian' both apply to the same reptiles, since the order Rhynchocephalia contains but one species. And any tuatara or rhynchocephalian is essentially a tuatara or rhynchocephalian, respectively, at least assuming common essentialist intuitions that would be shared by those who take essential application to amount to rigidity: so according to these theorists' account of rigidity, 'tuatara' and 'rhynchocephalian' are both rigid appliers for the same reptiles. But the order Rhynchocephalia could have contained many species: other orders contain many species. The order Rodentia contains mice, rats, hamsters, squirrels, gophers, porcupines, beavers, muskrats, and so on. Rhynchocephalia happens to be an extraordinarily spare order, but this is a contingent matter. As a result, '(x)(x is a tuatara ≡ x is a rhynchocephalian)' is contingently true even though the contained terms rigidly apply to just the same objects, on the account in question, as they are both essential appliers for the relevant reptiles.

2.2. Essential Application as a Component of Rigidity

Essential application fails to perform the basic duties of rigidity: so I have argued. If, as I have also argued, an alternative account that I have put forward *does* perform the basic duties of rigidity, then that alternative account is clearly to be preferred. Still, those attracted to essential application might be tempted to *add* the essentialist requirement, as some authors in effect do,[24] to an alternative account of rigidity like the one that I propose in the foregoing section (1.1.1) or (1.2.2), which by itself does not appeal to essential application but which achieves the right results for the relevant identity statements or identification statements. The result might be called "rigid and essential designation":

A predicate F *rigidly and essentially* designates Hs just in case, *for every possible world* w, (i) F applies to all and only Hs with respect to w, and (ii) any x that is an H at w is an H at all possible worlds at which x exists.

The resulting account would not recognize that 'rhynchocephalian' and 'tuatara' together rigidly designate tuataras; 'rhynchocephalian' would fail to rigidly designate tuataras, since this term applies to nontuataras with respect to some possible worlds. Hence, rigidity on the resulting account does not require the necessary truth of '(x)(x is a tuatara ≡ x is a rhynchocephalian)', which is as it should be. Of course, this desired result is simply the work of the account of rigid designation borrowed from section (1.2.2), here found in condition (i). The essentialism added by condition (ii) to the foregoing account is not necessary to give the desired result with respect to '(x)(x is a tuatara ≡ x is a rhynchocephalian)', since rigid designation is enough on its own (again, see §1.2.2); nor is the essentialism added by condition (ii) to the foregoing account *sufficient* to give the desired result (see §2.1).

The essentialism added by condition (ii) to the foregoing account of rigid and essential designation performs no work at all to achieve the right results with respect to '(x)(x is a tuatara ≡ x is a rhynchocephalian)'. It is hard to see what other productive work the essentialist requirement could do if, as I have argued, the basic duties of rigidity are manifested in the necessity of identity statements or identification statements (and closely related work: see note 22). Nor is the addition of an essentialist requirement to our account of rigidity for property terms a harmless superfluity: the work performed by rigidity in familiar arguments is undermined by the added requirement.

Familiar arguments from rigidity for appliers are rendered unnecessarily weak when they are formulated in terms of rigid and essential designation rather than in terms just of rigid designation. Thus, take the arguments concerning '(x)(x is water ≡ x is H$_2$O)' or 'water = H$_2$O': rigidity is supposed to assure the necessity of these statements. As I have indicated, there is no *need* to establish any premise to the effect that 'water' and 'H$_2$O' are essential appliers, in order to establish the relevant necessity, and if we insist on *adding* such essentialist premises to the argument for necessity, along with the usual premises to the effect that the relevant rigidity obtains, then we weaken the argument for necessity by burdening it with controversial essentialist premises that may call for rejection.[25]

Other arguments that appear sound when framed in terms of rigid designation are rendered entirely implausible on anyone's account, not just weakened or rendered controversial, when framed in terms of essential designation along with rigid designation. Compare the argument for the necessity of '(x)(x is white ≡ x is albescent)'. As I have indicated (in §1.1.2.1), this statement seems to be necessarily true: it contrasts with the contingently true '(x)(x is white ≡ x is the color of Antarctica)' in a way that rigidity underwrites. There is no need, of course, for the sake of establishing the necessity of '(x)(x is white ≡ x is albescent)', to establish that white, albescent objects are essentially white or albescent: this is fortunate, since white, albescent objects are *not* essentially white or albescent (or at least not typically: see note 26). K2 might have been blue, given faster global warming, and my white, albescent door might have been painted another color. If we insist on framing the argument for the necessity of '(x)(x is white ≡ x is albescent)' in terms of rigid and essential designation rather than in terms of rigid designation simpliciter, we include in the premises not only that 'white' is rigid for white, but that it is an essential applier, contrary to what we know: so we strip the argument of its plausibility.[26] Something similar holds for the singular statement 'white = albescent', which corresponds to '(x)(x is white ≡ x is albescent)'. And something similar applies to many other identification statements, or corresponding identity statements, that contain terms that evidently ought to be counted as rigid: 'loud', 'hot', 'diabetic', 'energetic', 'radioactive', and so on.[27]

Appeals to rigid and essential designation also bring trouble for disputes over identity or identification theories of mind. If proponents of the identification theory of mind, who are committed to rigidity (see §1.1.2.2 and §1.2.2), were to commit to rigid and essential designation, they would thereby take on a superfluous burden and antimaterialist arguments would come too easily. Let us revisit the relevant argument from rigidity.[28] '(x)(x is pain ≡ x is *pain*)' is obviously necessarily true. If we find or coin another word that rigidly designates what 'pain' rigidly designates, substituting it for one of the tokens of 'pain', the resulting statement will inherit this necessity. Thus, '(x) (x is pain ≡ x is *dolor*)' is necessarily true. It does not matter whether any pain (dolor, and so on) is essentially pain (dolor), in the way that any tiger might be essentially a tiger, or whether it is not the case that any pain (dolor) is essentially pain (dolor) any more than it is the case that anything white is essentially white. Regardless of whether any pain (dolor) is essentially pain (dolor) or whether it is not essentially so, '(x)(x is pain ≡ x is *pain*)' and '(x)(x is pain ≡ x is *dolor*)' are necessarily true.

The identification theorist maintains that, like 'dolor', 'c-fiber firing' rigidly designates what 'pain' rigidly designates; such rigid codesignation is needed in order to qualify '(x)(x is pain ≡ x is c-fiber firing)' to be a genuine theoretical identification statement (again, see §1.1.2.2 and §1.2.2). This itself is problematic: it is hard to see, at least prima facie, how we could be warranted in supposing that 'c-fiber firing' rigidly designates what 'pain' rigidly designates; on the contrary, it would seem that there are possible events to which 'c-fiber firing' applies but not 'pain'. But none of this concerns the essentialist claim that any pain or dolor or c-fiber firing is essentially so: the identity theorist need not take up whatever *further* troubles might attend *that* claim.[29]

If these observations are correct, then it is a mistake to associate essential application with rigidity and its attending arguments. Coupling a requirement of essentialism with the relevant account of rigidity borrows trouble for arguments and claims associated with rigidity. Philosophers committed to rigidity may, of course, wish to accept those troubles; but there is no need to do so, so far as rigidity is concerned.

2.3. *Essential Application and Anti-Descriptivism*

I have just argued (in §2.1 and §2.2) that essential application does not perform the work proper to rigidity's role; it only gets in the way of that work. Of course, there is some disagreement over just what work *is* proper to rigidity's role (as I have indicated in chapter 3, §2). A defender of essential application could try to deflect the foregoing criticisms (from §2.1 and §2.2) by pressing such disagreement, arguing that the work that I have taken essential application not to perform is not really work proper to rigidity's role anyway. So for Devitt, an important supporter of essential application, rigidity's *primary* duty with respect to singular terms and general terms is found not in rigidity's work securing necessity for identity statements (Devitt 2005, p. 153), as I have maintained, but rather in rigidity's work "undermining description theories" (Devitt 2005, p. 145; see also Devitt 2009, pp. 241f., 245; Orlando 2009, pp. 202–3). Essential application "does this perfectly," says Devitt (2005, p. 144; for related claims, see Gómez-Torrente 2009, pp. 135f., 138, 146) and hence essential application steps into rigidity's role, by his lights.

Because I have already argued that the primary duty of rigidity is not refuting descriptivism (chapter 3, §2.4), I will not go through that argument here. Instead, I will point out here just that even if refuting descriptivism *were* rigidity's primary duty, essential application would *still* fail to do a good job at performing rigidity's primary duty because essential application does not do a good job at performing the work of refuting descriptivism. The connection between nondescriptivism and essential application is thinner than first impressions suggest.

It is true that one can mount arguments against certain naïve description theories as follows: 'tiger' is an essential applier, 'the big, striped, ferocious, solitary carnivore of Asia' is not an essential applier, and hence these expressions are not synonymous. If all is well with this argument, then essential application does some work refuting description theories. It can be used to show that 'tiger' is not synonymous with the foregoing description (really ascription: see §1.1.1; but I will suppress that detail in what follows), which we might initially have thought to be synonymous with it. My own account of rigidity performs related work: 'tiger' rigidly designates tigerhood (according to the conception of rigidity offered in §1.1; according to the conception of rigidity offered in §1.2.2, 'tiger' rigidly designates tigers), 'the big, striped, ferocious, solitary carnivore of Asia' does not rigidly designate tigerhood, so these expressions are not synonymous.

But there are many descriptions that apply *essentially* and so that could be synonymous with 'tiger' or with other one-word essential appliers (as Devitt seems to agree: 2005 pp. 145, 147–8). 'The species with such and such genes or gene combinations' and 'the number succeeding 2', not to mention 'the color most easily seen against dark backgrounds in the possible world α', are essential appliers but are also descriptive: or at least it is as plausible to say that these descriptive expressions are essential appliers as it is to say that the terms to which Devitt appeals are essential appliers. So a single-word essential applier like 'tiger''s status as an essential applier would hardly provide the needed direction for sorting out its status as descriptive or nondescriptive. Since we cannot, on the basis of a term's status as an essential applier, reject a descriptive account of the term's semantics, it is hard to see how essential application could help very much at refuting descriptivism.

It might be suggested that even if not *all* essential appliers are nondescriptive, *only* essential appliers are nondescriptive, with respect to general terms anyway: so a term's essential application satisfies a *requirement* for the term to be nondescriptive and accordingly helps to confirm that the term is nondescriptive. This suggestion for preserving the alleged tie between essential application and nondescriptivism fails: it is not only essential appliers that are nondescriptive.

Devitt acknowledges that there *may* be a kind of exception to the rule that only essential appliers are nondescriptive general terms: *if* an artifact term like 'pencil' is causally grounded, then 'pencil', which is not an essential applier, would be nondescriptive: so not only essential appliers would be nondescriptive (2005, p. 162, note 18). But his discussion suggests that such terms as 'pencil' are unlikely to be exceptions, and are at best rare exceptions, to a general rule that only essential appliers are nondescriptive.

Whether artifact terms like 'pencil' fail to qualify as essential appliers but are nevertheless nondescriptive is an issue that I set aside: there are many other examples of general terms that fail to qualify as essential appliers but that enjoy the same claim to nondescriptivism as paradigm essential appliers like 'tiger', whose extension is not determined by what satisfies a description in the minds of speakers like 'the big, striped, ferocious, solitary carnivore of Asia' (see Kripke 1980, pp. 119ff.). Examples resembling 'tiger' in the relevant respect include 'loud', 'hot', 'diabetic', 'energetic', 'radioactive', 'white', and so on. Thus, the extension of 'loud' is not determined by what satisfies a description in the minds of speakers like 'what is distinctly heard or perceived by the ears', since a world in which all humans are deaf could still contain loud automobiles, say (cf. Kripke 1980, pp. 130–2, 134). The terms 'loud', 'hot', 'diabetic', 'energetic', 'radioactive', 'white', and so on, have the same claim to nondescriptive status as essential appliers, but these terms are not essential appliers: loud objects like fire engines might have been quiet instead. So it is not only essential appliers that are nondescriptive. Again, essential application fails to live up to its association with nondescriptivism.

I conclude that even if work undermining description theories were the primary duty of rigidity, that would not offer much support to the bid of essential application to serve as an account of predicates' rigidity, since there is not a close tie between essential application and nondescriptivism. As it happens, the primary work of rigidity seems to be elsewhere (again, see chapter 3): it is tied closely to the necessity of identity statements and identification statements. This work is performed by terms that are not essential appliers, like 'loud' and 'white', as well as by terms that are or are supposed to be essential appliers.

3. Conclusion

The rigid–nonrigid distinction for property designators may be upheld even if property designators are nonsingular. So I have argued in this chapter. Essential application (discussed in §2) cannot perform the work of rigidity, so it does not provide the basis of a proper rigid – nonrigid distinction for mere appliers; but I have articulated accounts of the rigid – nonrigid distinction for mere appliers that do the right work (in §1).

Because the rigid – nonrigid distinction characterizes mere appliers, the traditional arguments from rigidity concerning properties or kinds, and even the traditional arguments from rigidity concerning particulars like concrete objects, may be re-framed in a way that does not appeal to the rigidity of singular terms. Traditional arguments about properties or allegedly about properties may therefore be fashioned to suit theorists with different views concerning whether there are any properties and concerning what the semantic relationship is between a property, provided there are any properties, and its corresponding term.

It is time to take stock. In chapters 2 and 3, I defend my understanding of the rigid – nonrigid distinction for property designators, provided in chapter 1 (§3), from criticisms according to which some incoherence or confusion troubles my understanding. I treat property designators as singular in these early chapters, although the criticisms addressed in chapters 2 and 3 and the remedies are generally applicable whether property designators are to be construed as singular or nonsingular (but see chapter 2, note 3). Other criticisms of a rigid – nonrigid distinction for property designators turn on such matters of grammar: I address those criticisms in chapters 4 and 5. In chapter 4, I argue that uniformly singular treatments of property designators are available, given certain presuppositions. If uniformly singular treatments are available, then my account of the rigid – nonrigid distinction for property designators from chapter 1 accommodates property designators in general; there is no need for an alternative understanding to accommodate nonsingularity. Even so, it would be unfortunate were my account of the relevant distinction compatible only with a singular treatment of property designators. No shortcoming along such lines troubles my account of rigidity, I urge in the present chapter. Chapters 2–5 dispense, then, with salient worries concerning my preferred account of what the rigid – nonrigid distinction comes to, for property designators, and of how widely the rigid – nonrigid distinction applies to various property designators.

Even if I have correctly characterized the rigid – nonrigid distinction for property designators in the foregoing respects, I may have gone wrong somehow in evaluating the philosophical power of that distinction, which is manifested in its *use* in familiar arguments supporting or impugning various theoretical identity statements that would reveal the essences of interesting properties. These are matters for the remaining chapters.

It remains simplest, for the sake of exposition, to frame the lessons of rigidity by appeal to singular designation, even though, as I have argued in this chapter, we could accommodate theorists who would prefer to do otherwise. Accordingly, in the following chapters, I return to the usual practice of appealing to singular designators and to the identity statements in which they feature. The reader who prefers instead to work with predicates and identification statements is free to adjust what I say in ways that I have indicated.

Notes

1. Devitt (2005, p. 143) criticizes accounts of the rigid – nonrigid distinction like the one that I favor in earlier chapters on the grounds that they cannot accommodate nominalism. Collins outright rejects such accounts on grounds of nominalism (1988, pp. 203ff.). Many others suggest that any adequate defense of the rigid – nonrigid distinction ought to be able to accommodate nominalism: see, e.g., Haukioja (2006, pp. 159, 166–7), Martí (1998, pp. 487–9) and Schwartz (2002, pp. 267f.). The foregoing workers seem to share the conviction that a theory of semantics like the one at hand ought not to depend on a controversial position concerning the ontological status of properties. I sympathize (as I have indicated, in chapter 2 at note 1).
2. Theorists here would include Berger 2005, p. 89; Devitt (2005, pp. 141–3); Kaplan (in a conversation reported by Salmon 2005, p. 132, note 22); Macbeth (1995, pp. 263, 265f.); Rubin (2008, p. 512n.); Salmon (1981, pp. 70–2; 2005, p. 120); Schnieder (2005, pp. 228 ff.); Schwartz (2002, pp. 268f., 273); Soames (2002, p. 251; 2003, p. 427; 2004, pp. 95–7; 2006b, p. 712). As I indicate in chapter 4, various workers maintain that some first-order predicative expressions, namely general terms, may serve as higher-order *singular* terms: so some of the foregoing authors regard general terms as subject to the original rigid – nonrigid distinction for singular terms. Predicates *containing* general terms are a different matter: these might be merely predicative even if the general terms that they contain are not merely predicative (see note 3; for similar observations, see Robertson 2009, p. 136, note 23; Soames 2004, pp. 95–7; 2010, pp. 90f.; see also 2006b, p. 712; Inan 2008, p. 228).

Kripke may have supposed decades ago that mere appliers are subject to a rigid – nonrigid distinction (see chapter 1, note 15) but he does not try to characterize such a distinction; perhaps he never achieved clarity about the matter himself (as Soames reports: 2002, p. 366, note 22). No one after Kripke has clarified the matter either, or resolved the basic foregoing objection that mere appliers could not give rise to a rigid – nonrigid contrast. Various workers seem to follow Kripke in *thinking* of merely predicative expressions as subject to a rigid – nonrigid distinction (e.g., Sidelle 1989, p. 63), and just a few workers have proposed accounts to try to illuminate such a distinction, including López de Sa (2001, pp. 614, 617–21; 2006, § 1; 2008a, pp. 2–3), who accounts for the rigidity of mere predicates by appeal to the rigidity of "closely related singular terms" corresponding to predicates (López de Sa 2001, p. 617; for animadversions to approaches of this type, see Levinson 1978, pp. 17–20; Soames 2002, pp. 259–62; Schnieder 2005; López de Sa also gestures toward an alternative account, more in the spirit of uniformly singular accounts of rigidity that I discuss in the foregoing chapter 4, which dispenses with any correspondence between predicates and singular counterparts: López de Sa 2008a, pp. 3–4): of course, since my project in the present chapter is to accommodate, with a rigid–nonrigid distinction, the position that property designators are uniformly *non*singular, I am hardly entitled to join López de Sa by appealing to the rigidity of singular terms for properties, in proposing my predicative account. Martí (1998, pp. 487–9; see also 2002) also sketches an account of rigidity for mere appliers, which is again quite unlike the one that I will offer below: there are indications that this 1998 treatment has been abandoned (e.g., Martí 2004, p. 129, note 2).

3. In the previous chapter, I distinguish sharply between a property designator like 'white' and a predicate containing it, like '... is white' (see chapter 4, note 15; for further discussion, see the foregoing note 2 in the present chapter), in order to defend the singularity of the property designator without making any claim about the singularity of the predicate. But for purposes of the present chapter, I treat property designators and predicates alike as nonsingular: so there is no need to emphasize a distinction between them. The reason I treat them alike is because my question is whether the rigid – nonrigid distinction applies to *merely predicative* expressions, and that would certainly include predicates if it includes general terms. Of course, if terms for properties are to be treated as singular terms, second order or otherwise, and predicates are not to be treated as singular terms, then the rigid – nonrigid distinction that I articulate here for mere appliers should be taken to characterize predicates, like '... is white', but not the property designators that the predicates contain, like 'white'; 'white' would be rigid for familiar reasons that explain the rigidity of other singular terms. So even on a uniformly *singular* view of *property* designators (see chapter 4), a predicative account of rigidity might accurately characterize some expressions.

4. The use of singular terms allows me to say *which* properties different predicative designators rigidly designate. Fregeans, who deny that any property designators are singular, have notorious difficulties here: hence, the traditional problem of "the concept *horse*." To the question, Which property or concept does 'horse' stand for?, Fregeans seem unable to say. "It seems we can not reply," as Anthony Kenny (1965, p. 103) relates the familiar tale, without resorting to an expression like 'the property *horse*' or 'the property that the French word "cheval" stands for' which, "being grammatically a singular term," is evidently off-limits.

5. See also note 7. Compare Frege's use of the term 'Bedeutung', which, like 'designation' here, applies broadly to the relationship between a singular term and what it names, and also

to the relationship between a predicate and its concept, which is not named (for discussion, see Cocchiarella 1972, p. 182; Furth 1968; Linsky 1984, p. 275, note 15).
6. As I explain in chapter 2 (at note 1), a property can be thought of as having a *metaphysical* extension (Salmon 1981, p. 46), which contains, in any possible world w, those objects *instantiating* the property with respect to w. A predicate's *semantic* extension contains, with respect to any possible world w, those objects to which the predicate *applies* with respect to w. Thus, the property constraining the use of 'white' shares 'white''s extension, with respect to all possible worlds, because the property constraining the use of 'white' is instantiated by just the white objects in any possible world w, which are just those items to which the predicate 'white' applies (see note 26 below for discussion of a possible scruple concerning the nature of these extensions).
7. See note 6, on metaphysical extensions. This use of 'designate' accords with the spirit of Carnap's use of 'designate'. For Carnap, the predicate letters 'H' (for *human*) and 'F' (for *featherless biped*) co*designate*, just as they do on my proposal (see below, §1.1.2.1); on the proposal for 'designate' rejected in the foregoing paragraph of the text, by contrast, these predicates do not codesignate. On my proposed use of '*rigidly* designate' (below in the text), 'human' and 'featherless biped' do *not* rigidly designate the same property. For Carnap, they do not co-"*L*-designate," because they do not codesignate with respect to all possible worlds (1956: see pp. 4, 7, 163–4). L-designation is related to rigid designation, though Carnap does not distinguish designation with respect to all possible worlds, which is a requirement for rigid designation, from designation in virtue of meaning (see, e.g., pp. 7, 4), which is not. In speaking about rigid designation in this chapter, I ignore worlds in which the designata fail to exist, as I have done in treating singular terms for properties: for simplicity, I assume that properties exist in all possible worlds. This chapter's account of rigid designation could be further articulated in order to allow for weaker and stronger construals (cf. analogues for singular terms in §1.2 of chapter 1).
8. I assume here that there are relational properties (or that there are appropriate semantic surrogates: see §1.2.1). More generally, as I discuss rigid designators for predicables (in §1.1), I assume that the plenum of properties is rich. If properties are too sparse, then what is needed for arguments from rigidity that appeal to property designators is an account of rigidity that does not assume the existence of the properties: I save such an account for §1.2.
9. See, e.g., Devitt (2005, p. 140) and Schwartz (2002, p. 266) on the triviality worry; see also the references in note 2. A quite distinct worry that might occur to the reader is that an account according to which every designator rigidly designates something or other and nonrigidly designates some other thing might collapse into incoherence (Rubin discusses possible troubles in this neighborhood: 2008, p. 513).
10. Cf. Soames' (2002, pp. 254–6; 2006a, p. 650) similar use of 'identification statement'; Kripke also calls some statements "identifications" (e.g., in 1980, at p. 99), but the intent is less clear. I do not include mere conditionals, like '(x)(x is white $\rightarrow$ x is colored)', in the camp of "identification statements" of any kind. Nor would I count 'white is a color' as an *identity* statement, and for similar reasons, which I indicate at chapter 3, note 5.
11. This principle holds for artificial property designators as well as for natural property designators, as reflection on parallel statements containing natural and artificial designators indicates: thus, compare '(x)(x is a brontosaur $\equiv$ x is an apatosaur)' and '(x)(x is soda $\equiv$ x is pop)', on the one hand, with '(x)(x is a brontosaur $\equiv$ x is the herbivorous dinosaur genus

with chevron bones that resemble those of carnivorous marine reptiles)' and '(x)(x is soda ≡ x is the beverage Uncle Bill requested at our Super Bowl party)', on the other hand. The basic observations from earlier chapters (chapter 2, §1 and chapter 3, §2.2 and §2.3) to the effect that artificial property designators conform to a rigid – nonrigid distinction hold up, then (as I have promised, in chapter 2 at note 3), whether the designators in question are singular, as I treat them in those chapters, or merely predicative.

12. One might raise quibbles about whether the account on which I have elaborated applies to '7' or to 'Cicero' if Cicero is a simple: a Cartesian soul without parts, say. This is a scruple not likely to arise for the case of 'hesperus' or 'hesperus stuff'. The scruple need not detain us: terms like 'hesperus' or 'hesperus stuff', '7' or '7 stuff', and 'cicero' or 'cicero stuff' could be used for some of the relevant object which in the limiting case of a simple would have to include the whole object.

13. I hold, to the contrary, that 'H_2O' *rigidly* designates its intension: see chapter 6, §2.1.2, for arguments. In any event, keep in mind, for what follows, that 'h_i', 'w_i', and 'u_i' designate the relevant intension rigidly, whether or not 'H_2O' does.

14. I thank an anonymous referee for raising basically this objection. Applied to the account of rigidity that will be offered in §1.2, the objection becomes this: to say that F and G rigidly codesignate *H*s is to say no more or less than that F and G are necessarily coextensive.

15. Kripke regards this *conditional* claim as "self-evident" (1980, p. 4; the literature, too, testifies to the obviousness of the conditional: see chapter 3, note 2). To be sure, Kripke would at one time have rejected claims of *necessity*, which are *not* obviously true, but he would accordingly have denied that rigidity obtains, too. Eventually, Kripke explains, he came to see that the received resistance to the *necessity* of name-containing statements was "incorrect, that the natural intuition that the names of ordinary language are rigid designators can in fact be upheld" (1980, p. 5).

16. Because selective realism recognizes *some* properties, there is no trouble seeing how selective realism could be accommodated in *part* with an account of rigidity that commits to properties: either the original version of rigidity for singular terms or else the version of rigidity already offered in this chapter, either of which might apply to terms designating properties that remain. I discuss the relationship between selective realism and rigidity at greater length in chapter 7, §1.2.

17. Sullivan (2005, pp. 594–5 and especially 2007, pp. 6–7; see also Inan 2008, pp. 221, 224, 226–8) also indicates that the rigid–nonrigid distinction holds with or without nominalism, by arguments that are complementary to those here: indeed, he performs a similar clarificatory service with respect to a number of other issues that are inappropriately associated with rigidity.

18. This conception of properties is coarse-grained, not distinguishing between, say, the property of *being white* and the property of *being white in such a way that the successor of 2 is 3*. In order to represent finer-grained properties, one might construe properties as functions with more structure, as I suggest in a closely related discussion about coarse-grained and fine-grained *meanings* (chapter 2, note 10). For purposes here, coarse-grained properties, which satisfy what is arguably "the best-known candidate for an identity condition for properties," namely "necessary coextensiveness" (Swoyer 2008, §6.1), suffice. Nothing more fine-grained is needed in order to defend the a posteriori necessity of 'water = H_2O', say, or to raise the familiar troubles for 'pain = c-fiber firing'. I say more about the relevance of coarsely cut properties in chapter 8, §3.

19. Hence, for example, there is a so-called "Quine-Devitt" response (Balaguer 2008, §3) to realists' demand for an explanation of the fact that two snowballs are both white (Quine 1961, p. 10; Devitt 1980; Balaguer provides a nice overview of this response and, more generally, of the whole realism – nominalism debate). According to this response, we can explain why snowballs are white in terms of their both reflecting light of all wavelengths in the visible spectrum; but that or something like it is the explanation überhaupt. No further explanation like "snowballs reflect light of all wavelengths because they *share* the universal *reflecting light of all wavelengths*" is of any help (for further criticisms of such purported explanations, see Bruce Aune 2008, especially chapter 4: discussion with Bruce has helped me to see the force of nominalism, and has helped to clarify for me some issues that come into play in this section, §1.2).
20. Even Quine, who is the first nominalist to come to mind for many philosophers, is not as radical as Sellars (for a brief comparative discussion, see Loux 1998): Quine recognizes sets, though he would not recognize rigid designation because he would not recognize possible worlds or metaphysical necessity. Nominalism (eliminativism, etc.) about possible worlds is of course nominalism of a different sort than nominalism about properties. Nominalism about possible worlds can be set aside for purposes of this book, which aims to vindicate a rigid – nonrigid distinction for *property* designators specifically. In order to vindicate a rigid – nonrigid distinction for property designators specifically, there is no need to defend the usual appeal to possible worlds or to pursue surrogates in order to mollify nominalists of Quine's sort: if nominalism about possible worlds is a threat to the rigid – nonrigid distinction for *property* designators, that is only because it is a threat to the rigid – nonrigid distinction *itself*, and something similar may be said for Quinean skepticism about metaphysical necessity. I generally ignore qualms, especially qualms that have been as thoroughly scrutinized already as Quine's have, that concern *all* claims to rigidity, including claims about designators like 'Hesperus', which excite little controversy (see chapter 1, note 1 and the accompanying text).
21. Here 'F' is a dummy term for a word, while 'F' or 'Fs' is a dummy term for a word's extension, which corresponds in the expected fashion. Where I say "Fs," read this as shorthand for the more cumbersome "Fs, or what is F."
22. For discussion of the lessons of rigidity with respect to identity statements, see chapter 1, §1.1 and §2 as well as chapter 3, §1; for discussion of the lessons of rigidity with respect to identification statements, see §1.1.2 and §1.2.2 of the present chapter. To be sure, many of the effects of rigidity on identity statements or identification statements carry over certain other sorts of statements as well: see chapter 3, §2.1.
23. The terms would presumably rigidly apply just to actual bits of water or to the set of actual bits of water, and so on: this is how I understand the matter in the present section, §2.1, as it seems to be the usual way of understanding the matter (Cook, for example, suggests that the term 'cat' applies rigidly, as it happens, to the actual cats in the world, although 'cat' might have applied rigidly to other items had there been more cats: 1980, p. 63). In §2.2, I will address the suggestion that 'cat' or 'water' rigidly applies to something besides just *actual* cats or water quantities (see especially note 24).
24. Cordry (2004, pp. 250f.) adds essential application as one component of his account of rigidity. Gómez-Torrente, in rich and interesting work on predicative property designators (see, e.g., Gómez-Torrente 2004, pp. 42ff.), presents an account of rigidity that also, assuming certain objections can be surmounted, achieves effects similar to those obtained by adding an essentialist requirement to the account of rigidity that I propose here (in

§1.2.2). For Gómez-Torrente, in order for, say, 'rhynchocephalian' to rigidly apply to rhynchocephalians, 'rhynchocephalian' must apply and must *essentially* apply to all and only *actual and possible* rhynchocephalians, with respect to every possible world. *If* Gómez-Torrente's substantial commitment to a kind of "obstinate rigidity" for appliers is tenable (Gómez-Torrente, 2004, pp. 43ff.; cf. Soames 2004, pp. 87ff. for objections; for a discussion of obstinate rigidity, see chapter 1, §1.2) *and if* the relevant essentialist doctrines obtain, then Gómez-Torrente is able to accommodate the necessity of '(x)(x is water ≡ x is H_2O)'. He is also able to accommodate the non-necessity of statements like '(x)(x is a tuatara ≡ x is a rhynchocephalian)', since for him, 'rhynchocephalian' would fail to be rigid for *tuataras*: 'rhynchocephalian' applies not only to actual rhynchocephalians, which are all tuataras, but also to merely *possible* rhynchocephalians, some of which are not tuataras. However, the relevant essentialist requirements are not *needed* to account for the differing modal status of '(x)(x is water ≡ x is H_2O)' and '(x)(x is a tuatara ≡ x is a rhynchocephalian)', and the essentialist requirements bring not only those complications indicated already in this note, but much graver troubles as well to a proper account of rigidity that can handle the necessity on its own without the essentialist add-on: I discuss these matters further in the text below.

25. The claim that 'water = H_2O' is necessary is closely associated with the claim that the *property* or *kind* water is essentially H_2O, not with the claim that *bits* of water are *essentially* H_2O. Something similar holds, as I suggest in the foregoing paragraphs, for the corresponding biconditional, '(x)(x is water ≡ x is H_2O)'. The necessity of 'water = H_2O' or '(x)(x is water ≡ x is H_2O)' assures, with respect to any possible world w, that any water at w is H_2O at w, and vice-versa, but this is compatible with there being some metaphysically possible world w' that is distinct from w, in which a quantity of water from w loses a few subatomic particles in order to become non-H_2O, without becoming a different quantity of matter. It is just that this loss of subatomic particles at w' would have to result in the quantity's becoming not only non-H_2O but also non-water at w'. As one should expect, there are philosophers who favor essentialism about properties or kinds but who reject claims according to which particulars essentially instantiate those properties or kinds (Enç 1986; Lee 1979, pp. 294–5). So these authors, who can countenance rigidity, cannot countenance essential application as an add-on.

26. 'Trope of whiteness' or 'particular patch of whiteness', which applies, if it applies at all, to something like a particularized property or trope or mode, is different from 'white', in that it is plausibly regarded as an essential applier: that is because, although white objects like K2 could have been blue, particularized whitenesses present on K2's surface could presumably not have been present as particularized bluenesses. For this reason, if the issue at hand were that of establishing the necessity of '(x)(x is a particular patch of whiteness ≡ x is a particular patch of albescence)', essential application would not stand out so saliently as useless (see Oderberg 2007, chapter 9, note 17; Gómez-Torrente 2006, pp. 257–8). But the issue *here* is '(x)(x is white ≡ x is albescent)', not '(x)(x is a particular patch of whiteness ≡ x is a particular patch of albescence)'. If anyone would not recognize the intended reading of '(x)(x is white ≡ x is albescent)', I could stipulate the relevant use of 'white' and 'albescent', clarifying with subscripts.

27. This is not to mention terms for semi-artificial properties like 'waterlogged', 'coffeepot', or 'gilded', or terms for outright artificial properties like 'soda' or 'bachelor', which also seem to find a contrast in nonrigid designators: see chapter 2, §1 and chapter 3, §2.2. For further

discussion of how essentialist requirements would restrict rigidity excessively, see Inan (2008, pp. 216–18).

28. I model this presentation of the dispute over the identity theory of mind after the presentation in chapter 1, §2.2, though that chapter's presentation appeals to identity statements containing singular terms and here in the text I appeal to identification statements containing mere appliers. I might have stayed with identity statements, as Kripke does. I indicate how here: if 'pain = c-fiber firing' is a true theoretical identity statement, then 'pain' and 'c-fiber firing' are rigid designators for the same property, which is problematic enough, at least prima facie, for familiar reasons. The identity theorist is not burdened with *further* problems that she might draw by committing to the claim that pains are essentially pains. A fanciful example may illustrate. Even if there is some particular token event p, like your most recent toe-stubbing-associated mental event, that is in fact a pain but that might have been, say, a performance of Bach's Mass in B minor instead, it remains the case that the type *pain* is identical to the type *c-fiber firing* so long as 'pain' and 'c-fiber firing' are rigid designators of the same type, which would require only that p is a non-c-fiber-firing as well as a non-pain in worlds in which p is a performance of Bach's Mass in B minor instead of a pain bothering you. So although antimaterialist arguments directed at trouble arising from a materialist's commitment to essential application, as opposed to just rigidity, might tell against the identity theorist who embraces essential application, such arguments would not tell against identity theorists who reject essential application, as identity theorists are free to do. Kripke himself evidently slips over this point on occasion. "The identity of pain with the stimulation of C-fibers, if true, must be *necessary*," he insists, since "'pain' is a rigid designator of the type, or phenomenon, it designates: if something is a pain it is essentially so" (1980, pp. 148–9), and the same holds for 'c-fiber firing'. Kripke is right that type identity theorists are committed to the claim that 'pain' and 'c-fiber firing' *rigidly* designate the same type (Kripke never explains why they are so committed: see chapter 6, note 6) and hence to the *necessity* of 'pain = c-fiber firing'. But for all of this, identity theorists are *not* committed to the claim that any *particular* pain is essentially so: that claim swings free from appropriate claims about the rigidity and attending necessity. Even for someone who thinks on his feet as quickly as Kripke, such a slip would be easy to make in a talk: still, the confusion is unfortunate since it suggests a similar interpretation of some of Kripke's ensuing claims against identity theorists (e.g., 1980 at p. 151), thereby casting the arguments into needless doubt.

29. See note 28. The irrelevance of essentialism can be made clearer, perhaps, by a look at a corresponding argument concerning 'painful' and 'c-fiber firing-inducing', rather than the 'pain' and 'c-fiber firing', since it is obviously not generally the case that what is painful is so essentially: a painful cut, for example, could be rendered painless with the right anesthetic. 'Painful' is obviously not a rigid-cum-essential applier: even so, the relevant troubles for the identification theory are similar. '(x)(x is painful $\equiv$ x is painful)' and '(x)(x is painful $\equiv$ x is dolorous)' are clearly necessarily true by virtue of containing two rigid designators for the same property; '(x)(x is painful $\equiv$ x is c-fiber firing-inducing)' is another story. It is irrelevant that what is painful or dolorous or c-fiber-inducing is not necessarily so.

6

Rigidity – Associated Arguments in Support of Theoretical Identity Statements: on their Significance and the Cost of their Philosophical Resources

In chapters 2–5, I have defended a rigid – nonrigid distinction for property designators. I have said that the distinction is worth minding on account of rigidity's work in arguments aiming to establish or to impugn various theoretical identity statements, which express or would express theoretically interesting essences of various properties. There is much still to be done by way of defending these arguments. That is the work of the rest of this book.

To be sure, I have addressed a certain sort of doubt about the arguments aiming to establish or impugn theoretical identity statements: I have addressed doubts about whether, *if* property designators qualify as rigid according to my understanding of rigidity, they uphold the necessity, in case of truth, of identity statements containing them, as the relevant arguments suppose. To uphold this necessity is rigidity's role, so if property designators that qualify as rigid according to my understanding of the rigid – nonrigid distinction could not uphold the necessity, then that would indicate a problem with my understanding of the rigid – nonrigid distinction. Hence, it is in the course of defending my *understanding* of the rigid – nonrigid distinction for property designators that the foregoing doubt has come to attention (see chapter 3).

But there are plenty of doubts, about arguments aiming to establish or impugn theoretical identity statements, that would not threaten my understanding of a rigid – nonrigid distinction for property designators. These doubts would call into question rigidity's interest. They call for attention.

According to one doubt along the foregoing lines, even though rigidity would underwrite necessity if rigidity were to obtain, still identity statements that are supposed to contain rigid property designators might actually contain nonrigid ones. According to another doubt along the relevant lines, even if identity statements that are supposed to contain rigid property designators do so, conclusions obtained by appeal to rigidity, to the effect that this or that theoretical identity statement is true and therefore necessary, or that this or that theoretical identity statement is not necessary at least for all we can tell and therefore not true at least for all we can tell, are established by appeal not only to rigidity but to other resources that should be regarded with suspicion or worse. So the relevant conclusions about these theoretical identity statements are not established.

According to the foregoing worries, arguments supporting or impugning various theoretical identity statements fail to establish their conclusions. Besides such worries, there is also the worry that they establish their conclusions but that they give too prominent a place to rigidity, which is not of substantial help in *arriving* at the established conclusions. Finally, even if the arguments establish their conclusions and do so with substantial help from rigidity, those conclusions might be less interesting than I have taken them to be.

All of the foregoing worries have attended both arguments appealing to rigidity to support various theoretical identity statements and arguments appealing to rigidity to impugn various theoretical identity statements. All of the worries are to be addressed in the coming chapters, though not the foregoing order. The order in which they are to be discussed will respect the following division. In the final two chapters of the book, I will address criticisms that have most often and most clearly been directed against the skeptical arguments impugning psychophysical identities. These arguments have stimulated a great deal of discussion, mostly critical, from a diversity of workers throughout the discipline. In the present chapter, I will address criticisms that have tended to be more evenly directed against both sorts of argument, constructive and skeptical, or that have been directed mostly against constructive arguments associated with property designators' rigidity. Although constructive arguments will be the target of the objections as I formulate them, all of the objections have in some form or other also been directed at skeptical arguments and hence readers may make the necessary adjustments to my presentation of the objections and replies if they are interested.

I begin with a look at objections concerning how significant the constructive arguments appealing to property designators' rigidity are, at least provided that the arguments are also compelling. That is the subject of section (1). Then I will address objections according to which the constructive arguments are not compelling, costly as they are in terms of resources that they presuppose. That is the subject of section (2).

1. Significance

I will discuss three reservations concerning the significance of arguments appealing to rigidity to support theoretical identity statements. The first reservation addresses whether theoretical identity statements supported by the arguments are uninformative and trivial. The second and third reservations maintain that rigidity is not in the end important to *establishing* the theoretical identity statements supported by the arguments, whether or not the theoretical identity statements are informative: so the arguments are misleading because of their prominent appeal to rigidity.

1.1. *Are Theoretical Identity Statements Uninformative?*

Some philosophers hold that theoretical identity statements, because they contain rigid designators, are insignificant for how little they say. Michael Levin, for example, says that the necessity of 'water = H_2O' is hardly as "exciting" as philosophers have supposed; on the contrary, each term "lacks descriptive content and merely tags H_2O in all possible worlds," so that the statement "amounts to no more than 'water is water'" (Levin 1987, p. 287). Jaegwon Kim similarly seems to hold that "necessary identities with rigid designators" (2005, p. 132, note 23) express only trivial information[1]: 'water = H_2O' and 'water = water' apparently "report one and the same fact" (Kim 2003, p. 574). And again, the reason for the trivial content is apparently that the designators are rigid: thus, Kim recognizes that "contingent identities like 'Margaret Okayo was the women's winner of the 2003 New York Marathon'," which contain nonrigid designators, are informative (2005, p. 132, note 23).

If rigidity were to rob designators of theoretical content then indeed even a rigid theoretical designator like 'H_2O' would express little, sharing the content of 'water'; but there is scant reason to suppose that rigidity robs designators of theoretical content. Some rigid designators are fairly straightforwardly descriptive: thus, 'the positive square root of 16' seems as descriptive as 'the women's winner of the 2003 New York Marathon', but is straightforwardly rigid. Theoretical designators like 'H_2O' could similarly express theoretical content and yet be rigid. So there should be little motivation to resist prima facie considerations suggesting that theoretical designators, which are rigid, do express theoretical content. 'Water droplets pile up rather than flatten out because water is *H_2O*, and the components of that chemical cause it to form certain intermolecular bonds' seems to express more information, prima facie, than the corresponding but informatively meager 'water droplets pile up rather than flatten out because water is *water*, and the components of that chemical cause it to form certain intermolecular bonds': still, 'H_2O' is rigid (see the following section, §2.1.2). Other theoretical expressions like 'the motion of molecules' and 'the combination of all of the colors of the visible spectrum' seem even more plainly to express theoretical content; but again, they are rigid (or so I maintain in §2.1.2).

By all indications, then, theoretical identity statements express interesting theoretical information about the subject. They are informative. But there is more: the informativeness of theoretical identity statements does not *ride* on their expressing theoretical information about the subject. Even if theoretical expressions were not to *express* theoretical content semantically, contrary to considerations that I have just broached, it would be highly informative to learn of the truth of theoretical identity statements. Granted, the *propositions* that theoretical identity statements express would be trivial and uninformative: mere logical truths knowable a priori. But that would not detract from the informativeness of a *statement* of the sort in question, and for reasons I have already offered (see chapter 1, §1.3; for a similar discussion, see Witmer 2006, pp. 1140–1).

1.2. Is What is Designated What Matters, Not Designation?

Theoretical identity statements are not trivially true. So I have argued (in §1.1), thereby putting to rest a worry that could undermine the significance of arguments that appeal to rigidity in order to establish theoretical identity statements.

In the present section and in the section following, sections (1.2) and (1.3), I address a different sort of worry concerning the significance of those arguments. This sort of worry centers on the appeals to rigidity in the arguments. Even if theoretical identity statements established by the arguments are informative and interesting, there might be little reason to appeal to rigidity in order to establish those informative and interesting theoretical identity statements.

The first worry to be considered is the worry that rigidity is not relevant or at least not directly relevant to the truth of theoretical identity statements, since rigidity concerns words, in the first instance, not things and their properties. The items that theoretical identity statements discuss have their essential character entirely independently of how we might designate them, whether rigidly or not. To establish theoretical identities we should turn our attention straight to the subject matter of theoretical identities rather than to the topic of how we use words that theoretical identity statements contain. So goes the objection.[2]

The objection would seem to be founded on a truth: that the items discussed by theoretical identity statements have their essential character independently of how we might designate them. A conventionalist would, of course, disagree. A conventionalist would say that water, the stuff, owes its nature to our ways of thinking or naming. Although I will not criticize conventionalism here because there is no need for me to rule that position out, I am not disposed to accept it. *That water = H_2O seems to hold independently of any of our own referential practices. Nothing we could do by changing our referential practices or by any other means could cause water to be H_2O_2, say, instead of H_2O. On the contrary, it is a necessary truth that water = H_2O, and so true in all possible worlds, regardless of our referential practices or other behavior.

Still, rigidity is germane to whether the *statement* 'water = H_2O' is true: a statement owes its truth to how its terms hook up to items in the world. If we had used 'water' to designate sand or glass instead of water, 'water = H_2O' would not have been a true statement. And if we had used 'water' as a nonrigid designator without changing our use of 'H_2O', the resulting statement 'water = H_2O' would not have been *necessarily* true. Whether any statement is necessarily true, contingently true, false, and so on, depends on what it is expressing: and whether we use words rigidly or not in our statement is relevant, directly relevant, to what the statement expresses.

Rigidity is relevant to essences because it is relevant to the truth and modal status of theoretical identity statements. We could of course try to turn our attention away from *statements* like 'water = H_2O' and instead turn to the *content* of statements. We could argue directly for the truth or necessity of the proposition *that water = H_2O* without talking about words and whether or not they are rigid. But even to argue directly for the truth or necessity of the proposition *that water = H_2O* without talking about words, we still have to *use* words. So when it comes to *evaluating* what has been said, attention to rigidity can be enlightening. When we clarify the use of 'water' we clarify what we have been saying with it, which can cause us to rethink whether what we have said about *water*, as opposed to 'water', is true. That is why consideration of how words are used, by such time-honored tactics as consideration of what speakers would or should say in various circumstances (recall Twin Earth: Putnam 1975), can engender appreciation of metaphysical positions like essentialism. So we might come to the conclusion, after recognizing that 'water' rigidly designates H_2O, "Water is essentially H_2O after all. Something with another microstructure is undeserving of the label 'water'."

1.3. Do Mechanisms that Secure Rigidity Draw from Rigidity's Significance?

If rigidity is important in establishing the truth of theoretical identity *statements*, as I have argued, that is enough to assure its relevance to the truth and necessity of what is expressed by the statements. Yet there are doubts from some quarters about whether rigidity *is* important in establishing the truth of theoretical identity statements. Just how foundational a role rigidity plays in establishing these statements has been exaggerated in the tradition, according to some. Linguistic mechanisms or phenomena that are in some respects deeper or more fundamental than rigidity give rise to rigidity and the work associated with it. So we would do well to appeal to these *deeper* mechanisms, rather than to the *rigidity* to which the deeper mechanisms give rise, in our explanations of the necessity of theoretical identity statements and other statements containing rigid designators.

Even if rigidity is not of fundamental importance, we could still appeal to rigidity rather than to the deeper mechanisms issuing in rigidity, in building the case for necessity. This much is acknowledged by critics, who nevertheless point out that "there is nothing essential about this way of putting things" (Soames 2002, p. 311) and who urge furthermore that other ways of putting things are more illuminating. That rigidity is so dispensable indicates, according to Soames, a "demotion of the status of rigidity," and a corresponding promotion of the status of "other, more fundamental, semantic properties" (2002, p. 264). Devitt seems to agree. He is similarly inclined to say that rigidity lacks fundamental importance even if it explains in some respect the relevant necessity, since explanations appealing to rigidity are superficial, at best: "a deeper explanation" (Devitt 2005, p. 154) of the necessity that appeals to a semantic feature giving rise to rigidity is available and desirable (Devitt 2005, p. 145; see also Ahmed 2007, p. 58; 2009, p. 132).

I am convinced, although I will not argue, that linguistic mechanisms or phenomena that are in some respects deeper than rigidity give rise to rigidity and the work associated with it, as the foregoing authors claim. There is no need to endorse any specific mechanism. The more popular proposals seem to come from antidescriptivists, as my appeal to the above workers suggests. Many philosophers suggest that rigidity arises as a matter of course from direct reference (Cartwright 1998, pp. 72, 74; Kaplan

1989b, p. 571; King 2001, p. 311; Soames 2002 pp. 264–5, 310–11; Wolf 2006, p. 365; Wolter 2009, p. 455; and especially Sullivan 2007, pp. 7ff.; but cf. Martí 2003; Salmon 1981, p. 33, note 35), which, as I have observed, stands opposed to descriptivism (see chapter 1, §1.3). Devitt (2005, p. 145) maintains that *causal* mechanisms, which also testify against descriptivism, give rise to rigidity. I would recognize other mechanisms still; but again, specific candidates are not important. What *is* important here is that the fact, if it is a fact, that rigidity supervenes on deeper linguistic mechanisms, is no indication that rigidity is insufficiently deep or fundamental to merit the independent attention that it has received.

One indication that rigidity's importance is independent of the importance attached to natural mechanisms giving rise to rigidity is this: various fundamentally *different* mechanisms give rise to rigidity. So what is important about rigidity would seem to defy categorization in terms of one single natural mechanism or another giving rise to rigidity. The *de facto* rigidity of 'the square root of 9' or the *de jure* rigidity of 'the husband of Xantippe, in α' (see §2.1) is not secured by direct reference, or by causal mechanisms, or by any similar mechanism along the lines of the foregoing proposals. The reasons behind the rigidity of such expressions would seem to be different from the reasons behind the rigidity of directly referential or causally grounded terms. So no simple appeal to a natural mechanism other than rigidity would seem to render appeals to rigidity superfluous: rigidity remains important since it features, regardless of its source, in such familiar and general claims as the claim that when t and t' rigidly designate the same item, ⌜t = t'⌝ is not only true but necessarily true.

More importantly, even if some simple mechanism *could* account for all cases of rigidity, this would not show that rigidity does not have the explanatory power that it is supposed to have and therefore that it does not deserve the independent attention that it has received. A phenomenon is not stripped of its significance or proper role in explanations by arising from or supervening on other mechanisms or phenomena, even if these other mechanisms or phenomena support alternative, perhaps deeper explanations.

Consider a related example that keeps a little distance from the heart of the relevant controversy. Various mechanisms give rise to the phenomenon of intoxication and the traffic fatalities associated with it. So a deeper explanation of a fatal accident than "so and so was drunk and did not see the traffic light," could bypass direct appeals to intoxication: rather than to appeal to intoxication, the deeper explanation could appeal to specific events on which intoxication supervenes. The deeper explanation could make clear just how various molecules of alcohol were absorbed by an agent's digestive system, entered the bloodstream, interacted with other molecules, inhibited sufficient oxygen from reaching the right portions of the nervous system, interrupted this and that neural event, etc. The deeper explanation could make clear just how all of these events give rise to an alcohol-related accident.

Still, for all that the foregoing observations show, "so and so was drunk and did not see the traffic light" remains a proper explanation of how the fatal accident came to occur: it can meet the important explanatory needs of the occasion, as when an audience wonders whether the accident was caused by a malfunctioning traffic light, by ice on the road, and so on. So although there are explanations of traffic fatalities caused by drunk driving that are deeper than explanations appealing directly to intoxication, and deeper because these explanations appeal to phenomena that give rise to intoxication, that does not seem to be anything against the significance of intoxication as a phenomenon worth minding for its value in explaining the traffic fatalities for which it remains responsible.

Something similar would seem to hold for the phenomenon of rigidity. It might be that mechanisms or phenomena that are distinct from rigidity, perhaps mechanisms or phenomena that belie descriptivism, give rise to the phenomenon of rigidity. In that case, a deeper explanation for the necessity of a given identity statement than "both designators in the statement rigidly designate the same object" could bypass direct appeals to rigidity: rather than to appeal to rigidity, the deeper explanation could appeal to the mechanisms or phenomena on which rigidity supervenes. The deeper explanation could make clear just how these mechanisms give rise to rigidity-attended necessity.

Still, for all that the foregoing observations show, "both designators in the statement rigidly designate the same object" remains a proper explanation of the relevant necessity: it can meet the important explanatory needs of the occasion. History testifies that this explanation *has* met the important explanatory needs of salient occasions: thus, before such explanations caused rigidity's work to be appreciated, it was common to hold that a statement like 'Hesperus = Phosphorus' is contingently true. Explanations of rigidity's work have changed that (see chapter 1, §1.3). Indeed, explanations of rigidity's work have changed things without help from any settled resolution to fundamental issues concerning the phenomena on which rigidity might supervene, which phenomena lie close to the heart of the debate between descriptivism and antidesciptivism (see chapter 3, note 11). So although there may be explanations of the necessity attending rigidity that are deeper than explanations appealing to rigidity, that does not seem to be anything against the significance of rigidity as a phenomenon worth minding for its value in explaining the necessity for which it remains responsible.[3]

To be sure, a deeper explanation might amount to a more fundamental theory that commands *more* respect than the insights that it incorporates, as we see happening in science often enough: one thinks, for example, of how the remarkable observations concerning the relativity of space and time from the theory of special relativity follow from more general observations about gravity and space-time curvature from the theory of general relativity. Still, this is nothing against special relativity. No one is tempted to say that because the theory of special relativity follows from the theory of general relativity, special relativity loses interest and general relativity is what really matters. It is better to say that part of what is interesting about general relativity concerns its implications for the relativity of space and time, as explained by the theory of special relativity: special relativity retains its interest as part of a larger, more fundamental theory.

In the same way, credit for the successes of nondescriptive theories of reference is due to those workers (including Soames and Devitt) who have articulated those theories and who have shown, to whatever extent they have done so, how rigidity follows from those theories. But this credit does not draw from the credit due to these same theorists and others who have worked through the implications of rigidity.

2. Costs

In general, the rigidity-based arguments in support of theoretical identity statements are significant and uphold rigidity's significance, at least if they are convincing. But are they convincing? Salient objections commonly voiced in the literature charge that the arguments come at too high a price: that they carry costs or commitments that we would or should regard as prohibitive, so that the arguments should be regarded as unfortunately controversial or worse. I will argue, on the contrary, that alleged costs and controversial commitments are apparent rather than real. The arguments are backed by support that brooks little controversy.

In section (2.1) below, I address worries according to which significant portions of the community are committed, for substantial philosophical reasons, to resisting my position that the designators in familiar theoretical identity statements are rigid rather than nonrigid. In section (2.2), I address a salient worry that arises even if we may take for granted that the property designators in familiar theoretical identity statements are rigid rather than nonrigid. The worry is that even so, the arguments appealing to property designators' rigidity appeal also to controversial metaphysical input.

2.1. Rigidity Without Cost and Controversy

I have affirmed a tradition according to which rigidity underwrites the necessity of theoretical identity statements like 'heat = the motion of molecules' because both of the statement's designators are rigid. But detractors from the tradition have doubted that designators like 'heat' and 'the motion of molecules' are rigid: accordingly, these detractors would seem, at least on first glance, to present substantial reasons to resist the relevant necessity. I respond in this section. First I address name-like terms, such as 'heat', in section (2.1.1). Then I address theoretical expressions, such as 'the motion of molecules', in section (2.1.2).

2.1.1. On the Rigidity of Name-Like Subject Terms
Some philosophers who are skeptical about rigidity have focused on what I will call the "*subject* terms" of theoretical identity statements, like 'heat'. These philosophers have urged that the subject term is nonrigid: hence, they have urged, statements like 'heat = the motion of molecules' are contingently true, rather than necessarily true. Thus, Lewis maintains that 'heat' is shorthand for a description like 'the underlying physical phenomenon that happens to cause the boiling of water, the sensations that people feel when they touch fire, and so on', or, for short, 'the underlying phenomenon that happens to fill the *heat* role'. If this is so, then

'heat = the motion of molecules' is true but only contingently so. The statement is true, because "it is molecular motion that occupies the heat-role," but this is contingent because "it might have been molecular nonmotion, or caloric fluid, or what you will" (Lewis 1999a, p. 44; see also Roberts 2008, pp. 69–74): in other possible worlds 'heat = molecular nonmotion' or 'heat = caloric fluid' is true instead of 'heat = the motion of molecules'.

If indeed Lewis is right about the proper use of 'heat', then 'the motion of molecules' fails to express *what it is to be heat* or fails to express *that in virtue of which something counts as being heat*. After all, if Lewis is right, then it is possible for a phenomenon to be heat *without* being the motion of molecules and for a phenomenon to be the motion of molecules *without* being heat. But what it is to *be* heat could not be *separated* from heat in the way that, for Lewis, the motion of molecules can be separated from heat. If, as Lewis would have it, 'heat = the motion of molecules' is not necessarily true in virtue of 'the motion of molecules''s expressing what it is to be heat, but instead merely contingently true, then 'heat = the motion of molecules' fails to qualify as a genuine "theoretical identity statement" as I have understood that notion.[4]

Lewis represents, then, a disagreement between a tradition that I would defend with regard to the modal status of 'heat = the motion of molecules' and an alternative tradition. Even so, there is enough common ground between the traditions to reach agreement about the necessity of various theoretical identity statements. Agreement can be rendered clear with a little terminological negotiation: if 'heat' is nonrigid, we can simply *coin* a subject term that is *rigid* for what is, *in fact*, heat. Let us coin a name-like rigid designator 'heat★' in the foregoing manner for what is, in fact, heat. A look at the empirical world shows that such a term would rigidly designate the motion of molecules (on anyone's account).[5] Now we may produce (again, on anyone's account: see note 5) the desired necessarily true theoretical identity statement 'heat★ = the motion of molecules'. So when I, for one, use 'heat', let the reader who doubts the English version's claim to rigidity simply substitute 'heat★'.

2.1.2. On the Rigidity of Theoretical Expressions Doubts about the rigidity of theoretical expressions, such as 'the motion of molecules', 'the inability to metabolize glucose', and 'the combination of all of the colors of the visible spectrum', arise more frequently than do doubts about the rigidity of expressions like 'heat', 'diabetes', and 'white'. I will discuss salient doubts, in section (2.1.2.1). It is harder to defend the rigidity of theoretical expressions than to defend the rigidity of name-like expressions: there are pitfalls to be avoided, as I will indicate in section (2.1.2.2). Finally, I will argue that rigidity obtains, in sections (2.1.2.3) and (2.1.2.4).

2.1.2.1. Doubts In contrast to 'heat', 'white', and 'water', 'the motion of molecules', 'the combination of all of the colors of the visible spectrum', and even 'H$_2$O' are plausibly interpreted as descriptions. This alerts many to the possibility that theoretical expressions' claim to rigid status may be spurious (Bolton 1996, p. 148; Barnett 2000, pp. 108–9; Steward 1990, p. 393; see also Bealer 1987, p. 315; Bird and Tobin 2009, §3.3; Lowe 2008, p. 43): after all, descriptions are not always rigid. Even though *names* are uniformly rigid *de jure* (Kripke 1980, p. 21, note 21) according to Kripke's well-received account, and so, apparently, are various designators that are at least name-like, such as '4', descriptions are another matter. Some descriptions are rigid *de facto* (Kripke 1980, p. 21, note 21), such as 'the positive square root of 16', which is rigid since no number other than four satisfies the descriptive content of that expression in any possible world. But most descriptions we use are not rigid. A nonrigid description for four is 'the number of legs on most pets': although dogs and cats outnumber all other pets, snakes and goldfish might have done so and with respect to worlds in which they do, 'the number of legs on most pets' is zero, not four.

Because descriptions are often nonrigid, it would be hasty to affirm the rigidity of expressions like 'the motion of molecules' and 'the combination of all of the colors of the visible spectrum' without an argument. The need for an argument in favor of the rigidity of the relevant expressions is still more urgent in view of natural considerations favoring a nonrigid interpretation. According to a natural reading of 'the motion of molecules', it is a synonym for some expression like 'the motion that is exemplified in molecules'. Such a reading of 'the motion of molecules' seems to allow for the possibility that the same motion could have been exemplified in some other kind of particles. In the same way, a natural reading of 'the motion that I am showing with my arm' (I swing a racket), say, seems to allow for the possibility that the same motion could have been exemplified in other objects rather than by my arm: hence, I could correctly affirm 'the motion that I am showing with my arm is the motion that I want you to make'.

If 'the motion of molecules' is indeed to be read as something like a synonym for 'the motion that is exemplified in molecules', then 'the motion of molecules' is not clearly rigid. The reason is suggested by the foregoing parallel: with respect to worlds w that might plausibly be regarded as possible, molecules move in distinctive patterns quite unlike those in which they actually move. The description 'the motion that is exemplified in molecules' applies, as things are, to some pattern or type of motion *m* that is exemplified in molecules by virtue of the specific way that molecules happen to move; but with respect to worlds w, the description fails to apply to m, applying instead to some pattern or type of motion distinct from m that is characteristic of molecules in w but not molecules in the actual world.

That there is a natural nonrigid reading, or anyway a natural not-clearly rigid reading, for 'the motion of molecules' calls into question rigidity's alleged achievement of securing the necessity of 'heat = the motion of molecules'. Similar considerations could be adduced to call into question rigidity's alleged achievement of securing the necessity of 'white = the combination of all of the colors of the visible spectrum', 'water = H_2O', and so on (see also Salmon 2003, p. 488).

2.1.2.2. Facile Defenses of Rigidity to be Avoided

Some argument is needed to establish the rigidity of theoretical expressions if that rigidity is to be acknowledged with proper confidence. A couple of facile sources of support recommend themselves. A bit of reflection indicates that they are best avoided.

2.1.2.2.1. SUPPORT FROM ESSENTIALISM

One might turn, in order to support the rigidity of theoretical expressions like 'the motion of molecules', 'the inability to metabolize glucose', and 'the combination of all of the colors of the visible spectrum', to one's conviction that these theoretical expressions express the *essences* of heat, diabetes, and white, respectively. That would be a problematic source of support. Unfortunately, since explicit arguments to establish the rigidity of theoretical expressions are anything but common in the literature, the suspicion has occurred to various workers that essentialist intuitions are, in fact, the real reason driving philosophers to accept the relevant claims to rigidity (see Bolton 1996, p. 148; Martí 2004, p. 143; Steward 1990, pp. 393ff.). Let me explain why this would be unwelcome.

One problem with the foregoing source of support for claims of rigidity is that it introduces unwelcome circularity. The rigidity of the designators in statements like 'heat = the motion of molecules' is supposed to help to redeem essentialism. The theoretical virtues of the second designator, along with its rigidity, would seem to assure that the foregoing statement is "essentially informative," as Berger would say (2002, p. 58; see also chapter 1, §2 of this book). But if claims to the rigidity of 'the motion of molecules' get their support from intuitions to the effect that 'the motion of molecules' expresses heat's *essence*, then it is hard to see how the rigidity of 'the motion of molecules' could do much to support that very essentialist claim.

Even if the charge of circularity could be overcome, there would be a serious problem with drawing support for rigidity from essentialist intuitions. The course of reasoning in rigidity-affiliated arguments for necessity would "not proceed, as may first appear, from metaphysically innocuous premises" (Steward 1990, p. 396). Although the relevant necessity *appears* on face value to be supported just by innocuous linguistic observations and by the deliverances of the empirical sciences, opponents (like Steward 1990, p. 391) would turn out to be well positioned to resist, on skeptical grounds as old as philosophy, the relevant necessity and the "underhand" essentialism motivating it (Steward 1990, p. 387). The rigidity of theoretical expressions is best supported without the cost of any appeal to essentialist intuitions.

2.1.2.2.2. SUPPORT FROM STIPULATIONS THAT COME TOO EASILY

There is another source of support that will not do. My defense of the rigidity of theoretical expressions will in the end appeal to stipulation. But the most *straightforward* route to establishing rigidity by stipulation would fail to produce the needed theoretical designators.

The broad outline of my case for the rigidity of theoretical expressions is as follows. Suppose, as I have suggested, that theoretical expressions like 'the motion of molecules' have a *reading* or use on which they serve as definite descriptions whose rigidity cannot be taken for granted. If so, then even though theoretical expressions have a reading on which they might be nonrigid, they *also* have a reading on which they are *rigid*. The rigid readings secure the necessity of theoretical identity statements. Any nonrigid readings are properly discounted when the terms appear in sentences interpreted as theoretical identity statements.

Not only does 'the motion of molecules' have *a* reading on which it is rigid, it has *more than one* reading on which it is rigid: one reading on which it is rigid *de facto* and another reading on which it is rigid *de jure*. Each reading provides a natural construal of the expression. It is not obvious which construal, if either, represents the usage of various ordinary contexts. It may be that in ordinary contexts the expression 'the motion of molecules' is indeterminate with respect to the readings at hand (and perhaps other readings as well: chapter 3, note 10 offers a plausible way of reading at least many theoretical expressions which is different from anything broached here in chapter 6). Here is where stipulation comes into play. If ordinary contexts fail to provide a level of resolution fine enough to select one rigid reading that I will propose over another reading, rigid or nonrigid, we can introduce a *new* and more precise use of 'the motion of molecules' or context of use, by stipulation[6]: this rigid use, favoring one or another of the foregoing rigid readings, will follow closely enough the pretheoretic and inchoate use of natural English to be representative of what is of value in ordinary speech, at least for purposes of conveying matters relevant here.

The suggestion that we might relieve doubts about the rigidity of a theoretical designator by *stipulating* a use that is rigid recalls my treatment of names like 'heat' (in § 2.1.1). If 'heat' is nonrigid shorthand for 'the underlying phenomenon that happens to fill the heat role', and so designates the motion of molecules with respect to the actual world but not with respect to all possible worlds, then I have urged that we can arrange to express what we were supposed to express by 'heat' by coining instead 'heat★', which is stipulated to designate *rigidly* what is, in fact, heat. Unfortunately, this method will not relieve doubts about the rigidity of a *compositional* designator like 'the motion of molecules'. Doubts about the rigidity of compositional designators are harder to put to rest by stipulation than doubts about the rigidity of names or name-like expressions even though, as I have said, doubts about the rigidity of both can be put to rest by stipulation.

Complications for stipulating a rigid correlate of 'the motion of molecules' become apparent when we give stipulation a straightforward try, following the pattern introduced by 'heat★'. 'The motion of molecules★' could be stipulatively introduced to designate rigidly what is in fact the motion of molecules. This could be done in different ways: e.g., the referent of 'the motion of molecules★' could be *fixed* by the description 'the motion of molecules', or else 'the motion of molecules★' could be introduced as shorthand for the world-indexed description 'what is, in a, the motion of molecules', 'a' being a name for the actual world. But then 'the motion of molecules★', like 'heat★', would be a naming or name-like designator that could not be counted on to express essence in the way that theoretical expressions are supposed to do. Instead, 'the motion of molecules★' would resemble a name like 'Phosphorus' according to descriptive accounts of names for which the reference of 'Phosphorus' is fixed by the description 'the brightest nonlunar body in the morning sky' (see Kripke 1980, pp. 55ff.) or else for which 'Phosphorus' is synonymous with a world-indexed description like 'the brightest nonlunar body in the morning sky in α' (see chapter 3, §2.4). Such descriptions do not express or communicate essence, or enough essence, to allow 'Phosphorus', on this descriptivist interpretation, to qualify as a theoretical expression (as I observe in chapter 1, note 9); 'Phosphorus' remains a name or at least it remains close enough to a name, and distant enough from theoretical expressions, for which more of the designatum's essential nature is discernible by competent users who attend to composition, for it to be taken as a name by theorists sympathetic to descriptivism. With respect to other possible worlds, the designatum of 'Phosphorus', even on the foregoing descriptivist interpretation, may not be bright, may not appear in the morning, and may not even be a heavenly body, for all that we are assured by the term's descriptive content about bright, morning-sky, heavenly body-hood. Similar words apply to 'the motion of molecules*'. For that reason, 'the motion of molecules*' is not the stipulatively rigid, theoretically contentful counterpart to 'the motion of molecules' that is needed for theoretical identity statements, in the event that 'the motion of molecules' should turn out not to be rigid.

To see that 'the motion of molecules*' is not the stipulatively rigid, theoretically contentful counterpart to 'the motion of molecules' that is needed for theoretical identity statements, in the event that 'the motion of molecules' should turn out not to be rigid, suppose that indeed 'the motion of molecules' is not rigid: the actual designatum of 'the motion of molecules' is not the designatum with respect to certain other possible worlds, where the actual designatum is something else instead of molecular motion. In that case, 'the motion of molecules*', which is a rigid designator for the *actual* designatum of 'the motion of molecules', designates something *other than* molecular motion with respect to other possible worlds where the actual designatum is something other than the motion of molecules. Just what sort of entity the designatum is with respect to other possible worlds is not clear. Accordingly, the essence of the designatum is unclear: the essence is not, contrary to what we might have thought, to be the motion of molecules since the designatum is not the motion of molecules with respect to other possible worlds.

Since the essence associated with what was supposed to be the theoretical expression 'the motion of molecules*' is unclear, 'heat = the motion of molecules*' is not the essence-enlightening theoretical identity statement that we sought to obtain with the help of stipulation to assure rigidity. It resembles instead statements like 'Hesperus = Phosphorus' according to descriptivist accounts like those just mentioned for the names 'Hesperus' and 'Phosphorus'. Again, no one takes 'Hesperus = Phosphorus' to be a theoretical identity statement. Since the point of stipulation was to obtain a rigid designator that redeems the theoretical identity statement 'heat = the motion of molecules' or a suitable surrogate, a stipulative effort will have to be more subtle than the foregoing effort if it is to assure us that theoretical expressions rise to the standard of rigidity in such a way that they contribute to the construction of the relevant theoretical identity statements.

As I have indicated, my own defense of the rigidity of theoretical designators like 'the motion of molecules' is stipulative, at least insofar as I would appeal to stipulation in the event that the two rigid readings that I will propose should fail to be proper English. In that event, let 'the motion of molecules**' be stipulated to express the reading that I will propose in section (2.1.2.3), which renders the expression rigid de facto. Let 'the motion of molecules***' be stipulated to express the reading that I will propose in section (2.1.2.4), which renders the expression rigid de jure. 'The motion of molecules**' and 'the motion of molecules***' are not subject to the problems that beleaguer 'the motion of molecules*' because they express or communicate theoretical content in the way that a theoretical expression should, unlike 'the motion of molecules*'. So I will indicate.

2.1.2.3. A Defense of De Facto Rigidity One plausible reading of 'the motion of molecules' according to which this theoretical expression is rigid is a reading on which 'the motion of molecules' is a disguised description that is shorthand for something like, 'the property P such that: necessarily, P characterizes x if and only if x is a molecular motion' (cf. Salmon for a similar suggestion: 2003, pp. 486–7). This description is rigid de facto. What makes it rigid de facto, as opposed to rigid de jure, is not merely that it *is* a description; descriptions can be rigid de jure, at least according to certain sensible and fairly well-entrenched uses of 'de jure' (see §2.1.2.4). But it seems most appropriate *not* to call the description 'the property P such that: necessarily, P characterizes x if and only if x is a molecular motion' "rigid *de jure*": its constant tie to the designatum, molecular motion, is not assured directly by stipulating that the designator is to follow the same designatum from world to world.[7] Nor is the designator's constant tie to the designatum assured by devices whose sole purpose is to track the same designatum from world to world. Instead, what assures a constant tie is simply that the designator characterizes the designatum according to essential characteristics. That is the mark of de facto rigidity: as Baumann says, "an expression is rigid de facto if it just happens to be the case, metaphysically, that the expression cannot but denote a particular object" (Baumann 2010, p. 334, note 4).

That the rigidity in question is not assured directly by stipulating that the designator is to follow the same designatum from world to world, nor by devices whose sole purpose is to track the same designatum from world to world, is indicated by consideration of certain deviant metaphysical views that would lead one to deny that the designatum, molecular motion, satisfies the requirements for rigid designation: for example, consider the view that properties or kinds are only accidentally properties or kinds. On such a view, a given property might in some other worlds exist but as a non-property: perhaps it is a football or a number in such worlds. If the property P of being molecular motion is a property at all possible worlds that contain molecules in motion, but is a football or a number instead at worlds not containing molecules in motion, then P is *non*rigidly designated by 'the property P such that: necessarily, P characterizes x if and only if x is a molecular motion': the expression designates P as things are but does not designate P with respect to worlds in which P is not a property.

The reason for successful *designation*, in the circumstances entertained, is as follows. In all possible worlds *containing* molecules that are in motion, anything x is a molecular motion just in case P characterizes x, P being a property in all such worlds: so in *those* possible worlds, P characterizes x if and only if x is a molecular motion. In all of the remaining possible worlds, those *not* containing molecules in motion, P fails to characterize anything. So in those remaining possible worlds, too, anything x is characterized by P if and only if x is a molecular motion: this is trivially true with respect to such worlds. Hence, in *all* possible worlds, those containing molecules in motion and those not containing molecules in motion, P characterizes x if and only if x is a molecular motion. P is in fact a property and we may suppose, whether or not by way of metaphysical deviance, that no other property meets the foregoing requirements for being the designatum of the relevant description. So, P is *in fact* the designatum of 'the property P such that: necessarily, P characterizes x if and only if x is a molecular motion'.

But P is not the designatum of 'the property P such that: necessarily, P characterizes x if and only if x is a molecular motion' with respect to all possible worlds containing P, so P is not *rigidly* designated: in some worlds containing P, which is in fact a property, P is not a property but is instead a particular, according to the deviant metaphysical position entertained, so the description fails to apply with respect to those worlds. The description is accordingly not rigid.[8] That a claim to nonrigid designation could be supported straightforwardly by the foregoing sort of deviant metaphysical reasoning indicates that the relevant designator is not rigid de jure: if the expression were rigid de jure, it would be required by sheer stipulation or by linguistic rules to follow the same designatum from world to world.

Although 'the property P such that: necessarily, P characterizes x if and only if x is a molecular motion' is not rigid de jure, its rigidity could hardly be considered controversial (Salmon 2003, pp. 486–7 suggests agreement): it would be hard to find a philosopher with such deviant metaphysical views that she opposes the suggestion that such a designator designates the same property from world to world, if it designates at all. So if 'the motion of molecules' is shorthand for something like the foregoing, then its status as a rigid designator for the property seems assured.

Many other descriptive property designators might be analyzed in something like the same fashion, to the same effect: this would include not only other definite-description resembling expressions such as 'the inability to metabolize glucose' and 'the combination of all of the colors of the visible spectrum' but also descriptive expressions that lack the article, such as 'H_2O', 'tender loving care', or 'open-hearted friendliness'. So 'open-hearted friendliness', for example, might be analyzed as expressing something like *the property P such that: necessarily P characterizes x if and only if x is friendly in an open-hearted manner*. The rigidity of such a designator seems assured even if the rigidity is de facto. As Plantinga indicates, even if such designators are not names, they might as well be names so far as rigidity is concerned (1974, p. 31).

2.1.2.4. A Defense of De Jure Rigidity Expressions like 'the motion of molecules', 'open-hearted friendliness', and so on, might be construed along lines that would render them rigid de facto: so I have just argued (in §2.1.2.3). But there are other plausible construals, some of which would render such designators rigid de jure: as I have indicated, rigid de jure expressions are those that are "*stipulated*" (Kripke 1980, p. 21, note 21) to designate the same individual from world to world, or that are "linguistically mandated" to do so (Baumann 2010, p. 343), or that designate the same individual from world to world by way of linguistic "rules" (Stanley 1997a, p. 582, note 40; Almog 1986, pp. 223ff.) or by other such design.

If 'the motion of molecules' is rigid de jure, then that expression is not shorthand for a description like 'the property P such that: necessarily, P characterizes x if and only if x is a molecular motion'; this would only assure de facto rigidity (as noted in §2.1.2.3). However, *de jure* rigidity could be secured in something *like* the way described for de facto rigidity (and perhaps other ways as well: again, see chapter 3, note 10). 'The motion of molecules' would rigidly designate the appropriate property de jure if, for example, the linguistic rules or proper procedures associated with 'the motion of molecules' were to direct the expression, in effect, to designate, with respect to any possible world, the very item that is *in fact* the property P such that necessarily, P characterizes x if and only if x is a molecular motion. Perhaps 'the motion of molecules' expresses the same as the world-indexed description: 'the property P in α such that: necessarily, P characterizes x if and only if x is a molecular motion'. Or perhaps the reference of 'the motion of molecules' is *fixed* by a description like 'the property P such that: necessarily, P characterizes x if and only if x is a molecular motion'. We have seen the appeal to world indexing and reference fixing fail to secure a properly theoretical expression in the case of 'the motion of molecules★' (in § 2.1.2.2.2), which is also rigid de jure. But that is because the description associated with 'the motion of molecules★' was too thin in essence-relevant content to equip the designator to serve in a theoretical identity statement. Here that problem is remedied by a better description (and the reader is free to take the remedy further with descriptions still richer in essence-relevant content). 'The motion of molecules' is assigned to a designatum by means that assure that the designatum is associated with moving molecules with respect to all possible worlds containing them: that tells something crucial about the designatum's essence.

To be sure, according to the account of de jure rigidity just limned, we do not assign a designatum to 'the motion of molecules' without regard to the designation of its parts, in the way that we might do for apparently simple components like 'motion' (but see the end of note 9), and in the way that we do for proper names like 'Phosphorus'. Rather, the rules of our language allow us to *construct* designators like 'the motion of molecules' from component words, in a way that *assures* that the complex designators are linked with the designata we are after. But it should not be supposed that compositionality precludes de jure rigidity. Natural language testifies otherwise: it seems to feature compositional but rigid de jure designators. Thus, if 'Socrates' is rigid de jure, this de jurity would presumably be inherited by 'that which is Socrates' or 'the thing Socrates'. World-indexing also seems to allow for compositional designators that are "rigid de jure" on a plausible construal, as I have indicated. 'The husband of Xantippe, in α', is an expression that many would count as "rigid de jure" (Almog 1986, pp. 223ff.; Stanley 1997a, p. 582, note 40; see also Plantinga 1985, pp. 82–7 and for closely related examples, Kaplan 1989b, p. 577, note 25 and Sidelle 1992b, p. 414) even though we do not bestow rigid status by *stipulating*, "Let 'the husband of Xantippe, in α' designate, with respect to any possible world, the same individual." The expression describes the individual according to a characteristic he has with respect to all possible worlds. Still, the sole purpose of world indexing is to allow a denoting expression to track the same designatum from world to world, by tying a thread to the designatum, so to speak, at the present world and then following the thread to find that individual at different possible worlds. There are other plausible examples of rigid de jure but compositional designators from English, as well.[9]

We can stipulate that any compositional designator formed according to certain rules is to follow the *same* object from world to world, just as we can stipulate, for a simple name, that it is to follow the same object from world to world. The language would in that case provide rules for generating an actual designatum and add a further rule to the effect that the designatum is not to vary from world to world. Of course, the rules governing use may be established tacitly, whether they concern simpler designators like 'motion' or more complex designators like 'the motion of molecules'.

Perhaps, again, theoretical expressions like 'the motion of molecules' or 'the combination of all of the colors of the visible spectrum' are not rigid de jure in English, not even tacitly. Again, it does not matter: the rigid designators that would serve in theoretical identity statements need not come from unrefined natural language. Just as we could introduce a designator that behaves in the manner described in the foregoing section (§2.1.2.3), we could introduce a designator that behaves in the manner described in the present section (§2.1.2.4). In either case, we could obtain for ourselves a term to do the needed work in theoretical identity statements.

It is time to draw a close to section (2.1). I began this section with the worry that theoretical expressions fail to be rigid and hence fail to uphold the necessity of theoretical identity statements in which they are embedded. I broached a suspicion on the part of some theorists that controversial essentialist intuitions serve as the real motivation behind the usual conviction of rigidity, no better motivation being available: perhaps, for example, our conviction in the truth of 'heat = the motion of molecules' and the rigidity of its designators has its source in a conviction that 'the motion of molecules' expresses the essence of what we have named 'heat'. That source of support would carry an unwelcome metaphysical price tag. But the suspicion has now been put to rest. There is good reason, which is independent of controversial essentialist intuitions like the foregoing, to recognize the rigidity of 'the motion of molecules' and other theoretical expressions that are well suited to serve in theoretical identity statements.

2.2. Theoretical Identity Statements Without Hidden Essentialist Costs

I have addressed one form of a widespread suspicion according to which interesting conclusions about theoretical identity statements that are reached with the help of rigidity cannot be embraced without a more costly metaphysical investment than first meets the eye: in the form in which I have addressed it (in the foregoing §2.1), the suspicion is that controversial essentialist intuitions support claims to *rigidity*. But the basic worry that arguments appealing to rigidity carry hidden essentialist costs need not locate the costs in support for rigidity.

Philosophers who call attention to the worry according to which the arguments appealing to rigidity carry hidden essentialist costs, apart from any costs introduced by the appeal to rigidity itself, usually locate themselves in a tradition stemming from the careful and detailed work of Nathan Salmon (1981).[10] If Salmon is right, popular accounts of the way that speakers secure reference with 'water' and 'H_2O', say, do not assure the necessity of 'water = H_2O' without some substantial essentialist input, even given the rigidity of the designators.

I will agree in what follows that *popular* accounts of the necessity of familiar theoretical identity statements *do* hinge on substantial essentialist intuitions, just as Salmon would have it. I will go on, however, to contend that *my own* arguments for the necessity of theoretical identity statements need not owe anything to such substantial essentialist support.[11]

Here is why popular accounts of the way that speakers secure reference to 'water' and 'H_2O' do not assure the necessity of 'water = H_2O', even given the rigidity of the designators, without some substantial essentialist input: a term like 'water' is supposed to acquire its use in something like a baptismal ceremony during which the speaker makes a pronouncement like, "I use 'water', with respect to various possible scenarios, for a type of *substance*: the one that happens to fill *that* valley" (the speaker points to a body of water: see Kripke 1980 and Putnam 1975). In view of empirical investigation following a baptism like the foregoing, we might be *inclined* to conclude that 'water' designates the same type of *chemical* with respect to all possible worlds: the type of chemical that 'H_2O' also designates with respect to all possible worlds. If this is a correct conclusion, then since the chemical structure of a chemical like H_2O would be essential to that *chemical*,[12] we would evidently also be entitled to conclude that the substance water's chemical structure is essential to it, as Kripke and Putnam would hold.

But even if many of us would be inclined to conclude, in view of scientific work and a baptism like the foregoing, that 'water' designates the same type of chemical with respect to all possible worlds and hence that the chemical structure of water is essential to it, the science and baptism together do not alone *license* this conclusion: the baptism assures only that 'water' designates, rigidly, a type of *substance*, namely the one present in certain samples. Whether the *chemical* H_2O, which scientists tell us is present in the baptismal samples, would qualify as a type of *substance* and hence whether it is what is baptized as the designatum, or whether instead the chemical H_2O would only happen to be *coinstantiated* with the substance water that is baptized as the designatum, is another issue. A philosopher is free, as Salmon would point out, to endorse the deliverances of chemistry and the foregoing baptism of 'water' while also holding "that the actual chemical structure of the substance water is only an accidental feature of the substance, and that the very same substance water can have a different chemical structure in different possible worlds" (Salmon 1981, p. 186). Such a position is suggested by Mellor, for one, who disputes the intuition that 'water' designates H_2O from possible world to possible world: "why should it?," he asks rhetorically. "Because its microstructure is an essential property of water? Well, that is what's in question" (1991a, p. 127; for similar sentiments, see Ahmed 2007, p. 63; Lowe 2008, p. 45; Margalit 1979, p. 34; Steward 1990, p. 391).

The familiar arguments for 'water = H_2O''s status as a genuine, essence-revealing theoretical identity statement do appeal to controverted essentialist intuitions about substancehood, then, in order to establish their conclusions. Those arguments do not appeal just to uncontested premises from science or obvious truths about language: this is an interesting observation (as I indicate in effect in LaPorte 2004, where I discuss terms from natural language: see especially chapters 3–6; see also LaPorte 2010 at note 6). Still, *without* any appeal to controversial essentialist costs like those just indicated rigidity secures an abundance of interesting, essence-exposing theoretical identity statements.

Interesting, essence-exposing theoretical identity statements can be secured without controverted essentialist input provided the relevant designators are coined with the proper baptismal ceremony (Salmon indicates as much: 2003, p. 488; see also Coppock's helpful discussion: 1984, pp. 266–70). A particular group of speakers could opt to use 'water' as a *chemical* term rather than a *substance* term: a group of scientists might point to a sample of liquid with the baptismal pronouncement, "we use 'water' for *that chemical*," or perhaps, "we use 'water' as a rigid designator for the abstract entity that is, in all possible worlds, AU or H_2O or C_2H_6O, or whatever similar item is the majority such item instantiated in *this* sample." Such a baptism circumvents worries like the foregoing about the essential properties of *substances*, which worries would tend to be raised by the corresponding vernacular term's baptismal pronouncements. Given the foregoing scientific use of 'water', it would seem that the relevant statement 'water = H_2O', which exposes the essence of a theoretically interesting entity, is secured without controversial essentialist input in the form of philosophical intuitions to whose disputability the Salmonesque tradition rightly calls attention.

Scientists sometimes adopt a refined, somewhat technical use of terms in the manner just indicated, in order to reduce disagreement or indeterminacy surrounding lay speech (elsewhere I discuss examples: LaPorte 2010 at note 14). Appeals to refined scientific uses of terms cannot by fiat settle controversial questions about the essential nature of *substances* and other murky subjects whose nature is relevant to the vernacular use of pre-refined correlates to refined uses. Refining merely allows speakers to *circumvent* the foregoing controversial questions by directing attention to what might, for all that the relevant baptisms assure, be different designata: the designata of refined terms, whose natures are more straightforwardly discerned than are the natures of the designata of pre-refined terms. The reorientation to a new subject is a highly important service, if the designata to which our attention is newly directed, such as the designatum of the *chemical* term 'water', which is straightforwardly essentially H_2O, are what is really of interest to us or are a suitable alternative subject matter. A scientifically refined use of 'water' is sufficient for my purposes in this book, where representing natural language is secondary in importance to the investigation of what property designators' rigidity accomplishes in any interesting statements that we are able to use.

It is time to draw morals for section (2), which has discussed alleged costs associated with affirming rigidity or with affirming theoretical identity statements given rigidity. Rigidity and the theoretical identity statements like 'water = H_2O' that rigidity helps to establish can be affirmed without substantial cost or controversy. It is possible that 'water' needs refinement, in order to assure *rigidity*. It might also need refinement along scientific lines, in order to assure that the designatum has the right sort of essence. Theoretical expressions like 'H_2O' might also require refinement (to achieve similar ends: see note 12). Since little rides on proper vernacular use of words, I would be happy to use 'water$_{precisified}$' in place of 'water', to indicate properly refined use, whatever the motivating need. Similarly, I would be happy to use '$H_2O_{precisified}$', to indicate properly refined use (e.g., a use matching that of '$H_2O\star\star$' or '$H_2O\star\star\star$': see §2.1.2.2.2). The reader may perform the terminological substitution where I rely on context to clarify the intended uses. The necessity of 'water$_{precisified}$ = $H_2O_{precisified}$' depends, it would seem, just on uncontroversial observations about the use of 'water$_{precisified}$', which is clarified in the baptism discussed in the foregoing paragraphs, and on uncontroversial observations about the use of '$H_2O_{precisified}$' (described in §2.1.2) and on uncontroversial empirical observations from chemists.[13]

3. Conclusion

I have addressed in this chapter objections to rigidity-based arguments that are supposed to support theoretical identity statements. The objections concern whether the supporting arguments are significant and convincing. I have maintained that the arguments are significant and convincing. Hence, the arguments uphold the significance of rigidity.

It is time now to turn to the many objections that have tended to take aim just at skeptical arguments appealing to rigidity, which arguments center around psychophysical identity statements. These objections form a vast tradition focused more or less narrowly on the mind–body problem.

Notes

1. Kim's charge is even broader in scope than this: it threatens not only theoretical *identity* statements but also corresponding *biconditionals* (see, e.g., 2005, p. 137). So Kim's charge, if successful, would be especially destructive, relegating to insignificance even reformulations of arguments about identity, which discuss identi*fication* instead (again, see chapter 5, §1).
2. I thank Alvin Plantinga and Ori Simchen for articulating variations of the objection. It might not represent the considered view of either: it certainly does not represent the considered view of Plantinga, who recognizes a response to the objection similar to the response I provide.
3. The objection that some phenomenon other than rigidity, such as direct reference, gives rise to rigidity and thereby draws importance from rigidity, is apparently in some way inspired by a look at property designators (see, e.g., Soames 2002, pp. 262–4 and passim; see also 2006a, p. 651; Devitt 2005, p. 159 and passim), which is why I address the objection in detail; but the objection would seem to undermine the significance of rigidity in general if it undermines the significance of an extension of rigidity to property designators, as the relevant critics seem to recognize (Soames 2002, p. 264; Devitt 2005, pp. 140, 145, 148). For a brief rejoinder on behalf of rigidity that is similar in spirit to some of the foregoing, see Salmon (2005, p. 121).
4. Lewis would be under no illusions about the failure of 'heat = the motion of molecules', as he understands that expression, to expose what it is to be heat. A theoretical identity statement exposing *what it is to be heat* would not, according to Lewis, spotlight heat itself, the mere occupant of the heat role; instead, a theoretical identity statement exposing what it is to be heat would spotlight the "highly disjunctive and extrinsic" functional property of *occupying the heat role* (Lewis 1999a, p. 45. For Lewis' distinction between 'heat' and 'to be heat' or similar expressions, compare Lewis 1983c with Lewis 1983a, pp. 86–7; 1983b, p. 101; 1999c, p. 307; it might be necessary to clarify the right reading of 'to be heat' or substitutes, as I indicate in chapter 1, note 10; I characterize theoretical identity statements in chapter 1, §2 and I indicate why rigidity is a crucial component of theoretical identity statements in chapter 3 in a discussion at the end of §1).
5. 'Heat*' would rigidly designate the motion of molecules on either Lewis' preferred account or mine, at any rate, since 'heat*' is coined as a rigid designator for the actual designatum of 'heat', which Lewis grants is the motion of molecules. I would restate how to coin 'heat*' in order to accommodate an alternative functionalist position according to which 'heat' is a *rigid* designator for the functional property of *occupying the heat role*, rather than a *non*rigid designator for whatever *realizes* the relevant functional property (see chapter 7, note 6 for a discussion of these two varieties of functionalism).
6. Kripke, too, apparently favors stipulative measures to assure rigidity, where doubts arise. At one point he considers that a certain theoretical designator might turn out not to be rigid, but he dismisses the problem quickly. If the expression "is not a rigid designator, simply replace it by one which is, or suppose it used as a rigid designator in the present context" (1980, p. 149). But because it might easily be doubted whether a stipulative remedy could successfully secure rigidity for theoretical expressions (see the text below the marker for this note for complications introduced by these expressions), some explanation to assure that it could do so is desirable. Further, it is not obvious without explanation why a stipulative measure, or indeed any measure at all to assure the rigidity of name-like designators or theoretical expressions, is

needed if familiar theoretical statements containing these expressions, like 'heat = the motion of molecules' and 'pain = c-fiber firing', are to command the interest that is expected of them (for discussion of this further issue, see chapter 3, §1). Kripke seems to presuppose that rigidity is needed but one might suppose otherwise, in view of those who take such statements to be contingently true on account of nonrigidity (I have cited references in this chapter, §2.1.1; for more, see chapter 7, §1.2.1). Important Kripkean arguments turn on the matter. Indeed, one author claims that "the standard way for materialists or naturalists to avoid Kripke's concerns" is to deny the rigidity of terms like 'pain' (Polger 2004, p. 39; see also pp. 42–3): if nonrigidity issues in a sufficiently substantive, contingently true interpretation of 'pain = c-fiber firing', then we will have the psychophysical identity we are looking for, and we may accordingly ignore Kripke's criticisms as irrelevant, pertaining as they do to an alternative interpretation instead according to which the designators would be rigid (I oppose this strategy, whose appeal is strong even if overstated by Polger, in chapter 7, §1.2.1, including at note 6, where I presuppose the present chapter's establishment of rigidity: §2.1).

7. Of course, it is another matter whether a given use of 'the motion of molecules' is stipulated to be shorthand for 'the property P such that: necessarily, P characterizes x if and only if x is a molecular motion', as it *would* be on a use to which I might appeal in the event that natural language does not provide me with a rigid reading for 'the motion of molecules'. But *this* stipulation does not render the expression stipulatively *rigid* and hence de jure rigid.

8. I have shown how deviant reasoning could uphold the position that there are worlds at which the relevant designator fails to apply to P. Related deviant reasoning could uphold the position that there are worlds at which the relevant designator applies to some other property *rather than* P: perhaps at some or all worlds w at which P is an object of some other category, and at which something similar holds for other potential properties, there is just one property P_w, which exists at only a few worlds, none which contain molecules in motion or anything that instantiates P_w. If so, then P_w trivially satisfies the description at w (in affirming the described necessity, I ignore as usual worlds at which the designatum P_w fails to exist: see chapter 1, §1.2).

9. Further examples of rigid de jure but compositional designators from the language that we speak might be provided by complex numerals, say. No one has gone through and assigned, one by one, names in the form of numerals to each of the numbers for which our language permits ready designation in the form of a numeral; instead, we construct a numeral for a number like 40 or 40,000,000 out of the numerals '4' and '0', and assign the numeral its designatum in accordance with systematic rules. But that might not make numerals rigid *definite descriptions* (Kripke agrees in unpublished lectures: see Berger 2002, p. 62, note 23), which are the expressions with which Kripke associates de facto rigidity (1980, p. 21, note 21); consider, for example, that the instructions, so to speak, leading a complex numeral to attach to a designatum, might not be *expressed* by the numeral and so might not render the numeral descriptive (see chapter 8, §2.2.2). Even if the instructions *do* issue from a definite description expressing them, the numeral still might be rigid de jure: world-indexed definite descriptions are rigid de jure definite descriptions. There are yet further salient possibilities for the semantics of numerals that respect de jure rigidity (for an adaptable idea, see chapter 3, §2.4.1). If numerals rigidly designate numbers de jure, even if these expressions are constructed according to rules of numeral formation, then perhaps McCaffery is right to call them "compositional names" (1999, p. 427; see also Berger 2002, p. 62). Relevantly similar

expressions might include 'January 1, 2007', which has been proposed as a semantically complex name for a day (McCaffery 1999, p. 423; but cf. King 2001) and 'that England is a monarchy', which Russell apparently took at one time as a genuine, though semantically complex, name for a proposition (see the discussion in Kripke 2005, p. 1007, note 7). Other expressions that might plausibly be held to be both compositional and rigid de jure include general-term phrases (again, see chapter 3, §2.4.1) and certain general terms formed from other terms: e.g., 'Michigander' (from 'Michigan').

10. See, e.g., Drewery (2004, p. 315); Lowe (2007, pp. 31–2); Martí (2004, pp. 142–3); Mumford (2006, pp. 53f., 62); Steward (1990, pp. 385–6, note 1); Schwartz (2006, p. 285) makes closely related claims as does Mackie (2006, pp. 186ff.; see especially pp. 198–200), despite some sympathy for the position that the relevant essentialism follows from the theory of direct reference. I would deny that it does (see also Robertson 2009, pp. 135ff.), though there are notable points of agreement between Mackie's claims and mine. An exception who does not cite Salmon but who expresses much the same worry as those in the tradition is Collins (1988, p. 207). For further discussion of the Salmonesque tradition, see Bird and Tobin (2009, §3.4) and Beebee and Sabbarton-Leary (2010, §2.2).

11. Discussions in the Salmonesque tradition tend to suggest that, or at least fail to clarify whether, arguments from rigidity for theoretical identity statements' necessity are inevitably indebted to controversial essentialism: cf. some of the different sources cited in note 10. Such arguments are not inevitably so indebted. Salmon has indicated that he would not be under any illusions here (as I will suggest in the text).

12. A "chemical" may be understood by example to be the sort of entity that in fact serves as a designatum of a term like 'H_2O' and 'C_2H_6O'. It is easier to doubt whether a *substance* has the same chemical structure from world to world than whether a *chemical* does; but I address those who doubt whether a chemical has the same chemical structure from world to world, in effect, in §2.1.2 of this chapter. Arguments there, to the effect that chemical terms like 'H_2O' and 'C_2H_6O' rigidly designate, on the relevant readings anyway, assure that the terms rigidly designate what is, with respect to all possible worlds, H_2-O and C_2-H_6-O: i.e., what meets certain structural requirements.

13. An affirmation of 'water$_{precisified}$ = $H_2O_{precisified}$' commits one to *realism* about properties; but again, chapter 5 explains how to get around this commitment. There really is something of a free metaphysical lunch here. Or rather, it is better to say that the lunch has already been covered by the time we talk about the entities in question, as part of the cost of our using the relevant terms for the entities as we use them. Of course, we cannot be said to *generate* substantial essentialist truths on the cheap merely by adopting the right use of terms (at least not on my preferred account: see §1.2; cf. Lowe's worry: 2008, p. 25). But speakers sufficiently conscious about their use of terms to be able to use them in the first place in the manner I have specified would normally recognize upon reflection that they are thereby committed to the essentialism in question. Indeed, in order so much as to acknowledge singular rigid designation requires presupposing a minimum of essentialism: and it would seem to be because this connection is so clear that essentialism has been rendered popular by the broad acceptance of rigidity. Appeals to general terms' rigid designation would be less committal on this score (see chapter 5, §1.2.2), although I would argue that such appeals are not without their metaphysical commitments, too, however little controversy these commitments might prompt; at any rate, I will elaborate here on the singular case to give a sense

of some of the essentialist commitments that are undertaken in presupposing rigid designation. Cartwright observes suggestively, "The *name* 'Shakespeare' is rigid only if the *man* Shakespeare could not have existed without being Shakespeare – or, as we might equally well say, only if it is essential to Shakespeare that he is Shakespeare" (Cartwright 1998, p. 69). So if Shakespeare could have been Obama instead of Shakespeare, 'Shakespeare' would not be rigid. More basic still is the observation that an object has to be essentially itself and not another object in order to be the designatum of a rigid designator; otherwise the designator could not designate it and no other object with respect to all possible worlds, which is what a designator would have to do in order to qualify as rigid. But again, while essentialist input cannot be eliminated from appeals to singular rigid designation, essentialist input can be minimized, and more-or-less controversial essentialist input can be eliminated, by the right use of terms: this right use can, as I have emphasized, be established by stipulation if necessary.

7

The Skeptical Argument Impugning Psychophysical Identity Statements: on its Significance and the Cost of its Philosophical Resources

In the present chapter, I continue the discussion over whether rigidity-associated arguments supporting or impugning various theoretical identity statements are significant and convincing. I address objections directed primarily against the skeptical arguments associated with psychophysical identity statements (offered in chapter 1, §2.2). Most of the objections that I will entertain in the present chapter could be generalized, so readers inclined to direct one or another objection at constructive arguments supporting this or that theoretical identity statement can make the necessary adjustments to my presentation of the objection and the response.

In section (1), I address objections to the effect that the skeptical arguments, even if convincing, are not significant. Then, in section (2), I address objections to the effect that the skeptical arguments are not convincing, appealing as they allegedly do to resources that come at too high a cost.

1. Significance

Here I uphold the significance of the skeptical arguments, or of that skeptical argument that concerns the psychophysical identity of choice. If my defense stands, then whether the argument is convincing, a question for later, matters.

1.1. *Against Specific Psychophysical Identities, Not Materialism*

The conclusions endorsed here regarding psychophysical identity statements are weaker than Kripke's. At least some strands in Kripke suggest that he is out to undermine materialism with the conclusion that it is doubtful whether there is any true psychophysical identity statement like 'pain = c-fiber firing' or, to vary the subject matter, 'consciousness = pyramidal cell activity' (cf. Crick 1994, pp. 250–3; see also

256–7; Block and Stalnaker 1999, pp. 1, 43), 'phenomenal quality Q = cortico thalamic oscillation (of a certain sort)' (Block 2002, p. 394), and so on (see also Papineau 2002, pp. 141, 144). Thus, Kripke closes "Identity and Necessity" with the announcement that, "the analytical tools we are using go against the identity thesis and so go against the general thesis that mental states are just physical states" (1971, p. 163; see also 1980, pp. 100, 155). By contrast, the argument endorsed here does not conclude that it is doubtful whether there is any true psychophysical identity statement; instead it concludes, for any psychophysical identity statement, that it is doubtful whether that statement is true. Such a conclusion does not necessarily undermine materialism. The relevant contrast resembles that between saying that it is doubtful whether any lotto ticket has a winning number, on the one hand, and saying that for any given lotto ticket, it is doubtful whether it has a winning number, on the other hand. There might be reason to suppose that there are some winning tickets even if we are not in a position to say which tickets are winners so that there is scant reason to suppose that you or I hold a winner. In the same way, there might be reason to believe that there are true psychophysical identity statements, even if we are not in a position to say which psychophysical identity statements are true, and even if there is accordingly scant reason to suppose, of any given psychophysical identity statement, that it is true. I will argue that we are not in a position to say which psychophysical identity statements are true and that our position will not be improved by the progress of empirical science: psychophysical identity statements, the holy grail of theoretical identity statements, are out of reach.

In view of the contrast between the conclusion endorsed here and what seems to have been Kripke's original conclusion, the reader might wonder why I have not embraced the conclusion that no mental state is physical, and whether the alternative conclusion here is of interest. These are the questions that will occupy me in the present section (§1.1).

1.1.1. Why Not Conclude that No Psychophysical Identity Statement is True? Kripke's argument, according to which it is doubtful whether any psychophysical identity statement is true, is now dated. The argument criticizes an attempt to rescue materialism from unwelcome modal intuitions pressed by a tradition from Descartes. On its face, materialism calls for some apology: our modal intuitions suggest that material phenomena like c-fiber firing are separable from phenomenal properties like pain. Kripke recalls a prominent attempt to come to terms with this problem, "common to philosophical discussions of materialism" in his day: it was to claim that pain is *contingently* identical with c-fiber firing. Such thinking "enabled philosophers *simultaneously* to think of certain designators as if they were nonrigid (and hence found in 'contingent identities') *and* as if they were rigid" general names (1980, p. 4). Kripke points out that if *that* is the excuse for not following modal intuitions where they lead, materialism is a failure: "Someone who wishes to maintain an identity thesis cannot simply *accept* the Cartesian intuitions" that the mental and physical are separable, yet maintain identity between them (1980, p. 148). Nor can the Cartesian intuitions be handled in the way that they can be for 'water = H_2O', which on its face also seems to be a contingent identity; a closer look indicates that we can come to see that water and H_2O are not separable after all, given some empirical assumptions about the chemical structure actually underlying certain samples of matter baptized "water." 'Pain = c-fiber firing' cannot be secured in the same way as 'water = H_2O'. So if modal intuitions of what is separable and what is not have a claim on us, as "the usual forms of materialism" presupposed, and as Kripke seems to presuppose as well (1980, p. 155), a proper understanding of rigidity undermines materialism.

Philosophical presuppositions have changed. Having profited from Kripke's arguments, most philosophers today respond by rejecting outright the reliability of Cartesian modal intuitions according to which a mental state is separable from the corresponding physical state. "The majority of contemporary materialists" begin, as Papineau says, with an important "concession to the classic antimaterialist arguments" of Kripke and others (Papineau 2007b, p. 111). That concession is that the *concept* of a phenomenal property like pain that we form from the *internal* perspective of a pain-wracked patient is different from the concept that we form from the external or scientific perspective of a neurologist who studies pain, even though both concepts refer to the same thing. Conceptual dualism is coupled with ontological monism for these philosophers: there is only one property pain for them and it is a physical or functional property.

Since conceptual dualism is the most salient position in the field in the wake of Kripke's arguments,[1] it would be fruitless to continue to push Kripke's own arguments, which presuppose rather than directly argue that Cartesian modal intuitions have a prima facie claim to reflect ontology with accuracy. To push Kripke's arguments would beg questions against typical materialists.

By way of keeping Kripkean antimaterialist arguments current, we could turn our attention directly on the Cartesian intuitions whose prima facie claim to our allegiance Kripke presupposes: we could try to develop and generalize those intuitions with a view to vindicating them or at least making them coherent and attractive. Chalmers and others take up this cause. But I for one find Chalmers' modal rationalism, which rejects a tradition from the middle ages, according to which certain necessities are not discernible by our intellect, to be too potent (so, apparently, does Kripke: Chalmers, for example, rejects the claim that physical necessity might turn out to be full-scale necessity: 1999, pp. 483–5; Kripke remains open on this issue: 1980, p. 99; I discuss modal rationalism further in §2.3). More importantly, even though I find materialism problematic, as do Kripke and Chalmers, I do not know of any replacement for Chalmers' modal rationalism that I would find attractive and that would testify against materialism without begging important questions.

There is, however, a different sort of Kripkean argument that still finds traction against materialist accounts: arguments of this sort address materialist optimism about whether the empirical sciences are capable of confirming specific psychophysical identities. Even if the untrustworthiness of our modal intuitions renders us unable to conclude that materialism is false, it is hard to see how we could ever assure ourselves of identity in any given case. The Cartesian intuition of distinctness between the phenomenal and the physical, trustworthy or not, prevents us from seeing our way to identity by ordinary a priori reasoning. Nor can we confirm psychophysical identity statements in the same way as we do 'water = H_2O'. It is hard to see how else we could ever close off the possibility of separation between any phenomenal component and any physical or functional component of an alleged identity. Yet we cannot concede separability and appeal to contingent identity; that route is closed by consideration of rigid designation. So prospects seem grim that we will ever be in a position to learn the truth of a psychophysical identity statement that finally reveals for us the nature of pain or consciousness or the like. That is the thrust of the argument that I propose.

The argument that I propose remains telling, then, even if we concede with the majority of materialists today that we are modally blind in the relevant respect so that there is no good argument from conceivability against materialism. The argument also remains telling even if there *are* convincing arguments *for* materialism. So it may be that the ever-popular causal argument, which appeals to troubles attending would-be causal interactions between the mental and physical realms, establishes that some form of materialism or other obtains (Bates 2009, pp. 319–20; Levine 2001, p. 16; 1998, p. 475; Papineau 2002, chapter 1; Patterson recounts the tradition in favor, from recent decades: 2008, pp. 572ff.; Lucretius's focused discussion testifies to the ancient origin of the argument: *De Rerum Natura* III.161–78; for criticisms of the argument, see Bishop 2006; Kim 2005, p. 125; Chalmers 2003, p. 125; distinguished forbears include Aquinas: *Summa Theologiae* 1a.75.1; see also Locke's *An Essay Concerning Human Understanding* IV.3.6, pp. 539–43). But even if the causal argument establishes that some form of materialism or other obtains, we are still destined to remain, with the ancients who also enjoyed access to that argument, unable to specify in a satisfactory way the *essential nature* of mental phenomena that are at bottom physical or functional.

The skeptical argument presented here has no ambitions to refute materialism, then. Even so, the argument might be considered bad news for materialism. That is because it precludes our chances of obtaining what might otherwise be satisfying closure to the issue of the physical nature of phenomenal events, in the face of so much philosophical disagreement. The argument from causation for physicalism is not going to bring everyone together. The same can be said for other broad philosophical considerations. Compelling empirical evidence for a scientific identity, one might suppose, could do better: it has allowed us to come to agreement about whether Hesperus = Phosphorus and whether Brontosaurus = Apatosaurus. With a little more trouble (see chapter 6, § 2.2), we could produce agreement that water is identical with a certain chemical, that life is identical with a conjunction of functions like metabolism and reproduction that scientists have found common to life, and so on. Yet if the skeptical argument is sound then no such clear resolution, according to which pain is this or that physical or functional property, is forthcoming.[2]

1.1.2. Psychophysical Identities: Is What Eludes us Just Conceptual or Explanatory? Someone unconvinced that there is anything at stake might reason as follows. "Kripke's conclusion is about the nature of mental states: it purports to undermine materialism. The conclusion here is merely epistemic; it is not about the nature of mental states but rather concerns our cognitive position with respect to mental states. Does the conclusion amount to anything more than an affirmation of conceptual dualism, which is widely acknowledged anyway?"

The foregoing line of reasoning is mistaken on more than one salient score. The first point to observe, something of a detail, is that my argument *is* about the nature of mental states: the argument casts doubt severally on *specific* psychophysical identities, which concern the nature of pain and the like.

A second point to observe is that conceptual dualism, though familiar as a response to the mind – body problem, is a more potent position than the foregoing line of reasoning suggests: it stands opposed to the increasingly visible tradition of arguments offered on behalf of *scientific necessitarianism*, according to which physical necessity is metaphysically necessary too (as I will explain in chapter 8, §3). This conflict merits an investigation, which I will provide in effect, as I investigate the related conflict between the *skeptical argument* and arguments aiming to establish scientific necessitarianism. Although, as I will point out in a moment, the skeptical argument concludes with something more than mere conceptual dualism, both its conclusion and conceptual dualism stand opposed to the tradition of arguments aiming to establish necessitarianism. Indeed, much of what is interesting about the skeptical argument has to do with what it shows about our conceptual powers to discern the structure of how things are by necessity in the world (see chapter 8, §3.6). There is more at stake than materialism.

But the most important point to observe in response to the foregoing question as to whether the phenomenon to which I point is concept – property dualism is the answer to the question: the phenomenon to which I point is *not* concept – property dualism. I have argued that we face an *evidential* shortcoming, which undermines the identity theorist's entitlement to affirm 'pain = c-fiber firing'; I have not argued that we face a *conceptual* shortcoming to the effect that we cannot avoid thinking of a single property from something like two distinct perspectives. Perhaps we do suffer from a conceptual dualism in our thinking, some sort of inability to unite two distinct perspectives; but we suffer from a problem of an evidential nature too, which is distinct from conceptual dualism and which is disturbing if indeed there are true psychophysical identities.

What I have said about conceptual dualism applies also to the frequently mentioned "explanatory gap" (Levine 1983; 1993; 1998; 2001), which might be characterized as our "current inability to supply a suitably intelligible link" between pain and c-fiber firing (Van Gulick 2004, §5.2). Various laws and observations concerning brain functions do not reveal how c-fiber firing amounts to painfulness: some revelation like that is what closing the gap would require (Levine 2001, p. 74). But the problem with which I have been concerned is not that we are unable to provide an intelligible link between pain and c-fiber firing or to see how laws and observations about brain functions could reveal how c-fiber firing amounts to painfulness. The problem with which I have been concerned is that we are in no position to find grounds for affirming that c-fiber firing amounts to painfulness. The problems are distinct. It is one thing to ask for an *explanation* or some suitable *conceptual illumination* of an identity; it is another, as one author correctly observes, to "ask for *reasons to believe* that we've found a true identity, rather than a mere correlation of distinct entities" (Weisberg 2007, p. 85).[3]

The relationship between conceptual or explanatory difficulties and evidential ones is a delicate relationship that need not be sorted out in great generality here. But since some philosophers seem to believe, contrary to what I have just said, that evidential problems of the sort in question would follow straightforwardly from a conceptual or explanatory gap (see, e.g., Kim 2005, p. 138; for similar claims see Clark 1997, p. 46), I take a moment to indicate that things are more complicated. To see that evidential problems do not follow as a matter of course from explanatory and conceptual problems, consider a related case helpfully positioned some distance away from the controversial terrain of psychophysical identities: your observations of bees might leave you with a conceptual or explanatory gap that has no evidential correlate. Careful observation leaves you with enough *evidence* that bees' wing motion lifts them into the air so that 'flight = what bees actually achieve with their wings' is true. Even so, the best available calculations and current understanding of principles and laws might indicate that flight by means of this type of flapping *should* be aerodynamically "impossible," as puzzled scientists have pronounced it (Altshuler et al. 2005, p. 18213; see also Caltech Media Relations 2005). Hence, you might have trouble, with many others since the 1930s, explaining how flight could be what bees actually achieve with their wings. You might also, it would seem, be unable to reconcile two distinct ways of *thinking* about what bees achieve with their wings: you recognize that bees achieve flight with their wings, because you watch bees fly as they flap their wings; but you may also think of what bees achieve with their wings as what should amount to such and such sequence of awkward, lift-free interactions with the environment. If the foregoing considerations are right, then you might be troubled by a salient explanatory gap and an awkward two-fold way of thinking about the subject matter, even though you do not seem to lack any *evidence* concerning the truth of the relevant attending identity statement.

One way to establish identity between a subject under investigation and a theoretical property would be to *see* that the instantiation of either *necessitates* the instantiation of the other. For that, we would need to be able to close whatever cognitive gaps might have prevented us from seeing the necessity (again, I discuss prospects of establishing psychophysical identities by this route in chapter 8, §3). But there might be other ways to establish identity. A proponent of conceptual dualism, who denies that we can see our way through the relevant necessity, is not obviously thereby precluded from optimism concerning our evidential prospects with respect to whatever identities she acknowledges, whether psychophysical identities or some other sort of theoretical identities; mere adherence to dualism is not much testimony that Papineau and others are on a wrong track when they acknowledge only a "temporary ignorance" of the truth of specific theoretical identity statements (Papineau 2007a, p. 491; see also Musacchio 2005, p. 435; Polcyn 2005, pp. 50, 53; Polger 2004, p. 58). Similar words apply to the explanatory gap: those who would embrace the relevant explanatory troubles are not obviously thereby committed to recognizing the evidential troubles (again, practice suggests as much: see for references Patterson 2008, pp. 571f.). If adherents to conceptual or explanatory difficulties are not entitled to optimism concerning the establishment of psychophysical identities specifically, this needs to be shown.

In sum, then, conceptual or explanatory difficulties must be distinguished from evidential ones. And if the relevant conceptual or explanatory difficulties are acknowledged, there is still work to be done to establish that there are also evidential difficulties. The skeptical conclusions that I defend concerning our evidential position are not stripped of significance by the broad acknowledgement of familiar conceptual and explanatory problems.

1.2. Is Type Identity Irrelevant?

I have urged that psychophysical identity statements are out of reach, in that we are not and should expect not to be in any position to confirm them by way of gathering evidence of a sort that might confirm certain other theoretical identity statements. But perhaps the loss of psychophysical identity statements is not really so grave a matter after all. Some materialists suggest, along these lines, that psychophysical identity statements are irrelevant or dispensable, from the perspective of a right-minded materialist, because they concern *types*. If that is right then the familiar skeptical arguments concerning psychophysical identity statements may be dismissed as inconsequential: such arguments show only that we cannot know the truth of statements that are irrelevant or dispensable anyway.

The reason type identity is often said to be irrelevant or dispensable is that materialists[4] are free to endorse multiple realizability, and in particular functionalist versions of multiple realizability according to which no *biological* type, like a specific brain state, could amount to pain. On such a position, the type pain could be realized not only in organisms like us with brains of carbon but also in silicone beings (Patterson recounts the tradition of appealing to multiple realizability instead of type identity: 2008, pp. 545, 552, 554f, 573; for an extended discussion of multiple realizability, see Bickle 2008). So even if materialists should identify each particular pain, which is one of many *tokens* all of which belong to the type pain, with a particular brain event, it is much less clear that they should identify the type pain with any type of brain event. Perhaps it is token identity that matters, if identity matters at all, and not type identity that matters.

Or perhaps identity as a whole matters less than philosophers have thought and we ought to concern ourselves with supervenience. If pain *supervenes* on some physical property like brain state C, then necessarily something with brain state C is in pain; but something might be in pain without being in brain state C, since that mental property can have multiple supervenience bases (Kim 1993, pp. 65, 98–9; 1998, pp. 7–10). Kim accordingly explains why supervenience has drawn so much attention from multiple-realizability theorists: "in allowing multiple supervenience bases for supervenient properties, it offered a perfect scheme for accommodating the multiple realizability of mental properties" (1998, pp. 7–8). Again, the importance of identity might seem to be eclipsed.

It might appear, then, that the skeptical argument concerning prospects for confirming psychophysical identities (from chapter 1, §2.2) is an argument of no consequence, concerning as it does type identity statements: that is the threat at hand. I will argue, in response, that the skeptical argument is of consequence. There are a few points to be made in this connection. The first point is this: provided that pain can be realized by any number of properties, as the objection would have it, then pain is also *identical* to some theoretical property that is multiply realized. So multiple realizability is after all compatible with type identity. I will argue for this first point in section (1.2.1). A second point on behalf of the skeptical argument, which concerns type identity, is that to give up the search for psychophysical identities and to turn our attention instead to supervenience or token identity would be to concede unwelcome defeat: statements of supervenience or token identity are no replacement, in terms of the information that they provide, for theoretical identity statements about types. I will argue for this point in section (1.2.2). A third and final point to be made on behalf of the skeptical argument against psychophysical identities is that the skeptical argument can be adjusted to address supervenience instead of type identity. It can also be adjusted to address token identity. So even if type identity *were* to yield its importance to supervenience or token identity, the skeptical argument could be recast to restore its significance. I will argue for this point in section (1.2.3.).

1.2.1. Type Identity Obtains if Multiple Realizability Does If we grant that there are true claims of multiple realizability, then we should grant that there are corresponding true claims of type identity: theoretical identity statements (cf. by contrast Carruthers 2000, p. 48; Kirk 2003, pp. 52–4; Sidelle 1992a, p. 276). Consider diabetes, which is realized by the body's inability to produce insulin, a hormone that is needed for metabolism. This inability to produce insulin is not what diabetes *is*. On the contrary, diabetes arises also if the body *produces* the insulin but is unable to *use* it, owing to a problem with insulin receptors. Further, *each* of these routes to obtaining diabetes can have various sources: a viral attack on the pancreas or any of various genetic defects can lead to production difficulties. So diabetes is realized by any number of conditions none of which is identical to that malady. Surely if there *is* such a property as diabetes to be realized by these diverse conditions, then there would have to be some accurate account, at least in principle, of *what* diabetes is. So some theoretical identity statement or other, however subtle, would truthfully expose what diabetes is. As it happens, diabetes is the inability to metabolize glucose, so the relevant theoretical identity statement would be 'diabetes = the inability to metabolize glucose'.[5]

What applies to diabetes applies to pain, too: if there *is* such a property as pain to be realized by different conditions, then there would have to be some accurate account, at least in principle, of *what* pain is. So some theoretical identity statement or other, however subtle, would express what it is. Given functionalism, that theoretical identity statement would have to appeal, on the side that designates by way of a theoretically laden expression, to the proper functional role, which might be subtle and complicated, which any token pain would need to fill by virtue of being a pain. Because 'pain' designates, according to the functionalist position in question, a multiply realized functional property, the relevant theoretical identity statement would be 'pain = the state of occupying functional role P', where 'P' abbreviates the right multiply realized functional property.

Some functionalists complicate the foregoing line of thinking somewhat; but they do not upset it. "Realizer" functionalists maintain that 'pain' does not designate rigidly a *functional* property but instead designates nonrigidly what realizes a functional property: brain state C, say, in this world, and brain state B in some other world (Lewis 1983b, pp. 101–2; 1999b, pp. 248–9, 257; 1999c, pp. 303ff.; Jackson, Pargetter, and Prior 1982, pp. 216–19; Carruthers is also sympathetic: 2000, pp. 47–8; cf. Tye, for contrast: 2006, pp. 151, 164–5; Bennett 2007 helpfully discusses the contrast). Although for realizer functionalists 'pain' nonrigidly designates what realizes a functional role, 'to be pain' or 'pain as such' rigidly designates the functional role itself. '*To be* pain = to occupy functional role P' would accordingly become a theoretical identity statement about the functional property for these theorists, where 'P' abbreviates the right multiply realized functional property. It would be possible to formulate an alternative theoretical identity statement about the realizer, too.[6]

Multiple realizability theorists, and functionalists specifically, cannot give up type identity. I do not mean to suggest that this has escaped the notice of philosophers in general, but common terminology suggests otherwise. So Michael Tye, say, would presumably recognize that he is a type identity theorist strictly speaking, even though in his own terminology "type" theorists hold, incorrectly for Tye, that pains and other phenomenal types are identical with neurophysiological states or properties. "Functionalists, by contrast, hold that consciousness and its various species are identical with *functional-role* states or properties" (Tye 2006, p. 166: my emphasis; see also Bates 2009, p. 316; Block and Stalnaker 1999, p. 24; Levin 2010, §1).

Since functionalists, who hold that pain is multiply realized, should recognize theoretical identity statements about phenomenal properties, the skeptical argument applies to functionalism. In representing the theoretical identity statement evaluated by the argument, I will typically use 'pain = c-fiber firing', but let functionalists or others substitute their preferred theoretical identity statement, which might be 'pain = functional property P', 'to be pain = to be the occupant of functional role P', etc. Similarly where I speak of "psychophysical identities," functionalists may substitute 'psychofunctional identities'. The skeptical argument applies with a minimum of adjustments, thereby accommodating multiple realizability theorists.

In observing that multiple-realizability theorists are committed to type identity, we must distinguish multiple-realizability theorists from *eliminativists* about higher-level properties that would be multiply realized. Eliminativists concerning higher-level properties agree that different so-called "lower-level" properties, such as this or that brain state, give rise to pain and other alleged "higher-level" properties. But eliminativists concerning higher-level properties do not regard pain to be a property at all; it is, for them, a mere heterogeneous collection of phenomena sharing a name. Accordingly, they reject multiple realizability, understood as the thesis "that a single mental kind (property, state, event) can be realized by many distinct physical kinds" (Bickle 2008, opening paragraph): no higher-level property is multiply realized according to the eliminativist position at issue (for discussion, see, on the side of eliminativism, Armstrong 1997, pp. 26–8 and Mellor 1991b; cf., by contrast, Jubien 1989, pp. 168–9; Ladyman 2004; Lewis 1999c, p. 307; Ross and Spurrett 2004).

Eliminativists about higher-level properties, unlike multiple-realizability theorists, are entitled to reject identity statements like 'pain = c-fiber firing' and the necessity that must attend them: after all, eliminativists do not recognize *pain*. Even so, eliminativists about higher-level properties cannot escape type identity or its lessons any more than multiple-realizability theorists can. There are a couple of reasons for this.

First, even if higher-level properties or types like *pain* do not exist, the arguments concerning identity may be reformulated, without ontological commitment, in terms of theoretical *identification* statements like '(x)(x is pain $\equiv$ x is c-fiber firing)': so I have argued in chapter 5 (§1.2.2). Hence, the substantial *lessons* of type identity hold up even if we must drop our commitment to the types and reformulate.

But second, eliminativists about higher-level properties do *not* drop their commitment to types, in general; they drop their commitment only to *higher-level* types. They still recognize so-called "lower-level" types, and that is enough for the identity theorist to work with, in formulating close variants of the usual arguments from rigidity that bear comparable significance. The search for theoretical identity statements like 'pain = c-fiber firing' and 'diabetes = the inability to metabolize glucose' can be redirected and refined into a search for statements like 'type-1 pain = type-1 c-fiber firing' and 'type-1 diabetes = the type-1 inability to metabolize glucose' (others also defend type identities on these grounds: see, e.g., Lewis 1999c, p. 306). Although 'type-1 diabetes = the type-1 inability to metabolize glucose' would seem to admit confirmation at least in principle for familiar reasons (see chapter 1, §2.2), 'type-1 pain = type-1 c-fiber firing' seems unfortunately to be as dubious as its more general correlate, 'pain = c-fiber firing', for analogous reasons. So even if 'pain = c-fiber firing' itself were irrelevant because there are no higher-level properties, rigidity-associated skeptical arguments concerning psychophysical identity statements in general would retain their power and significance, with a little adjustment to the direction of fire.

1.2.2. Why Type Identity Matters and Why Supervenience or Token Identity is No Substitute There is no escaping type identity; so I have argued. There is no escaping type identity's informative value, either: so I will argue. Theoretical identity statements about types matter. It would not do to ignore them in favor of some other notion like supervenience or token identity.

A theoretical identity statement expresses what the subject amounts to: what its nature is. A statement affirming supervenience does not. This difference in information highlights the unique interest of theoretical identities, which is not to be captured by supervenience. Similar words apply to kindred phenomena of dependence[7]; but I will point up the basic issues with an examination of supervenience.

Consider again diabetes, which supervenes on any number of conditions, none of which it is identical to. The truth of 'diabetes supervenes on the inability to produce insulin' does not indicate much about what interesting connection unites *all* of the diverse bases on which diabetes supervenes; 'diabetes = the inability to metabolize glucose' does.

Further, diabetes is not the *only* malady that arises from all of its diverse supervenience bases. The property of *having a fatal disease*, or the property of *having a food intolerance* is not the same as diabetes, but is one of many properties that supervenes on each one of the sources. So even if there were only one property on which diabetes supervenes, we would not learn much about the nature of diabetes to be told that it supervenes on that source; a variety of properties do the same.

Clearly 'diabetes = the inability to metabolize glucose' tells us far more about what it is to be diabetes than a statement like 'diabetes supervenes on the inability to produce insulin'. It might be suggested that diabetes is interestingly related by supervenience to the whole *list* of the hundreds of abnormalities that are known or suspected to give rise to diabetes, as opposed to each item on the list taken severally, so that the list therefore holds the key to the nature of the disease. Diabetes might be unique insofar as it is the *one and only* natural condition that arises from *all and only* underlying abnormalities on the list. But that would appear not to be so: the list could not be expected to be *accurate* and so some abnormalities currently listed would surely turn out not really to give rise to diabetes. The list is also *incomplete*: other abnormalities off the list will no doubt turn out to give rise to diabetes, too.

The inaccuracy and incompleteness of the list might be remedied, in principle if not in practice. Still, efforts to remedy the list's shortcomings are instructive. These efforts suggest that in thinking through the condition of diabetes, the theoretical identity statement enjoys a certain priority over the list (see also Emmeche et al. 1997, pp. 103–4). I will argue that this is in fact so: the theoretical identity statement could be used to correct the list but not vice-versa because of the different information the two convey. I will point out some other related ways the theoretical identity statement has priority, too.

The list is wanting even if it conveys the same information as the theoretical identity statement. First, a theoretical identity statement that captures the nature of diabetes promises to be simple and handy for explanatory purposes (discussed further in chapter 6, §1.3). The long list to which we compare the theoretical identity statement would be so unwieldy as to be worthless as an account of what diabetes is, from a practical point of view, given the number of conditions.

There is more: each condition on the list would itself have to be hugely complex. To say that diabetes supervenes on the inability to produce insulin is an oversimplification that I have tolerated until now for ease of exposition. But any supervenience base property would have to be far more complex: it would have to give rise *necessarily* to diabetes. And the mere *inability to produce insulin* might have *failed* to give rise to diabetes, with vaccines or genetic engineering or whatnot. There is a hugely complex property in the list, in place of *the inability to produce insulin*: the relevant property would be something along the lines of *the inability to produce insulin in circumstances in which none of the following obtains: insulin comes with the meal on account of . . . or . . . or . . . or an insulin substitute is naturally available in . . . or in . . . or in . . . , etc.* Other base properties would be similarly unwieldy.

The list as a whole is unwieldy and so are the individual base properties taken severally. So even if an accurate, complete list of abnormalities giving rise to diabetes were to convey the same information as what is summarized in a theoretical identity statement, the theoretical identity statement would still have unique value for its manageability. Further, as I have indicated, the foregoing list would not convey the same information as what is summarized in a theoretical identity statement; the list would leave out important information conveyed by the theoretical identity statement.

First, consider that while the completeness of the list would assure that abnormalities *off* the list never *in fact* give rise to diabetes, abnormalities off the list *might have* given rise to diabetes though they do not in fact give rise to it. Nothing in the list would indicate what could make something off the list a source of diabetes; a theoretical identity statement, by contrast, would indicate that. Second, consider that while the accuracy of the list would assure that abnormalities on the list do give rise to diabetes, there is no guarantee that diabetes is the *only* natural condition to which they give rise. Diabetes might be a broad type having one or more subtypes nested within it that, like diabetes itself, supervene on each of the underlying abnormalities in the list and only them. Alternatively, diabetes might be a subtype of wider natural conditions that also supervene on each of the underlying abnormalities on the list and only them. By going over the list we would not specify the nature of *diabetes* any more than we would specify the nature of other conditions to which the list might also give rise.

A list, however accurate and complete, of conditions actually serving as bases for diabetes, fails to convey the same important information about the nature of diabetes that a theoretical identity statement conveys. And the information that the list does provide about the nature of diabetes is unwieldy. 'Diabetes = the inability to metabolize glucose' enlightens us about what diabetes fundamentally amounts to. A list of supervenience bases does not.

But what if our interest is narrower than that of someone seeking an account of diabetes? What if we are interested not in diabetes in general but only in the narrower form or forms it actually takes? We might suppose that for that purpose it is enough to know what diabetes supervenes on, in the actual world. Similarly, we might wish to understand the nature not of pain in general but only of the form of pain that humans actually experience: type-1 pain, say. And we might suppose, with Peter Carruthers, that we will know what that type of pain is, when we know "what pain is *constituted* by" in the actual world for humans: so if we were to know that pain is constituted by brain state C and so supervenes on brain state C, then "there would be nothing left unexplained" about what type-1 pain, our type of pain, *is* (Carruthers 2000, p. 48). To understand the nature of type-1 pain, according to this account, "requires only a logical supervenience claim, not a necessary identity" (Carruthers 2000, p. 48).

But in fact, supervenience or constitution is no substitute for identity, even if we are interested only in type-1 pain, the specific type of pain that humans experience. Knowing that human pain is constituted by brain state C in the actual world fails to tell us that type-1 pain amounts to brain state C, or what type-1 pain does amount to; a theoretical identity statement like 'type-1 pain = brain state C' tells us that. That human pain is constituted by brain state C in the actual world is compatible with type-1 pain amounting to a wider type than brain state C instead of amounting to brain state C itself: for all type-1 pain's constitution by brain state C tells us, type-1 pain could have been constituted by brain state D or E, other members of the family of brain states whose actual representative is C, instead of by C itself. Perhaps type-1 pain would have felt different had it been realized by D or E, which are never in fact instantiated.

That human pain is constituted by brain state C in the actual world is compatible not only with type-1 pain amounting to a wider type than brain state C instead of amounting to brain state C itself, but also with brain state C amounting to a wider type than type-1 pain: for all type-1 pain's constitution by brain state C tells us, it might be that while brain state C in fact generates just type-1 pain, brain state C might under other nonactual circumstances have generated type-2 pain or type-3 pain, which might be distinguished because they feel different, instead of type-1 pain.

So even if pain is in fact constituted by brain state C in humans, whose pain is just type-1 pain, there could be different relationships between type-1 pain and brain state C: I have mentioned a couple of salient possibilities. These possibilities, which are not exhaustive, indicate that we are nowhere close to giving an account of the nature of type-1 pain when we observe that pain for humans is actually constituted by brain state C or supervenes on it. Type-1 pain's nature is not necessarily *to be* brain state C, or anything else for that matter, for all constitution has to tell us. Again, to give an account of the nature of type-1 pain, we need a theoretical identity statement, along the lines of 'type-1 pain = brain state C', not a statement about constitution and hence supervenience.

I have been comparing theoretical identity statements concerning types with supervenience claims. The former are more interesting and informative, I have argued: so it would be a loss to give up on them. It would also be a loss to give up on type identity in favor of token identity. As interesting as it is to be told the nature of a particular case of diabetes, it matters also what the nature is of diabetes in general, and what the nature is of the salient type instantiated in this or that paradigm case of diabetes. Thus, we might uncover the nature of one token case and investigate whether some other sample is a case of the same type. Token identity does not supplant type identity in importance.

1.2.3. How to Redirect the Skeptical Argument to Address Supervenience and Token Identity Instead of Type Identity Suppose, contrary to what I have argued, that type identity were rendered false by multiple realizability, so that the only viable psychophysical identities were token identities: in that case, any skeptical argument impugning type identities would be superfluous. Or suppose supervenience or token identity were to capture all the interest of type identities: in that case a skeptical argument impugning type identities could be ignored as indicating no loss. But even so, the skeptical argument could be rendered significant because it could be adjusted to target supervenience or token identities, instead of type identities (see also Shoemaker 2011, pp. 331–3).

That the skeptical argument could be adjusted to address supervenience should be clear simply from my attention throughout this book on the possible absence of painfulness despite c-fiber firing rather than the possible absence of c-fiber firing despite painfulness. If painfulness supervenes on c-fiber firing, then c-fiber firing necessarily generates painfulness.

The relevant arguments could also be adjusted to address theoretical identities about *token* pains. Here is a straightforward first-try argument. Suppose that token materialism is true and that it underwrites this theoretical identity statement: 'P = Jones' token c-fiber firing event Y'. Even if that were the case, we would not be in any position to *recognize* or to come to recognize the statement's status as a true theoretical identity statement; on the contrary, for all that we know, some subtle change of conditions could leave Y painless, a possibility that would strip the statement of truth.

Straightforward arguments like the foregoing first-try argument against token psychophysical identities are commonly dismissed as weak or moot because they rely on easily challenged intuitions about the essences of events (Chalmers 1996, pp. 147–9; Fitch 2004, pp. 132–3; Hughes 2004, pp. 200ff.; Feldman has been an important influence: 1973; 1974; 1980; but he seems doubtful, by 1980 anyway, about prospects for psychophysical identity statements about tokens: see 1980, p. 151). It might be protested that if the token brain state Y were to stop issuing in painfulness, it would lose something essential and so cease to exist, just as the pain P would lose something essential and so cease to exist. Or it might be protested that even though Y would lose nothing essential were it to become painless, and so would go right on existing, the same could be said for P: P would also lose nothing essential and so would go right on existing as a painless event. Either way, painlessness would not ruin identity.

Let me address first the possibility that P would become painless if Y did. Kripke regards that idea as "self-evidently absurd" (1971, p. 162, note 17). For him, P is essentially painful. The problems, if there are any, for one who hopes to confirm token identity might initially appear to settle here, in a standoff with Kripke over clashing essentialist intuitions (see, e.g., Fitch 2004, p. 133). But in fact we can press on, setting aside Kripke's intuition about P's essential painfulness.

The basic trouble with the affirmation of 'P is accidentally painful' is that it adopts an unhelpful use of 'P'. As an expression for the pain event, 'P' was supposed to help us to zero in on what is, from world to world, phenomenal, so that we could use 'P' in a theoretical identity statement that would identify the phenomenal with the physical or functional. If 'P' is not a word that stays with the phenomenal in alternative circumstances featuring the corresponding physical event, then we have to coin another expression to follow the physical event just in its phenomenal condition, to express what we want to express. Let us coin '$P_{mode\ painful}$' for that purpose.

'$P_{mode\ painful}$' rigidly designates a mode of an event, which I will understand, adapting from Chisholm (1973, p. 602; see also Rea 1997, p. lvi, note 43) to be an event-like particular that exists just in case a particular event exemplifies a certain property. Now we may reconstruct the argument concerning tokens by appeal to $P_{mode\ painful}$ instead of P.

'$P_{mode\ painful}$ = Y' is false, given the rigidity of the designators, because Y could fail to be painful, by hypothesis, but $P_{mode\ painful}$ could not fail to be painful. What we need for a theoretical identity statement, which would express the physical or functional essence of $P_{mode\ painful}$ and tell us therefore what it is in physical or functional terms, without leaving any mysterious phenomenal residue unaccounted for, is a richer entry on the theoretical side of the statement. It may help to consider an analogous item of investigation: some physically tractable mode of Jones himself, who endures Y. The essence of Jones, if a Kripkean line is right, would be to have come from a particular sperm and egg. But again, suppose our aim is not to give an account of Jones' essence but rather the essence of one of Jones' modes: we want to understand, from a scientific perspective, what it is to be Jones-as-white, say, or Jones-as-this-specific-white (the shade actually instantiated by Jones, which, we will suppose for simplicity, is a function of Jones' diet or disease, so clearly accidental to him). It would not do to propose as our theoretical identity statement, 'Jones $_{mode\ white}$ = the product x of sperm S and egg E such that x is white', since this fails to illuminate in scientific terms what is specific to the mode under investigation: but that is just what we are trying to account for in scientific terms when we investigate the relevant *mode* of Jones instead of investigating Jones plain and simple. Fortunately, an account of the mode is available that is more satisfying, from the perspective of a scientist: a scientist might say that the mode is the product x of sperm S and egg E such that x reflects light in such and such manner from all wavelengths of the color spectrum.

Provided we wish to produce a similarly satisfying account of $P_{mode\ painful}$, from a scientific perspective, we need to say something about what, from a scientific perspective, it is to be Y's painfulness. The relevant theoretical identity statement will be some statement like '$P_{mode\ painful}$ = Y in conditions C', where 'C' abbreviates a limited range of the physically or functionally articulated conditions that could attend Y. That statement is impugned on familiar grounds: it is hard to see how we could assure ourselves that Y could not fail under conditions C to issue in painfulness, or how we could assure ourselves that Y could not be painful in the absence of C.

Related considerations allow us to circumvent the question of whether Y is essentially painful. (Here I will go back to using 'P' instead of '$P_{\text{mode painful}}$'.) Suppose that in order to be Y, an event would have to be painful: in the (impossible) event that Y should have been painless, "it" (so to speak) would in virtue of that painlessness thereby count as a numerically *distinct* c-fiber firing Y_{minus} instead of Y. In that case, if P is physically or functionally tractable and is identical with Y, then there are physical or functional conditions C, essential to Y, that distinguish Y from Y_{minus} which, barring C, would be present in place of Y. Without some physical or functional condition like C to distinguish Y from Y_{minus}, Y and therefore P would differ only in being phenomenal, not in any physical or functional respect. So the theoretical identity statement we seek in order to expose P's physical or functional nature will be something like 'P = what amounts to Jones' c-fiber firing Y (the alternative being that nothing amounts to Y on account of Y's matter comprising Y_{minus} instead of Y) in virtue of C'. But of course the usual troubles are now evident: it seems, again, that we have no way to assure ourselves that P could not arise without C or fail to arise despite C, in unusual circumstances.

Even if type identity were of no consequence because it ceded its importance to supervenience or token identity, which is not so, the problems that we have seen for affirming psychophysical identity statements about types would be significant because they carry over to statements affirming supervenience and token identity. The skeptical argument does not lack significance for its connection to type identity.

2. Costs

The skeptical argument at hand is significant: or at least it is significant if it is convincing. The question that remains is whether it *is* convincing. I divide doubts about whether the skeptical argument concerning psychophysical identity statements is convincing into a couple of broad, roughly characterized divisions. Not much rests on how natural the underlying taxonomy is, so long as these divisions allow me to cover the relevant objections in an order readers find handy enough.

One sort of criticism according to which the skeptical argument at hand is not convincing maintains that the argument carries extravagant costs: that it takes for granted resources in establishing its conclusion that are controversial or worse. Perhaps the argument assumes that we enjoy powers that we do not after all enjoy, to establish the separability of physical and phenomenal events, say. I will address objections along these lines in the present section of the present chapter (§2). As a skeptical argument, the argument under scrutiny is also subject to doubts from the other direction: one might worry that the argument is too parsimonious in the resources that it is willing to countenance. Again, the argument might overlook powers that we enjoy to establish the statements concerning which the argument is skeptical. I save worries along these lines, which arise with great frequency in the literature, for a separate chapter: chapter 8.

I turn now to objections according to which the argument presupposes costly resources. I begin by discussing a genuine cost (in §2.1), which I call the cost of acknowledging a *privileged insider's perspective*: it is a cost that eliminative materialists will find too high but few philosophers will suppose that we can get by without it. Then I will discuss a couple of non-commitments which accordingly add no cost.

2.1. *The Privilege of an Insider's Perspective: a Cost Too High for Eliminative Materialists*

The argument that I favor presupposes that we have a privileged insider's perspective on what counts as a pain: we can identify pain introspectively when we experience it, imagine it, remember it, and so on. We know by acquaintance pain's essence or at least we know by acquaintance that if an experience feels like *this*, there is pain (call to mind how it feels to stub your toe hard) and if it feels like *that*, there is no pain (call to mind blissful freedom from anything unpleasant). To be sure, we could imagine someone's situation as feeling a certain way or we could seemingly recall our own situation as feeling a certain way when really it did not: we suppose someone felt like *this* (call to mind the sensation of stubbing a toe) but they did not, say, or we misremember feeling so when we did not. But if we imagine or remember a situation correctly, as presenting *this* (call to mind that *ouch*), then we have imagined or remembered pain. The trouble generated by this assumption, as the skeptical argument goes (again, see chapter 1, §2.2), arises because we are unable to assure ourselves that what we identify by introspection as pain is the same as this or that property that we recognize in physical or functional terms.

The acknowledgement that there is a privileged insider's perspective on phenomenal states is a cost. But it is not prohibitive for many philosophers, most of whom are strongly committed against the alternative to paying: that is to accept eliminative materialism.

Perhaps it is best to remove a possible confusion at the outset. To be privileged with knowledge by way of an insider's perspective is not necessarily to enjoy knowledge that is demon-proof or infallible; to be demon-proof or infallible is too much to ask of any knowledge, regardless of the source. My awareness that I am in pain is not necessarily guaranteed to be authentic in the presence of deceptive Cartesian demons (cf. Mandik and Weisberg 2008, pp. 237–40). Still, there is no *special* problem here for any position in the philosophy of mind. Fallibilism is a *general* problem that must be defused by way of some general response. My preferred response to fallibilism is to say that it is correct to say we "know" this or that in contexts in which certain defeaters, including the possibility that evil demons deceive, are not appropriately entertained. But there are other responses to the threat of fallibilism: what is important here is that whatever response is given, the response should respect that we do have knowledge even though we are not immune to error on account of demonic deception – or on account of having missed too much sleep or of having taken the wrong drugs, and so on. Despite these vulnerabilities, we have knowledge about lots of matters, from the weather today to geometry: and one of the things that we know, or so I presuppose, is that something is in pain if it feels like *this* (call to mind what it feels like to stub your toe hard), that something is not in pain if it feels like *that* (call to mind blissful freedom from anything unpleasant), and so on.

Because we honor knowledge obtained by way of the privileged insider's perspective, we trust pain reports, by and large. If it were to turn out that patients report sincerely that they feel pain even though we find this surprising since the patients are undergoing just *d*-fiber firing, where in the past it had been thought that pain was correlated just with c-fiber firing, we would adjust our assessment of whether it is just c-fiber firing that causes pain, rather than dismiss the report as an error (see also Kirk 2003, p. 53). Just so, when patients report sincerely that they experience a visual impression of red, yet we learn that the cause is the perception of light that is low on green rays rather than light containing red rays, we trust patients. Rather than dismiss them as mistaken about having an experience of being appeared to redly we adjust our assessment of the physical paths by which things appear red to us, concluding "that our eyes don't discriminate specific wavelengths of light. Our perceptions of color are, in effect, mental constructs somehow" (Hazen 2001, p. 47). Again, patients might misremember their experiences or get muddled, on account of demonic mischief or just sleepiness or drugs. But again, fallibilism is not enough to remove the status of a patient's internal perspective as a source of knowledge.

To claim that there is some way accurately to distinguish, by introspection, pains from non-pains, is not universally accepted, even given qualifications to allow for fallibilism: such a claim would be rejected by a minority of philosophers. Obviously the claim would be rejected by avowed eliminative materialists, who deny that pain exists, to be identified from the inside and distinguished from the absence of pain. A more interesting conflict with the position that we can diagnose whether or not we have pain by way of introspection comes, in practice, from "analytic functionalism" (see Block 1980, p. 268; Burge 1992, p. 40; Levin 2010, §3.2; Lewis 1999b, p. 248; 1999c, pp. 301–2) or "folk-psychological functionalism," as I will call it following Sprevak (2009) and others.

Folk-psychological functionalism, which acknowledges pain, is thereby more plausible on its face than bare eliminativism. But unless it is adopted in conjunction with an acknowledgement of a privileged insider's perspective, the position becomes so revisionist as to collapse into eliminativism. This observation, that unless it is adopted in conjunction with an acknowledgement of the privileged insider's perspective the position collapses into eliminativism, is no more applicable to folk-psychological functionalism than to any other version of functionalism or to any other materialist account of what phenomenal events are; I make the observation in connection with folk-psychological functionalism only because practice suggests that the position might as well be taken straight, without an acknowledgement of the privileged insider's perspective. Still, there is no obligation in principle for folk-psychological functionalists to take the position straight, as I will explain.

Folk-psychological functionalism holds that what a phenomenal term like 'pain' expresses can be analyzed as something like *the role-filler for the role of what usually causes avoidance, contortions, wincing, and so on; and what is caused by bodily injury, and so on.* The tie between 'pain' and these ordinary, folk observations about pain's role is conceptual and a priori.

David Lewis is probably the first folk-psychological functionalist to come to mind (see any of the foregoing discussions of the position). Armstrong (1968) offers a closely related account that is also paradigmatic of folk-psychological functionalism. I will explain how Lewis' position is a form of eliminativism, intuitively and for purposes here. Something similar could be said for the position of Armstrong, for whom it is "peculiarly easy" (1968, p. 123) to be sure when someone else is in pain, say, since it is only a matter of verifying the presence of physical conditions, and not a matter of being sure in addition that those conditions feel like this or that (call to mind how it feels to stub a toe and so on) (Armstrong 1968, pp. 123–5; for discussion, see Nagel 1980, p. 206); but I will focus on Lewis.

Although Lewis would not deny that we can recognize pain in our everyday world when we sit on a cactus or hammer our thumb, he would not acknowledge that you identify pain if I ask you, setting aside any question of functions and physical states, to focus on *that* (imaginatively introspect a state you cannot tell apart from the cactus episode). You cannot know whether what you imagine is really pain in this hypothetical case without the information, explicit or tacit, that you are in the expected brain states playing the expected functional roles. This rejection of a privileged internal perspective shows Lewis' close affinities to eliminativism: there is no feeling of painfulness that can be identified from inside, to serve as an independent standard for whether one is in pain. Lewis himself concedes, after denying that one can pick out what would or would not be a pain introspectively by recognition or imagination, by virtue of knowing just what it is like to be in pain, that "It is not altogether wrong to call him an 'eliminativist'" (1999d, p. 329; 'him' refers to Lewis and those in his camp: see pp. 327–9).

Lewis is not vulnerable to Kripke-style arguments, including that of chapter 1 (§2.2), which presuppose internalism about our access, or at least one route of access, to whether we are in a state like pain or painfulness. It would be possible for a folk-psychological functionalist to be more sympathetic to the privileged insider's perspective, in which case she would find herself in the company of realists: what sets realists apart, intuitively and for purposes here, is in acknowledging that pain is that unwelcome sensation that we detect from the inside when we imagine pain, remember pain, and so on. Its *feltness from the inside* is both necessary and sufficient for there to be pain, in the realist sense (cf. Kripke 1971, p. 163, note 18).[8] So we can tell by introspection that this or that state which we entertain would or would not be pain by how it would seem from the inside.

Were a folk-psychological functionalist to embrace the internal perspective, then she would find herself subject to the Kripkean argument (from chapter 1, §2.2): now she has two distinct routes by which she takes herself to secure reference to pain, the first by the *ouch* sensed from the inside and the second by a description provided by the analysis. It is hard to see how she could ever assure herself that what she secures reference to in the one case is the very same thing that she secures reference to in the other case. Let us consider a tough case, for which a folk-psychological functionalist would want to say that there *is* pain (or at least Lewis would want to say that there is pain, as I will explain; if the peculiarities of a different folk-psychological-functionalist's account happened to call for an absence of pain in this case, then we could make minor adjustments to pose a similar problem with that judgment as well). Consider an individual who is knocked out by a paralyzing accident. Pain-associated behavior like wincing, moaning, aversion, etc. is out of the question after the accident. Because the patient in the thought experiment cannot exhibit pain behavior, the state *earlier* associated with the behavioral role for the patient, or else the state associated with the behavioral role for the *species*, would be what determines the case according to Lewis. We may suppose that for the patient's species, and for the patient prior to the accident, pain behavior like wincing, moaning, and aversion, is associated with brain state C. Since, for the patient before the accident and for the species, brain state C is what is associated with pain behavior, being in brain state C would qualify the individual to be in pain (see Lewis 1983c, pp. 126–7, 129).

We could try to pose a difficulty for Lewis: "suppose that when the patient were undergoing brain state C, it seemed from the inside like *this* (imagine what it feels like to be blissfully free from any unpleasant feeling whatsoever). Surely there would be nothing painful?" But Lewis, who rejects the privileged insider's perspective, would feel no rub. We could not *tell* that the patient is in pain by introspective reflection on what it seemed like to the patient, for Lewis: there is no special ability that we enjoy to pick out pain by recalling the unpleasant sensation or freedom from it. So it is irrelevant that, as we have described the case, you are unable to tell this state apart, by introspective focus on what it is like, from a painless state. For Lewis, introspection leaves you without information. So information from introspection cannot compete with the verdict of his analysis: again, there is no rub. Introspection leaves you without information because all that there is to pain is a brain state in a role and we cannot discern the nature of *that* by how things feel from the inside – "Making discoveries in neurophysiology is not so easy!" (Lewis 1999d, p. 329). That is all there is to discern.

By contrast, a folk-psychological functionalist who defers to the privileged insider's perspective would find herself in tension over the case. She would acknowledge that the patient is in pain if and only if she is in brain state C, in accordance with her analysis (again, supposing for simplicity that her analysis agreed with Lewis' over this case). But she would also trust her powers of introspection to discern a real difference in mental states when she typically compares *this* (call to mind placid freedom from any painful sensation) to *that* (call to mind that unpleasant *ouch*): and she would accordingly acknowledge that the patient is not in pain if the patient feels the former. That creates tension. We must find some way around saying that the patient would both be and not be in pain.

The natural response from any folk-psychological functionalist who embraces the privileged insider's perspective would be to emphasize that the cognitive tension at hand is no disproof of folk-psychological functionalism because the conceivability or apparent conceivability of the case at hand might indicate only that we can conceive or apparently conceive what is metaphysically impossible. It might be that our cognitive position allows us to conceive or apparently conceive of a patient in brain state C, with its associated roles, who feels from the inside like *this* (again, call to mind freedom from pain), even though the brute fact is that such a patient would have to feel from the inside like *that* (call to mind what it felt like last time you stubbed your toe) or like *that* (call to mind what it felt like when you hammered a thumb) or something recognizably similar.

Whatever the merits of such a response as a defense of the favored folk-psychological functionalist account against an objection according to which we can reject it on the basis of our intuitions, troubles remain for ever *confirming* that the particular analysis at hand has it right. And the same goes for any other folk-psychological-functionalist analysis you replace it with. That is where the argument from chapter 1 takes hold. It is hard to see how we could be confident that the feeling whose phenomenal character we identify introspectively and whose physical nature we seek to articulate would *have* to go with the state-cum-functions associated with the feeling by our folk-psychological functionalist analysis: how we could be confident that the sensation and the state-cum-functions, which we independently identify, are inseparable.

Folk-psychological functionalists sympathetic with the privileged insider's perspective have options for responding to the skeptical argument that have analogues in the options of other materialists who are sympathetic with the privileged insider's perspective. First, a folk-psychological functionalist could hope that a more accurate or less vague analysis of what functions the folk associate with 'pain', which are those functions that the subject is supposed to amount to, could help: such an analysis would concern just what behavior, from toe curling to bed rest, is associated by the folk with the label 'pain'. It has to be said that prospects for any such a response to the skeptical argument are dim: no such effort is going to generate an analysis that is immune to conflict with our introspective judgment of whether pain is present, in a cleverly described thought experiment.

Scientific functionalists, who turn to science to articulate functions (see, e.g., Levin 2010, §3.2 for discussion), or others who hope that scientists will uncover some theoretical property that redeems theoretical identity statements concerning phenomenal states, might hope that a more accurate understanding of functions or brain states provided by advancing science will replace the apparently contingent connections we make, between any physico-functional event and corresponding feeling, with a conceptually necessary connection. I will suggest that the empirical sciences cannot provide that service though (see chapter 8, §3.5.2). So folk-psychological functionalists are no worse off for not appealing to science to articulate functions as far as this matter goes of finding a conceptual link between what is perceived internally as phenomenal and what is expressed scientifically as a function.

There remain a couple of other salient options available to folk-psychological functionalists sympathetic to the privileged insider's perspective, for responding to the skeptical argument concerning whether we could ever be in a position to affirm specific psychophysical identity statements. I will discuss these options in greater detail later (in chapter 8). First, folk-psychological functionalists who retain the privileged insider's perspective could argue that empirical observation could establish *inductively* that properties correlated empirically are probably identical. That might give us grounds to *confirm* identity, even if we cannot perceive by reflection on what we identify by one means and represent on the one side of the identity statement that it is necessarily inseparable from what we identify by other means and represent on the other side of the identity statement. Perhaps it is by induction that we confirm 'flight = what bees actually achieve with their wings', which again has posed conceptual problems even though it seems clearly true (see §1.1.2). Perhaps we observe a correlation between flight and wing behavior and thereby inductively confirm identity, even if we do not see how wing action *could* give rise to flight. Granted, 'flight = what bees actually achieve with their wings' is not a theoretical identity statement; on the contrary, flight might not have been achieved by bees at all, for all this statement indicates, and bees might have achieved nothing more with their wings than to warm themselves. So the statement does not inform us about the essence of flight (for further discussion of the poverty of such statements by comparison with theoretical identity statements, see chapter 6, §2.1.2.2.2). Even so, if induction helps to confirm the identity statement 'flight = what bees actually achieve with their wings', it might also help to confirm theoretical identity statements, including psychophysical identity statements. Again, I will examine the prospects in chapter 8.

The second salient option for responding to the skeptical argument is to urge that a deeper conceptual investigation into the theoretical underpinnings of our words' proper use could expose conceptual connections binding apparently distinct properties. This is not the claim that what will help is a more accurate analysis of just what functions are associated by the folk with 'pain', but rather a claim that what will help is a better understanding of just how our word 'pain' needs to have the connections it has to both the internally recognized phenomenal aspect of the designatum and to the relevant functions, in order to be used meaningfully. Such understanding might expose the necessary connections we are looking for between what we perceive with the privileged insider's perspective and what we are talking about in our analysis.

The foregoing salient options for responding to skepticism are available, with adjustments, to other physico-functionalists who retain the privileged insider's perspective, as well as folk-psychological functionalists who do so. Again, I save until chapter 8 evaluation of these options for responding to the skeptical argument in question.

I conclude section (§2.1) by way of summary. The skeptical argument pressed in this book (chapter 1, §2.2) presupposes the privileged insider's perspective, a cost that eliminative materialists are unwilling to pay. This presupposition does not necessarily force a break with folk-psychological functionalism; but folk-psychological functionalists or other physico-functionalists are free to reject the privileged insider's perspective.

If they do reject it, they thereby embrace a revisionism so strong that their position becomes a form of eliminative materialism. Because only "a distinct minority" of philosophers can tolerate the poverty of eliminative materialism, as Chalmers observes (2003, p. 112; see also 1996, pp. 165–6), whether the eliminativism is explicit or whether it is implicit in the rejection of a privileged insider's perspective to attend physico-functionalism, most philosophers will not be alienated by the cost of presupposing the privileged insider's perspective.

2.2. *Two Dimensionalism: No Commitment, No Cost*

Although there is no fear of offending a great many theorists by cutting away eliminative materialism, broadly though I have construed it, one might wonder about some other possible costs for my arguments. In particular, I will discuss a couple of other possible commitments associated with Chalmers, with controversial price tags. I will point out that these are not genuine commitments.

The first of these possible commitments is two-dimensionalism. Kripkean conclusions, especially with regard to psychophysical identity statements, are often held in connection with two-dimensionalism (e.g., in Chalmers 1996; Jackson 1998) so it might occur to readers to wonder: to what extent are rigidity, as I have articulated it, and the uses to which I have put rigidity, indebted to two-dimensionalist semantics, about which I have said so little throughout this book? In this brief section, I clarify that there is no debt at all. We may safely ignore the ubiquitous worries that two-dimensionalism has provoked, then: that is why I *have* until now ignored worries associated with two-dimensionalism despite its high profile in the Kripkean tradition.

We can get a handle on two-dimensionalism by attending to 'Brontosaurus = Apatosaurus': I have taken statements like this to be true and therefore necessarily true by virtue of rigid designation even though it took empirical observation to determine the necessary truth (see chapter 1, §2.1). With respect to a world in which scientists use different sample specimens in baptismal ceremonies to coin *their* words 'Brontosaurus' and 'Apatosaurus', 'Brontosaurus = Apatosaurus' is still true, even though in some such worlds w_d, what speakers call "Brontosaurus" turns out to be a different genus from the one that they, in w_d, call "Apatosaurus." In those worlds w_d, speakers correctly *reject* "'Brontosaurus = Apatosaurus'". The reason that our statement 'Brontosaurus = Apatosaurus' is still true with respect to worlds w_d is because in *our* language 'Brontosaurus' and 'Apatosaurus' designate the same genus of apatosaurs with respect to all possible worlds, including those worlds w_d in which this genus has different names and in which other items instead of this genus have the names that it has in our actual world (see chapter 1, §1.2).

Our statement 'Brontosaurus = Apatosaurus' has a content that is necessarily true, then. That is as far as my commitments about content go. By contrast, two-dimensionalists like Chalmers and Jackson would qualify: they would recognize a *double* content for the statement 'Brontosaurus = Apatosaurus': there is "epistemic content," on the one hand, and "subjunctive content," on the other. Double content is supposed to be attractive for its help in redeeming the epistemic status of a sentence like 'Brontosaurus = Apatosaurus' as a posteriori, as well as necessary. A two-dimensionalist says that the sentence is *metaphysically* necessary in virtue of its "subjunctive content" and that it is *epistemically* contingent and therefore a posteriori in virtue of its "epistemic content" (Chalmers' terminology: other names are used by other writers). The foregoing two types of content make up the "complex content" of the sentence, which "subsumes both of these and possibly more" (Chalmers 2002, p. 165; see also Chalmers 1996, p. 62). Both contents, for two-dimensionalists, are bona fide truth-bearing semantic contents. 'Brontosaurus = Apatosaurus' is not true in an *unqualified* way with respect to all worlds including w_d. The statement has a true subjunctive content with respect to all worlds, including w_d; but it has a false epistemic content with respect to w_d (Chalmers 2002, p. 166; see also 2006a, p. 134; 2006b, pp. 596ff.; for a similar view, see Jackson 1998, pp. 84–6).

The two-dimensional semantic framework is irrelevant to the arguments that I endorse. I recognize no content that is distinct from the content that is responsible for 'Brontosaurus = Apatosaurus''s *necessity*, as I have indicated. I claim that we know a posteriori the truth, with respect to all possible worlds, of the *statement* 'Brontosaurus = Apatosaurus'; but for all that I say, the relevant *content* is known a priori to be true, with respect to all possible worlds (see chapter 1, §1.3). There may, then, be no content that is knowable only a posteriori to be true with respect to all possible worlds. But if there *is* such a posteriori content, as seems plausible for at least some identity statements like 'water = H_2O' (for related discussion, see chapter 6, §1.1), it is a further question, concerning which again I make no commitments, whether such a posteriori content would be distinct from the subjunctive content that is true with respect to all possible worlds in virtue of the rigidity of the two designators. There is no need for me to take a position with respect to these matters, either for or against semantic contents beyond the one that I recognize.

2.3. Modal Rationalism and Apriority: No Commitment, No Cost

Just as my arguments do not commit to two-dimensional semantics, my arguments do not commit to "modal rationalism" (Chalmers 1999, p. 479 note 3; see also 1999, pp. 483ff.; 2006b, §3.1 and §5). According to modal rationalism, any scenario that rational reflection in certain ideal epistemic circumstances cannot rule out as metaphysically impossible is metaphysically possible. Such ideal epistemic circumstances might obtain, for example, after scientists have done their work discovering the microstructural compositions of our substances. In such circumstances, the possibility of a world in which water fails to be H_2O can be ruled out but the possibility of a world in which pain fails to arise despite c-fiber firing cannot: so, for modal rationalists, a world in which pain fails to arise despite c-fiber firing is metaphysically possible (see Chalmers 1996, pp. 136–8; see the related claims of Jackson 1998, p. 83).

No such position is endorsed here. For all that I have said, c-fiber firing in the absence of pain or vice-versa is a metaphysical *im*possibility. It is just that we do not have much evidence of that: for all that we know or have evidence for believing now or after the relevant scientific information is in, c-fiber firing without pain and pain without c-fiber firing are possible. So for all that we know, there is no identity. Thus, my arguments evade objections directed at the modal rationalism underlying well-known antimaterialist arguments (see, e.g., Soames 2005, chapter 9, e.g., pp. 206ff.).

"Modal rationalism" is closely associated with two-dimensional semantics, as I have indicated (Chalmers even proposes "two-dimensionalism" as an alternative rubric for modal rationalism: 1999, p. 479 note 3). So is the position that metaphysical possibility and necessity are discernible a priori: partly because of this association with two-dimensionalism, controversies have surrounded the a priori.[9] Some philosophers go so far as to suggest that there is no a priori at all (Devitt and Sterelny 1999, p. 103; Stalnaker 2003, p. 18; Putnam 1983, pp. 87ff.). A commonly offered reason for rejecting the a priori is that any belief is revisable in light of empirical evidence to the contrary (see, e.g., Putnam 1983, pp. 87ff.). This familiar Quinean observation would not seem to support a convincing case against the a priori: even if any belief might be rationally *relinquished* on the basis of empirically acquired information, e.g., on the basis of testimony, some knowledge may still be rationally *acquired* without the need for empirical investigation (as Plantinga, for one, has observed: Plantinga 1993, pp. 110–13; also pp. 18–19). Perhaps other arguments against apriority fare better: in any event, what is important here is that there is nothing in my arguments requiring the a priori.

To be sure, I appeal to *analysis* of language or concepts, in order to determine that which we designate with a term. We have to examine how we employ a term like 'water', for example, by looking at how we would apply it in various counterfactual scenarios, if we hope to see whether it designates H_2O with respect to other possible worlds or whether it designates instead just anything that is clear, drinkable, and so on. The enterprise of analysis is traditionally *thought* to be a priori. Yet it is possible for all that I claim here that the work of learning about how we would use a word in various circumstances is in the end not an a priori exercise in ratiocination but an empirical, sociological investigation into what speakers say in various circumstances or with various promptings (Devitt and Sterelny 1999, pp. 103, 179–84; Levine 1998, pp. 159–60). It does not matter here whether work determining what we would say in various circumstances, which is the work of linguistic or conceptual analysis, is empirical or whether it is a priori. What matters is that such work is needed, in order to determine what we have designated by the use of a term. To that I am committed.

Of course, that analysis is needed at all, a priori or otherwise, might itself be regarded as a cost to my position. But analysis is widely used in philosophy and it is hard to see how to get by without it: there would need to be a salient alternative to the use of analysis for the commitment to analysis to count as a genuine cost. So I will address the suggestion that we might dispense with analysis in the context of a broader suggestion that I have overlooked alternative resources that would do instead and that would allow us to confirm psychophysical identities (chapter 8). Here it has been enough to observe that a commitment to analysis is not a commitment to modal rationalism or to apriority, which raise controversy that the skeptical argument circumvents.

3. Conclusion

The skeptical argument at hand is significant. And it does not carry costly presuppositions in the form of an appeal to metaphysical or epistemic resources that raise controversy. The argument does presuppose that we can identify something, namely pains, by how matters seem to us from the inside. That presupposition carries a cost that eliminative materialists are unwilling to pay. But again, it is only a minority of philosophers who can live with the poverty of eliminativism. The skeptical argument does not help itself to more controversial resources: to two-dimensional semantics, to lofty estimates of our ability to discern necessity in the world, or even to our capacity for a priori knowledge.

Perhaps the skeptical conclusion can still be resisted. Although it is good that the skeptical argument is modest in its appeal to resources, it might be objected that the argument is *too* modest. There might be philosophical resources that the argument overlooks that could be marshaled to the cause of establishing psychophysical identity statements. This is the topic of chapter 8.

Notes

1. Conceptual dualism is sometimes cited as the orthodoxy (e.g., by Papineau 2002, p. 5; see also Papineau 2003, p. 217; 2007a, pp. 483ff., and Shoemaker's helpful discussion: 2011, pp. 335–42). That seems accurate or close to accurate. Many express sympathy for the position (including Balog 2012 forthcoming; Block 2003, p. 763; Campbell 2009, pp. 49–50; Carruthers 2000, pp. 55–6; Hill and McLaughlin 1999, p. 453; Loar 1997, pp. 599–603; 2003, p. 125; 2007, pp. 456, 463; Macdonald 2004, pp. 506, 515, 520; Polger 2004, chapter 2; see also Levine 1993, p. 123; 2001, pp. 68, 91; Musacchio 2005, p. 435; Nagel 1974, p. 446, note 11; and the further references cited in chapter 8). Even so, there are positions other than conceptual dualism to contend with. I will evaluate eliminativism and folk-psychological functionalism below (in §2.1). There and elsewhere I evaluate an argument that has attended that functionalism historically, according to which we may deny the skeptical argument's premise that psychophysical identity statements are by virtue of rigidity necessarily true if they are true (see first, on this head, chapter 6, note 6). I evaluate scientific necessitarianism in chapter 8 (§3).
2. In chapter 8, I will revisit these would-be parallel discoveries of identity.

    There are some who would take my conclusion to serve as a premise for an argument against materialism that is distinct from Kripke's (Horgan 2006, pp. 587–8; see also Patterson 2008, pp. 576f.; cf. by contrast, McGinn 1999b and Levine 2001, p. 10; 1998, p. 475); as I have indicated, I would not press such an argument even though I take my argument to spoil prospects for the foregoing satisfying resolution to philosophical controversy in favor of physicalism and even though I would not accept that there are true psychophysical identities (my resistance could be exaggerated: it is not clear to me that the big-picture metaphysics that I favor would be unable to accommodate the truth of 'pain = c-fiber firing'). My claims about our ignorance of the truth of specific psychophysical identity statements accord with currents in the work of Levine, McGinn, and Nagel (1974). Of course there are salient differences between these authors and me as well as differences that distinguish them from each other.

3. Levine, who might accept the distinction here between evidential problems and explanatory ones (2001, p. 91; 1998, pp. 473, 475; 1993, pp. 123, 126), focuses on explanatory matters; but in an early paper, he argues in effect not only for an explanatory gap but also, briefly, for something like the evidential trouble that I recognize (Levine 1983, pp. 354, 359–60) which should be clearly distinguished.

4. Here the materialism is of a modest sort compatible with functionalism, according to which humans are in fact composed entirely of inorganic matter (see Block 1996 for more discussion). There is no commitment on whether phenomenal properties are natural from the perspective of physics (see LaPorte 2004, pp. 23–4) or on whether there could have been, perhaps are somewhere, spiritual instantiations of functional properties that are phenomenal.

5. Levine (1998, pp. 471f.) argues, just as I do but by a different route, that "materialism is committed to some sort of identity theory" of types (p. 472). In defending type identity, I have followed the usual policy of ignoring objections directed at rigidity in general, as opposed to objections directed at rigidity as it applies to property designators specifically. Accordingly, I have ignored well-known and popular Quinean worries to the effect that one could not, even in principle, produce two expressions to capture just the same entity in all modal contexts: it is too late for such worries, or for Quinean worries about necessity, after we have committed ourselves to *any* rigid co-designation *at all*, along with the attending necessarily true identity statements. I begin the book with such a commitment, in accordance with a general consensus (at chapter 1, note 1 and accompanying text; for related discussion concerning mutual antagonism between popular Quinean positions about *analyticity*, on the one hand, and popular claims about rigid designation, on the other hand, see LaPorte 2004, chapter 6).

6. 'Pain = brain state C' is not the theoretical identity statement about the realizer; since 'pain' is nonrigid according to realizer functionalists, 'pain = brain state C' is contingently true. But then the realizer is separable from pain and thus to be the realizer is not what it is to be pain: hence 'pain = brain state C' is not a theoretical identity statement, which would express what it is to be pain (for more on theoretical identity statements, see chapter 1, §2). To frame a theoretical identity statement we need a rigid designator for the intended subject. A rigid designator for the *realizer* would be 'pain★', which is stipulated to refer rigidly to *the actual occupant of the role* (for further discussion and references, see chapter 6, §2.1.1): so 'pain★' would rigidly designate brain state C. Really, then, there are two theoretical identity statements to be honored by a realizer functionalist: 'to be pain = to be the occupant of functional role P', and 'pain★ = brain state C'. Which does the skeptical argument concerning psychophysical identities target? The answer to this question is: whichever theoretical identity statement is supposed to have as its subject matter *the phenomenon saliently present in* this *and* that *experience* (call to mind what it is like to stub a toe hard or hammer a thumb, etc.) *but not this* other *experience* (call to mind freedom from any distress). In principle either of the foregoing sentences could be taken to have for a subject the relevant phenomenon causally identified

by introspection because either 'to be pain' or 'pain★' could be thought to designate a property whose essential nature is both to be like *this* or *that* (call to mind the relevant painful experiences) *and* to be functional (as *to be pain* is, for realizer functionalists) or physical (as *pain★* is, for realizer functionalists). Which, if either sentence is supposed to have the relevant phenomenon causally identified by introspection for a subject matter depends on how the functionalist position is developed. If a functionalist will not allow that *either* 'to be pain = to be the occupant of functional role P' or 'pain★ = brain state C' has the phenomenal subject matter causally identified by introspection, then the skeptical argument fails to apply; the functionalist has in effect retreated to eliminativism about pain(s), while retaining 'pain' language in reformed use. Here I anticipate the discussion in §2.1.

7. The central observations of this section apply whether we are talking about supervenience or other related notions of dependence that are, like supervenience, asymmetric. For F to be held in virtue of G's being held, or for G to constitute F, etc., is not for F to *be* G, any more than for F to supervene on G is for F to be G. For F to be G has its own interest. So the central observations of this section can be transferred from supervenience to more basic phenomena that might explain the necessity captured by supervenience, should these phenomena interest us more than supervenience (see, e.g., Melnyk 2003, p. 71). And the observations apply whether we take supervenience to incorporate these more basic phenomena of dependence (Kim 1993, p. 67; 1998, p. 11) or not. Someone could argue that for F to be, by virtue *of its nature, precisely* G, or for F to amount to G in the strong respect that to be G is the essence of F, etc., is for an asymmetric relation to hold between F and G, contrary to what I might suggest at various points in the text. And this relation *would* capture all that theoretical identity statements offer. How would I respond? Let me concede all, for the sake of argument (although I doubt that the asymmetry is genuine). The relevant in-virtue-of relation is a potent one: to be informed that that strong relation holds between F and G would suffice to be informed that a theoretical identity, F = G, also holds. So there is no shortcut here by way of attending to some asymmetric notion of dependence that bypasses identity to capture the nature of F.

8. There might be some question in English concerning the use of 'pain' if the physical state constituting pains comes in different degrees of intensity that are felt more or less intensely. If necessary, refine 'pain' to exclude physical states like these when they are of such low intensity that they cease to be felt. By the same token, I do not mean to suggest that for any introspected condition, it is clearly either painful or painless. There are borderline cases.

9. Chalmers calls the position that some form of content for the relevant sentences is knowable a priori a "core claim" of two-dimensionalism (2006b, §3.1; see also Jackson 1998, pp. 84–6). In the course of defending identity claims, materialists often reject or downplay the role of the a priori (Marras 2005, pp. 347–52; Block and Stalnaker 1999, pp. 13–16; Papineau 2002, p. 157; for related criticisms, see Nimtz 2004).

8

The Skeptical Argument Further Examined: on Resources, Allegedly Overlooked, for Confirming Psychophysical Identities

I have indicated that among the various arguments that I have discussed that make use of rigidity for properties, the skeptical arguments concerning mind (chapter 1, §2.2) stand out as unique for their cold reception, broadly speaking, in the philosophical community. Optimistic rejoinders are popular. In the present chapter, I continue to defend the skeptical argument that I favor from prominent rejoinders.

I concluded chapter 7 by rejecting the concern that the skeptical argument appeals to objectionable metaphysical or epistemic resources. In this chapter, I will reject the concern that the skeptical argument overlooks *un*objectionable resources that could help to establish psychophysical identities.

In sections (2) and (3), I examine two broad movements in the philosophical tradition that suggest that important resources are available for confirming the truth and necessity of psychophysical identity statements. But the movements do not help. Correlation and the scientific method do not help: so I conclude in section (2). Scientific necessitarianism does not help either: so I conclude in section (3). A look at why the skeptical argument survives these movements builds an appreciation for the skeptical argument. After discussing these matters, I conclude in section (4).

Before I begin the main work of the chapter, it will be helpful to rehearse my favored argument, amplifying some aspects: I do this in section (1). The conclusion, again, is that we could never be in a position to endorse a psychophysical identity statement, such as 'pain = c-fiber firing': any such statement will remain doubtful even with further advances in empirical science. Something similar applies to psychofunctional identity statements. As I have said (chapter 7, §1.1; but see there note 2 and accompanying text), the conclusion of my argument is not that materialism is false. For simplicity, we may assume from the outset that materialism is true.

1. Psychophysical Identity Statements' Support is Undermined by Missing De Jure Connections to Physically Described Matter

'Water = H_2O' serves as the usual model of a true theoretical identity statement. This statement is indeed a true theoretical identity statement, if 'water' and 'H_2O' both rigidly designate the same item; otherwise, it is not. Fortunately, we have every reason to suppose that 'water' and 'H_2O' both rigidly designate the same item. So I have argued.[1]

Unfortunately, our impressive grounds for affirming 'water = H_2O' are not matched by any impressive grounds, or even prospects of acquiring any impressive grounds, for affirming a statement like 'pain = c-fiber firing'. Like 'water = H_2O', 'pain = c-fiber firing' is a true theoretical identity statement if and only if 'pain' and 'c-fiber firing' both rigidly designate the same item; but in this case, we have *no* good reason to suppose that they do so.

The disparity arises for the following reasons. 'Water' is rigid *de jure*, or rigid by design, for: that underlying chemical, whatever it is, that is properly correlated with samples that speakers are able to identify in the actual world (see chapter 6, §2.2). Since 'water' is rigid by design for the chemical, whatever it is, that is properly correlated with certain particular quantities of matter in the actual world, a scientific discovery that H_2O is the chemical that is properly correlated with these items is clearly also a discovery that 'water' rigidly designates H_2O: it is a discovery that 'water = H_2O' is a true theoretical identity statement.

'Pain = c-fiber firing' admits no similar confirmation. If something like it is a true theoretical identity statement, as something like it must be if physicalism obtains (see chapter 7, §1.2), then the statement's status as a true theoretical identity statement must be confirmed by some alternative route that is not at all like the foregoing.[2] But it is hard to see how any alternative route could bring confirmation. So there are strong grounds for pessimism concerning our prospects for confirming 'pain = c-fiber firing'.

The familiar trouble, or the specific version of it that will articulate and defend, is that 'pain', unlike 'water', is not *rigid de jure*, or rigid by design, for anything like: the underlying neurophysiological property, whatever it is, that is properly correlated with certain unpleasant phenomena that speakers are unfortunately all too able to pick out in the actual world. So a scientific discovery that c-fiber firing is the relevantly salient underlying neurophysiological property correlated with the unpleasant phenomena at issue is *not* clearly also a discovery that 'pain' rigidly designates c-fiber firing. 'Pain' is a rigid designator for the sensations themselves as selected de jure from the inside by their phenomenal aspect. Since a scientific discovery that c-fiber firing is the underlying phenomenon behind the unpleasant sensations is *not* also a discovery that 'pain' rigidly designates c-fiber firing, it is not a discovery that 'pain = c-fiber firing' is a true theoretical identity statement.

As I have just framed the argument, it impugns statements identifying pain with a neurophysiological type. But with minor adjustments the argument targets statements identifying pain with a functional type.

The argument impugns statements identifying pain with a functional type quite straightforwardly if 'pain' is *not* rigid *de jure* for whatever *functional* type is supposed to be identical with the relevant unpleasant sensations. In that case, we may substitute an expression for the relevant functional type in the place of 'c-fiber firing' in the argument and make a few other obvious corresponding changes, in order to generate an argument impugning psycho-functional identity statements (for further details, see chapter 7, §1.2).

But for some functionalists 'pain' (or alternatively 'to be pain' — I will include this alternative only tacitly, often) *is* rigid de jure for a functional type: "analytic" or "folk-psychological functionalists" in particular (see chapter 7, §2.1) hold that 'pain' or 'to be pain' is rigid de jure for what it is *to be the state (e.g., brain state) typically resulting from bodily damage and issuing in avoidance behavior, etc.* The skeptical argument defended in this chapter presupposes that 'pain' or 'to be pain' is straightforwardly rigid de jure for a sensation discerned by introspection (see chapter 7, §2.1), rather than for any physical or functional type; so if 'pain' or 'to be pain' is rigid de jure for a functional type, then the skeptical argument does not apply without modification. However, minor adjustments render the argument applicable.

Even if 'pain' is straightforwardly rigid de jure for a functional type, the skeptical argument finds a purchase, so long as painfulness can be identified also independently by introspection as the sensation that 'pain', a functional term, designates. I have already argued for this, in essence (in chapter 7, §2.1): here I will draw on that earlier discussion, refocusing and refining to suit.

Some who maintain that 'pain' is rigid de jure for a functional type would *deny* that painfulness is also something that could be identified independently by introspection. Such functionalists thereby adopt a version of eliminativism, so it is not surprising that the skeptical argument here concerning psychofunctional identity statements should not have much to say to them (again, see chapter 7, §2.1).

But consider a functionalist for whom the relevant sensation, which is allegedly functional, can be identified also independently by introspection. Such a functionalist will find herself vulnerable to a skeptical argument. The specific form taken by the skeptical argument will depend on the connection that the functionalist recognizes between 'pain' and that which is introspected. A few salient options present themselves. According to the first, a folk-psychological functionalist maintains that 'pain' is *defined*, de jure, according to functional role alone, even though the referent might also be identified introspectively or in other ways not associated with 'pain''s meaning. This option for functionalists robs the skeptical argument of a handy word that is guaranteed de jure to stay with the introspectively identified phenomenal sensation. But we may reformulate the skeptical argument by coining a new expression, instead of 'pain' which the functionalist redeploys: again, the functionalist in question acknowledges the power of introspection to pick out the relevant sensation, so she should have no objections to our naming the sensation in a causal baptism by way of samples obtained introspectively. Let 'P_s,' designate, de jure, *that* (introspect painfulness). Although 'pain' or 'to be pain' is rigid de jure for a functional property according to the present story, 'P_s' is not. Now the skeptical argument can be formulated by reference to P_s, instead of pain. The argument could become this: the information that some functional property P_f is correlated with P_s fails to indicate that 'P_s' rigidly designates that functional property, and accordingly fails to indicate that '$P_s = P_f$' is true. In the newly formulated argument, '$P_s = P_f$' has become the theoretical identity statement in doubt. I will continue to speak of 'pain' rather than 'P_s' as the subject term of the theoretical identity statement cast into doubt by the skeptical argument, tacitly supposing that 'pain' rigidly refers de jure to the introspectively identified phenomenon. But the reader with doubts is free to substitute 'P_s' for 'pain'.

There are other options for the folk-psychological functionalist who honors introspection but the effect is similar. The functionalist could try defining 'pain' by reference both to a functional role and also by reference to *that* (introspect painfulness), as two necessary conditions, jointly sufficient for the application of 'pain'. But here again, the expression 'pain' is redeployed for something that is unhelpful for articulating the question here, which is whether *that* (introspect painfulness) could come apart from the functional role. So again, the interesting question would become whether '$P_s = P_f$' could be established. The skeptical argument would maintain that it could not.

The likeliest option for the functionalist (and the option I tacitly attribute to her in chapter 7, §2.1; see also Senderowicz 2010, p. 88) would be, in effect, for the functionalist to offer *two* analyses, one analysis according to which 'pain' is to be used just for such and such functional role and the other analysis according to which 'pain' is to be used just for *that* (introspect painfulness): this sort of repeated defining is not uncommon in science (see LaPorte 2004, especially chapter 5). If this is the functionalist's position, then the properly adjusted skeptical argument would urge that for all we know there is a metaphysical possibility of separation between what is recognized from the inside perspective and the relevant functional correlate, which possibility would cause the twice-defined 'pain' to lack a straightforward designatum, and which possibility would accordingly cause the psychofunctional identity statement that contains 'pain' as a subject term to lack any straightforward truth value. Precisification or refinement is the remedy needed: the ill-defined term 'pain' must be replaced. We may use 'P_s' or 'P_f' but we must choose.

2. Why Not Dispense with De Jure Connections in Favor of Correlation and Scientific Induction?

I have stressed (in §1) that 'pain' is not rigid *de jure* for an underlying phenomenon or substance; but 'water' is. This claim or something close to it will be accepted by most philosophers and by most philosophers who accept materialism (see chapter 7, §1.1.1, and also chapter 7 §2.1 where I address exceptions) and apparently by most interested scientists as well, who routinely limit themselves to a search for "correlates" to phenomenal properties (e.g., Crick 1994, p. 9; Crick and Koch 1990, p. 264), mathematical or physical "parallels" to phenomenal properties (e.g., Page 2003, p. 468), and so on, implicitly or explicitly acknowledging "a distinction between what appears to be these two different aspects of reality" (Page 2003, p. 472).

But while my claim that 'pain' is not rigid de jure for an underlying phenomenon might pass with little controversy, my claim that this absence of the right de jure ties creates confirmational troubles can be expected to arouse opposition. There is a chorus of witnesses who testify, contrary to what I have claimed, that mere correlation will suffice, without help from any de jure ties, for purposes of confirming the truth of psychophysical identity statements. If this chorus is right, then we are entitled, "purely on the basis of direct correlational evidence," as Papineau would say (2002, p. 158; see also Bates 2009, p. 315), without help from any analyzable reference-establishing conditions associated de jure with its terms, to infer the truth of statements like 'pain = c-fiber firing'. Such statements could stand secure as "inductively established identities," as Marras holds (2005, p. 351; see also Marras 2005, p. 350 and Levine 1998, p. 459). According to the relevant chorus, the license to infer the truth of psychophysical identity statements on the basis of observed correlation is an inductive license that issues from broad methodological principles familiar from empirical science, like parsimony or simplicity or inference to the best explanation (Bates 2009, p. 315; Block and Stalnaker 1999, pp. 29–30; Clark 1997, p. 47; Hardcastle 1997, pp. 64–5; Heinzel and Northoff 2009, pp. 19f., 24; Hill and McLaughlin 1999, p. 451; cf. p. 447; McLaughlin 2001, p. 329, note 5; see also p. 320; Melnyk 2005; see also Mandik and Weisberg 2008, pp. 243–4; Patterson discusses forbears: 2008, pp. 544, 576).

I will argue, by appeal to confirmationally impoverished identity statements that seem easier to come to grips with than do the psychophysical identity statements at the center of controversy, that correlation as thorough as one might hope to obtain along with the best inductive practices at our disposal should give us little confidence of any theoretical identity statement's truth, without the right de jure ties. I present this case in section (2.1) below. Then in the following section (2.2), I address worries to the effect that in presenting my case in section (2.1), I overlook well-known resources for dispensing with the de jure ties that I deem to be so important, resources from widely embraced and plausible theories in the philosophy of language: recognitional and direct theories of reference.

2.1. Why De Jure Connections Must Attend Correlation and Scientific Induction

Water provides the classic case of a properly *confirmed* theoretical identity statement: 'water = H_2O'. But any confirmational merit that 'water = H_2O' enjoys or confirmational demerit that 'water = H_2O' suffers could not be expected to transfer to psychophysical identity statements because the means of confirmation is not the same. Merit or demerit that transfers would come instead from an identity statement about water any confirmational merit for which is obtained by the empirical observation of correlation in the absence of de jure ties to anything like: whatever *chemical* is instantiated in such and such baptismal sample. Fortunately, there are such statements available for comparison: 'water = $^{1-3}H_2O$' is one example.[3]

2.1.1. Problematic Theoretical Identity Statements and Correlation 'Water = $^{1-3}H_2O$' enjoys as much support from correlation as 'water = H_2O', but does not profit from de jure ties to anything like: whatever chemical is instantiated in such and such baptismal sample. Let me explain. '$^{1-3}H_2O$' is a name that I introduce for *H_2O made with ^1H, ^2H, or ^3H*, which are the three different isotopic varieties in which the element hydrogen happens to come. ^1H, ^2H, and ^3H have different weights, but share the same atomic number and hence are all hydrogen. Quantities of matter are H_2O just in case they are also $^{1-3}H_2O$: so chemists tell us, having observed a strict correlation between hydrogen and $^{1-3}$hydrogen. *Correlation* supports 'water = $^{1-3}H_2O$' as strongly as 'water = H_2O', since every sample of either H_2O or $^{1-3}H_2O$ is a sample of both. But 'water = $^{1-3}H_2O$' is hardly well confirmed, in the way that 'water = H_2O' is.

The reason that empirical inquiry puts speakers in a position to say that the facts about correlation vindicate 'water = H_2O', but not 'water = $^{1-3}H_2O$', is again that 'water = H_2O' profits from 'water''s *de jure connections*, which determine *what should be called "water"* in conceivable or apparently conceivable worlds in which the various types of properties that are *actually* correlated with water *come apart*: e.g., worlds in which some H_2O is not $^{1-3}H_2O$. Consider a Twin-Earth-type place or a possible world w featuring H_2O that is not $^{1-3}H_2O$, since w contains ^5H_2O, as our world does not. We would or should say, "in w, water is not all $^{1-3}H_2O$; rather, some of it is ^5H_2O." We should say this because 'water' rigidly designates, de jure, the underlying *chemical* present in a baptism; 'water' does not rigidly designate, de jure, anything like the underlying isotopically delimited chemical *variety* so present, though as it happens the isotopically delimited chemical variety $^{1-3}H_2O$ is present with the chemical H_2O in the baptismal sample and indeed in all samples of either H_2O or $^{1-3}H_2O$ in the actual world, where there is perfect correlation. Because 'water' rigidly designates, de jure, the relevant underlying chemical, 'water' applies to *all* varieties of that chemical, including ^5H_2O, with respect to possible worlds w that do not honor the correlation observed in the actual world between the chemical H_2O and the variety $^{1-3}H_2O$.

'Water = $^{1-3}H_2O$' is not true with respect to w, which contains ^5H_2O. But in that case, 'water = $^{1-3}H_2O$' is not true with respect to the actual world, any more than it is true with respect to w, even though the actual world does *not* contain any ^5H_2O to spoil a perfect correlation between water and $^{1-3}H_2O$ in the way that w does: if the identity statement were true with respect to the actual world, then it would be true with respect to all possible worlds, including w, since a true theoretical identity statement contains two rigid designators for the same property (see note 1), and so is true with respect to all possible worlds. 'Water = $^{1-3}H_2O$' is therefore false.

Or at least we may say that 'water = $^{1\text{-}3}\text{H}_2\text{O}$' is false if we are optimistic about our powers of discerning genuine metaphysical possibility by reflection on what is conceivable or apparently conceivable, in view of scientific deliverances. We can be more cautious. A more cautious line of thinking stops short of outright denial, maintaining not that 'water = $^{1\text{-}3}\text{H}_2\text{O}$' is necessarily *false*, but rather that we have little warrant for taking 'water = $^{1\text{-}3}\text{H}_2\text{O}$' to be *true*.[4] The cautious response remains open to the prospect that w, with its $^5\text{H}_2\text{O}$, is only *apparently* conceivable though *not really* metaphysically possible. But though we might wish to remain *open* in this way to the metaphysical impossibility of w, we certainly cannot say that scientific results about *correlation* give us any reasonable *grounds* for saying that w really *is* impossible. For all that scientists may assure us about correlation in the actual world, in which H_2O is all $^{1\text{-}3}\text{H}_2\text{O}$ and vice-versa, w with its attending $^5\text{H}_2\text{O}$ is truly metaphysically possible: new forces or conditions might, for all that our information indicates, produce $^5\text{H}_2\text{O}$. Given that scientific work does not indicate the metaphysical impossibility of w, and given that we should apply 'water' but not '$^{1\text{-}3}\text{H}_2\text{O}$' to $^5\text{H}_2\text{O}$ in w, we cannot be at all confident that the identity statement 'water = $^{1\text{-}3}\text{H}_2\text{O}$' is true. Even after the scientific research confirming correlation is completed, there is little evidence to support the identity statement.

I select 'water = $^{1\text{-}3}\text{H}_2\text{O}$' for an example in part because it is not patently false (see note 4): in that way it resembles psychophysical identity statements. But the cost of broaching an example of this sort is that it might lead the reader to suspect that, contrary to what I have said, this statement enjoys after all 'water = H_2O''s confirmational success: and so would any other statement that also measures up to 'water = H_2O' so far as support from correlation is concerned. Such doubts may be put to rest by consideration of certain identity statements that *are* patently false in a way that 'water = $^{1\text{-}3}\text{H}_2\text{O}$' is not: compare 'water = triplestatestuff'. 'Triplestatestuff' rigidly designates, de jure, an artificial type of matter whose instances in any possible world w are the same as the instances of whatever single chemical naturally occurs in w on Earth in three states: solid, liquid, and gaseous. Water is all of one chemical, the only chemical that happens naturally to occur in three states on Earth. So 'triplestatestuff' and 'water' apply, with respect to the actual world, to the same quantities of matter. What entitles us to favor 'water = H_2O' over 'water = triplestatestuff', despite the coapplication of 'water' and 'triplestatestuff', is again de jure connections, which determine *what should be called "water," "triplestatestuff," and so on*, with respect to worlds in which various correlated types *come apart*. Consider worlds w with respect to which *mercury* is the chemical that occurs naturally in three states on Earth: we should say that *'water'* fails to apply this time to what the other term, 'triplestatestuff', applies. We should say this because 'water' rigidly designates, de jure, the *chemical* present at baptism: so 'water' could hardly apply to matter of a different chemical like mercury, even with respect to worlds in which that different chemical comes in three states. 'Triplestatestuff', on the other hand, rigidly designates, de jure, something in a different and more artificial category. 'Triplestatestuff' rigidly designates, de jure, a type of stuff whose extension contains matter belonging to different chemicals with respect to different possible worlds in which different chemicals come in three states. So with respect to the foregoing worlds w in which mercury comes in three states, we should say "with respect to w, the triplestatestuff is present in the mercury, but the water is present in the H_2O." Such considerations undermine 'water = triplestatestuff' and support 'water = H_2O'.

Now I turn to psychophysical identity statements, to which similar words apply: correlation can not assure us that 'pain = c-fiber firing' is true any more than it can assure us that 'water = $^{1-3}H_2O$' is true or that 'water = triplestatestuff' is true. To confirm the psychophysical identity statement, we have to consider what we should say with respect to conceivable or apparently conceivable worlds in which salient correlated properties come apart, including worlds in which some c-fiber firing is not attended by painful sensations. Consider a Twin-Earth-type place or a possible world w featuring c-fiber firing that is not attended by painful sensations, since anesthesiologists there find a way to bring complete relief to patients experiencing that unpleasant sensation, by medical means that do not interfere with c-fiber firing. We would or should say, with respect to w, "c-fiber firing occurs without pain." We should say this because 'pain' rigidly designates, de jure, a *sensation* as selected by its phenomenal aspect from the inside rather than something like: the candidate that is present at baptism from such and such physical category. As in the foregoing cases concerning water and $^{1-3}H_2O$ or triplestatestuff, correlation between the phenomenon baptized 'pain' and the theoretical phenomenon c-fiber firing is not enough to qualify c-fiber firing, which we recognize in its own right, to be the referent.

'Pain = c-fiber firing' is not true with respect to w, which contains sensationless c-fiber firing. But in that case, 'pain = c-fiber firing' is not true with respect to the actual world, any more than it is true with respect to w, even though the actual world does *not* contain any sensationless c-fiber firing: if the statement were true with respect to the actual world, it would be true with respect to all possible worlds, including w, since a true theoretical identity statement contains two rigid designators for the same property (again, see note 1), and so is true with respect to all possible worlds. 'Pain = c-fiber firing' is therefore false.

Or at least we may say that 'pain = c-fiber firing' is false if we are optimistic about our powers of discerning genuine metaphysical possibility by reflection on what is conceivable or apparently conceivable, in view of the deliverances of science. Of course, we can be more cautious. A more cautious line of thinking stops short of outright denial, maintaining not that 'pain = c-fiber firing' is necessarily *false* but rather that we have little warrant for taking 'pain = c-fiber firing' to be *true*. Again, the cautious response remains open to the prospect that w, which features sensationless c-fiber firing, is only *apparently* conceivable though *not really* metaphysically possible. But again, even though we might wish to remain *open* to the metaphysical impossibility of w, we certainly cannot say that the scientific results about correlation give us any reasonable grounds for saying that w *is* impossible. For all that scientists can assure us about correlation in the actual world, in which painful sensations are all c-fiber firings and vice-versa (or so we may suppose),[5] w with its attending sensationless c-fiber firing is truly metaphysically possible: new forces or conditions might, for all that our information indicates, render c-fiber firing sensationless. Given that scientific work about correlation does not indicate the metaphysical impossibility of w, and given that we should apply 'c-fiber firing' but not 'pain' to sensationless c-fiber firing in w, we cannot be at all confident that the identity statement 'pain = c-fiber firing' is true. Even after the scientific research confirming perfect correlation is completed, there is little evidence to support the identity statement.

I will close this section (§2.1.1) by getting its central claim into a little sharper focus and casting it in more general terms than I have. As I have indicated, both subject terms 'water' and 'pain' are causally grounded in samples. Items qualify as candidates for reference, at the outset, by virtue of belonging to some *category* associated with the term de jure, however implicitly (or, more generally, by virtue of having some *descriptional or recognitional profile* associated de jure with the term: see §2.2): the de jure tie connecting the term to its referent by way of some category (or descriptional or recognitional profile: I will suppress this added precision in the following paragraphs, for simplicity) is what allows us to pick the referent out from competitors of the wrong category that are present in the same places and times. So again, to be able to pick out H_2O as the referent of 'water' we need to be able to recognize it as that *chemical* instantiated in this or that sample (other categories would do: see chapter 6, §2.2). '$^{1-3}H_2O$', by contrast, is fashioned to pick out a certain *isotopically limited* chemical *variety*, not a chemical. So the designatum of '$^{1-3}H_2O$' is not a candidate to be 'water''s designatum in the straightforward respect that H_2O is and that other chemicals are as well, like CO_2. Just so, to be able to pick out P_s as the referent of 'pain' we need to be able to recognize it from the inside perspective as that *phenomenal sensation* saliently exemplified in this toothacheish sensation, that stubbed-toeish sensation, etc. Since the referent of 'c-fiber firing' is picked out via some physically specified conditions, not phenomenally specified conditions, it fails in the most straightforward respect to be a candidate for 'pain''s reference.

The now more or less familiar observations from the foregoing paragraph might not on first glance seem worrisome. Even though the designatum of two terms in an identity statement like 'pain = c-fiber firing' or 'water = $^{1-3}H_2O$' are properly picked out de jure via distinct routes, we might still hope to find out what the designatum is for each term *independently* and *then*, by correlation, establish that the designatum of the one term is in fact identical with that of the other. We might for example propose to pick out "water" de jure as a certain *chemical* and to pick out "$^{1-3}H_2O$" de jure as a certain chemical *variety*, notice that their extensions are copresent, and infer identity from copresence; or we might propose to pick out "pain" de jure as a certain phenomenal sensation and to pick out "c-fiber firing" de jure as a certain neurophysiological type and again infer identity from copresence. But the trouble with this proposal is, in general, that if we *could* establish identity from copresence, then we would not need de jure ties to establish a designatum for each term in the relevant identity statement to begin with. But we do need de jure ties to establish a designatum for each term in the relevant identity statement to begin with.

In more detail, the problem is as follows (see the end of §2.1.2 for nuances): given that ⌜t⌝ and ⌜t'⌝ designate what is copresent, the category associated de jure with ⌜t⌝, in which we must recognize t, in order to *establish* that t *instead of distinct but copresent candidates* is the referent of ⌜t⌝, is a category in which we must *also* recognize t', in order to *establish* that t' *instead of distinct but copresent candidates* is also the designatum of ⌜t⌝, if we are to *establish* that t = t'. And in the case of problematic theoretical identity statements, including psychophysical identity statements, we are unable to discern that t', which is present with t along with other candidates for designation, belongs to the category that we would have to see that t' belongs to in order to establish that t' *instead of distinct but copresent candidates* is the designatum of ⌜t⌝ and hence that t = t'. The relevant de jure ties are missing. Hence, so far as we are able to discern, t' is not the item of the relevant category present in that place and time; t' is some other item present in that place and time.

So again, 'water' singles out for its referent one contender among many with copresent extensions: the *chemical* present in such and such location. But having established that 'water' designates a certain chemical (the one so present: H_2O), we could be assured that this designatum of 'water' is identical with $^{1-3}H_2O$ or $^{1-4}H_2O$, or $^{1-5}H_2O$ or whatnot, only if we could be assured that $^{1-3}H_2O$ or $^{1-4}H_2O$ or $^{1-5}H_2O$ or whatnot is also a *chemical*, namely H_2O, the designatum of 'water': being a chemical is what qualifies H_2O to *be* the designatum, so for that reason (among other reasons: chapter 6 note 12) there is no question that H_2O is a chemical, given that it is the designatum of 'water', and of course we are trying to discern whether the *variety* in question is also identical to this designatum. Unfortunately, we fail to see that the variety $^{1-3}H_2O$, as opposed to $^{1-4}H_2O$ or $^{1-5}H_2O$ or whatnot, is a chemical, as H_2O is: and similar doubts attend the alternatives $^{1-4}H_2O$ and $^{1-5}H_2O$, as well as any number of other copresent chemical varieties. We may be able to rule out some options by experiment: e.g., by producing ^4H_2O in the lab, thus defeating coextensiveness between $^{1-3}H_2O$ and the chemical H_2O and thereby ruling out $^{1-3}H_2O$ as the designatum of our term 'water'. But this is little help in narrowing us down to the right variety, assuming there is one, from among the candidates correlated with water.

Similarly, having established that 'pain' designates a certain *phenomenal sensation* (the one so present: P_s) and even perhaps having established (via some general argument: see chapter 7 §1.1.1) that P_s is some neurophysiological type or other, or some functional type or other, we could be assured that this designatum of 'pain' is identical with c-fiber firing or c-fiber firing-cum-conditions c or c-fiber firing-cum-conditions c' or whatnot, only if we could be assured that c-fiber firing or c-fiber firing-cum-conditions c or c-fiber firing-cum-conditions c' or whatnot is *also* a phenomenal sensation (identified from the inside: see chapter 7, §2.1), namely P_s, the designatum of 'pain': being a phenomenal sensation is what qualifies P_s to *be* the designatum, so for that reason (among other reasons) there is no question that P_s is a phenomenal sensation, given that it is the designatum of 'pain', and of course we are trying to discern whether the *neurophysiological type* in question is also identical to this designatum. Unfortunately, we fail to see that the neurophysiological type c-fiber firing, as opposed to c-fiber firing-cum-conditions c or c-fiber firing-cum-conditions c' or whatnot, is a phenomenal sensation, as P_s is: and similar doubts attend the alternatives c-fiber firing-cum-conditions c and c-fiber firing-cum-conditions c', as well as any number of other copresent neurophysiological or functional alternatives. We may be able to rule out some options by experiment a posteriori by seeing, say, that there are no conditions c attending certain pain-wracked patients, thus defeating coextensiveness between c-fiber firing-cum-conditions c and the phenomenal sensation pain, and thereby ruling out c-fiber firing-cum-conditions c as the designatum of our term 'pain'. But this is little help in narrowing us down to the right neurophysiological or functional candidate for reference, from among the candidates correlated with pain.

2.1.2. Problematic Theoretical Identity Statements and Broad Inductive Principles Testifying to Identity Something about the foregoing lesson may appear to be at odds with ordinary scientific practice, in which the confirmation of identity is commonplace. Taxonomists have confirmed, as I have said, that Brontosaurus = Apatosaurus. Astronomers have confirmed that Hesperus = Phosphorus. Historians have confirmed that Mark Twain = Samuel Clemens, or could do so if called upon. Surely, we might suspect in light of scientists' routine confirmation of identity, 'pain = c-fiber firing' ought to be tractable if true.

A suggestion that naturally comes to mind on consideration of historical cases is that I might have neglected, in my skeptical evaluation of 'pain = c-fiber firing''s prospects (§2.1.1), to take into account that theories about identity find scientific support not just in correlation but also in inductive principles. Thus, the scientist who discovered that Brontosaurus = Apatosaurus had to sort out the likelihood, by broadly inductive methods, that the specimen grounding 'Brontosaurus' is of the same genus as the specimen grounding 'Apatosaurus', rather than a quite distinct genus, as former scientists had thought on account of differences in size. Scientists confirming that Hesperus = Phosphorus had to sort out the likelihood, by broadly inductive methods, that Hesperus and Phosphorus are the same heavenly body with a relatively natural pattern of motion across the sky rather than distinct planets that take very unnatural turns when we cannot observe them: and so on. Philosophically minded scientists might in these cases appeal to the simplicity of positing identity or centrality of identity in the leading theory, and so on: in any event, identity seems to find support in a body of broadly inductive "methodological principles whose power and importance are widely acknowledged even if no one has ever been able to formulate them precisely" (Block and Stalnaker 1999, p. 21). Perhaps these broadly inductive methodological principles are enough to secure identity, without any help from de jure ties, when scientists are able to confirm identity, even though correlation in space and time alone is not enough to secure identity. But I will argue that broadly inductive principles are not enough; scientists must rely on de jure ties in conjunction with the relevant inductive principles.

Consider the confirmation of 'Brontosaurus = Apatosaurus'. De jure ties attaching this statement's terms to their designata are conveniently clear: Marsh deliberately coined two *genus* terms 'Brontosaurus' and 'Apatosaurus', using a different sample specimen for each. Had he intended instead when he coined these terms to name a *species* or a taxon of some other rank, he would have had to choose names with a different form, according to the explicit directives of nomenclatural codes. So a taxonomic name like 'Brontosaurus' or 'Apatosaurus' is explicitly tied, de jure, to genus or species or whatever the rank may be.

The most reasonable theory, by the appropriate broadly inductive standards, turned out to support identity between the genus designated by the one term and the genus designated by the other term. The sample specimen used to ground the genus term 'Brontosaurus' in a baptism, a particular dinosaur that Marsh exhumed and tagged "YPM 4633," turned out by the most reasonable theory to be a more mature specimen of the same genus as the sample specimen used to ground the genus term 'Apatosaurus', a particular dinosaur that Marsh exhumed and tagged "YPM 1860."

The de jure ties connecting 'Brontosaurus' and 'Apatosaurus' to the *genus* of the respective sample are presupposed in the language used to reason about identity. That the identity 'Brontosaurus = Apatosaurus' owes its favorable epistemic status to these de jure ties is clear from a comparison to alternative identity statements containing different names that were coined by appeal to the same samples: names with their own de jure ties explicitly distinct from the de jure ties of the names in 'Brontosaurus = Apatosaurus'. '*Apatosaurus Ajax*' is the *species* term corresponding to the genus term 'Apatosaurus'. This species term was grounded using the same sample specimen, namely YPM 1860. But '*Apatosaurus Ajax*' enjoys unique de jure connections allowing it to designate the *species* of the individual YPM 1860 instead of the genus of that individual.

Because '*Apatosaurus Ajax*' is a species term instead of a genus term, the same theoretical information as supports 'Brontosaurus = Apatosaurus' cannot begin to support 'Brontosaurus = *Apatosaurus Ajax*' or 'Apatosaurus = *Apatosaurus Ajax*', although it could support '*Brontosaurus excelsus = Apatosaurus Ajax*', which concerns species only, provided that YPM 4633, the particular dinosaur grounding '*Brontosaurus excelsus*', as well as 'Brontosaurus', is of the same species as YPM 1860, which again is the particular dinosaur grounding '*Apatosaurus Ajax*', as well as 'Apatosaurus'.

We are not entitled to say that the *genus* Brontosaurus is identical to the species *Apatosaurus Ajax* even though both the genus Brontosaurus (Apatosaurus) and the species *Apatosaurus Ajax* are present in the sample individual YPM 4633. The most that can be inferred reasonably about the relationship between the genus and the species is expressed by the statement 'Brontosaurus (Apatosaurus) and *Apatosaurus Ajax* are copresent in the sample specimen YPM 4633' or similar statements affirming *copresence* instead of identity. Identity would foreclose the possibility that the genus and species should ever come apart in other sample specimens: any specimens belonging to the same genus but different species would defeat the coextensiveness of 'Brontosaurus' and '*Apatosaurus Ajax*', thereby ruling out identity. And although we *can* establish the necessary coextensiveness of 'Brontosaurus' and 'Apatosaurus' by establishing that they are both names for the *same genus*, designating it rigidly or with respect to every possible world, no world of which features the genus coming apart from *itself* of course, the empirical observations and broadly inductive principles used to establish the necessary coextensiveness of 'Brontosaurus' and 'Apatosaurus' leave us helpless to establish the necessary coextensiveness of a name for the *genus* and a name for one of its *species* despite rigidity. Here it does not matter whether or not we have yet *found* any specimens that belong to the genus without belonging to the species: that concerns correlation. Even should we have good reason to think there *are no* such specimens to be found, given the conditions under which new species are able to take hold and given the stringent ecological requirements of that genus, still that would not show that it would be metaphysically impossible for the genus to produce new species. Any genuinely possible separation belies identity between species and genus. Sound inductive principles do not license 'Apatosaurus = *Apatosaurus Ajax*' nor any other identity statement similarly lacking more cooperative de jure ties between the statement's expressions and their designata.

Identity statements about concrete objects uphold the same lesson. We can imagine later historians motivating a theory of identity with claims like, "Look at the 'coincidences' in which we find both Mark Twain and Samuel Clemens present doing the same things. They must be the same person, since the theory that they are identical is so much simpler than alternative theories according to which two people somehow happen to duplicate each other's lives" (cf. Block and Stalnaker 1999, p. 24; see also Levine 1998, pp. 460–1). Here it might seem to be especially straightforward to confirm identity: scientists simply reconstruct history, using trustworthy inductive resources to reconstruct the spatio-temporal paths of Mark Twain and Samuel Clemens, finding them to be the same. There would be no need for the terms both to designate, de jure, anything like: the *person* meeting such and such conditions. Without such de jure ties we might establish that 'Mark Twain' and 'Samuel Clemens' designate the right person empirically just by tracing the concrete referent of each term, as David Hull would have it in accordance with this natural line of thinking, "back in time to see if they intersect at the naming ceremony. If so, the name rigidly designates the entity" (Hull 1988, p. 500). Thomas Kuhn agrees: to put an end to the question whether Mark Twain is also Samuel Clemens, "we simply trace his life history or lifeline backward in time to see whether it includes the appropriate act of baptism or dubbing" as 'Samuel Clemens' (Kuhn 2000, p. 198).

As natural as the foregoing line of thinking is, it is not correct: if 'Mark Twain' were an ordinary *person*-term and 'Samuel Clemens' were a "persisting-officer" term instead (see chapter 2, §2.1), for an item constituted first by Mark Twain and then by the person, if anyone, who succeeds Mark Twain as the highest-profile figure in the Congo Liberation Movement, then 'Mark Twain = Samuel Clemens' would be false, or at least we would have no reason to suppose it is true, whatever we learn of the spatio-temporal coincidence between Mark Twain and "Samuel Clemens" at the time of baptism or during a longer span of time, such as the person's or persisting officer's life (for closely related arguments see, again, chapter 2, §2.1). All that a reasonable inference could come to is 'Mark Twain [the person] and Samuel Clemens [the persisting officer] are copresent in the same matter at various events in which they are found doing the same things'. Identity would foreclose the possibility of their ever *not* being copresent; but scientific reasoning will not license us to close that possibility. We so naturally and effortlessly use 'Samuel Clemens' as a *person* term that we easily overlook the de jure connections that enable us to conclude, in view of the empirical information, that we have designated the ordinary person Mark Twain with the term, rather than a persisting officer or some other kind of entity.

Similar words apply to 'Hesperus = Phosphorus'. Again, contrary to appearances, it is not true that spatio-temporal "continuity of the entity being named permits disambiguation," and hence establishes a definite designatum in the absence of de jure ties (Hull 1998, p. 500; see also p. 497; see also Collins 1988, pp. 202–3, 206; Kuhn 2000, pp. 198–200, 205, 312–13). Were 'Hesperus' an ordinary planet term and 'Phosphorus' an office-planet term for an item constituted at any time by the brightest planet at that time, then the inductive principles that confirmed 'Hesperus = Phosphorus' could not have confirmed it. Those principles, here in this case as before, license us to affirm identity only with the help of de jure ties.

By way of closing this section (2.1.2) let me address briefly a few details which settle into place without affecting the main point. First, it makes no difference to the argument in question if some speakers borrow reference conditions of terms for historical figures or other objects from other speakers. If speakers' use is to underwrite the truth of 'Mark Twain = Samuel Clemens', then since today's speakers have not themselves, with something like a baptismal pronouncement, secured both terms to a person, as opposed to something else like a persisting officer, they have to have borrowed the terms from other speakers who have secured the terms appropriately in this way. I have left out causal chains to simplify the presentation.

Another substantial simplification that I have made in presenting de jure connections here and elsewhere is to ignore various complex types of de jure conditions on reference, such as we see in de jure conditions on reference that apply defeasibly on condition that certain presuppositions are met. Thus, we recognize 'Samuel Clemens' to be a person term, *in view of what we have found*. Had we found a robot's innards during an autopsy, then the conditions for 'Samuel Clemens' to be a person-term would presumably not properly be recognized as obtaining. We would say that 'Samuel Clemens'' status as a person term was defeated: the status held, de jure, on condition that a person and not something like a robot was present at baptism. These complications would seem not to affect the main point here. Even if the type of item to which

'Mark Twain' and 'Samuel Clemens' should refer is determined in part, de jure, by empirical input, the type of item to which each of these terms should refer would be sensitive to empirical input in the *same* way. So the truth of 'Mark Twain = Samuel Clemens' seems assured, in view of *any* autopsy, as long as the referents share the body on which the autopsy is performed. Barring exotic skeptical possibilities, both terms are *person* terms rather than, say, robot terms; but if 'Samuel Clemens' were to turn out to be a robot term, so would 'Mark Twain' and hence the identity would be upheld.

2.2. Are De Jure Connections Controversial?

I have argued, in section (2.1), that correlation and the scientific method, without the right de jure connections allowing us to pick out the referent from a field of competitors in the wrong category present at the same places and times, is useless for purposes of securing the truth of theoretical identity statements. Although I am certainly not the first to point to the need for something like a "mediating category" (as Bealer would say: 1987, p. 351) to this end, the idea of a mediating category can be expected to arouse widespread suspicion or worse.

It might be granted easily enough that de jure connections dovetail with *descriptive* theories of reference, according to which a term's dubber might offer descriptive information de jure in order to select a referent for a term she dubs. Thus, let us consider a recent and informed version of descriptivism: the so-called "causal-descriptive" theory, according to which there is a causal element to reference, as is manifested by ostension at baptism, but according to which there is also a descriptive element to reference. According to the causal-descriptive theory of reference, the right referent is "picked out by the descriptions associated with the term in the grounding" (Devitt and Sterelny 1999, p. 92; for a similar position, see Stanford and Kitcher 2000). So 'water' might have been baptized with a pronouncement to the effect that it is to name a *"chemical"* (the speaker points); 'triplestatestuff' would have a very different baptism, since it names not a *chemical* but rather a somewhat artificial type of material that is *coinstantiated* with one or another of different chemicals in different possible worlds. Given baptismal pronouncements like the foregoing ones honored by the causal-descriptive theory of reference, descriptive specifications do the needed work of attaching terms, de jure, to underlying properties in a way that licenses the confirmation of 'water = H_2O', though not 'triplestatestuff = H_2O' or 'water = triplestatestuff'.

But while the causal-descriptive theory of reference, or a more heavily descriptive account of reference, clearly accommodates the de jure ties whose crucial role in confirmation I have been emphasizing, it is much less clear from the outset whether theories of reference that are known for dispensing with descriptions can also accommodate de jure ties. There are two such theories that enjoy prominence. I will discuss them in turn in sections (2.2.1) and (2.2.2).

2.2.1. The Recognitional Theory of Reference The best alternative (alleged alternative anyway: see Stanford and Kitcher 2000, p. 102) to a causal-*descriptive* theory of reference, and the only competing theory of reference enjoying much currency in today's market, is the "recognitional" theory of reference, according to which speakers responsible for establishing reference, including dubbers or experts on whom ordinary speakers rely for their borrowed use of a term, have to be able to *recognize* the referent in various possible scenarios, given the right conditions and information, even if they need not be able to provide explicit *descriptive* information in order to establish reference (Brown 1998; Haukioja 2006, §2; Miller 1992, p. 428; Sterelny 1983, p. 116). This view is popular with identity theorists (see, e.g., Carruthers 2000, pp. 55ff.; cf. pp. 47–8; Hill and McLaughlin 1999, p. 448; Loar 1997, pp. 600–4; Marras, 2005, p. 347; Papineau 2002, pp. 86–7; Tye 2006, pp. 151–2, 166).

The recognitional theory of reference may *appear* to show the way around de jure ties. If, as a recognitional view would maintain, there is no descriptive de jure connection that speakers have explicitly articulated, or perhaps that speakers even *could* explicitly articulate, between 'water' and a "chemical," then it might appear that there are no de jure connections *at all* binding 'water' to this or any other type of underlying entity. In that case, our knowledge about 'water = H_2O''s necessity could hardly owe anything to de jure connections of the relevant sort: and there would be nothing to prevent us, impoverished as we are with respect to the relevant de jure connections, from obtaining similar knowledge about the necessity of psychophysical identity statements. The recognitional theory might look especially promising, then, to theorists interested in locating a resource that will license them to do without any commitment to de jure ties. But a closer look at the theory will disappoint.

What the recognitional theory suggests is that 'water' does not *explicitly* designate, de jure, anything like: the underlying chemical present at baptism. But the recognitional theory does not suggest that 'water' has no de jure ties. On the contrary, the recognitional theory is hospitable to the position that de jure ties somehow or other bind words like 'water' to the appropriate designata: indeed the recognitional theory is *committed* to the position that de jure ties do this work. The theory offers an explanation of how speakers could secure a term to the candidate that the term really designates, without the use of *descriptive* connections that might distinguish the real designatum from decoys present at the same time and place as the real designatum: the explanation is in effect that *tacit, recognitional* de jure connections secure designation, instead of *explicit* de jure connections. If there is a tacit, recognitional de jure connection of the relevant sort, then the dubber is unable to articulate at water's baptism, say, that she is coining a *chemical* term rather than an *in-a-particular-number-of-terrestrial-states* term for stuffs: but she would *recognize* the *chemical, H_2O* (or the chemical H_2O_2 or XYZ or whatever, as the circumstances warrant) rather than the *in-a-particular-number-of-terrestrial-states* type of stuff *triplestatestuff*, as the proper referent, in view of the relevant scientific work following baptism. In this way, she uses 'water', de jure, in *deed* and tacitly, even if not in word and explicitly, as a rigid designator for the underlying chemical present at baptism.

The recognitional theory of reference can recognize the necessity of 'water = H_2O', because *tacit* de jure links of the sort recognized by this theory can secure the necessity of the statement, just as explicit de jure links can, in a way that bare correlation can not. What the recognitional theory can *not* do is to show how the necessity of 'water = H_2O' could be secured *without* de jure links, which is the hope that motivated an investigation of the recognitional account here in the first place. The investigation leaves us, then, where we started: with no plausible account of how the necessity of 'water = H_2O' could be secured on the basis of bare correlation, without the relevant de jure connections.

2.2.2. The Theory of Direct Reference As I have said, the recognitional theory is one of a *pair* of well-known theories in the philosophy of language that can appear on a first glance to be incompatible with my case on behalf of de jure connections' indispensability for confirming the truth of theoretical identity statements: the *other* such theory is the theory of *direct reference*.[6] If a term like 'pain' *directly* refers, it could easily seem as if there is no room for mediation between the word and its referent, by way of de jure ties binding the word to whatever candidate for reference satisfies the right conditions. Still, we might hope to confirm the necessity of theoretical identity statements containing such directly referring subject terms. So it is not surprising that philosophers who are optimistic about prospects for confirming psychophysical identity statements frequently maintain that terms like 'pain' and corresponding concepts, "directly pick out certain physical states, without remainder," as Loar holds (2003, p. 120). These "basic unstructured terms" (Papineau 2003, p. 216) are supposed to lack descriptive associations that would put requirements on designation: instead, they are supposed to "refer directly in their own right" (Papineau 2002, p. 158n.; see also pp. 92–3; 2006; Balog 2012, §2 and §3; Macdonald 2004, p. 517; Marras 2005, pp. 347–8; a similar position is found in the work of earlier generations: see Patterson 2008, p. 572).

I will argue that it is a mistake to suppose that the direct-reference theory tells against de jure ties. Direct-reference theorists can and should acknowledge de jure ties, as recognition theorists do.

Whether direct-reference theorists *should* acknowledge de jure ties can be resolved quickly at this point. Although direct-reference theorists are not *committed* to de jure ties by virtue of *being* direct-reference theorists, for reasons I will indicate soon, direct-reference theorists should acknowledge de jure ties for the reasons everyone else should: as I have already argued, de jure ties are needed to establish a designatum. If 'Samuel Clemens' were not, de jure, something like an *ordinary*-person term rather than an *office*-person term, it could not designate Mark Twain instead of an office person copresent with Mark Twain. If 'water' were not, de jure, something like a *chemical* term rather than an *in-a-particular-number-of-terrestrial-states* term, it could not designate H_2O rather than triplestatestuff.

But even if direct-reference theorists *should* acknowledge de jure connections, it might be questioned whether they *can*. They can. Any account of de jure conditions on reference lies outside the scope of the direct-reference theory. This is because the direct-reference theory tells us *what* it is that terms and statements express, not *how* they manage to express what they express. Though the direct-reference theory does not speak to whether there are any de jure conditions on reference, direct-reference theorists are as entitled as anyone else to the usual position concerning *how* the referent of 'Samuel Clemens' or 'water' qualifies as the referent: by virtue of being the *person* or *chemical* present at a *baptism*, at which the dubber has the needed recognitional capacities or utters the right descriptive baptismal pronouncement, and so on. The typical direct-reference theorist helps herself to the usual position accordingly (see note 7). What distinguishes a direct-reference theorist *as* a direct-reference theorist is her additional commitment to the claim that 'Samuel Clemens' or 'water' *expresses* nothing about the foregoing matters. What the terms express has nothing to do with all of the manifold factors *allowing* for them to do so. Accordingly, what 'Mark Twain = Samuel Clemens' says or expresses has nothing to do with persons or baptisms or pointing; the statement just says *that Mark Twain = Mark Twain*.

An economical way of putting the situation is as follows. Direct-reference theorists are free to acknowledge that there are conditions associated de jure with any given designator and that a successful candidate for designation must satisfy these de jure conditions. What direct-reference theorists are *not* free to acknowledge is that such conditions are *semantic*. They must regard the conditions as *metasemantic* (Kaplan 1989b, pp. 573–6; Stalnaker 2003, pp. 15, 166–7, 174; 2007, pp. 253–4).[7]

3. De Jure Connections Supplied by way of Scientific Necessitarianism?

Scientific observation confirming correlation, along with methods like scientific induction, are not enough to assure that two terms in a theoretical identity statement like 'pain = c-fiber firing' rigidly designate the same item: so I have argued (in §2). We need more by way of instructions associated de jure with the relevant terms, so to speak, to tell the terms how to find their designata. But such de jure instructions fail to help secure the truth of 'pain = c-fiber firing'. So as helpful as science is in establishing correlation (which we might even agree amounts to coinstantiation: see note 5), it is not easy to see how science could confirm psychophysical identity statements.

There is a second broad, salient proposal in the literature, on behalf of science's efficacy for establishing the truth of psychophysical identity statements. I will evaluate that proposal, before I conclude that science's prospects for confirming psychophysical identity statements are dim. The proposal is that while mere correlation, along with traditional methods like scientific induction, can not vindicate theoretical identity statements, more potent reasoning associated with scientific necessitarianism *can* vindicate theoretical identity statements (Garrett 2009, §3; Gozzano 2010, p. 124; Shoemaker: see 1998, p. 76, and 11; 2011, p. 341; see also Matson 2011, p. 153 and for a critical discussion see Moffett 2010, §4). The proposal rests on two claims. The first and more important claim is that *physically* necessary correlation between phenomena like pains and c-fiber firings must also be *metaphysically* necessary: this specific application of scientific necessitarianism, the general view that physical necessity is necessity in the strongest sense, is the basis of the proposal in question to vindicate science's authority to confirm problematic theoretical identity statements of the sort at issue. The second and auxiliary claim needed to establish science's authority to confirm problematic theoretical identity statements of the sort at issue is the claim that properties are coarsely individuated, so that if it is a matter of *metaphysical necessity* that all pain is c-fiber firing and vice-versa, then this is sufficient to establish *identity* between these seemingly different types of phenomena.[8] Let me say a bit more about how these two claims would work together, according to the proposal in question.

Triangularity and trilaterality are necessarily coinstantiated: we can be confident of that, but our warrant for confidence here is not matched by any *similarly* obtained warrant in the case of pain and c-fiber firing (as I explain in chapter 1, note 12). We must turn elsewhere for help securing the metaphysical necessity. This is where scientific necessitarianism promises to help, maintaining as it does that pain and c-fiber firing are correlated as a matter of metaphysical necessity if they are found to be correlated as a matter of physical necessity. We might accordingly suppose then that scientists can, by establishing that pain and c-fiber firing are correlated as a matter of physical necessity, establish that pain and c-fiber firing are correlated as a matter of metaphysical necessity.

Of course, even if scientists can confirm metaphysically necessary coinstantiation for pain and c-fiber firing, we are not yet licensed to affirm an *identity* statement like 'pain = c-fiber firing' unless we are taking properties to be very coarsely individuated. But the claim that properties are so coarsely individuated need not invite any controversy. For our purposes, anyway, triangularity and trilaterality may be said to be *identical*. The same applies to pain and c-fiber firing, provided that *they*, too, are coinstantiated by virtue of metaphysical necessity.[9] To the objection, "surely we want to distinguish a property like triangularity from a property like trilaterality," we may reply, with David Lewis, "Sometimes we do, sometimes we don't." For Lewis, there is not to be found here any "matter for dispute. Here there is a rift in our talk of properties, and we simply have two different conceptions" (1986, p. 55). Let us adopt a coarse conception of properties then, with Lewis and others (Lewis 1986, pp. 55ff.; Loar 2003, p. 125; Shoemaker 1984, p. 225; 2002, pp. 61–2), as at least one helpful explication of 'property'.

A coarse understanding of properties, especially in coordination with scientific necessitarianism, promises to redeem any number of theoretical identity statements, including but not only including psychophysical identity statements. Thus, as a matter of *physical* necessity, water expands when it freezes. This unusual action has to do with the water molecule's peculiar structure and the various bonds that hold within and between water molecules: most chemicals become *denser* when they freeze since the molecules pack more tightly together. In fact, water appears to be the only compound that expands like this. Since any other chemical's behavior in this regard, like water's behavior in this regard, is a matter of physical law, it appears to be physically necessary that water is the one compound that expands when it freezes. Even if such a generalization should be regarded as provisional at this point, we can suppose that it holds for the sake of illustration: so given that the relevant physically necessary behavior is also metaphysically necessary, and given a coarse construal of properties, 'water = the chemical compound that expands when it freezes' or 'water = the chemical compound that behaves aqueously' (where "aqueous" behavior includes, along with expansion upon freezing, also water's transparency in its pure liquid state, its boiling point, its freezing point, and so on), can be counted as a true theoretical identity statement.[10] Something similar might hold for 'water = $^{1-3}H_2O$', discussed in the previous section, which is perhaps a more doubtful case. It is not clear whether restrictions on the range of water in the actual world, from ^1H_2O to ^3H_2O, represent physically necessary law or accident, since the range of isotopes in some elements has been increased under unusual circumstances introduced in the laboratory; but the former possibility, according to which the range is established by law, suggests that 'water = $^{1-3}H_2O$' might be vindicated after all.

A coarse construal of properties, combined with scientific necessitarianism, issues a generous license to recognize a variety of otherwise objectionable identity statements, then. Even so, I suggest that the license is not *so* generous that it can be rejected out of hand. Even if the license honors 'water = the chemical compound that expands when it freezes' and perhaps also 'water = $^{1-3}H_2O$', that would seem to be appropriately in harmony with the spirit behind the coarse construal. The license issued by a coarse construal is *not* so liberal as to honor even a statement like 'water = triplestatestuff', say, to which few would be inclined to commit. H_2O and triplestatestuff are correlated only as a result of a mere geological accident, and not as a result of anything like physical necessity: so there is no need to recognize identity here, even on a coarse construal of properties combined with scientific necessitarianism.

I have noted that a coarse construal of properties is unobjectionable, or at least the present use of it is, even if scientific necessitarianism is also unobjectionable, in which case we are committed to upholding a surprisingly vast range of theoretical identity statements. But scientific necessitarianism is *not* unobjectionable. I will argue that scientists are unable, by observing physical necessity, to establish the relations of metaphysical necessity that would secure identity between properties. So after the information from scientists about physical laws is in, psychophysical identity statements like 'pain = c-fiber firing', as well as similarly problematic theoretical identity statements concerning other subjects like water, such as 'water = the chemical compound that expands when it freezes' and 'water = $^{1-3}H_2O$', will remain unconfirmed by science. In sections (3.1)–(3.4), I will discuss distinct strategies on the part of scientific necessitarians to show that scientists *can*, contrary to what I claim, establish the relevant metaphysical necessity. I will point out reasons to resist.

3.1. From Subject Terms to Properties to Law-Governed Behavior: the Missing De Jure Link?

Different strains within scientific necessitarianism suggest in different ways that the relevant de jure links are there to be found, or at any rate something reflecting the spirit of de jure links is there to be found, to tell us how to single out the designatum of a term like 'pain' from a variety of coinstantiated candidates, even if the relevant links are not so obviously positioned as those linking 'water', say, to whatever *chemical* might be present at baptism. In the following four sections (3.1)–(3.4), I will present four different attempts to locate subtly positioned de jure links, or something like them, which would be capable of vindicating psychophysical identity statements and other similarly problematic theoretical identity statements like 'water = the chemical compound that expands when it freezes' or 'water = the chemical compound that behaves aqueously'.

The first of the attempts to locate subtly positioned de jure links is the most straightforward. This attempt urges that any property term is linked, de jure, to those law-governed behaviors that actually attend the designated property, because those behaviors are the criteria we use to determine what counts as the designatum with respect to other possible worlds. Here Sydney Shoemaker comes first to mind, for his seminal suggestion that "semantic intuitions" support "the claim that the causal features of properties are essential to them" (1998, p. 63), so that the laws of nature, which govern those properties, hold in all metaphysically possible worlds: "it is impossible that the same properties should be governed by different causal laws in different possible worlds" (1984, pp. 222–3; see also 1998, pp. 61, 69–70; 2007, pp. 142–4). The suggestion here, allegedly supported by intuitions about our "criteria" for using a term like 'water' properly (2007, p. 143), is that we would refrain from *calling* the stuff in our oceans "water" if it were not to expand upon freezing. To be worthy of the name 'water', a substance has to behave as water *does* behave when stimulated in the same causally relevant ways, and water expands. On the foregoing grounds, we might conclude that 'water expands when it freezes' is necessary: and related reasoning apparently promises to redeem the still stronger necessity behind 'water = the chemical compound that expands when it freezes' (see the paragraphs introducing §3).

What applies to 'water' applies to 'c-fiber firing'. According to the argument under consideration, we would refrain from calling the relevant units of our nervous system "c-fibers" if they were sensationless upon firing. To be worthy of the name 'c-fibers', organic material must behave as c-fibers *do* behave when stimulated in the same causally relevant ways, and c-fibers issue in pain when stimulated to fire. On these grounds, we might affirm the metaphysical necessity of 'c-fiber firing issues in pain' and, after more extensive reasoning along similar lines, 'pain = c-fiber firing'. In general, our scientific terms would have no application in worlds with different physical laws. So goes the line of reasoning.

I do not share the foregoing semantic intuitions with respect to the proper use, de jure, of property designators, with respect to counterfactual situations, but these intuitions are not my target here. There is no need to dispute them: even if the intuitions are sound, they do not vindicate theoretical identity statements of the interesting variety we are after. Let us suppose, for the sake of argument, that sound intuitions inform us that the proper use of 'water' forbids the application of 'water' to matter in other possible worlds that is otherwise like water but that contracts when frozen: in that case, we can know that it is metaphysically impossible for *water* to contract when frozen. Even so, we may coin 'sch-water' as a substance term that is not so restrictive in its possible application as 'water' turns out to be (for related appeals to schm-entities, see Botterill 2005, p. 121; Handfield 2005, p. 82; Lange 2004, pp. 229ff.; Levin 1987, pp. 291–2; Sidelle 2002). 'Sch-water' is a term that applies just as 'water' does except with respect to possible worlds in which would-be water contracts when frozen or behaves in ways otherwise out of accordance with our physical laws: with respect to those worlds, 'sch-water' applies to the contractive substance even though 'water' does not. In addition to 'sch-water', there is 'sch-c-fiber firing', and so on.

If you think that 'water' and 'c-fiber firing' are best given the restrictive use described, rephrase what I say about "water" and "c-fiber firing" in order to put it instead in terms of "sch-water" and "sch-c-fiber firing." Given a restrictive use of 'water', we can find out that '*water* expands when it freezes' expresses a metaphysically necessary truth by finding out that it expresses a physically necessary truth; but we still cannot find out that '*sch*-water expands when it freezes' expresses a metaphysically necessary truth by finding out that it expresses a physically necessary truth. And the substantive issue here is the metaphysical necessity or contingency of *sch-water*'s expansion: the issue is whether there could be something that is *just like* the water in your glass *except* that it would not expand if it froze. Again, it does not matter whether we would still use the *label* 'water' for this substance, which is indistinguishable by all chemical accounts, so semantic intuitions about how we should apply that specific label are irrelevant. Because we are in no position to say that 'sch-water = the chemical compound that expands when it freezes', expresses a truth, the *substance* of the lessons to this point for 'water = the chemical compound that expands when it freezes' remains intact.

In the same way, given the restrictive use of 'c-fiber firing', we can find out that '*c*-fiber firing generates painful sensations' expresses a metaphysically necessary truth by finding out that it expresses a physically necessary truth; but we still cannot find out that '*sch*-c-fiber firing generates pain' expresses a metaphysically necessary truth by finding out that it expresses a physically necessary truth. And the substantive issue here is the metaphysical necessity or contingency of *sch-c*-fiber firing's generation of pain: the issue is whether there could be something that is *just like* the particular c-fiber firing occurring now as you stub your toe *except* that there is no attending painfulness.[11] It does not matter whether we would still use the *label* 'c-fiber firing' for this event type, which is indistinguishable by all physical accounts, so semantic intuitions about how we should apply that specific label are irrelevant. Because we are in no position to say that 'pain = sch-c-fiber firing' expresses a truth, the *substance* of the lessons to this point for 'pain = c-fiber firing' remains intact.

Scientific necessitarians are chary about addressing the metaphysical possibility of schm-entities with exotic properties that defy our physical laws (as Botterill observes: 2005, p. 121). But sometimes they do address the issue explicitly. Ellis does: he "would certainly deny that real possibilities can just be invented like this. Real possibilities have to be discovered" (2004, p. 76). One problem with Ellis' response is that people who call attention to schm-entities do not claim to have *invented* a metaphysical possibility. For my part, I do not even claim that contractive sch-water, painless sch-c-fiber firings and the like are a *genuine* metaphysical possibility: only that they are a metaphysical possibility for all that we *know*. But if contractive sch-water, painless sch-c-fiber firings and the like are indeed possible, as they might be for all that our information indicates, then I did not invent their possibility: the phenomena were surely possible before I did anything at all by way of calling attention to the possibility.[12]

Mere semantic intuitions, concerning whether we would still apply 'c-fibers' if their firing failed to be painful, or concerning whether we would still apply 'water' if its freezing failed to issue in expansion, seem unable to provide substantive relief for doubts over the metaphysical necessity of interesting claims about the designata. A *substantive* argument for the metaphysical necessity of 'water = the chemical compound that expands when it freezes', 'pain = c-fiber firing', and so on, would be an argument that could be reformulated, to the same effect, by appeal to sch-entities in place of familiar entities. Such an argument is still needed.

3.2. From Subject Terms to Constitution to Law-Governed Behavior: the Missing De Jure Link?

Fortunately, there *is* a proposal in the literature, related in spirit to the proposal considered in the foregoing section (3.1), that suggests a *substantive* vindication of the metaphysical necessity at issue. The proposal is that 'water', 'c-fiber firing', and so on are linked, de jure, to something like a microstructural property: but any term or concept for a microstructural property is in turn linked by discernible necessity, given the scientific theory responsible for enlightening us about the relevant microstructural property, to the manifest, superficial properties realized or caused by that microstructural property. So to give up the link between the relevant *microstructure* and manifest properties would be to forfeit our grip on the theory that gives any content to property terms linked, de jure, to microstructure.

Kuhn suggests a position like the foregoing. For Kuhn, since "one can in principle predict the superficial properties of water," given chemical theory, we must grant that these "so-called superficial properties are no less necessary" than the underlying structural properties. "In order to use the label" as we do, we are bound to agree that water could only act aqueously. Other chemicals that do *not* in fact act aqueously *could* not do so. This includes any chemical with a long, complicated chemical formula of the sort Putnam (1975) famously discusses under the abbreviation 'XYZ'. No such substance *would* act aqueously: the "substance would, among other things, be too heavy to evaporate at normal terrestrial temperatures" (1990, p. 310). So no such substance *could* act aqueously: it would be heavy in virtue of its massive XYZ constitution but also light in virtue of its easy evaporation into clouds. The theory responsible for giving content to the microstructural formula abbreviated 'XYZ' would in ways like this collapse into incoherence.

Kuhn is not alone in recognizing something like a de jure link between our microstructural terms, to which ordinary naming or name-like subject terms are linked de jure, and corresponding manifest or superficial properties. McGinn suggests an especially strong link here. For him, manifest "secondary properties are to be *identified* with primary properties," such as microstructural properties, so that the relevant ordinary subject terms "must be related rigidly" to superficial properties as well as microstructural ones (1999a, p. 53): accordingly, he says, anything with the constitution of gold, say, could never have "the gross properties of rubber" (p. 56; for similar thoughts or discussion of them, see Berger 2002, p. 67, note 25; Brown 2002, pp. 146–7; Drewery 2006, pp. x–xi; Kuhn 2000, pp. 83–4; Seddon 1972, pp. 483, 485).

If the Kuhnian line of reasoning is successful, then it might provide relief from triviality threatened by sch-properties. Kuhn does not address sch-properties, but he might have said, in accordance with his position, that just as the host term 'water' depends, for its proper use, on "modern chemical theory" (Kuhn 1990, p. 310), so the *derivative* term 'sch-water' would depend, for its proper use, on that *same* theory. So if this dependence demands necessity on the part of certain statements formulated with the host term, it would make corresponding demands on statements formulated with the derivative term. Hence, if the Kuhnian line of reasoning establishes that 'water expands when it freezes' could not fail to be true, then that same line of reasoning would presumably also establish that 'sch-water expands when it freezes' could not fail to be true, in which case 'sch-water expands when it freezes' would collapse into incoherence since it *has* to be capable of falsity, according to the definition of 'sch-water': so this statement's alleged contingency is incapable of trivializing the necessity of the host statement 'water expands when it freezes'.

If the Kuhnian line of reasoning is successful, then it might provide relief from triviality threatened by sch-properties: so I have claimed. But unfortunately the Kuhnian line of reasoning is *not* successful. It does *not* establish the necessary truth of 'water expands when it freezes' or the more ambitious statements 'water = the chemical compound that expands when it freezes' and 'water = the chemical compound that behaves aqueously'. So this line of reasoning, despite its initial air of hope, cannot in the end deliver substantive vindication for problematic theoretical identity statements like those I have been discussing, including psychophysical identity statements. The chief trouble is that even if, as we presume, the chemical theory that underwrites our use of 'H_2O' and that by extension underwrites our use of 'water' is a theory that describes accurately H_2O's expansion when it is frozen in circumstances that we have been able to *investigate*, that theory still does not account for H_2O's behavior in the presence of unfamiliar interfering forces or disrupting circumstances. Such forces or circumstances could prevent H_2O, and hence water, from expanding.

There is no need to appeal to exotic forces to illustrate that law-governed or law-like behavior that we would typically expect to observe in a substance or object can be upset by counteracting forces. Gravity pulls a bus toward Earth, so the bus' pressing against the ground presently is governed by laws: but other forces like chemical forces could prevent the bus from pressing against the ground. The bus could hang ten meters off the ground, bound by the chemical bonds of a sturdy chain or glue. Gravity pulls the bus in a law-governed manner, but this does not necessarily bring about the outcome that would obtain in the absence of certain counteracting forces.

And of course, even when we do not *know* of forces that could disrupt well-understood, law-governed or law-like behavior in a substance or object, we cannot rule out the *possibility* of interference. The chemical theory explaining water's expansion, upon freezing, does not address every source of interference that might be encountered: nor does any physiological theory that might explain c-fibers' painfulness, upon firing, address every source of interference that might be encountered. So any de jure connection of the Kuhnian sort between 'water' or 'c-fiber firing' and the superficial properties that might be explained in relation to the relevant structures is a connection that would support, at best, the necessity of statements like 'by disposition, water expands when it freezes' or 'by disposition, c-fibers generate pain when they fire': the attending dispositions bring about their effects *ceteris paribus*.[13] Unfortunately, something stronger than dispositional necessity is needed here: even if it is necessary that c-fibers *tend* by disposition to generate pain when they fire, unless they generate the pain in every physically possible circumstance, pain is more than c-fiber firing and 'c-fiber firing' is not a rigid designator for pain. Accordingly, the theoretical identity statement 'pain = c-fiber firing' is not established by appeal, however solid, to the necessity of the relevant dispositions, and something similar holds for 'water = the chemical compound that expands when it freezes' or 'water = the chemical compound that behaves aqueously'. Despite all the dispositional necessity that Kuhnian reasoning might establish, that reasoning leaves the truth of the foregoing theoretical identity statements moot.

3.3. From Subject Terms to Constitution to Fundamental-Law Governed Behavior

I have discussed an initially hopeful route to defending the metaphysical necessity, indeed the *substantive* metaphysical necessity, of psychophysical identity statements like 'pain = c-fiber firing' and similarly problematic theoretical identity statements having nothing to do with psychophysical phenomena, like 'water = the chemical compound that expands when it freezes' and 'water = the chemical compound that behaves aqueously'. According to the foregoing defense, any statement like 'it is not necessarily the case that water expands when it freezes' or 'it is not necessarily the case that c-fiber firing generates painful sensations', whose truth would be devastating for the corresponding theoretical identity statement, is *not* true; it fails to express what it is supposed to express, since the denial empties key property terms of their intended content. So goes the relevant defense, which unfortunately stumbles over the way that chemical or physiological laws H governing the behavior of H_2O or c-fiber firing are or could be subject to exceptions, in view of forces from outside the governance of H, which might interfere with H in some physically possible circumstances. This suggests that we might try turning to *fundamental* laws, as opposed to the higher-level laws of *chemistry* and *physiology*, in order to overcome such troubles.

Suppose that just one fundamental law F or a small number of fundamental laws that operate in harmony, underlies all physical possibility. Then no physical forces described by higher-level laws that are *not* governed by F ever interfere with the governance of F, in the actual world or indeed in any physically possible world; otherwise F would not be truly fundamental, as it is by hypothesis. So provided that F calls for expansion on the part of water or painfulness on the part of c-fibers, in certain conditions, we might naturally conclude that water and c-fibers must behave accordingly, by metaphysical necessity. The case that water and c-fibers must behave accordingly might seem easiest to build in the event that there are no possible alternatives to F, or anyway no possible alternatives that govern in any worlds like ours by virtue of containing, say, complex denizens such as our atoms and molecules. Although I will evaluate this suggestion later (in §3.4), in the present section (3.3) I evaluate a clever proposal according to which, even if the relevant fundamental laws should turn out to brook a wide range of variations governing possible worlds more or less like ours, our investigation of those fundamental laws could reveal the necessity of chemical or physiological behavior issuing from those laws.

Alexander Bird suggests that the right ties between higher-level phenomena concerning water and the relevant underlying fundamental laws might assure us that "God could not have created a world" (Bird 2005b, p. 547; for a similar position, see Wilson 2005, pp. 437, 445–6, 456, note 19) in which water does not act aqueously.[14] In its broad outlines, the argument is this:

(i) we could learn that our actual fundamental laws, and sufficiently close "cousins" (Bird 2005b, pp. 535, 538) to those laws, require that water (H_2O) expands when it freezes.

But

(ii) we could also learn that worlds without either the *actual* fundamental laws or cousins that *similarly* require water to expand when it freezes are metaphysically incompatible with the presence of *water*.

Hence,

(iii) we could learn that it is metaphysically necessary for water to expand when it freezes.

Similar reasoning would seem to apply to c-fiber firing and painfulness.

Premise (ii) stands most obviously in need of support. But Bird musters a simple and powerful case on its behalf. The suggestion is that we might learn, depending on empirical investigation of our laws, that a world without *either* our basic laws of quantum mechanics, say, *or* some variant law close enough that it *also* calls for water's *expansion* and c-fibers' *painfulness* in the right circumstances, would be a world without *our* substances, like *water*, and without our biological materials, like *c-fibers*. So this would not be a world in which water's freezing fails to issue in expansion or in which c-fibers' firing fails to issue in painful sensations. We might learn all of this because our information about just how our fundamental laws ultimately direct expansion and painfulness might show that any possible laws that sometimes direct different behavior would be *markedly different* and not just slightly different from actual laws: even if the alternative laws often prescribe familiar behavior, and even if the matter that those alternative laws govern could not be distinguished from actual matter by means of an isolated investigation, however detailed, of the matter's intrinsic features, the alternative fundamental laws might have to be markedly different from actual ones by virtue of being highly complex and gerrymandered, to account for exceptional behavior. Bird would argue that a world with alternative laws that are so markedly different would be one whose substances *mimic* our substances, at best. The substances would not be our substances, for Bird, because our substances are *essentially* held together by the forces that *actually* hold them together, in accordance with our laws or something close: an atom, say, that is "held together by completely different laws would not be an atom of any substance we have in this world" (Bird 2002, p. 260; see also 2005b, pp. 535–7, 547). Similar words apply to molecules *made up* of the foregoing atoms or materials made up of those molecules.

Bird defends premise (ii) in impressive detail; I will not, but will instead take (ii) for granted: there would be no water, I concede, if the fundamental physical laws that govern our actual world were to be replaced by fundamental laws so different that would-be water could sometimes contract or hold its volume, when it freezes. There might be *Twin*-water (Bird 2002, pp. 261, 268; cf. Putnam 1975) but there would not be *water*.

Taking (ii)'s soundness for granted, I will point out trouble with premise (i): that our actual fundamental physical laws and their suitably close cousins require that water expands when it freezes. I concede that our fundamental physical laws and close variants might be found, in the following respect, to require that water expands when it freezes: so long as nothing interferes with these fundamental laws' governance, water inevitably expands when it freezes. We might learn just how water will go about expanding, as a consequence of the roomy stacking configuration that molecules will take, when a freezing event occurs according to the directives of the relevant fundamental law.

But the foregoing concession is not strong enough to license the conclusion that water must indeed expand when it freezes: the trouble is, again, that something might interfere, for all that has been said, with the governance of the relevant laws. This point can escape notice now that *fundamental* laws are the laws at issue, since it is not *physically* possible that a force should interfere with the fundamental laws. By virtue of the relevant laws' being fundamental physical laws, all forces submit in any physically possible world. Still, there is a residual problem. The problem is not the *physical* possibility of interference but the *metaphysical* possibility of interference. Even if, in physically possible circumstances, no interference in the fundamental laws' governance frustrates the expansion of water when it freezes, it might well be that in physically *im*possible circumstances that are nonetheless metaphysically possible, there is interference preventing water's expansion: for all that has been said, there might be metaphysically possible worlds containing forces that engage with our familiar matter to produce metaphysically possible changes. The idea is a Newtonian one: just as, for Newton, God could (and does, for Newton) step in to interrupt the activities of a physical system that has its own forces and direction, in order to alter the positions of certain objects, so God might, for all that we are assured, be able to introduce some force to disrupt the ordinary operation of our fundamental laws, holding back or redirecting the natural, straightforward progression of law-governed events that would otherwise ensue, without thereby *removing* the laws whose powers are overridden on occasion, from the world.[15] To *interfere* with the fundamental laws F would of course not be the same as to *supplant* F with other laws, at least according to the characterization of laws relevant to the arguments in question (see below, in this section); on the contrary, the very same powers of governance could be present with the interference as are present without the interference, even though the powers would be overridden and thereby prevented from issuing in *behavior* in the event of interference. Since a world w^f in which F is troubled by interference from some force that is not physically possible has the same fundamental laws as the actual world a, there can be no objection that different fundamental laws would obtain in w^f than in a, and so preclude the instantiation of genuine *water*, as opposed to Twin-water. So there can be no objection to the claim that in w^f, it is *water* that fails to expand when it freezes.

Just as a non-actual but metaphysically possible force might interfere with the tendency of water to expand when it freezes, such a force might also, of course, interfere with the tendency of c-fiber firing to issue in painful sensations. We cannot, for all that has been said anyway, rule out the metaphysical possibility of such interference, even if we are able to learn that painfulness, like expansiveness, inevitably arises, provided that the fundamental law or something close to it governs the world. Even in this ideal state of knowledge, we could not confirm the necessity of 'water expands when it freezes' or 'c-fibers generate pain when they fire'.

Before drawing a close to the section, let me address a possible objection that might have occurred to the reader. I have said that the very same laws could govern the world with interference as without, even though the *power* of those laws would sometimes be overridden in some measure so that the behavior in the physical world that the laws would otherwise bring about is prevented or modified. So to interfere with laws F is not the same as to supplant F with other laws. In claiming this I presuppose a specific though commonly accepted conception of laws, according to which laws have real *power*, as it might be put, to "*make things happen in certain ways*" (Hoefer 2008, §2.4), whether that is because laws "are relations of necessity between universals, or the rules God uses for deciding how the universe is going to evolve, or whatever" (Beebee 2000, p. 572). A law, as understood here, *governs* and hence any law "possesses nomic *necessity*" (Butts 1995, p. 423). I leave it open whether the necessity is *full-strength*, metaphysical necessity (as Bird thinks: 2005a) which obtains in all possible worlds or whether it is *weaker* than full-strength metaphysical necessity, holding only in a limited range of possible worlds in which those laws govern (as, say, Armstrong would have it: 1983, pp. 85–8, 92; see also Armstrong 1993, p. 422). Either way, it is real necessity with "modal force" that is causal and that "arranges the temporal order of events" (Schrenk 2005, pp. 855–6).[16]

Although the governing conception of laws is not universally accepted, criticism of my presupposition would be out of place. The argument here (in §3) is that even *given* scientific necessitarianism, which might appear to offer help, problematic theoretical identity statements remain problematic. Scientific necessitarianism is committed to the claim that laws govern. So we may take for granted that laws do govern for purposes of this section; otherwise the scientific-necessitarianism driven proposal that I investigate cannot get going in the first place.

3.4. From Fundamental Laws to Fatalism to Identity

I have discussed one argument according to which, provided that *fundamental* laws call for expansion on the part of water or painfulness on the part of c-fibers, in certain conditions, we should conclude that water and c-fibers must behave accordingly, by metaphysical necessity. There is another such argument to be considered.

It might be claimed that the *final theory* or the *theory of everything* concerning the most basic laws, for which some physicists are searching, might vindicate fatalism: "The hope here is that logical consistency" in the formulation of any such theory "may dictate a unique way the world is" (as Redhead puts it: 1995, p. 67). Thus, one hopeful physicist suggests in an interview that "If you can somehow argue" that there is only one consistent theory of everything, then you would find that God has no freedom, that "in the beginning, there was mathematical consistency. Everything else follows, including us [laughs]" (David Schramm, quoted in Lightman and Brawer 1990, p. 449). It might even be said that "it is an empirical question," as Drewery maintains (2005, p. 392), because it is a question for physicists to answer, whether "there is just one way the world could be" (p. 391).

If we could somehow discover that there is just one consistent theory so that God had no choice but to permit the actual unfolding of the universe and no other, then our discovery would allow for confirmation of 'pain = c-fiber firing': a discovery of *correlation* between pain and c-fiber firing would be a discovery of *identity*. To be sure, I have already argued that correlation is too weak to deliver identity. The pain in the world might well be just the c-fiber firing in the world even if the two are separable in principle, I have argued (see §2.1): just so, the water in the world is just the triplestatestuff in the world but the two are correlated only accidentally. But when I argued that correlation is too weak to establish identity, I was operating under the natural and familiar presupposition that there are plenty of other possible worlds including, for all we know, worlds in which c-fiber firing is not painful. A discovery that there is only one metaphysically possible world changes matters. If there are no other ways the universe could have unfolded, in which matter might have behaved differently, then if *in fact* the pain in the world is just the c-fiber firing in the world, there is no metaphysical possibility that it should *not* have been: again, in that case, there is no metaphysical possibility of any universe other than our own. So pain and c-fiber firing are not, after all, separable in principle. Neither are water and triplestatestuff, accidental though the connection would ordinarily be taken to be. Hence, by verifying correlation, we would confirm 'pain = c-fiber firing', as well as 'water = triplestatestuff' (given a favorable construal of property identity: see the start of §3). Any two properties that share the same extension in the actual world share that extension with respect to all possible worlds, given fatalism: even properties seemingly accidentally correlated.

Given a fatalism-assuring final theory, 'pain = c-fiber firing' can be confirmed if we can confirm the designators' actual coextension. Confirming coextension even in the actual world is no mean feat, but suppose it could be done by induction: in this section (§3.4) I will broach salient reasons even so to be less than optimistic about the foregoing route for confirming the relevant theoretical identity statement.

First, for humans to use the relevant theory to establish fatalism, the final theory would have to be one that humans have the cognitive wherewithal to discover. And about that there is uncertainty. Indeed, there is uncertainty whether a final theory exists in order to be discovered (Barrow 1991, p. 89; Penrose, Randall, Rovelli, and Weinberg in t'Hooft et al. 2005; Rees 2003, pp. 149, 154; see also Hawking 1988, pp. 12–13).

Even if the final theory exists and humans have the wherewithal to discover it, it might lack various features it would need to have in order to establish fatalism. The final theory might lack, for example, the feature of ruling out the possibility of variants of our world, which is one feature it would need in order to establish fatalism. Scientists are not confident that the theory would have this feature (Barrow 1991, p. 90; Weinberg 1993, p. 191 and Weinberg's contribution in t'Hooft et al. 2005). It is uncertain whether even variant worlds with relatively close cousins of our laws could be ruled out. It would be harder still to rule out the possibility of worlds with laws more radically different than ours (see Ellis's contribution in t'Hooft et al. 2005; Giberson and Artigas 2007, p. 115; Page 2010, §4; Redhead 1990, p. 152; 1995, pp. 67–8, 85–6; Weinberg 2009, p. 22; for related thoughts, see Levin 1987, pp. 288–9) such as universes with gruesome laws: gruesome laws look like simple laws with dramatic exceptions here or there. In the same way that it is hard to rule out the possibility of universes with gruesome laws, it is hard to rule out the possibility of interference in genuinely simple laws, resulting in exceptions here or there.

Physicists have not indicated that they have thought much about whether we can rule out the possibility of universes under the governance of gruesome laws or universes whose simple laws are subject to interference that would have the same effect on our observations, so far as we could tell. They generally speak casually when they sound fatalistic. Hence, the distinguished cosmologist Don Page cautions us about interpreting his colleagues naïvely: when "people say that there might be only one consistent theory, I think what they mean is only one *fairly simple* theory that might be consistent" (recorded in Lightman and Brawer 1990, p. 408). But to be relevant here, a final theory ruling out other possible universes would have to be much stronger than that. It would have to rule out more than alternative universes whose laws or courses of events can be characterized smoothly in terms of simple physical *laws* alone. And it would have to rule out more than alternative universes whose laws or courses of events can be characterized smoothly in terms of physical laws that *govern* simply because strictly without interference. Metaphysical possibilities that would complicate the universe count in a context in which broad metaphysical possibility is at issue. But such possibilities seem to be left open in the brief treatments physicists might appear to offer on behalf of fatalism.

Another example of a feature the final theory might lack, and thereby fail to rule out fatalism, is the feature of being deterministic. Indeterministic laws would allow for the possibility of our exposing c-fiber firings to different experimental conditions in the universe, which might for all we know refute 'pain = c-fiber firing', since indeterministic laws would allow for a span of different metaphysically possible ways, varying in probability, that the world could turn out. Yet for considerations related to quantum mechanics, as well as other salient considerations, modern physicists are sympathetic to the possibility that our world and laws are at bottom indeterministic (Page 2003, p. 470; Redhead 1995, pp. 66–7). So again, physicists' degree of confidence in a fatalism-sustaining final theory should be understood accordingly.

So the suggestion that a final theory could establish psychophysical identities by way of establishing fatalism seems unpromising. Further, even if fatalism *could* redeem the truth of 'pain = c-fiber firing' and other problematic identity statements, fatalism would do so without illuminating us conceptually about the nature of the subject matter and what makes it what it is, which is what scientists investigating subjects like pain, water, and so on seek to do: not only 'pain = c-fiber firing', 'water = the chemical compound that behaves aqueously', and other problematic identity statements that we hoped in the spirit of scientific necessitarianism to redeem, but also statements like 'pain = what Jones talks about with his doctor', 'water = triplestatestuff', 'white = Mill's favorite example of a color', 'Obama = the 44th president of the U.S.A.', and so on, would be confirmed as necessarily true. Yet barring fatalism these would be counted as accidentally true. We do not enjoy insight into what about the subject makes them true, in view of how we use the designators, in the way that we do for theoretical identity statements like 'water = H_2O', 'white = the combination of all of the colors of the visible spectrum', and 'Obama = the product of S and E'. And no theory establishing fatalism can give us that insight: so I will argue in the following section (§3.5).

3.5. Dissolving the Problem with Scientific Development

Perhaps the whole problem in seeing how we could ever with more empirical information discern the necessity of any psychophysical identity is a problem that will go away as science develops. This could be because a different sort of scientific theory is on the horizon or it could be because more business as usual with theories much like those we now accept will gradually remove the scales from our eyes, until we see clearly the necessary connections between phenomenal properties and physical or functional ones. I will discuss these prospects in order.

3.5.1. A New Sort of Theory Fundamental theories in physics have a salient way of challenging our basic categories: e.g., blurring the distinction between a wave and a particle or between space and time. De jure specifications on the reference of terms make use of categories, which play a key role in the problem at hand. So it might be natural to turn for hope once again to fundamental physics. This time the hope is that the discipline will supply a new theory that reshapes our old categories: "with a new physics, things might be different," as Chalmers puts the idea. What we learn by "a radically different theoretical framework might be sufficient to entail and explain consciousness" (Chalmers 1996, p. 162; see also Garrett 2006, pp. 587–8). Again, the final theory comes to mind, promising as it does to put an end to the search for more fundamental laws and categories underlying all physical phenomena.

But a final theory in physics is not likely to alter categories from biology or psychology. "A final theory is not going to help us cure cancer or understand consciousness," as Weinberg concedes (2009, p. 3). So the final theory will not answer whether, regardless of various conditions that might attend c-fiber firing, c-fiber firing has to be attended by pain. Nor will the final theory in physics answer whether hydrogen could have more isotopes or whether H_2O could contract when it freezes. In fact, as Sir Martin Rees says, "A so-called theory of everything would actually offer absolutely zero help to ninety-nine percent of scientists" (2003, p. 151). Many questions and problems even in physics will remain untouched (Redhead 1995, pp. 68–9; Weinberg 1993, p. 191; 1999, p. 75).

Conceptually, it seems, matters of fundamental physics are too far removed from other areas of science, including other areas within physics, to illuminate metaphysically necessary connections in those diverse areas. Thus the Nobel laureate P. W. Anderson testifies in his classic essay on this subject that the discovery of simple fundamental laws governing all matter does not give us the conceptual leverage "to start from those laws and reconstruct" how matter must behave in chemistry or biology or psychology or even in many areas of physics. On the contrary, the more that "physicists tell us about the nature of the fundamental laws, the less relevance they seem to have to the very real problems of the rest of science" (Anderson 1994, p. 1). It seems unlikely that we will be able to use anything like the final theory in physics to see our way into the metaphysical necessity underlying the physical nature of consciousness.

If any discipline were capable of producing new theories that could break down our categories and help us to see how psychophysical identities could hold up, fundamental physics would seem capable. Accordingly, it is very hard to see how any sort of new theory, strikingly different from the sorts of theories with which we are familiar, could open our eyes to the necessity behind psychophysical identities and thereby dissolve what would appear to be an insoluble problem. Scientists who frame future theories, like scientists who frame current theories, will establish reference with the help of de jure connections. There is no other way to establish reference (see §2). They will continue to establish reference to 'pain' from the inside, by its feel. And they will continue to establish reference to 'c-fiber firing' from a third-person, scientific perspective. So it is hard to see how it could be that we will ever get beyond familiar problems, how it could be that scientific work "will yield a conceptual breakthrough," as Levine (1998, p. 472) among others hopes, that allows us to see the truth of what the sciences now seem helpless to allow us to see.

3.5.2. Familiar Work on Familiar Sorts of Theories If it is hard to see how a *new* sort of theory could allow us to see how empirical work could ever establish the metaphysical necessity upholding psychophysical identities, it is also hard to see how familiar work on familiar theories and others like them could allow us to see how empirical work could ever establish the metaphysical necessity upholding psychophysical identities.

Recall (from §2.1.2) that no amount of empirical investigation into sample specimens could establish that 'Brontosaurus' designates a species. The best that ordinary scientific advancement in systematics might show is that all of the brontosaur samples that there are belong to the same species, perhaps even as a matter of biological laws or law-like generalizations concerning ecological competition and conditions necessary for the inception of species or whatever. Even if ordinary scientific advancement, at its best, were to show that, 'Brontosaurus' would still designate the genus Brontosaurus to which the samples all belong and not the species, so far as we could tell. So we could not affirm '*Apatosaurus Ajax* = Brontosaurus': lacking insight as we would into any metaphysically *necessary* connection between the respective designata, we would have to leave open the possibility that some brontosaurs could have belonged to other species instead of *Apatosaurus Ajax*. Similarly, the best that ordinary scientific advancement in brain science, or in the discipline of choice for investigating psychological functions, might show is that pains are all c-fiber firings and vice-versa (but see note 5), perhaps even as a matter of neurophysiological laws. Even if ordinary scientific advancement, at its best, were to show that, 'pain' would still designate a phenomenal sensation detected from the inside and not the neurophysiological type c-fiber firing, so far as we could tell. So we could not affirm 'pain = c-fiber firing': lacking insight as we would into any metaphysically *necessary* connection, we would have to leave open the possibility that some c-fiber firings could have been painless.

The salient argument to the contrary according to which ordinary empirical advances can overcome the relevant conceptual barriers, cites precedent. "We've been in this situation before in the history of science," John Searle insists (1996; for similar sentiments see Garrett 2003; 2006; de Sousa 2000, p. 320; for related discussion see Chalmers 1996 pp. 108–9, 370, note 8). People thought at one time that *life* could not be understood as a biochemical phenomenon. The thought is that we did not coin 'life' for a biochemical phenomenon and we did not see how 'life' could conceivably turn out, whatever our empirical findings, to name one. But gradual empirical work taught us that 'life' could conceivably turn out to name a biochemical phenomenon, and indeed that it does so. "The mechanists, as they were called, won the battle and the vitalists lost," and this happened "because we got a much richer theory of the mechanisms," by gradual advances in biology (Searle 1996). What it took "to dispel the mystery is to understand the processes" (Searle 1984, p. 23).

Something like the foregoing account of the vitalism–mechanism debate's resolution is common and natural. But I will argue that it does not do justice to the resolution, which provides no helpful precedent for the case at hand. The resolution to the vitalism–mechanism debate, insofar as there is one, does not show that scientific advancement has the power to clear up how empirical work could ever expose necessary connections between physically or functionally understood behavior and phenomena that were designated in a way that the designata seemed incapable, whatever empirical findings should turn up, of being understood physically or functionally.

Vitalism is not a single well-defined position. Vitalists loosely adhered to "a multitude of theories," as C. D. Broad observed (Broad 1925, p. 44; see also McDougall 1938, p. 75). Different positions in the cluster were adopted by different vitalists in an evolving tradition. Some of the positions on the vitalists' side left it clearly an empirical matter whether 'life' designates something biochemical or biochemically realized. Accordingly, the refutation of these vitalistic positions can not show how gradual progress in biology could reveal, without help from cooperative de jure ties allowing the term 'life' to designate something biochemical or functional given the right empirical results, how the term could turn out to designate something biochemical or functional. Other positions on the vitalists' side have never been resolved to the general satisfaction of scientists and philosophers so they do not provide the needed precedent for enlightenment either.

Consider first the vitalistic position that only living tissues can produce organic chemicals. This has not turned out to be so. Have scientists thereby become informed that 'life' could after all be understood as a biochemical phenomenon? They should have been so informed if, say, they had coined 'life' de jure as "what is responsible for the production of organic chemicals, whether biochemically tractable or not," as various workers did on different occasions, in effect, to suit the purposes of various specific contexts; but then the de jure specifications on the term's use with respect to those contexts had allowed us to see all along how the referent might turn out to be a set of processes that accord with biochemical explanations. Friedrich Wöhler's artificial synthesis of urea was the first in a line of empirical discoveries to indicate that the referent would in fact be just that (see, e.g., Cohen and Cohen 1996; Noble 2008, pp. 16–17).

Similar words apply to the vitalistic position that there is a principle at work to regulate development that is not biochemical or subject to physical laws: this vitalistic position, held most notably by Hans Driesch (Driesch 1908; 1914; see for discussion Medawar and Medawar 1983; Bechtel and Richardson 1998), is now discredited. Have scientists thereby become informed that 'life' could after all be understood as a biochemical phenomenon? They should have been if, say, they had coined 'life' de jure as "what allows for development in organisms, whether or not that is biochemically tractable," as various workers did on different occasions, in effect, to suit the purposes of various specific contexts; but then the de jure specifications on the term's use with respect to those contexts had allowed us to see all along how the referent might turn out to be a set of biochemically tractable processes, depending on how empirical investigations into development should turn out.

The foregoing vitalist positions have been resolved to the general satisfaction of biologists; but they do not show how such resolutions could come in the absence of cooperative de jure ties for 'life' that clearly allow in advance of a resolution for the term to designate something biochemically or functionally tractable depending on empirical results. Still, according to some authors there is more to the now resolved – because now refuted – vitalist line of thinking, which causes that thinking to parallel the reasoning behind my skeptical argument. Dennett, for example, presents us with a fictional vitalist who complains to molecular biologists that physical and functional behavior could never amount to life, so far as we could discern. Dennett's fictional vitalist holds that, "We can imagine something that was capable of reproduction, development, growth, metabolism, self-repair and immunological self-defense, but that wasn't, you know, *alive*" (Dennett 1997, p. 33). Sometimes vitalists sound as if this is their line of thinking. John Burroughs, for example, writes that it is not enough to "look upon the body as only the sum of its physical and chemical activities"; a vitalist such as Burroughs will "feel the need of accounting for life itself – for that something which confers vitality upon the heretofore non-vital elements" (1915, p. 73). But Burroughs immediately proceeds to indicate his reason for thinking so: namely that the vital activities of "growth, assimilation, metabolism, reproduction," and so on require a non-physical cause: we cannot "get these things out of the old physics and chemistry without some new factor or agent or force" (1915, p. 73). So the thought is not that physics and chemistry could account for all of life's activities and still there be no life. The thought is rather that physics and chemistry can *not* account for all of life's activities: and this much more tractable thought can be resolved in the course of doing those sciences.[17]

I have discussed salient vitalist positions that have been more or less resolved to the general satisfaction of biologists, although the resolutions fail to show how what has been thought to be inconceivable whatever the deliverances of science could be found after an examination of biological processes to be conceivable after all. By contrast, some salient "vitalist" positions have never been clearly resolved. Consider the position that "biology has its own problem and its definite point of view," independent of the problems and point of view of chemistry and physics: this is a position of the great experimentalist and "physical vitalist" Claude Bernard (Bernard 1957, p. 95). Bernard and many contemporaries defended "vitalism" on the grounds that biology is not just applied physics and chemistry (see, on this point, Gregory 1977, p. 166), while mechanists attacked vitalism on the grounds that physiology would dissolve into physics and chemistry (see, e.g., Coleman 1977, p. 151). Bernard's position is not obviously one that has been refuted or that is subject to empirical refutation. So no appeal to his position's demise illustrates that gradual advances in the special sciences have removed conceptual blindness to what "just seems obvious to us" now (Searle 1996). Further, for Bernard the behavior of living organisms is physically and chemically determined (see, e.g., Goodfield 1960, p. 162; Olmsted and Olmsted 1952, p. 214): so even if his position were to have been refuted by way of a decisive resolution, his position's demise would not illustrate how the special sciences allowed vitalists to overcome a former blindness concerning whether life could be biochemical or realized in matter obeying just physical laws.

There are other salient positions associated with vitalism that have not been resolved to the general satisfaction of informed scientists and philosophers. One such position is that phenomenal events are not physical (Wheeler 1939, 250–1). Clearly this is not the precedent for which optimistic physicalists are searching.

In sum, it is a distorting oversimplification to suppose that the resolution of the debate between vitalism and mechanism provides precedent indicating that difficulties for securing psychophysical identities will be dissolved by enough scientific business as usual. The resolution of the vitalism-mechanism debate is piecemeal. Where it is solid, that is because empirical work has routed vitalism with the help of cooperating de jure ties, which rendered it all along clear how the right empirical results could undermine vitalism by indicating that 'life' refers to something biochemically tractable. There was no difficulty to be dissolved, in understanding how empirical results could be relevant, where resolution has come. But cooperating de jure ties do not attend phenomenal expressions and so cannot show how phenomenal expressions could refer to something physical or functional: here there is a difficulty. It remains hard to see how the difficulty could ever be dissolved by the ordinary progress of science.

3.6. Where We Are Left: Scientific Empiricism

Scientific necessitarians, at their best (e.g., Bird 2001), work to articulate conceptual connections that would license us to take physical necessity for full-blown metaphysical necessity. This type of reasoning is broadly reminiscent of early modern rationalism. According to that rationalism, the causal order in the world and perhaps even the world itself "has necessary existence, and that necessity is something like logical necessity." Accordingly, the world's structure "tends to be read as a matter of logical deduction," by way of reasoning that makes use of limited empirical information (this depiction of continental rationalism is from Lennon and Dea 2008, §1; for closely related characterizations or discussion, see Beebee and Leary 2010, pp. 13–15; Magee 1988, pp. 111–12, 115–16; Matson 2011, pp. 153, 198).

The hope with which we began section (3) was the hope that somehow we would be able to see a connection between what we know that it *is* fundamentally to be water, given our information, and water's aqueousness or between what we know that it is to be c-fiber firing, given our information, and painfulness. But we seem destined to be left without conceptual leverage to make a connection to water's aqueousness or c-fiber firing's painfulness. Even after we have a satisfactory account of the makeup of a parcel of matter and indeed even after we have a successful final theory and know that we do, if we are to learn the behavior of physical matter exposed to different conditions, we must resort to further "experimental results to complete the story" about what the matter will do in the actual world, as one physicist puts it (from t'Hooft et al. 2005, p. 258), to say nothing of other physically and metaphysically possible worlds. Something similar applies to the special sciences. So we seem to be left with an empiricist alternative to the broadly rationalistic perspective of scientific necessitarianism. What we might call "scientific empiricism" is again evocative of its early modern counterpart, with its emphasis on contingency and the obligation to check the empirical world for connections that could come apart, at least for all we know.

A present-day scientific empiricist who is thoroughgoing (the early modern tradition is eclectic: see Bealer 1987, pp. 299–30; BonJour 1998, p. 17) must update to accommodate complications added by the necessary a posteriori. Given the accuracy of empirical work to expose the chemical nature of samples of water, it is no longer an empirical matter for experiments to resolve whether *water is essentially H_2O*: on the contrary, given the accuracy of empirical work to expose the chemical nature of samples of water, the connection between water and H_2O is not one that could for all we know come apart. We are in a conceptual position to affirm essence at that point. It is not my business to argue for either an empiricist understanding of this necessary a posteriori information (for relevantly updated empiricisms stronger than I would embrace, see Sidelle 1989; Mackie 1976) or a rationalist understanding (Bealer 1987). The empiricism that I embrace here concerns necessity more elusive than that binding water and H_2O.

Given the accuracy of chemistry, water that is not H_2O is not possible; but *nonaqueous* water or painless c-fiber firing *is* metaphysically possible, so far as we are in a position to determine now or after further scientific work. Further empirical experiments might leave untouched the correlation so far observed between aqueousness and water or between painfulness and c-fiber firing, under various different conditions to which we have access; but such experiments cannot close off the possibility that matter will defy the correlation so far observed, under other conditions that are physically or metaphysically possible so far as we are in a position to determine. So after the science is in, the relevant necessity, if that is what it is, will remain hidden: "we shall never discover a reason, why," as David Hume insisted, a certain physical event would have to give rise to a phenomenal one if it would have to do so. Our poverty extends to various other scientifically established connections as well. The possibility of separation remains open (*A Treatise of Human Nature*, Bk 1, Pt IV, Sect 5).

4. Concluding Remarks

Even after scientists have told us all that they can tell us, 'pain = c-fiber firing' might for all that we will know be false. Unknown conditions, present in the actual world or in other possible worlds, could render the c-fiber firing painless at the hands of skilled anesthesiologists.

'Water = H_2O' is, of course, different: information from chemistry along with information about the proper use of 'water', which proper use is established de jure at baptism, assures us that 'water = H_2O' is true. To be sure, various *other* identity statements about water fail to measure up to the confirmational success of 'water = H_2O': so psychophysical identity statements are not alone in presenting the confirmational troubles that they present. The more problematic statements about water include 'water = the chemical compound that expands when it freezes'. 'Water = H_2O' is special, because even if H_2O is misbehaved in other possible worlds, because, say, it contracts when it freezes, we still apply 'water' with respect to those worlds, just to the H_2O in them, assuming that scientists have their chemistry right and the samples we have baptized as "water" are comprised of H_2O. We have secured 'water', de jure, to whatever chemical is present in certain samples. By contrast, we have not secured 'water' de jure to anything like a behavior-restricted entity: so with respect to the relevant worlds in which some H_2O contracts, we do not apply 'water' just to expansive H_2O. Since we cannot rule out the genuine metaphysical possibility of refractory worlds like the foregoing in which H_2O is misbehaved, any statement like 'water = the chemical compound that expands when it freezes' is questionable at best, even provided that water is in fact comprised of the chemical compound that expands when it freezes, as scientists tell us. But 'water = H_2O' is secure, provided that water is in fact comprised of H_2O, as scientists tell us.

The lesson here does not address the tenability of physicalism in general (but see chapter 7, note 2 and accompanying text). The lesson addresses the tenability of specific theoretical identity statements, like 'pain = c-fiber firing' or 'consciousness = pyramidal cell activity'. The lesson here is that, if the relevant phenomenal properties are identical to the relevant physical properties, we are in no position ever to recognize it. So we are in no position to grasp the essence of pain or consciousness in physical terms. If there are true theoretical identity statements linking the mental and the physical, their truth will remain unknown to us after scientists have done all the work that they can do.

Notes

1. In chapter 1, §2, I introduce an argument that in view of certain features of its component terms, including 'H_2O''s theoretical content, 'water = H_2O' is a true theoretical identity statement if and only if 'water' and 'H_2O' both rigidly designate the same item. I also introduce parallel claims about 'pain = c-fiber firing' and its component terms. I elaborate on these arguments in chapter 6, §2, where I go on to argue in detail that 'water' and 'H_2O' both rigidly designate the same item, and in chapter 7, §1.2.1.
2. So although 'pain', unlike 'water', is not rigid de jure for a physical or functional property, it is rigid de facto for one if physicalism is true. But because of this difference, "some very different philosophical argument from the sort which has been given" for 'water = H_2O' is needed to support 'pain = c-fiber firing': "a deeper and subtler argument" (1971, p. 163; see also 1980, pp. 150, 154, 98–100), as Kripke says.
3. So rather than resembling the usual subjects of comparison including 'water = H_2O', which are non-psychophysical theoretical identity statements that reflect successful reduction, psychophysical identity statements resemble statements like 'water = $^{1-3}H_2O$', with respect to the matter at hand, which is whether correlation, without help from de jure ties, can assure us of identity. There are other parallels between psychophysical identity statements and statements like 'water = $^{1-3}H_2O$'. Some authors (Block 2002, p. 424; Levin 2010, §5.5.2; Levine 1998, p. 465; see also p. 467; 1983, pp. 358–9; Loar 2003, p. 125) suggest that psychophysical identities are unique in putting us in epistemic tension by virtue of being plausibly taken to be metaphysically necessary even while they continue to present themselves conceptually as contingent after we have done the empirical work to learn of the relevant facts about physical constitution or correlation. But if scientific necessitarianism is thought to be plausible, even though indemonstrable (as I will argue in §3), then statements like 'water = $^{1-3}H_2O$' put us in similar epistemic tension.
4. Even if both 'water = H_2O' and 'water = $^{1-3}H_2O$' could be true together, as a coarse individuation of properties might allow (see §3), the difference in confirmational merit obtains.
5. Correlation does not *assure* even that all c-fiber firings are pains and vice-versa, even given the assumption of physicalism; ocean waves are correlated with froth but they are not froth even though both ocean waves and froth are physical. But let us take for granted that any particular pain *is* a c-fiber firing and vice-versa, just as any particular bit of water is a bit of $^{1-3}H_2O$ as well as a bit of triplestatestuff, and vice-versa.
6. It might appear that the direct-reference theory and the recognitional theory are allies, somehow, in a struggle against descriptive theories like the causal-descriptive theory that I have just discussed. This is not so: rather, the salient rivalry here is between the recognitional theory and the causal-descriptive theory. The theory of direct reference takes no part in this rivalry since it addresses *semantic* issues while the other two theories address *meta*semantic issues, the nature of which I will explain in the text that follows (in §2.2.2). More precisely, that is how matters stand with the theories as I have articulated them, in a typical form true to the usual spirit in which they are proposed. But while recognitional theories and descriptive theories (pure or augmented by causal elements) *need* not address semantic issues, either one *might*: accordingly, *versions* of these theories that are more elaborate than the basic versions that I have articulated here sometimes assign semantic work as well as metasemantic work to

recognition, to descriptions, to causal chains, and to other mechanisms that are supposed to secure the right designatum for a term: *this* generates conflict between the theory of direct reference, on the one hand, and the relevant version of *either* a recognitional *or* a descriptive theory on the other hand (see, e.g., Devitt 1989, pp. 215ff.; 1996, pp. 179–86; 2005, p. 161, note 10; forthcoming 2012, §3.1, §3.2 and passim; cf. Salmon 1986, pp. 70–1). I thank Jason Stanley for discussion that has helped me to articulate these important relationships and closely associated material to follow in this section (§2.2.2).

7. It may surprise the reader that Kaplan, the original champion of direct reference, remains open to the possibility that *descriptive* information mediates between a directly referring term and its referent (1989b, p. 568, note 5). Descriptivism about how terms come to have the right referent is compatible with the theory of direct reference so long as whatever "mechanisms there are that govern the search for the referent, they are irrelevant to the propositional component, to content", as Kaplan maintains (1989b, p. 569). Soames, another distinguished direct-reference theorist, acknowledges familiar observations about the right candidate for reference having to *meet* various *conditions*: indeed, he takes such observations to be "platitudes," but urges, like Kaplan, that any such conditions binding a term to its designatum are not relevant to the theory of direct reference since they are not about semantics proper (2007, p. 41, note 10; see also 2007, p. 40, note 9; 2005, pp. 182ff.); Soames' "platitudes" concerning what conditions do the mediating are available to opponents of direct reference, too, of course, who regard the mediation as semantic (e.g., Devitt in references cited in the foregoing note 6; Lewis 1999e, pp. 353–4, note 22). Kripke, who does not rule out the theory of direct reference (1979; 1980, pp. 20–1), explicitly acknowledges that "criteria" associated de jure by speakers with a name permit the name to secure a referent (in Harman et al. 1974, p. 510; see also pp. 513, 515, 517–18; 1980, pp. 96–7, 118–19, 124, 126). Each of the foregoing direct-reference theorists and sympathizers (and others still: e.g., Perry 2001, pp. 32; 188–95) acknowledges, in effect, that a de jure connection to a type of property or item present at baptism is perfectly compatible with direct reference.

8. This second, auxiliary claim allows me to frame the issues in terms of identity rather than identification. On a finer conception of properties than the second claim honors, 'pain' and 'c-fiber firing' could not be counted on to designate the very same property even if they could be shown to designate properties that are necessarily coinstantiated: so we would have to do more than secure necessary coinstantiation in order to secure the identity statement 'pain = c-fiber firing'. I have argued at length (in chapter 5) that the central arguments tied to rigidity, which would of course include the ones addressed in the present chapter concerning psychophysical identity statements, may be restated without appeal to identity. Accordingly, in building a case for science's authority to confirm that the relevant psychophysical statements are necessarily true, someone ill-disposed to coarsely cut properties or indeed to properties of any kind could dispense with the commitment to coarsely cut properties or to properties of any kind, and appeal only to scientific necessitarianism: the relevant psychophysical statements would then be *identification* statements like 'for all x, x is *pain* if and only if x is *c-fiber firing*' (or correlates: see note 9), rather than identity statements like 'pain = c-fiber firing'.

9. The way in which pain and c-fiber firing, like triangularity and trilaterality, would have to be necessarily correlated is by way of necessary *coinstantiation*. Again, I have accepted, for the sake of argument, that correlation is or indicates coinstantiation: see note 5. Otherwise the

present case for the truth and consequent necessity of theoretical *identity* statements would have to be weakened into a case for the necessity of a disappointingly thin variety of theoretical *identification* statements like 'for all x, x is a pain if and only if x *is correlated with c-fiber firings*'. Of course, even to establish the necessity of such thin theoretical identification statements would be far more interesting than to establish mere facts about correlation with respect to the *actual* world.

10. In this chapter, I have been counting as "theoretical identity statements" statements like 'water = $^{1-3}H_2O$', and now 'water = the chemical compound that expands when it freezes', in a liberal spirit encouraged by a coarse construal of properties. Such a loose use of the label 'theoretical identity statements' might be questioned. Do these statements expose *the* essence of the relevant property? They must, in order to count as "theoretical identity statements," as I understand those. Still, they might sensibly be said to count as "theoretical identity statements" in some contexts or in a derivative manner. Accordingly, I will continue, in this chapter, the generous practice of calling such statements "theoretical identity statements," to simplify the presentation.

11. Or perhaps we should say that the issue is whether there could be something that is just like the particular c-fiber firing occurring now except that there is no attending *sch-painfulness*(!), 'sch-painfulness' being a designator for what would be called "painfulness" if only it never failed to attend c-fiber firing.

12. Ellis finishes his thought by addressing the possibility of sch-protons that are like protons but that can have half the mass. He complains that, if anything like sch-protons with only half of the expected mass "were considered to be a real possibility, then we should certainly have heard of it by now" (2004, p. 76). This, too, is inadequate as grounds for dismissing schm-entities. No one supposes that any scientist has discovered *actual* sch-protons with half the mass of protons: we would have heard of *that*. But an acknowledgement that scientists consider schm-entities with unusual properties like this to be *metaphysically possible* could hardly be expected to make headlines. Further, there is only a limited amount that scientists can say about schm-entities with unusual properties since no one has a very good idea about what the ramifications would be for the world as a whole if we were to tinker with this or that law, constant, and so on. Even so, there is some discussion on the part of cosmologists who are willing to consider "surreal" (Barrow and Webb 2005, p. 63) conditions in which the "number and strength" of nature's forces undergo adjustment (Barrow, 2002, p. 283). Various scientists are open to the possibility that such conditions are possible or even actual in remote corners of the world (see also Lightman and Brawer 1990, p. 414; contributions by Susskind and Witten in t'Hooft et al. 2005, p. 257).

13. Ceteris paribus conditions are notorious for the difficulties that they bring (for discussion see, e.g., Mumford 1998, pp. 86–7, 224). Substitutes might do similar work (see, e.g., Molnar 2003, chapter 4 for one proposed substitute; but cf. Beebee 2005, p. 676). The central lesson here regarding ceteris paribus generalizations holds also for probabilistic generalizations: so even if law-like probabilistic correlations are necessary (as they are for Smith 2001, pp. 35–7), and even if the identity between c-fiber firing and pain is law-like, the *identity* theory needs more. For identity, it has to be necessary that c-fiber firing actually *generates* pain and even that c-fiber firing does so without exception; any correlation weaker than this is not enough. It is implicit here and in the text that 'pain = c-fiber firing', to be relevant, is to be read categorically as a statement about what pain *amounts to* instead of dispositionally as a statement

about what pain tends to be like, whatever its true underlying nature; otherwise the statement fails to be a genuine theoretical identity statement exposing the nature of pain. The same applies to other theoretical identity statements like 'water = H_2O'. To be sure, what something like c-fiber firing or H_2O *is* fundamentally might itself be understood dispositionally; but all of the arguments in the text can accommodate such an understanding without any adjustment at all.

14. Bird concedes, at least for the sake of argument, that the fundamental physical laws permit a lot of variation. Bird would also concede that, for all that we can say without reference to fundamental laws, interference in the operation of higher-level chemical laws could prevent water from expanding when it freezes, say: higher-level laws govern *ceteris paribus*. So Bird's ingenious case for the metaphysical necessity of water's behavior (Bird 2001; 2002; 2007, pp. 178–9; 2008, p. 54; 2009) is, where Bird makes no reference to fundamental laws, carefully qualified to allow that the necessity is dispositional (2001, pp. 273–4; 2002, pp. 267–8; for similar concessions, see Harré and Madden 1975: see pp. 140–1, 149, 153; see also Bigelow 1999, p. 50; Ellis 2001, p. 219). Despite these concessions, Bird suggests that the right ties between higher-level phenomena concerning water and the relevant underlying *fundamental* laws might turn out to show us that water *had* to manifest the behavior that it does manifest (2005b: see pp. 533, 535, 537, and especially 546, 547; 2009, p. 517).

Because of the concessions that I have just noted on Bird's part, the criticism of the foregoing section (§3.2) should not create problems for him. However, the criticism that I will raise against Bird in *this* section (§3.3) applies to the targets of that earlier section (§3.2), as well. In general, the criticisms of sections (3.1)–(3.3) become more inclusive: so later criticisms apply, or at least promise to do so with a little adjustment, to earlier-considered arguments.

15. The basic Newtonian position has been held by many since: see, e.g., Lightman and Brawer 1990, pp. 407–8; Plantinga 2010, §3.2; van Inwagen 2003, p. 359. It could be maintained on the basis of intuitions about what we should properly call "*our* fundamental laws F" that any interference from forces not subject to physical possibility would result in different fundamental laws entirely, ones that resemble ours but that are distinct since they do not hold strictly but suffer from occasional interference. Tactics like this have already been addressed: they fail for lack of substance. The trouble is that even if so-called fundamental laws "F" fail to govern in interference-plagued worlds w^f, fundamental laws sch-F do not fail to govern in w^f. Laws sch-F apply the same causal powers, the same "*oomph*" (Schrenk 2005), to affect matter's behavior in the same way as do laws F. The difference is just that laws sch-F would still properly be said to govern in the possible but not actual event that interference should hold back the powers from pushing into effect what they are disposed to push into effect. Laws F, by contrast, would not properly be said to govern in the possible but not actual event of interference; they would properly be said, by virtue of the interference, to be absent since anything with the label 'law F' is required by definition to be strict. We have seen (in §3.2) that it is sometimes possible to neutralize sch-arguments on Kuhnian grounds according to which, in this case, appeal to sch-F would suffer from something like incoherence, because by separating the behavior associated with F from the use of 'sch-F' we would thereby dissociate 'sch-F' from the behavior-causing *source* that gives meaning to 'F' and that is supposed to give meaning to 'sch-F'; but those grounds do no neutralizing here. Laws designated by 'sch-F' apply the same causal powers to affect

matter's behavior in the same way as do laws designated by 'F'; it is only interference that causes behavior to vary, not a different causal source (see §3.2).

16. So if the *interference* in the laws that I discuss were only metaphysically possible but not actual, then the actual course of the physical universe might be accounted for by appeal to a few simple, powerful laws. But nothing like simplicity or explanatory power in any description of the physical world would *make* the relevant laws *laws* according to the present conception (in contrast to a Humean conception of laws, for discussion of which see the sources in the paragraph corresponding to this note): as I have indicated, some genuine necessity is needed, which would be mind-independent in a way that simplicity and explanatory power are not (or at least human-mind independent; laws might for all I say here depend on some sort of mind like that of God to issue them, as Plantinga 1997 and Foster 2004 would maintain).

17. Again, Burroughs notes that complexity and organization are not enough to account for life, as a steam engine is no more alive than a wheelbarrow (1915, p. 97). But again, he is thinking of how a steam engine cannot carry out vital functions: "the steam-engine cannot remove its own ash; the 'living machine' can" (1915, p. 92). That there could be a fake organism carrying out the various vital functions yet without life is not what he is saying. Something similar would seem to hold for Nehemiah Grew, whom Brian Garrett (2006) resourcefully adduces as a historical figure who endorsed the equivalent in biology of zombie arguments in the philosophy of mind. According to Grew, it is impossible that "the finest Engine made by Humane art, or by Nature, become vital" any more than a kite is vital. "Were then, a Man, or other animal, nothing else but an Organized Body; let his several Organs be never so artificially made, and Variously and Regularly moved: Yet after all, he would be no more, than a finer sort of [puppet]" (Grew 1701, p. 33). But Grew, who does not elaborate further, gives scant indication in this one odd passage that he supposes that it is conceivable that there could be reproduction, development, growth, metabolism, self-repair and immunological self-defense, and so on, as opposed to great complexity and robot-like movement, that did not amount to life. Observe that even if that *were* Grew's idea (or that of Burroughs or other vitalists), the idea might easily be subject to familiar empirical scrutiny because the idea might simply be that there are empirical grounds for holding that vital functions *in fact* conform to no physical or functional account, so those functions are *in fact* driven by a vital principle: so therefore with respect to counterfactual worlds, where these or superficially *similar* functions *do* conform to a physical or functional account, there is no *life* (what *we* would call "life" in this world: see chapter 1, §1.2) but only what we might call "*twin*-life," the biological equivalent of XYZ (cf. Putnam 1975). In any event, Grew's cryptic point about the puppet, however it is to be understood, is not a salient or recurring point for him much less the vitalist tradition, as Garrett concedes; by contrast, "the inability of reigning mechanist models to account for vital phenomena" is a salient and abiding theme (Garrett 2003, p. 78; see also pp. 73–4, 79). To account for the vital processes, it was maintained, "a Vital or Directive Principle, seemeth of necessity to be assistant to the Corporeal" (Grew 1701, p. 35).

References

Ahmed, Arif. 2007. *Saul Kripke*. London: Continuum.
——. 2009. "Rigidity and Essentiality: Reply to Gómez-Torrente." *Mind* 118: 121–33.
Almog, Joseph. 1986. "Naming Without Necessity." *The Journal of Philosophy* 83: 210–42.
Altshuler, Douglas L., et al. 2005. "Short-Amplitude High-Frequency Wing Strokes Determine the Aerodynamics of Honeybee Flight." *Proceedings of the National Academy of Sciences* 102: 18213–18.
Anderson, P. W. 1994. "More Is Different." In *A Career in Theoretical Physics*, pp. 1–4. New Jersey: World Scientific.
Anscombe, G. E. M. and Geach, P. T. 1961. *Three Philosophers*. Ithaca: Cornell University Press.
Aquinas, Thomas. 1920. *The Summa Theologica of St. Thomas Aquinas*. 2nd ed., ed. Kevin Knight, trans. Fathers of the English Dominican Province. http://www.newadvent.org/summa/index.html.
Ariansen, Per. 2001. Logic for Dummies. Textbook for "Logic," Department of Philosophy, Classics, History of Art and Ideas, University of Oslo. http://folk.uio.no/perar/EngLogic.html.
Armstrong, D. M. 1968. *A Materialist Theory of the Mind*. London: Routledge & Kegan Paul.
——. 1978. *A Theory of Universals*. Cambridge: Cambridge University Press.
——. 1983. *What is a Law of Nature?* Cambridge: Cambridge University Press.
——. 1993. "The Identification Problem and the Inference Problem." *Philosophy and Phenomenological Research* 53: 421–2.
——. 1997. *A World of States of Affairs*. Cambridge: Cambridge University Press.
Aune, Bruce. 2008. *An Empiricist Theory of Knowledge*. Hist-Analytic. http://www.hist-analytic.org/ETK.pdf.
Balaguer, Mark. 2008. "Platonism in Metaphysics." *The Stanford Encyclopedia of Philosophy* (Fall 2008), ed. Edward N. Zalta. http://plato.stanford.edu/archives/fall2008/entries/platonism/.
Balog, Katalin. 2012 forthcoming. "In Defense of the Phenomenal Concept Strategy." *Philosophy and Phenomenological Research* 84.
Barnett, David. 2000. "Is Water Necessarily Identical to H_2O?" *Philosophical Studies* 98: 99–112.
Barrow, John. 1991. *Theories of Everything*. Oxford: Oxford University Press.
——. 2002. *The Constants of Nature*. New York: Pantheon.
——. and Webb, John. 2005. "Inconstant Constants." *Scientific American* 292 (June): 56–63.
Bates, Jared. 2009. "A Defence of the Explanatory Argument for Physicalism." *The Philosophical Quarterly* 59: 315–24.
Baumann, Pierre. 2010. "Are Proper Names Rigid Designators?" *Axiomathes* 20: 333–46.
Bealer, George. 1982. *Quality and Concept*. Clarendon: Oxford University Press.
——. 1987. "The Philosophical Limits of Scientific Essentialism." *Philosophical Perspectives* 1: 289–365.
——. 1989. "Fine-Grained Type-Free Intensionality." In *Properties, Types and Meaning*, eds. C. Gennaro, B. H. Partee, and R. Turner, pp. 177–230. Dordrecht: Kluwer Academic Publishers.

Bealer, George. 1994. "Property Theory: The Type-Free Approach v. the Church Approach." *Journal of Philosophical Logic* 23: 139–71.

———. and Mönnich, Uwe. 1989. "Property Theories." In *Handbook of Philosophical Logic*, vol. 4, ed. D. Gabbay and F. Guenthner, pp. 133–251. Dordrecht: D. Reidel.

Bechtel, William and Richardson, Robert. 1998. "Vitalism." In *Routledge Encyclopedia of Philosophy*, vol. 9, ed. Edward Craig, pp. 639–42. London: Routledge.

Beebee, Helen. 2000. "The Non-Governing Conception of Laws of Nature." *Philosophy and Phenomenological Research* 61: 571–94.

———. 2005. Review of *Powers: a Study in Metaphysics*, by George Molnar. *Philosophical Quarterly* 55: 674–7.

Beebee, H. and Sabbarton-Leary, N. 2010. "Introduction." In *The Semantics and Metaphysics of Natural Kinds*, pp. 1–24. New York: Routledge.

Bennett, Karen. 2007. "Mental Causation." *Philosophy Compass* 2: 316–37.

Berger, Alan. 2002. *Terms and Truth: Reference Direct and Anaphoric.* Cambridge, MA: MIT Press.

———. 2005. "General Terms, Anaphora, and Rigid Designation." In *General Terms, Anaphora, and Rigid Designation*, ed. by David Oderberg with a Foreword by P. F. Strawson. Cambridge MA: MIT.

Bernard, Claude. 1957. *An Introduction to the Study of Experimental Medicine.* Translated into English by Copley Green, with an Introduction by Lawrence J. Henderson and a Foreword by I. Bernard Cohen. New York: Dover. Originally published as *Introduction à l'étude de la Médecine expérimentale.* Paris: J. B. Baillière, 1865.

Besson, Corine. 2009. "Externalism, Internalism, and Logical Truth." *The Review of Symbolic Logic* 2: 1–29.

Bickle, John. 2008. "Multiple Realizability." *The Stanford Encyclopedia of Philosophy* (Fall 2008), ed. Edward N. Zalta. http://plato.stanford.edu/archives/fall2008/entries/multiple-realizability/.

Bigelow, John. 1999. "Scientific Ellisianism." In *Causation and Laws of Nature*, ed. H. Sankey, pp. 45–59. Dordrecht: Kluwer.

Bird, Alexander. 2001. "Necessarily, Salt Dissolves in Water." *Analysis* 61: 267–74.

———. 2002. "On Whether Some Laws Are Necessary." *Analysis* 62: 257–70.

———. 2005a. "The Dispositionalist Conception of Laws." *Foundations of Science* 10: 353–70.

———. 2005b. "Unexpected A Posteriori Necessary Laws of Nature." *Australasian Journal of Philosophy* 83: 533–48.

———. 2007. *Nature's Metaphysics: Laws and Properties.* Oxford: Clarendon Press.

———. 2008. "Remarks on Our Knowledge of Modal Facts." *Norsk filosofisk tidsskrift* 43: 53–9.

———. 2009. "And Then Again, He Might Not Be." *Australasian Journal of Philosophy* 87: 517–21.

Bird, Alexander and Tobin, Emma. 2009. "Natural Kinds." *The Stanford Encyclopedia of Philosophy* (Spring 2009), ed. Edward N. Zalta. http://plato.stanford.edu/archives/spr2009/entries/natural-kinds/.

Bishop, Robert C. 2006. "The Hidden Premise in the Causal Argument for Physicalism." *Analysis* 66: 44–52.

Block, Ned. 1980. "Are Absent Qualia Impossible?," *The Philosophical Review* 89: 257–74.

———. 1996. "What is Functionalism? A revised version of the entry on functionalism in *The Encyclopedia of Philosophy Supplement*, Macmillan. http://www.nyu.edu/gsas/dept/philo/faculty/block/papers/functionalism.pdf.

———. 2002. "The Harder Problem of Consciousness." *The Journal of Philosophy* 99: 391–425.

———. 2003. "Consciousness, Philosophical Issues about." In *Encyclopedia of Cognitive Science*, ed. Lynn Nadel, pp. 760–70. New York: Nature Pub. Group.

———. and Stalnaker, Robert. 1999. "Conceptual Analysis, Dualism, and the Explanatory Gap." *Philosophical Review* 108: 1–46.

Boër, Steven E. 1985. "Substance and Kind: Reflections on the New Theory of Reference." In *Analytical Philosophy in Comparative Perspective*, ed. B. K. Matilal and J. L. Shaw, pp. 103–50. Dordrecht: D. Reidel.

Bolton, Cynthia J. 1996. "Proper Names, Taxonomic Names and Necessity." *The Philosophical Quarterly* 46: 145–57.

BonJour, Laurence. 1998. *In Defense of Pure Reason*. Cambridge: Cambridge University Press.

Botterill, George. 2005. Review of *Scientific Essentialism*, by Brian Ellis. *Philosophical Books* 46: 118–22.

Broad, C. D. 1925. *The Mind and Its Place in Nature*. New York: Humanities Press.

Brock, S. 2004. "The Ubiquitous Problem of Empty Names." *Journal of Philosophy* 101: 277–98.

Brown, James R. 2002. Review of *Thomas Kuhn*, by Alexander Bird. *British Journal for the Philosophy of Science* 53: 143–9.

Brown, Jessica. 1998. "Natural Kind Terms and Recognitional Capacities." *Mind* 107: 275–303.

Burge, Tyler. 1982. "Other Bodies." In *Thought and Object*, ed. A Woodfield, pp. 97–120. Oxford: Oxford University Press.

———. 1992. "Philosophy of Language and Mind: 1950–1990." *Philosophical Review* 101: 3–51.

Burroughs, John. 1915. *The Breath of Life*. Boston: Houghton Mifflin.

Butts, Robert E. 1995. "Lawlike Generalization." In *The Cambridge Companion to Philosophy*, ed. Robert Audi, p. 423. Cambridge: Cambridge University Press.

Caltech Media Relations. "Deciphering the Mystery of Bee Flight," news release, November 29, 2005. http://pr.caltech.edu/media/Press_Releases/PR12772.html.

Campbell, Neil. 2009. "Why We Should Lower Our Expectations about the Explanatory Gap." *Theoria* 75: 34–51.

Carnap, Rudolf. 1956. *Meaning and Necessity: a Study in Semantics and Modal Logic*. Chicago: University of Chicago Press.

Carney, James. 1982. "A Kripkean Approach to Aesthetic Theories." *British Journal of Aesthetics* 22: 150–7.

Carruthers, Peter. 2000. *Phenomenal Consciousness: A Naturalistic Theory*. Cambridge: Cambridge University Press.

Cartwright, Richard. 1998. "On Singular Propositions." In *Meaning and Reference*, ed. Ali A. Kazmi, pp. 67–83. Calgary: University of Calgary Press.

Chalmers, David. 1996. *The Conscious Mind*. Oxford: Oxford University Press.

———. 1999. "Materialism and the Metaphysics of Modality." *Philosophy and Phenomenological Research* 59: 473–96.

———. 2002. "On Sense and Intension." *Philosophical Perspectives* 16: 135–82.

———. 2003. "Consciousness and its Place in Nature." In *The Blackwell Guide to Philosophy of Mind*, ed. Stephen Stich and Ted Warfield, pp. 102–42. Malden, MA: Blackwell.

Chalmers, David. 2006a. "The Foundations of Two-Dimensional Semantics." In *Two-Dimensional Semantics: Foundations and Applications*, ed. M. Garcia-Caprintero and J. Macia, pp. 55–140. Oxford: Oxford University Press.

———. 2006b. "Two-Dimensional Semantics." In *The Oxford Handbook of Philosophy of Language*, ed. E. Lepore and B. Smith, pp. 574–606. Oxford: Oxford University Press.

Chisholm, Roderick. 1973. "Parts as Essential to Their Wholes." *Review of Metaphysics* 26: 581–603.

Clark, Thomas. 1997. "Function and Phenomenology: Closing the Explanatory Gap." In *Explaining Consciousness: the Hard Problem*, ed. Jonathan Shear, pp. 45–60. Cambridge, MA: MIT Press.

Cocchiarella, Nino. 1972. "Properties as Individuals in Formal Ontology." *Noûs* 6: 165–87.

Cohen, Paul S. and Cohen, Stephen M. 1996. "Wöhler's Synthesis of Urea: How Do the Textbooks Report It?" *Journal of Chemical Education* 73: 883–6.

Coleman, William. 1977. *Biology in the Nineteenth Century: Problems of Form, Function, and Transformation.* Cambridge: Cambridge University Press.

Coleman, Keith A. and Wiley, E. O. 2001. "On Species Individualism: A New Defense of the Species-as-Individuals Hypothesis." *Philosophy of Science* 68: 498–517.

Collins, Arthur. 1988. "Types, Rigidity, and A Posteriori Necessity." In *Midwest Studies in Philosophy, 12: Realism and Antirealism*, ed. Peter French, Theodore Uehling Jr., and Howard Wettstein, pp. 195–224. Minneapolis: University of Minnesota Press.

Cook, Monte. 1980. "If 'Cat' is a Rigid Designator, What Does it Designate?" *Philosophical Studies* 37: 61–4.

Coppock, Paul. 1984. Review of *Reference and Essence*, by Nathan Salmon. *The Journal of Philosophy* 81: 261–70.

Cordry, Ben. 2004. "Necessity and Rigidly Designating Kind Terms." *Philosophical Studies* 119: 243–64.

Crane, Judith K. 2004. "On the Metaphysics of Species." *Philosophy of Science* 71: 156–73.

Crick, Francis. 1994. *The Astonishing Hypothesis: The Scientific Search for the Soul.* New York: Scribner.

Davidson, Matthew. 2003. "Introduction." In *Essays in the Metaphysics of Modality*, by Alvin Plantinga, ed. Matthew Davidson, pp. 3–24. Oxford: Oxford University Press.

Dennett, Daniel. 1997. "Facing Backwards on the Problem of Consciousness." In *Explaining Consciousness: The Hard Problem*, ed. Jonathan Shear, pp. 33–6. Cambridge, MA: MIT Press.

De Sousa, Ronald. 1984. "The Natural Shiftiness of Natural Kinds." *Canadian Journal of Philosophy* 14: 561–80.

———. 2000. Review of Joëlle Proust, *Comment l'esprit vient aux bêtes: Essai sur la représentation. Dialectica* 54: 320–8.

Devitt, Michael. 1980. "'Ostrich Nominalism' or 'Mirage Realism'?" *Pacific Philosophical Quarterly* 61: 433–9.

———. 1989. "Against Direct Reference." In *Midwest Studies in Philosophy, 14, Contemporary perspectives in the philosophy of language II*, ed. P. French, T. Uehling, and H. Wettstein, pp. 206–40. Notre Dame: University of Notre Dame Press.

———. 1996. *Coming to Our Senses.* Cambridge: Cambridge University Press.

———. 2005. "Rigid Application." *Philosophical Studies* 125: 139–65.

———. 2009. "Buenos Aires Symposium on Rigidity: Responses." *Análisis Filosófic* 29: 239–51.

———. 2012 forthcoming. "Meaning: Truth-Referential or Use?" In *Current Issues in Theoretical Philosophy vol. 3: Prospects for Meaning*, ed. Richard Schantz. Berlin: Walter de Gruyter.

———. and Sterelny, Kim. 1999. *Language and Reality: An Introduction to the Philosophy of Language*. 2nd ed. Cambridge, MA: MIT Press.

Donnellan, Keith. 1973. "Substances as Individuals." *Journal of Philosophy* 70: 711–12.

———. 1983. "Kripke and Putnam on Natural Kind Terms." In *Knowledge and Mind*, ed. C. Ginet and S. Shoemaker, pp. 84–104. New York: Oxford University Press.

Drewery, Alice. 2004. "A Note on Science and Essentialism." *Theoria* 51: 311–20.

———. 2005. "Essentialism and the Necessity of the Laws of Nature." *Synthese* 144: 381–96.

———. 2006. "Introduction." In *Metaphysics in Science*. Oxford: Blackwell.

Driesch, Hans. 1908. *The Science and Philosophy of the Organism*. London: A. and C. Black.

———. 1914. *The History and Theory of Vitalism*. London: Macmillan.

Dummett, Michael. 1981. *Frege: Philosophy of Language*, 2nd ed. Cambridge, MA: Harvard University Press.

———. 1991. *The Logical Basis of Metaphysics*. Cambridge, MA: Harvard University Press.

Ellis, Brian. 2001. *Scientific Essentialism*. Cambridge: Cambridge University Press.

———. 2004. "Marc Lange on Essentialism." *Australasian Journal of Philosophy* 83: 75–9.

Emmeche, Claus, Simo Køppe, and Frederik Stjernfelt. 1997. "Explaining Emergence: Towards an Ontology of Levels." *Journal for General Philosophy of Science* 28: 83–119.

Enç, Berent. 1986. "Essentialism without Individual Essences: Causation, Kinds, Supervenience and Restricted Identities." In *Midwest Studies in Philosophy 11, Studies in Essentialism*, ed. P. French, T. Uehling, and H. Wettstein, pp. 403–26. Minneapolis: University of Minnesota Press.

Ereshefsky, Marc. 2002. "Linnaean Ranks: Vestiges of a Bygone Era." *Philosophy of Science* 69: S305–15.

———. 2007. "Foundational Issues Concerning Taxa and Taxon Names." *Systematic Biology* 56: 295–301.

Feldman, Fred. 1973. "Kripke's Argument Against Materialism." *Philosophical Studies* 24: 416–19.

———. 1974. "Kripke on the Identity Theory." *Journal of Philosophy* 71: 665–76.

———. 1980. "Identity, Necessity, and Events." In *Readings in Philosophy of Psychology*, vol. 1, ed. Ned Block, pp. 148–55. Cambridge MA: Harvard University Press.

Fitch, G. W. 1976. "Are There Necessary *A Posteriori* Truths?" *Philosophical Studies* 30: 243–7.

———. 2004. *Saul Kripke*. Chesham: Acumen.

Fitting, Melvin. 2011. "Intensional Logic." *The Stanford Encyclopedia of Philosophy* (Spring 2011), ed. Edward N. Zalta. http://plato.stanford.edu/archives/spr2011/entries/logic-intensional/.

Forbes, Graeme. 1981. "An Anti-Essentialist Note on Substances." *Analysis* 41: 32–7.

Foster, John. 2004. *The Divine Lawmaker: Lectures on Induction, Laws of Nature, and the Existence of God*. Oxford: Clarendon.

Frege, Gottlob. 1952a. "On Concept and Object." In *Translations from the Philosophical Writings of Gottlob Frege*, trans. and ed. P. Geach and M. Black, pp. 42–55. Oxford: Blackwell.

———. "On Sense and Meaning." In *Translations from the Philosophical Writings of Gottlob Frege*, trans. and ed. P. Geach and M. Black, pp. 56–78. Oxford: Blackwell.

Frege, Gottlob. 1979. "Comments on Sense and Meaning." In *Posthumous Writings*, trans. Peter Long and Roger White, ed. Hans Hermes, Friedrich Kambartel, and Friedrich Kaulbach, pp. 118–25. Chicago: University of Chicago Press.

Furth, Montgomery. 1968. "Two Types of Denotation." In *Studies in Logical Theory*, American Philosophical Quarterly monograph series, monograph no. 2, pp. 9–45. Oxford: Blackwell.

Gampel, Eric H. 1997. "Ethics, Reference, and Natural Kinds." *Philosophical Papers* 26: 147–63.

Garcia, Laura L. 2007. "Human Rights and Natural Kinds." *UFL Annual Proceedings: UFL Life and Learning Conference* 17: 257–76. http://www.uffl.org/vol17/LGARCIA07.pdf.

Garrett, Brian Jonathan. 2003. "Vitalism and Teleology in the Natural Philosophy of Nehemiah Grew," *The British Journal for the History of Science* 36: 63–81.

———. 2006. "What the History of Vitalism Teaches us About Consciousness and the Hard Problem." *Philosophy and Phenomenological Research* 72: 576–88.

———. 2009. "Causal Essentialism versus the Zombie Worlds." *Canadian Journal of Philosophy* 39: 93–112.

Gaskin, Richard. 2008. *The Unity of the Proposition*. Oxford: Oxford University Press.

Geach, P. T., Ayer, A. J., and Quine, W. V. 1951. "Symposium: On What There Is." *Proceedings of the Aristotelian Society Supplementary Volumes* 25: 125–60.

Gendler, Tamar and Hawthorne, John. 2002. "Introduction." In *Conceivability and Possibility*, ed. Tamar Gendler and John Hawthorne, pp. 1–70. New York: Oxford University Press.

Gert, Joshua. 2009. "Toward an Epistemology of Certain Substantive A Priori Truths." *Metaphilosophy* 40: 214–36.

Ghiselin, Michael. 1987. "Species Concepts, Individuality, and Objectivity." *Biology and Philosophy* 2: 127–43.

Gibbard, Allan. 1975. "Contingent Identity." *Journal of Philosophical Logic* 4: 187–221.

Giberson, Karl and Artigas, Mariano. 2007. *Oracles of Science*. Oxford: Oxford University Press.

Girle, Rod. 2003. *Possible Worlds*. Montreal: McGill-Queen's University Press.

Glüer, Kathrin and Pagin, Peter. 2011. "General Terms and Relational Modality." *Noûs*: 1–41. Early View version (online).

Gómez-Torrente, Mario. 2004. "Beyond Rigidity? Essentialist Predication and the Rigidity of General Terms." *Crítica: Revista Hispanoamericana de Filosofía* 36: 37–54.

———. 2006. "Rigidity and Essentiality." *Mind* 115: 227–59.

———. 2009. "Essentiality and Theoretical Identifications: Reply to Ahmed." *Mind* 118: 135–48.

Goodfield, G. J. 1960. *The Growth of Scientific Physiology*. London: Hutchinson.

Gould, Stephen J. 1980. "The Return of Hopeful Monsters." In *The Panda's Thumb*, pp. 186–93. New York: W. W. Norton & Co.

———. 1991. *Bully for Brontosaurus: Reflections in Natural History*. New York: W. W. Norton & Co.

Gozzano, Simone. 2010. "Multiple Realizability and Mind–Body Identity." In *EPSA Epistemology and Methodology of Science*, vol 1, ed. M. Suárez, M. Dorato, and M. Rédei, pp. 119–27. New York: Springer.

Gregory of Nyssa. 2009. "On the Soul and the Resurrection." *In Nicene and Post-Nicene Fathers, Second Series, vol. 5*, translated by William Moore and Henry Austin Wilson, ed. Philip Schaff and Henry Wace (Buffalo, NY: Christian Literature Publishing Co., 1893), revised and edited for New Advent by Kevin Knight. http://www.newadvent.org/fathers/2915.htm.

Gregory, Frederick. 1977. *Scientific Materialism in Nineteenth Century Germany*. Dordrecht: D. Reidel.

Grew, Nehemiah. 1701. *Cosmologia Sacra: or a Discourse of the Universe as it is the Creature and Kingdom of God*. London. Printed for W. Rogers, S. Smith, and B. Walford. http://www.archive.org/details/cosmologiasacrao00grewuoft.

Hall, Everett. 1952. *What is Value? An Essay in Philosophical Analysis*. London: Routledge & Paul.

Handfield, Toby. 2005. "Lange on Essentialism, Counterfactuals, and Explanation." *Australasian Journal of Philosophy* 83: 81–5.

Hardcastle, Valerie Gray. 1997. "The Why of Consciousness: A Non-Issue for Materialists." In *Explaining Consciousness: The Hard Problem*, ed. Jonathan Shear, pp. 61–8. Cambridge, MA: MIT Press.

Harman, G., Quine, W. V., Kripke, S., Lewis, D., Dummett, M. A. E., and Partee, B. 1974. "Second General Discussion Session." *Synthese* 27: 509–21.

Harré, R. and Madden, E. H. 1975. *Causal Powers: a Theory of Natural Necessity*. Totowa, N.J.: Rowman and Littlefield.

Haukioja, Jussi. 2006. "Proto-Rigidity." *Synthese* 150: 155–69.

———. 2010. "Rigidity and Actuality-Dependence." *Philosophical Studies*. Online First version.

Hawking, Stephen. 1988. *A Brief History of Time: From the Big Bang to Black Holes*. New York: Bantam Books.

Hazen, Robert. 2001. *The Joy of Science*, part 4. Chantilly, VA: The Teaching Company.

Heintz, John. 1973. *Subjects and Predicables*. The Hague: Mouton.

Heinzel, Alexander and Northoff, Georg. 2009. "Kripke's Modal Argument Is Challenged by His Implausible Conception of Introspection." *Kriterion—Journal of Philosophy* 22: 13–31.

Hill, Christopher S. and McLaughlin, Brian P. 1999. "There Are Fewer Things in Reality than Are Dreamt of in Chalmer's Philosophy." *Philosophy and Phenomenological Research* 59: 445–54.

Hirsch, Eli. 1993. *Dividing Reality*. New York: Oxford University Press.

Hoefer, Carl. 2008. "Causal Determinism." *The Stanford Encyclopedia of Philosophy* (Spring 2008), ed. Edward N. Zalta. http://plato.stanford.edu/entries/determinism-causal/ .

Horgan, Terry. 2006. Review of *Purple Haze: The Puzzle of Consciousness*, by Joseph Levine. *Noûs* 40: 579–88.

Hughes, Christopher. 2004. *Kripke: Names, Necessity, and Identity*. Oxford: Clarendon.

Hull, David L. 1988. *Science as a Process: An Evolutionary Account of the Social and Conceptual Development of Science*. Chicago: The University of Chicago Press.

Hume, David. 1896. *A Treatise of Human Nature by David Hume, reprinted from the Original Edition in three volumes and edited, with an analytical index, by L. A. Selby-Bigge, M.A.* Oxford: Clarendon Press. http://oll.libertyfund.org/?option=com_staticxt&staticfile=show.php%3Ftitle=342&Itemid=27.

Inan, Ilhan. 2008. "Rigid General Terms and Essential Predicates." *Philosophical Studies* 140: 213–28.

Jackson, Frank. 1998. *From Metaphysics to Ethics*. Oxford: Clarendon.

———. 2003. "Armchair Metaphysics." In *Meaning*, by Mark Richard, pp. 317–37. Oxford: Blackwell.

———. 2004. "Why We Need A-Intensions." *Philosophical Studies* 118: 257–77.

———. 2007. "Reference and Description from the Descriptivists' Corner." *Philosophical Books* 48: 17–26.

Jackson, Frank, Pargetter, Robert, and Prior, Elizabeth. 1982. "Functionalism and Type-Type Identity Theories." *Philosophical Studies* 42: 209–25.

Johnson, David M. 1990. "Can Abstractions be Causes?" *Biology and Philosophy* 5: 63–77.

Jubien, Michael. 1989. "On Properties and Property Theory." In *Properties, Types and Meanings, Volume 1: Foundational Issues*, ed. Gennaro Chierchia, Barbara Partee, and Raymond Turner, pp. 159–75. Dordrecht: Kluwer.

Justice, John. 2003. "The Semantics of Rigid Designation." *Ratio* 16: 33–48.

Kaplan, David. 1973. "Bob and Carol and Ted and Alice." In *Approaches to Natural Language*, ed. J. Hintikka, J. Moravcsik, and P. Suppes, pp. 490–518. Dordrecht: Reidel.

———. 1989a. "Demonstratives." In *Themes From Kaplan*, ed. J. Almog, H. Wettstein, and J. Perry, pp. 481–563. Oxford: Oxford University Press.

———. 1989b. "Afterthoughts." In *Themes From Kaplan*, ed. J. Almog, H. Wettstein, and J. Perry, 565–614. Oxford: Oxford University Press.

Kenny, Anthony. 1965. Review of *Three Philosophers*, by G. E. M. Anscombe and P. T. Geach. *Mind* 74: 92–105.

Kim, Jaegwon. 2003. "Supervenience, Emergence, Realization, Reduction." In *The Oxford Handbook of Metaphysics*, ed. Michael Loux and Dean Zimmerman, pp. 556–84. Oxford: Oxford University Press.

———. 2005. *Physicalism, or Something Near Enough*. Princeton: Princeton University Press.

King, Jeffrey C. 2001. "Remarks on the Syntax and Semantics of Day Designators." *Philosophical Perspectives* 15: 291–333.

Kirk, Robert. 2003. *Mind & Body*. Montreal: McGill-Queen's University Press.

Kripke, Saul. 1971. "Identity and Necessity." In *Identity and Individuation*, ed. M. K. Munitz, pp. 135–64. New York: New York University Press.

———. 1977. "Speaker's Reference and Semantic Reference." In *Midwest Studies in Philosophy, II, Studies in the Philosophy of Language*, ed. P. French, T. Uehling, and H. Wettstein, pp. 225–76. Morris, MN: University of Minnesota Press.

———. 1979. "A Puzzle About Belief." In *Meaning and Use*, ed. A. Margalit, pp. 239–83. Dordrecht: D. Reidel.

———. 1980. *Naming and Necessity*. Cambridge, MA: Harvard University Press. 2005. "Russell's Notion of Scope." *Mind* 114: 1005–37.

Kuhn, Thomas S. 1990. "Dubbing and Redubbing: The Vulnerability of Rigid Designation." In *Minnesota Studies in the Philosophy of Science*, vol. 14, ed. C. Wade Savage, pp. 298–318. Minneapolis: University of Minnesota Press.

———. 2000. *The Road Since Structure*, ed. James Conant and John Haugeland. Chicago: University of Chicago Press.

Ladyman, James. 2004. "Supervenience: Not Local and Not Two-Way." *Behavioral and Brain Sciences* 27: 630.

Lange, Marc. 2004. "A Note on Scientific Essentialism, Laws of Nature, and Counterfactual Conditionals." *Australasian Journal of Philosophy* 82: 227–41.

LaPorte, Joseph. "Rigidity and Kind." *Philosophical Studies* 97: 293–316.

———. 2004. *Natural Kinds and Conceptual Change*. New York: Cambridge University Press.

———. 2010. "Theoretical Identity Statements, their Truth, and their Discovery." In *The Semantics and Metaphysics of Natural Kinds*, ed. H. Beebee and N. Sabbarton-Leary, pp. 115–24. New York: Routledge.

———. 2011. "Rigid Designators." *The Stanford Encyclopedia of Philosophy* (Summer 2011 Edition), ed. Edward N. Zalta. http://plato.stanford.edu/archives/sum2011/entries/rigid-designators/.

Lee, Jig-chuen. 1979. "Must a Cause be Contingently Related to its Effects?," *Canadian Journal of Philosophy* 9: 289–98.

Lennon, Thomas M. and Dea, Shannon. 2008. "Continental Rationalism." *The Stanford Encyclopedia of Philosophy* (Fall 2008 Edition), ed. Edward N. Zalta. http://plato.stanford.edu/archives/fall2008/entries/continental-rationalism/.

Leonhard, Gordon, Michel, Jan G. and Prien, Bernd. 2008. "On Swinburne and Possible Worlds." In *Richard Swinburne*, ed. N. Mößner, S. Schmoranzer, C. Weidemann, pp. 99–112. New Brunswick: Ontos Verlag.

Levin, Janet. 2010. "Functionalism." *The Stanford Encyclopedia of Philosophy* (Summer 2010 Edition), ed. Edward N. Zalta. http://plato.stanford.edu/archives/sum2010/entries/functionalism/.

Levin, Michael. 1987. "Rigid Designators: Two Applications." *Philosophy of Science* 54: 283–94.

Levine, Alex. 2001. "Individualism, Type Specimens, and the Scrutability of Species Membership." *Biology and Philosophy* 16: 325–38.

Levine, Joseph. 1983. "Materialism and Qualia: the Explanatory Gap." *Pacific Philosophical Quarterly* 64: 354–61.

———. 1993. "On Leaving Our What It's Like." In *Consciousness*, ed. M. Davies and G. Humphreys, pp. 121–36. Oxford: Basil Blackwell.

———. 1998. "Conceivability and the Metaphysics of Mind." *Noûs* 32: 449–80.

———. 2001. *Purple Haze: the Puzzle of Consciousness*. New York: Oxford University Press.

Levinson, Jerrold. 1978. "Properties and Related Entities." *Philosophy and Phenomenological Research* 39: 1–22.

Lewis, David. 1983a. "How to Define Theoretical Terms." In *Philosophical Papers*, vol. 1, pp. 78–95. Oxford: Oxford University Press.

———. 1983b. "An Argument for the Identity Theory." In *Philosophical Papers*, vol. 1, pp. 99–107. Oxford: Oxford University Press.

———. 1983c. "Mad Pain and Martian Pain." In *Philosophical Papers*, vol. 1, pp. 122–32. Oxford: Oxford University Press.

———. 1983d. "Scorekeeping in a Language Game." In *Philosophical Papers*, vol. 1, pp. 233–49. Oxford: Oxford University Press.

———. 1986. *On the Plurality of Worlds*. Oxford: Blackwell.

———. 1999a. "New Work for a Theory of Universals." In *Papers in Metaphysics and Epistemology*, vol. 2, pp. 8–55. New York: Cambridge University Press.

———. 1999b. "Psychophysical and Theoretical Identifications." In *Papers in Metaphysics and Epistemology*, vol. 2, pp. 248–61. New York: Cambridge University Press.

———. 1999c. "Reduction of Mind." In *Papers in Metaphysics and Epistemology*, vol. 2, pp. 291–324. New York: Cambridge University Press.

———. 1999d. "Should a Materialist Believe in Qualia?" In *Papers in Metaphysics and Epistemology*, vol. 2, pp. 325–31. New York: Cambridge University Press.

———. 1999e. "Naming the Colours." In *Papers in Metaphysics and Epistemology*, vol. 2, pp. 332–58. New York: Cambridge University Press.

Lightman, Alan and Brawer, Roberta. 1990. *Origins: The Lives and Worlds of Modern Cosmologists*. Cambridge, MA: Harvard University Press.

Linsky, Bernard. 1984. "General Terms as Designators." *Pacific Philosophical Quarterly* 65: 259–76.

———. 2006. "General Terms as Rigid Designators." *Philosophical Studies* 128: 655–67.

———. 2011. "Kripke on Proper and General Names." In *Saul Kripke*, ed. Alan Berger, pp. 17–48. Cambridge: Cambridge University Press.

Loar, Brian. 1995. "Meaning." In *The Cambridge Companion to Philosophy*, ed. Robert Audi, pp. 471–6. Cambridge: Cambridge University Press.

———. 1997. "Phenomenal States." In *The Nature of Consciousness: Philosophical Debates*, ed. Ned Block, Owen Flanagan, and Güven Güzeldere, pp. 597–616. Cambridge, MA: MIT Press.

———. 2003. "Qualia, Properties, Modality." *Philosophical Issues* 13: 113–29.

———. 2007. "Thinking About Qualia." In *Situating Semantics: Essays on the Philosophy of John Perry*, ed. Michael O'Rourke and Corey Washington, pp. 451–67. Cambridge, MA: MIT Press.

Locke, John. 1975. *An Essay Concerning Human Understanding*, ed. Peter H. Nidditch. Oxford: Oxford University Press.

López de Sa, Dan. 2001. "Theoretical Identifications and Rigidity for Predicates." In *Congress, Formal Theories and Empirical Theories*, ed. José M. Sagüillo, José L. Falguera, and Concha Martínez, pp. 611–21. Santiago de Compostela: Universidade de Santiago de Compostela.

———. 2006. "Flexible Property Designators." *Grazer Philosophische Studien* 73: 221–30.

———. 2007. "Rigidity, General Terms, and Trivialization." *Proceedings of the Aristotelian Society* 107: 117–23.

———. 2008a. "Rigidity for Predicates and the Trivialization Problem." *Philosopher's Imprint* 8: 1–13.

———. 2008b. "The Over-Generalization Problem: Predicates Rigidly Signifying the 'Unnatural'." *Synthese* 163: 263–72.

Loux, Michael. 1998. "Nominalism." In *Routledge Encyclopedia of Philosophy*, vol. 7, ed. Edward Craig, pp. 17–23. London: Routledge.

Lowe, E. J. 1997. "Ontological Categories and Natural Kinds." *Philosophical Papers* 26: 29–46.

———. 2006. "Powerful Particulars: Review Essay on John Heil's *From an Ontological Point of View*." *Philosophy and Phenomenological Research* 72: 466–79.

———. 2007. "Does the Descriptivist/Anti-Descriptivist Debate Have Any Philosophical Significance?" *Philosophical Books* 48: 27–33.

———. 2008. "Two Notions of Being: Entity and Essence." *Philosophy* 83: 23–48.

Lucretius. 1994–2009. *De Rerum Natura (On the Nature of Things)*. Trans. William Ellery Leonard. http://classics.mit.edu/Carus/nature_things.1.i.html.

Ludlow, Peter. 2009. "Descriptions." *The Stanford Encyclopedia of Philosophy* (Spring 2009 Edition), ed. Edward N. Zalta. http://plato.stanford.edu/archives/spr2009/entries/descriptions/.

Macbeth, Danielle. 1995. "Names, Natural Kind Terms, and Rigid Designation." *Philosophical Studies* 79: 259–81.

Macdonald, Cynthia. 2004. "Mary Meets Molyneux: The Explanatory Gap and the Individuation of Phenomenal Concepts." *Noûs* 38: 503–24.

Mackie, J. L. 1976. *Problems from Locke*. Oxford: Oxford University Press.

Mackie, Penelope. 2006. *How Things Might Have Been: Individuals, Kinds, and Essential Properties*. Oxford: Oxford University Press.

Magee, Bryan. 1988. *The Great Philosophers*. Oxford: Oxford University Press.

Maier, Emar. 2009. "Proper Names and Indexicals Trigger Rigid Presuppositions." *Journal of Semantics* 26: 253–315.

Maitra, Keya. 2003. *On Putnam*. Belmont, CA: Wadsworth.

Mandik, Pete and Weisberg, Josh. 2008. "Type-Q Materialism. In *Naturalism, Reference, and Ontology*, ed. Chase B. Wrenn, pp. 224–46. New York: Peter Lang.

Margalit, Avishai. 1979. "Sense and Science." In *Essays in Honour of Jaakko Hintikka*, ed. E. Saarinen, R. Hilpinen, I. Niiniluoto, and M. P. Hintikka, pp. 17–47. Dordrecht: D. Reidel.

Marras, Ausonio. 2005. "Consciousness and Reduction." *British Journal for the Philosophy of Science* 56: 335–61.

Martí, Genoveva. 1998. "Rigidity and the Description of Counterfactual Situations." *Theoria* 13: 477–90.

——. 2002. Review of Scott Soames, *Beyond Rigidity: The Unfinished Semantic Agenda of Naming and Necessity*. *Notre Dame Philosophical Reviews* (December). http://ndpr.nd.edu/reviews.cfm.

——. 2003. "The Question of Rigidity in New Theories of Reference." *Noûs* 37: 161–79.

——. 2004. "Rigidity and General Terms." *Proceedings of the Aristotelian Society* 104: 129–46.

——. and Martínez, José. 2007. "General Terms and Non-Trivial Rigid Designation." In *Current Topics in Logic and Analytic Philosophy*, ed. Concha Martínez, José L. Falguera, and José M. Sagüillo, pp.103–16. Santiago de Compostela: Universidad de Santiago de Compostela.

——. and Martínez, José. 2010. "General Terms as Designators: A Defense of the View." In *The Semantics and Metaphysics of Natural Kinds*, ed. H. Beebee and N. Sabbarton-Leary, pp. 46–63. New York: Routledge.

Matson, Wallace. 2011. *Grand Theories and Everyday Beliefs*: Oxford: Oxford University Press.

May, Robert. 2003. "Comments on Nathan Salmon 'Are General Terms Rigid?'." Unpublished Manuscript. http://kleene.ss.uci.edu/~rmay/Salmon.pdf.

McCaffery, Stephan. 1999. "Compositional Names." *Linguistics and Philosophy* 22: 423–45.

McDougall, William. 1938. *The Riddle of Life*. London: Methuen.

McGinn, Colin. 1999a. "A Note on the Essence of Natural Kinds." In *Knowledge and Reality: Selected Essays*, pp. 49–56. Oxford: Clarendon.

——. 1999b. *The Mysterious Flame: Conscious Minds in a Material World*. New York, N.Y.: Basic Books.

McKenna, Michael. 2009. "Compatibilism and Desert: Critical Comments on Four Views on Free Will." *Philosophical Studies* 144: 3–13.

McLaughlin, Brian. 2001. "In Defense of New Wave Materialism: A Response to Horgan and Tienson." In *Physicalism and its Discontents*, ed. Carl Gillett and Barry Loewer, pp. 319–30. Cambridge: Cambridge University Press.

Medawar, P. B. and Medawar, J. S. 1983. *Aristotle to Zoos: A Philosophical Dictionary of Biology*. Cambridge, MA: Harvard University Press.

Mellor, D. H. 1991a. "Natural Kinds." In *Matters of Metaphysics*, pp. 123–35. Cambridge: Cambridge University Press.

——. 1991b. "Properties and Predicates." In *Matters of Metaphysics*, pp. 170–82. Cambridge: Cambridge University Press.

Melnyk, Andrew. 2003. "Physicalism." In *The Blackwell Guide to Philosophy of Mind*, ed. Stephen Stich and Ted Warfield, pp. 65–84. Malden, MA: Blackwell.

Melnyk, Andrew. 2005. Review of *Physicalism, Or Something Near Enough*, by Jaegwon Kim. *Notre Dame Philosophical Reviews* (July). http://ndpr.nd.edu/review.cfm?id=3321.

Menzel, Christopher. 1993. "The Proper Treatment of Predication in Fine-Grained Intensional Logic." *Philosophical Perspectives* 7: 61–87.

———. 2008. "Actualism." *The Stanford Encyclopedia of Philosophy* (Spring 2008), ed. Edward N. Zalta. http://plato.stanford.edu/archives/spr2008/entries/actualism/.

Mill, John Stuart. 1843. "A System of Logic, Ratiocinative and Inductive." In *Collected Works of John Stuart Mill*, vol. 7, ed. J. M. Robson, 1963ff. Toronto: University of Toronto Press.

Miller, Richard B. 1992. "A Purely Causal Solution to One of the Qua Problems." *Australasian Journal of Philosophy* 70: 425–34.

Moffett, Marc. 2010. "Against A Posteriori Functionalism." *Canadian Journal of Philosophy* 40: 83–106.

Molnar, George. 2003. *Powers: a Study in Metaphysics*, ed. with an Introduction by Stephen Mumford and a Foreword by D. M. Armstrong. Oxford: Oxford University Press.

Mondadori, Fabrizio. 1978. "Interpreting Modal Semantics." In *Studies in Formal Semantics*, ed. F. Guenther and C. Rohrer, pp. 13–40. Amsterdam: North-Holland Publishing Co.

Mueller, Axel. 1995. "Natural Kinds and Projectible Predicates." *Sorites* 1: 13–45.

Mumford, Stephen. 1998. *Dispositions*. Oxford: Oxford University Press.

———. 2006. "Kinds, Essences, Powers." In A. Drewery (ed.), *Metaphysics in Science*, pp. 47–62. Oxford: Blackwell.

Musacchio, José M. 2005. "Why Do Qualia and the Mind Seem Nonphysical?" *Synthese* 147: 425–60.

Nagel, Thomas. 1974. "What Is It Like to Be a Bat?" *Philosophical Review* 83: 435–50.

———. 1980. "Armstrong on the Mind." In *Readings in Philosophy of Psychology*, vol. 1, ed. Ned Block, pp. 200–6. Cambridge MA: Harvard University Press.

Neale, Stephen. 1990. *Descriptions*. Cambridge MA: MIT Press.

———. 2005. "A Century Later." *Mind* 114: 809–71.

———. 2008. "Term Limits Revisited." *Philosophical Perspectives* 22: 375–442.

Nimtz, Christian. 2004. "Two-Dimensional and Natural Kind Terms." *Synthese* 138: 125–48.

Noble, Denis. 2008. "Claude Bernard, the First Systems Biologist, and the Future of Physiology." *Experimental Physiology* 93, 16–26.

Noonan, Harold. 2008. "Identity." *The Stanford Encyclopedia of Philosophy* (Fall 2008), ed. Edward N. Zalta. http://plato.stanford.edu/archives/fall2008/entries/identity/.

Oderberg, David S. 2007. *Real Essentialism*. New York: Routledge.

Okasha, Samir. 2002. *Philosophy of Science: A Very Short Introduction*. Oxford: Oxford University Press.

Oliver, Alex. 2005. "The Reference Principle." *Analysis* 65: 177–87.

Olmsted, J. M. D. and Olmsted, E. Harris. 1952. *Claude Bernard and the Experimental Method in Medicine*. New York: Henry Schuman.

Orlando, Eleonora. 2009. "General Term Rigidity as Identity of Designation: Some Comments on Devitt's Criticisms." *Análisis Filosófic* 29: 201–18.

Page, Don. 2003. "Mindless Sensationalism: A Quantum Framework for Consciousness." In *Consciousness: New Philosophical Perspectives*, ed. Quentin Smith and Aleksandar Jokic, pp. 468–506. Oxford: Oxford University Press.

———. 2010. "Scientific and Philosophical Challenges to Theism." In *Science and Religion in Dialogue*, ed. Melville Stewart, pp. 396–410. Oxford: Blackwell.

Papineau, David. 2002. *Thinking About Consciousness*. Oxford: Oxford University Press.
———. 2003. "Could There Be a Science of Consciousness?" *Philosophical Issues* 13: 205–20.
———. 2006. "Comments on Galen Strawson." In *Consciousness and Its Place in Nature: Does Physicalism Entail Panpsychism?*, ed. Anthony Freeman, pp. 100–9. Charlottesville, VA: Imprint Academic.
———. 2007a. "Kripke's Proof Is Ad Hominem Not Two-Dimensional." *Philosophical Perspectives* 21: 475–94.
———. 2007b. "Phenomenal and Perceptual Concepts." In *Phenomenal Concepts and Phenomenal Knowledge: New Essays on Consciousness and Physicalism*, ed. Torin Andrew Alter and Sven Walter, pp. 111–44. New York: Oxford University Press.
Patterson, Sarah. 2008. "Philosophy of Mind." In *The Routledge Companion to Twentieth Century Philosophy*, ed. Dermot Moran, pp. 525–82. London: Routledge.
Perry, John. 2001. *Reference and Reflexivity*. Stanford: CSLI.
Peterson, Philip L. 1986. "Revealing Designators and Acquaintance with Universals." *Noûs* 20: 291–311.
Plantinga, Alvin. 1974. *The Nature of Necessity*. Oxford: Clarendon.
———. 1985. "Self-Profile." In *Alvin Plantinga*, ed. J. Tomberlin and P. van Inwagen, pp. 3–97. Dordrecht: D. Reidel.
———. 1993. *Warrant and Proper Function*. Oxford: Oxford University Press.
———. 1997. "Methodological Naturalism?" *Perspectives on Science and Christian Faith* 49: 143–54.
———. 2003. *Essays in the Metaphysics of Modality*, ed. Matthew Davidson. Oxford: Oxford University Press.
———. 2010. "Religion and Science." *The Stanford Encyclopedia of Philosophy* (Summer 2010 Edition), ed. Edward N. Zalta. http://plato.stanford.edu/archives/sum2010/entries/religion-science/.
Polcyn, Karol. 2005. "Phenomenal Consciousness and the Explanatory Gap." *Diametros* 6: 49–69.
Polger, Thomas. 2004. *Natural Minds*. Cambridge, MA: MIT Press.
Putnam, Hilary. 1975. "The Meaning of 'Meaning'." In *Mind, Language and Reality*, pp. 215–71. New York: Cambridge University Press.
———. 1983. *Realism and Reason*. Cambridge: Cambridge University Press.
———. 1992. "Is it Necessary that Water is H_2O?" In *The Philosophy of A. J. Ayer*, ed. L. E. Hahn, pp. 429–54. La Salle, Illinois: Open Court.
Quine, W. V. 1960. *Word and Object*. Cambridge, Mass: MIT Press.
———. 1961. *From a Logical Point of View*. Cambridge, MA: Harvard University Press.
Rea, Michael. 1997. "Introduction." In *Material Constitution*, ed. M. Rea, pp. xv–lvii.
Read, Rupert and Sharrock, Wes. 2002. "Thomas Kuhn's Misunderstood Relation to Kripke–Putnam Essentialism." *Journal for General Philosophy of Science* 33: 151–8.
Redhead, Michael. 1990. "Explanation." In *Explanation and its Limits*, ed. Dudley Knowles, pp. 135–54. Cambridge: Cambridge University Press.
———. 1995. *From Physics to Metaphysics*. Cambridge: Cambridge University Press.
Rees, Martin. 2003. *Our Final Hour*. New York: Basic Books, 2004.
Richard, Mark. 1993. "Articulated Terms." *Philosophical Perspectives* 7: 207–30.
Roberts, John. 2008. *The Law-Governed Universe*. Oxford: Oxford University Press.

Robertson, Teresa. 2009. "Essentialism And Reference To Kinds: Three Issues In Penelope Mackie's *How Things Might Have Been: Individuals, Kinds, And Essential Properties.*" *Philosophical Books* 50: 125–41.

Ross, Don and Spurrett, David. 2004. "What to Say to a Skeptical Metaphysician: A Defense Manual for Cognitive and Behavioral Scientists." *Behavioral and Brain Sciences* 27: 603–27.

Rubin, Michael. 2008. "Is Goodness a Homeostatic Property Cluster?" *Ethics* 118: 496–528.

Russell, Bertrand. 1905. "On Denoting." *Mind* 14: 479–93.

———. 1912. *The Problems of Philosophy*. Oxford: Oxford University Press.

———. 1919. "Descriptions." In *Introduction to Mathematical Philosophy*, pp. 167–80. London: George Allen and Unwin.

Sainsbury, Mark. 1991. *Logical Forms*. Oxford: Basil Blackwell.

Salmon, Nathan. 1979. Review of *Names and Descriptions*, by Leonard Linsky. *Journal of Philosophy* 76: 436–52.

———. 1981. *Reference and Essence*. Princeton: Princeton University Press.

———. 1986. *Frege's Puzzle*. Cambridge, MA: MIT Press.

———. 2003. "Naming, Necessity, and Beyond." *Mind* 112: 475–92.

———. 2005. "Are General Terms Rigid?" *Linguistics and Philosophy* 28: 117–34.

———. 2007. "Demonstrating and Necessity." In *Content, Cognition, and Communication: Philosophical Papers Volume 2*, pp. 67–99. Oxford: Oxford University Press.

Schnieder, Benjamin. 2005. "Property Designators, Predicates, and Rigidity." *Philosophical Studies* 122: 227–41.

———. 2006. "Canonical Property Designators." *American Philosophical Quarterly* 43: 119–32.

———. 2008. "Further Remarks on Property Designators and Rigidity (Reply to López de Sa's Criticisms)." *Grazer Philosophische Studien* 76: 199–208.

Schrenk, Markus. 2005. "The Bookkeeper and the Lumberjack: Metaphysical vs. Nomological Necessity." In *Kreativität. XX. Deutscher Kongress für Philosophie. Sektionsbeiträge Band 1*, ed. G. Abel, pp. 850–6. Universitätsverlag der Technischen Universität.

Schwartz, Steven P. 1977. "Introduction." In *Naming, Necessity, and Natural Kinds*, pp. 13–41. Ithaca: Cornell University Press.

———. 1978. "Putnam on Artifacts." *The Philosophical Review* 87: 566–74.

———. 1980. "Formal Semantics and Natural Kind Terms." *Philosophical Studies* 38: 189–98.

———. 2002. "Kinds, General Terms, and Rigidity, A Reply to LaPorte." *Philosophical Studies* 109: 265–77.

———. 2006. "General Terms and Mass Terms." In *The Blackwell Guide to the Philosophy of Language*, ed. Michael Devitt and Richard Hanley, pp. 274–87. Oxford: Blackwell.

Searle, John. 1984. *Minds, Brains and Science*. Cambridge, MA: Harvard University Press.

———. 1996. "How to Study Consciousness Scientifically." Lecture 9 of his audio-recording *The Philosophy of Mind*, Springfield, VA: The Teaching Company.

Seddon, George. 1972. "Logical Possibility." *Mind* 81: 481–94.

Sellars, W. 1963. *Science, Perception and Reality*. London: Routledge & Kegan Paul.

———. 1967. "Abstract Entities." In *Philosophical Perspectives*, pp. 229–69. Springfield IL: Charles C. Thomas.

Senderowicz, Yaron. 2010. *Controversies and the Metaphysics of Mind*. Philadelphia: John Benjamins Publishing Company.

Shoemaker, Sydney. 1984. "Causality and Properties." In *Identity, Cause, and Mind*, pp. 206–33. Cambridge: Cambridge University Press.

———. 1998. "Causal and Metaphysical Necessity." *Pacific Philosophical Quarterly* 79: 59–77.

———. 2002. "Kim on Emergence." *Philosophical Studies* 108: 53–63.

———. 2007. *Physical Realization*. Oxford: Oxford University Press.

———. 2011. "Kripke and Cartesianism." In *Saul Kripke*, ed. Alan Berger, pp. 327–42. Cambridge: Cambridge University Press.

Sidelle, Alan. 1989. *Necessity, Essence, and Individuation: A Defense of Conventionalism*. Ithaca: Cornell University Press.

———. 1992a. "Identity and the Identity-like." *Philosophical Topics* 20: 269–92.

———. 1992b. "Rigidity, Ontology, and Semantic Structure." *The Journal of Philosophy* 89: 410–30.

———. 1995. "A Semantic Account of Rigidity." *Philosophical Studies* 80: 69–105.

———. 2002. "On the Metaphysical Contingency of Laws of Nature." In *Conceivability and Possibility*, ed. Tamar Gendler and John Hawthorne, pp. 309–36. New York: Oxford University Press.

Smith, Quentin. 2001. "The Metaphysical Necessity of Natural Laws." *Philosophica* 67: pp. 31–55.

Soames, Scott. 2002. *Beyond Rigidity: The Unfinished Semantic Agenda of Naming and Necessity*. New York: Oxford University Press.

———. 2003. *Philosophical Analysis in the Twentieth Century, vol. 2: The Age of Meaning*. Princeton: Princeton University Press.

———. 2004. "Reply to Ezcurdia and Gómez-Torrente." *Crítica, Revista Hispanoamericana de Filosofía* 36: 83–114.

———. 2005. *Reference and Description: The Case Against Two-Dimensionalism*. Princeton: Princeton University Press.

———. 2006a. "Précis of Beyond Rigidity." *Philosophical Studies* 128: 645–54.

———. 2006b. "Reply to Critics." *Philosophical Studies* 128: 711–38.

———. 2007. "The Substance and Significance of the Dispute Over Two-Dimensionalism." *Philosophical Books* 48: 34–49.

———. 2010. *Philosophy of Language*. Princeton: Princeton University Press.

Sosa, David. 2001. "Rigidity in the Scope of Russell's Theory." *Noûs* 35: 1–38.

———. 2006. "Rigidity." In *The Oxford Handbook of Philosophy of Language*, ed. Ernest Lepore and Barry C. Smith, pp. 476–89. Oxford: Oxford University Press.

Sprevak, Mark. 2009. "Extended Cognition and Functionalism." *The Journal of Philosophy* 106, 503–27.

Stalnaker, Robert C. 2003. *Ways a World Might Be: Metaphysical and Anti-Metaphysical Essays*. Oxford: Oxford University Press.

———. 2007. "Critical Notice of Scott Soames's Case against Two-Dimensionalism." *Philosophical Review* 116: 251–66.

Stamos, David N. 2003. *The Species Problem: Biological Species, Ontology, and the Metaphysics of Biology*. Lanham, Maryland: Lexington Books.

Stanford, P. Kyle and Kitcher, Philip. 2000. "Refining the Causal Theory of Reference for Natural Kind Terms." *Philosophical Studies* 97: 99–129.

Stanley, Jason. 1997a. "Names and Rigid Designation." In *A Companion to the Philosophy of Language*, ed. Bob Hale and Crispin Wright, pp. 555–85. Oxford: Blackwell.

Stanley, Jason. 1997b. "Rigidity and Content." In *Language, Thought, and Logic: Essays in Honour of Michael Dummett*, ed. Richard Heck, pp. 131–56. Oxford: Oxford University Press.
———. and Szabó, Zoltán. 2000. "On Quantifier Domain Restriction." *Mind and Language* 15: 219–61.
Sterelny, Kim. 1983. "Natural Kind Terms." *Pacific Philosophical Quarterly* 64: 110–25.
Steward, Helen. 1990. "Identity Statements and the Necessary A Posteriori." *Journal of Philosophy* 87: 385–98.
———. 2005. "Rigid Designation, Direct Reference, and Modal Metaphysics." *Pacific Philosophical Quarterly* 86: 577–99.
Sullivan, Arthur. 2007. "Rigid Designation and Semantic Structure." *Philosophers' Imprint* 7: 1–22.
Swinburne, Richard. 2007. "From Mental/physical identity to substance Dualism." In *Persons: Human and Divine*, ed. Peter Van Inwagen and Dean Zimmerman, pp. 142–65. Oxford: Oxford University Press.
Swoyer, Chris. 2008. "Properties." *The Stanford Encyclopedia of Philosophy* (Fall 2008 Edition), ed. Edward N. Zalta. http://plato.stanford.edu/archives/fall2008/entries/properties/.
Ter Meulen, Alice. 1981. "An Intensional Logic for Mass Terms." *Philosophical Studies* 40: 105–25.
Thomason, Richmond H. 1969. "Species, Determinates and Natural Kinds." *Noûs* 3: 95–101.
T'Hooft, Gerard, Susskind, Leonard, Witten, Edward, Fukugita, Masataka, Randall, Lisa, Smolin, Lee, Stachel, John, Rovelli, Carlo, Ellis, George, Weinberg, Steven, and Penrose, Roger. 2005. "A Theory of Everything?" *Nature* 433: 257–9.
Tye, Michael. 1981. "On an Objection to the Synonymy Principle of Property Identity." *Analysis* 41: 22–6.
———. 2006. "Absent Qualia and the Mind–Body Problem." *Philosophical Review* 115: 139–68.
Van Brakel, J. 2005. "On the Inventors of XYZ." *Foundations of Chemistry* 7: 57–84.
Vander Laan, David A. 1997. "The Ontology of Impossible Worlds." *Notre Dame Journal of Formal Logic* 38: 597–620.
Van Gulick, Robert. 2004. "Consciousness." *The Stanford Encyclopedia of Philosophy (Fall 2004 Edition)*, ed. Edward N. Zalta. http://plato.stanford.edu/archives/fall2004/entries/consciousness/.
Van Inwagen, Peter. 2003. "The Compatibility of Darwinism and Design." In *God and Design*, ed. Neil Manson, pp. 348–63. New York: Routledge.
Wald, David J. 1979. "Geach on Atomicity and Singular Propositions." *Notre Dame Journal of Formal Logic* 20: 285–94.
Weinberg, Steven. 1993. *Dreams of a Final Theory: the Search for the Fundamental Laws of Nature*. London: Vintage.
———. 1999. "A Unified Physics by 2050?" *Scientific American* 281 (December): 68–75.
———. 2009. *Lake Views: This World and the Universe*. Cambridge, MA: Harvard University Press.
Weisberg, Josh. 2007. "The Problem Of Consciousness: Mental Appearance And Mental Reality." PhD diss., The City University of New York. http://www.joshweisberg.com/Weisberg-dissertation.pdf.
Wheeler, L. R. 1939. *Vitalism: Its History and Validity*. London: Witherby.
Wiggins, David. 1984. "The Sense and Reference of Predicates: A Running Repair to Frege's Doctrine and a Plea for the Copula." *The Philosophical Quarterly* 34: 311–28.
Wilson, Jessica. 2005. "Supervenience-based Formulations of Physicalism." *Noûs* 39: 426–59.

Witmer, D. Gene. 2006. Review of *Physicalism, or Something Near Enough*, by Jaegwon Kim. *Mind* 115: 1136–41.

Wolf, Michael P. 2006. "Rigid Designation and Anaphoric Theories of Reference." *Philosophical Studies* 130: 351–75.

———. 2007. "Reference and Incommensurability: What Rigid Designation Won't Get You." *Acta Analytica* 22: 207–22.

Wolter, Lynsey. 2009. "Demonstratives in Philosophy and Linguistics." *Philosophy Compass* 4: 451–68.

Wolterstorff, Nicholas. 1970. *On Universals: An Essay in Ontology*. Chicago: University of Chicago Press.

Wright, Crispin. 1998. "Why Frege Did Not Deserve His *Granum Salis*: A Note on the Paradox of 'The Concept Horse' and the Ascription of Bedeutungen to Predicates." *Grazer Philosophische Studien* 55: 239–63.

Zalta, Edward N. 2006. "Deriving and Validating Kripkean Claims Using the Theory of Abstract Objects." *Noûs* 40: 591–622.

Index

actuality operator, *see* descriptions—world-indexed descriptions
adjectives 68, 69, 71, 76–7, 97
Ahmed, Arif 19 n. 11, 128, 142
Almog, Joseph 62 n. 11, 63 n. 12, 139, 140
ambiguity 33–4; 84 n. 7
analysis 172, *see also* analyticity
analytic functionalism, *see* functionalism
analyticity 52, 174 n. 5; *see also* causal theory of reference
Anderson, P. W. 207
Anscombe, G. E. M. and Geach, P. T. 85 n. 11, 99 n. 11, 108
Apatosaurus, *see* Brontosaurus
aposteriority 60 n. 8
  necessary aposteriority 16 n. 4, n. 5, 17 n. 6, 19–20 n. 12, 42–3, 46, 51, 59 n. 5, 212
  for non-theoretical identity statements 8–9, 18–19 n. 11
  permitted by rigidity 4–7, 95–6, 98–9, 101, 109, 120 n. 18; *see also* essence
  see also artificial-; causal theory of reference; direct reference; two-dimensionalism
application of words, as opposed to naming 64, 69, 84 n. 6, 8; *see also* descriptions—definite descriptions—vis-à-vis definite ascriptions; Mill
apriority 171–2, 175 n. 9; *see also* analyticity; aposteriority
Aquinas, Thomas 151
Ariansen, Per 64, 86 n. 15
Armstrong, David M. 78 , 107, 157, 164, 166, 204
artificial-property designators 22–5, 52–3, 111, 119–20 n. 11; *see also* causal theory of reference; descriptivism
Artigas, *see* Giberson and Artigas
Aune, Bruce 57, 121 n. 19

Balaguer, Mark 121 n. 19
Balog, Katalin 173 n. 1, 192
Barnett, David 132
Barrow, John 205, 216 n. 12
Barrow, John and Webb, John 216 n. 12
Bates, Jared 151, 156, 180
Baumann, Pierre 62 n. 11, 137, 139
Bealer, George 21 n. 16, 76, 80, 81, 107, 133, 190, 212
Bealer, George and Mönnich, Uwe 80, 107
Bechtel, William and Richardson, Robert 210

Beebee, Helen 204, 216 n. 13
Beebee, H. and Sabbarton-Leary, N. 19, 146 n. 10, 212
bees' flight, *see* evidential gaps
Bennett, Karen 156
Berger, Alan 59, 90, 117 n. 2, 134, 145 n. 9, 199
Bernard, Claude 211
Besson, Corine 4, 84 n. 9
Bickle, John 154, 157
Bigelow, John 217 n. 14
Bird, Alexander A. 201–2, 204, 211, 217 n. 14
Bird, Alexander and Tobin, Emma 12, 28, 38 n. 1, 133, 146 n. 10
Bishop, Robert C. 151
Block, Ned 149, 165, 173 n. 1, 174 n. 4, 214 n. 3
Block, Ned and Stalnaker, Robert 149, 156, 175 n. 9, 180, 186, 188
Boër, Steven E. 17 n. 8, 20 n. 13, 50, 64, 85 n. 12, 111
Bolton, Cynthia J. 19, 43, 132, 134
BonJour, Laurence 212
Botterill, George 197, 198
Bricker, Phil 17 n. 8
Broad, C. D. 209
Brock, S. 4
Brontosaurus, discovery and baptism 8–9, 186–88, 208
Brown, James R. 199
Brown, Jessica 191
Burge, Tyler 60 n. 7, 165
Burroughs, John 210, 218 n. 17
Butts, Robert E. 204

Caltech Media Relations 153
Campbell, Neil 173, n. 1
Carnap, Rudolf 91, 119 n. 7
Carney, James 50, 61 n. 9
Carruthers, Peter 43, 50, 155–6, 106, 160, 173 n. 1, 191
Cartesian intuition, *see* conceptual dualism; Kripke—on materialism
Cartwright, Richard 50, 61 n. 9, 128, 147 n. 13
categories, *see* mediating categories
causal-interactions argument for materialism 151
causal theory of reference 39 n. 4, 189–92
  and qua problem, *see* mediating categories
  relationship to theory of rigid designation 21 n. 15, 49–50, 129
  'rigidity' as a causally grounded term 52–3

ceteribus paribus, *see* laws
c-fiber firing, *see* skeptical argument against psychophysical identities
Chalmers, David 150–1, 161, 170–2, 175 n. 9, 207, 209
characterization as opposed to naming, *see* application of words
chemicals 141, 146 n. 12; *see also* de jure
Chisholm, Roderick 162
Clark, Thomas 153, 180
classification as opposed to naming, *see* application of words
Cocchiarella, Nino 119 n. 5
Cohen, Paul S. and Cohen, Stephen M. 210
coinstantiation, *see* correlation
Coleman, William 211
Coleman, Keith A. and Wiley, E. O. 90
Collins, Arthur 27, 117 n. 1, 146 n. 10, 189
compositionality 54, 139–40, 145–6 n. 9
conceptual dualism 150, 152–4, 168, 173 n. 1, 206; *see also* evidential gaps
concrete-object designator, *see* designation; neutrality; rigid designators; theoretical identity statements
confirmation, *see* evidential gaps; theoretical identity statements—problematic
context, *see* descriptions; problem of securing; shadowing; singular terms; grammatically
conventionalism 127
Cook, Monte 23, 111, 121 n. 23
Coppock, Paul 142
copresence, *see* correlation
copula 69, 70, 71, 75, 76, 77, 78–9, 86 n. 15, n. 17, n. 18, 86–7 n. 20, 87 n. 21; *see also* predicative use of 'is'
Cordry, Ben 39 n. 5, 47, 121 n. 24
correlation 176, 179–89, 193, 196, 204–5, 214 n. 5; *see also* necessity—of identity—on account of rigidity; shadowing
count nouns 13, 68, 69, 76–7, 97
Crane, Judith K. 90
Crick, Francis 148, 180

Davidson, Matthew 48, 62 n. 11
Dea, *see* Lennon and Dea
de facto – de jure distinction, *see* rigid designators
de jure connections for establishing reference 177–213, 214 n. 2; *see also* mediating categories; theoretical identity statements—problematic
definite ascriptions, *see* descriptions
Dennett, Daniel 210
denotation, *see* descriptions; descriptivism
dependence 158, 175 n. 7
descriptions:
    as nonrigid designators 23–4, 66, 71, 75
    as de facto or de jure rigid designators 65–6, 137, 145 n. 9

definite descriptions
    problem of securing a unique designatum 32–6
    Russellian construal 4, 65–8, 86 n. 16, 100; *see also* rigid–nonrigid distinction—whether
    vis-à-vis definite ascriptions 85 n. 11, 91, 99, 108
    world-indexed descriptions 18 n. 9, 56, 62–3 n. 12, 139, 140
    see also ambiguity; compositionality; descriptivism; mediating categories; theoretical expressions
descriptivism:
    arguments against: error and ignorance 56, 62 n. 12
    causal descriptivism 190, 214–15 n. 6
    naïve varieties associated with Frege and Russell 5, 55, 99
    associated descriptions not essence revealing 18 n. 9
    not central to rigidity's role 51–7, 61 n. 9, 62 n. 11, 111, 114
    not refuted by essential application 114–16
    rejected as an account of artificial-property designators 53–5
    rejected as an account of phrases like 'eligible unmarried male' 53–5; *see also* theoretical expressions—as compositional
    sophisticated varieties 56, 62 n. 11
    see also compositionality; descriptions; direct reference; mediating categories; pragmatics; reference fixing
designation:
    applies to either singular or purely predicative terms 20 n. 14, 91, 119 n. 7
    of concrete objects
        conform as well as property designators do to a uniformly singular or nonsingular treatment 83–4 n. 5
    see also neutrality; rigid designators
    see also meanings, mediating categories
designators, *see* property designators; rigid designators
De Sousa, Ronald 50, 209
Devitt, Michael 29, 39 n. 5, 43, 52, 61 n. 9, 61 n. 10, 62 n. 10, 91, 111, 114, 115, 117 n. 1, 117 n. 2, 119 n. 9, 121 n. 19, 128, 129, 131, 144 n. 3, 215 n. 6, 215 n. 7
Devitt, Michael and Sterelny, Kim 62 n. 12, 172, 190
diabetes 155–61
direct reference
    compatible with mediating categories 192–3, 215 n. 7
    implications for necessary aposteriority 4–7

relationship to rigidity 61 n. 9, 62 n. 11, 128–9, 144 n. 3
  see also descriptivism; pragmatics; two-dimensionalism
dispositions, *see* necessity
Donnellan, Keith 12, 20 n. 13, 50, 59, 65, 85 n. 12
Drewery, Alice 146 n. 10, 199, 204
Driesch, Hans 210
'dthat', *see* descriptions—world-indexed descriptions
dualistic treatments as opposed to uniform treatments, *see* designation; property designators; rigid–nonrigid distinction
Dummett, Michael 62 n. 12, 85 n. 12, 86 n. 15

eliminative materialism, *see* eliminativism
eliminativism:
  about higher-level properties 157
  about pain(s) 164–6, 170, 173 n. 1, 175 n. 6, 178
Ellis, Brian 198, 205, 216 n. 12, 217 n. 14
Emmeche, Claus, Simo Køppe, and Frederik Stjernfelt 158
empirical investigation, *see* aposteriority; causal theory of reference
empiricism, *see* induction; rationalism
Enç, Berent 122, n. 25
English-like refined languages 76, 99, 132, 134–7, 139, 142–3, 144–5 n. 6, 146 n. 12, n. 13; *see also* formalization; functionalism—analytic; grammar; Kripke
Ereshefsky, Marc 50, 61 n. 9
essence:
  of pains, *see* Kripke
  whether presupposed in arguments associated with rigidity 131, 134, 140–3, 146–7 n. 13
  associated with necessary aposteriority 6–7
  associated with rigidity 45–6
  trivial or uninformative 17 n. 7
  see also aposteriority; causal theory of reference; descriptivism; essential application; essential-property attributing statements; necessity; origins; scientific necessitarianism; theoretical identity statements
essential application 62 n. 10, 90, 110–16
essentialism, *see* essence
essential-property attributing statements 46–9, 59–60 n. 5
evidential gaps or shortcomings 152–4, 171–2, 173 n. 72, 198; *see also* final theory; skeptical argument against psychophysical identities; theoretical identity statements—problematic; vitalism

explanation 129–30, 158–79
explanatory gap, *see* conceptual dualism
extension:
  coextensiveness, *see* copresence
  for predicative and singular terms 11–12, 20 n. 13
  metaphysical- or semantic- extension or intension 23, 38 n. 1, 69, 91–2, 97, 102–3, 119 n. 6
externalism, *see* causal theory of reference

fallibilism, *see* privileged insider's perspective
fatalism 204–6
Feldman, Fred 161
final theory 204–6, 207–8, 212
first-order languages, *see* formalization; property designators; singular terms
Fitch, G. W. 3, 5, 6, 21 n. 15, 64, 161, 162
Fitting, Melvin 41 n. 10
Forbes, Graeme 85 n. 12
formalization of reasoning expressed with designators 71–4; *see also* property designators
Foster, John 218 n. 16
freezing of water, *see* theoretical identity statements—problematic
Frege, Gottlob 5, 6, 16 n. 3, 17 n. 6, 55, 75, 86 n. 15, 89, 99, 108, 119 n. 5; *see also* descriptivism
functionalism:
  analytic or folk-psychological functionalism 165–9, 173 n. 1, 178–9
  broadly materialist 174 n. 4
  realizer functionalism, *see* folk-psychological functionalism; multiple realizability; theoretical identity statements
Furth, Montgomery 119 n. 5

Gampel, Eric H. 49, 50
Garcia, Laura L. 50
Garrett, Brian J. 193, 207, 209, 218 n. 17
Gaskin, Richard 78
Geach, P. 85 n. 11, 108; *see also* Anscombe and Geach
Gendler, Tamar and Hawthorne, John 59–60 n. 5
General Principle on the Necessity of an Identity Statement 43–4
general terms:
  as higher-order singular terms, *see* property designators
  as merely predicative, *see* property designators
  see also designation; extension; grammar; singular terms
general-term phrases, *see* compositionality
genus terms, *see* Brontosaurus
Gert, Joshua 51
Gibbard, Allan 6

Giberson, Karl and Artigas, Mariano 205
Girle, Rod 45
Ghiselin, M. 57
Glüer, Kathrin and Pagin, Peter 47, 55
Gómez-Torrente, Mario 39 n. 3, 39 n. 4, 47, 48, 52, 61 n. 9, 64, 68, 84 n. 8, 86 n. 15, 111, 114, 121–2 n. 24, 122 n. 26
Goodfield, G. J. 211
Gould, Stephen J. 9
Gozzano, Simone 193
grammar 69–71, 84 n. 9, 84–5 n. 10; 85 n. 11; *see also* predicative use of 'is'; singular terms
Gregory of Nyssa 8, 18 n. 9
Gregory, Frederick 211
Grew, Nehemiah 218 n. 17
Grice, P., *see* pragmatics
$^{1-3}H_2O$, *see* theoretical identity statements—problematic

Hall, Everett 84 n. 9
Handfield, Toby 197
Hardcastle, Valerie G. 180
Harré, R. and Madden, E. H. 217 n. 14
Haukioja, Jussi 39 n. 5, 47, 50, 51, 55, 90, 117 n. 1, 191
Hawking, Stephen 205
Hawthorne, *see* Gendler and Hawthorne
Hazen, Robert 165
Heintz, John 84–5 n. 10, 85 n. 11, 89, 91
Heinzel, Alexander and Northoff, Georg 180
high-order languages, *see* formalization; property designators
Hill, Christopher S. and McLaughlin, Brian P. 173 n. 1, 180, 191
Hirsch, Eli 85 n. 12
Hoefer, Carl 204
Horgan, Terry 173 n. 2
Hughes, Christopher 1, 5, 6, 60 n. 5, 161
Hull, David L. 61 n. 9, 188, 189
Hume, David 213, 218 n. 16

identification statements 93–4, 110, 144 n. 1, 215 n. 8, 216 n. 9; *see also* necessity
identity statements, *see* de jure connections; essential-property attributing statements; identification statements; induction; multiply realizability; necessity; rigid–nonrigid distinction; singular terms; theoretical identity statements; token materialism
Inan, Ilhan 39 n. 5, 117 n. 2, 120 n. 17, 123 n. 27
induction as a means to confirm identity 169; *see also* methodological principles
intoxication, *see* explanation
introspection, *see* privileged insider's perspective

isotopically limited varieties, *see* theoretical identity statements—problematic

Jackson, Frank 15 n. 1, 60 n. 5, 62 n. 11, 170, 171, 175 n. 9
Jackson, Frank, Pargetter, Robert, and Prior, Elizabeth 21 n. 16, 156
Johnson, David M. 50
Jubien, Michael 84 n. 8, 107, 157
Justice, John 62 n. 11

Kaplan, David 3, 5, 63, 84 n. 9, 86 n. 15, 87 n. 20, 117 n. 2, 128, 140, 193, 215 n. 7
Kenny, Anthony 119 n. 4
Kim, Jaegwon 126, 144 n. 1, 151, 153, 155, 175 n. 7
King, Jeffrey C. 129, 146 n. 9
Kirk, Robert 155, 165
Kitcher, *see* Stanford and Kitcher
Køppe, *see* Emmeche, Køppe, and Stjernfelt
Kripke, Saul 1, 2, 3, 4, 5–6, 7, 9, 10, 11, 12, 13, 15, 15 n. 1, 16 n. 2, 16 n. 4, 16 n. 5, 17 n. 6, 19 n. 11, 20 n. 12, 20–1 n. 15, 21 n. 16, 41 n. 9, 41 n. 10, 44, 48, 50, 51, 52–3, 57, 58, 59–60 n. 5, 60 n. 6, 60 n. 7, 60 n. 8, 61 n. 9, 62 n. 11, 62 n. 12, 68, 77, 82, 86 n. 15, 89, 93, 95, 98, 99, 105, 115, 116, 118 n. 2, 119 n. 10, 120 n. 15, 128 n. 28, 133, 136, 139, 141, 144–5 n. 6, 145–6 n. 9, 148–9, 150, 152, 161–2, 166, 173 n. 2, 214 n. 2, 215 n. 7
on de facto and de jure rigidity 133, 139, 145 n. 9
on direct reference and semantic mediation 61 n. 9, 62 n. 11, 215 n. 7
distinguishes rigidity from easily- or often-confused notions 3–4, 53, 60 n. 7, 61 n. 9, 62 n. 11, 83 n. 1
Kripkean agenda of book 1, 9, 11, 15, 92
on materialism 20 n. 12, 123 n. 28, 148–50, 152, 166, 170, 173 n. 2, 214 n. 2
on pain's essential painfulness 123 n. 28, 161–62
on the rigidity of property designators 7, 11, 12, 13, 20–1 n. 15, 21 n. 16, 52–3, 58, 68, 89, 118 n. 2, 119 n. 10
on sense, meaning 41 n. 10
on stipulating rigidity 144–5 n. 6
Kuhn, Thomas S. 57, 188, 189, 198, 199

Ladyman, James 157
Lange, Marc 197
LaPorte, Joseph 15 n. 1, 19 n. 11, 39 n. 5, 61 n. 10, 142, 143, 174 n. 4, 174 n. 5, 179
laws, physical 152–3, 195–211
fundamental 200–7, 217 n. 14, 217–18 n. 15
governing conception of 202, 204, 218 n. 16

unable to govern behavior that is influenced by countervailing circumstances 200, 202–3, 217–18 n. 15, 218 n. 16
  see also fatalism
Leary, Nigel Sabbarton-, see Beebee and Sabbarton-Leary
Lee, Jig-chuen 122 n. 25
Lennon, Thomas M. and Dea, Shannon, 212
Leonhard, Gordon, Michel, Jan G., and Prien, Bernd 61 n. 9
Levin, Janet 156, 165, 168, 214 n. 3
Levin, Michael 60 n. 5, 126, 197, 205
Levine, Alex 50, 61 n. 9, 151, 152
Levine, Joseph 152, 172, 173 n. 1, 173 n. 2, 174 n. 3, 174 n. 5, 180, 188, 208, 214 n. 3
Levinson, Jerrold 86 n. 19, 118 n. 2
Lewis, David. 18 n. 10, 40 n. 8, 45, 62 n. 11, 85 n. 12, 107, 131–2, 144 n. 4, 144 n. 5, 156, 157, 165, 166–7, 194, 215 n. 7
life, see vitalism
Linsky, Bernard 17 n. 8, 21 n. 16, 33, 38 n. 1, 39 n. 5, 74, 75, 78, 85 n. 11, 85 n. 12, 85 n. 13, 86 n. 15, 86 n. 16, 86 n. 20, 87–8 n. 22, 199 n. 5
Loar, Brian 86 n. 15, 173 n. 1, 191, 192, 194, 214 n. 3
Locke, John 8, 18 n. 9, 151
López de Sa, Dan 15, n. 1, 18 n. 10, 39 n. 5, 50, 60 n. 8, 77, 118
Loux, Michael 107, 121 n. 20
Lowe, E. J. 15 n. 1, 17 n. 8, 106, 133, 142, 146 n. 10, 146 n. 13
Lucretius 151
Ludlow, Peter 40 n. 8

Macbeth, Danielle 38 n. 3, 50, 117 n. 2
Macdonald, Cynthia, 173 n. 1, 192
Mackie, J. L. 212
Mackie, Penelope 48, 60 n. 5, 146 n. 10
Madden, see Harré and Madden
Magee, Bryan 212
Maier, Emar 61 n. 9
Maitra, Keya 60 n. 7
Mandik, Pete and Weisberg, Josh 164, 180
Margalit, Avishai 142
Marras, Ausonio 175 n. 9, 180, 191, 192
Martí, Genoveva 33, 39 n. 5, 66, 83 n. 1, 90, 107, 117 n. 1, 118 n. 2, 129, 134, 146 n. 10
Martí, Genoveva and Martínez, José 39 n. 5, 41 n. 9, 50, 64, 90
Martínez, see Martí
materialism: see causal-interactions argument for materialism; eliminativism; evidential gaps; functionalism; induction; Kripke; multiple realizability; rationalism; scientific necessitarianism; skeptical argument against psychophysical identities; supervenience; token materialism; two-dimensionalism
Matson, Wallace 193, 212
May, Robert 64, 84 n. 7, 85 n. 12
McCaffery, Stephan 145–6 n. 9
McDougall, William 209
McGinn, Colin 173–4 n. 2, 199
McKenna, Michael 50
meanings:
  not what rigidity keeps constant 36–7, 57
  fine-grained and coarse-grained 41 n. 10, 120 n. 18
meaning postulates 85 n. 13
McLaughlin, see Hill and McLaughlin
Medawar, P. B. and Medawar, J. S. 210
mediating categories 184, 190, 215 n. 7
Mellor, D. H. 106, 142, 157
Melnyk, Andrew 175 n. 7, 180
Menzel, Christopher 4, 80, 81, 86 n. 19, 88 n. 23, 107
metaphysical extension, see extensions
metasemantics 60 n. 7, 193, 214–15 n. 6
methodological principles 179–80, 186–90
Michel, see Leonhard, Michel, and Prien
Mill, John Stuart 20 n. 13, 64, 68, 69, 70, 84 n. 6, 84 n. 7, 84 n. 8, 84 n. 9, 206
  on applying 64, 69, 70, 84 n. 6, n. 8
  on naming 69, 70
  see also direct reference; property designators
Miller, Richard B. 191
modal rationalism, see rationalism
modes of a physiological event 162
Moffett, Marc 194
Molnar, George 216 n. 13
Mondadori, Fabrizio 20 n. 13, 85 n. 12, 86 n. 19, 107
Mönnich, see Bealer and Mönnich
Mueller, Axel 61 n. 9
multiple realizability 154–7; see also theoretical identity statements—realizer
Mumford, Stephen 146 n. 10, 216 n. 13
Musacchio, José M. 154, 173 n. 1

Nagel, Thomas 166, 173 n. 1, 174 n. 1
name-like terms 8, 96, 98, 131; see also compositionality; descriptivism; reference fixing
natural-kind designators, see artificial-property designators; properties
natural-property designators, see artificial-property designators; properties
nature, see essence
Neale, Stephen 40, 83 n. 3, 83 n. 4
necessary and sufficient conditions, see necessity

necessity:
    dispositional 200, 216–17 n. 13, 217 n. 14
    of identity statements and identification statements 92–106, 109–10
        on account of rigidity 1–10, 13, 16 n. 2, 19 n. 11, 48–9, 66, 67, 93–5, 100
            contrasted with contingency, see rigid designators
            without rigidity 42–3
    of non-identity statements, see essential-property attributing statements
    physical necessity, see fatalism; laws; scientific necessitaritanism
    what rigidity is necessary, as opposed to sufficient for, see essence
    see also aposteriority; evidential gaps; General Principle; rigid designators; rigid–nonrigid distinction; scientific necessitarianism; supervenience; theoretical identity statements
neuroscience, see functionalism; multiple realizability
neutrality:
    with respect to whether concrete-object designators are predicative 83–4 n. 5
    with respect to whether kinds are properties, see properties
    with respect to whether names are rigid 45, 59 n. 2
    with respect to whether terms in necessary statements are rigid, see General Principle
    of rigid–nonrigid distinction for property designators
        with respect to pragmatics vs. semantics 40 n. 8
        with respect to whether properties are nameable 89–90, 116
        with respect to nominalism and selective realism 28, 38 n. 1, 83 n. 5, 91, 106–7, 116, 117 n. 1, 146 n. 13, 215 n. 8
    see also essences; rigid designators—for concrete objects
Newton, Isaac 203, 217 n. 15
Nimtz, Christian 175 n. 9
Noble, Denis 210
nominalism 38 n. 1, 89–90, 91, 106–10
nonrigid designators, see necessity; rigid–nonrigid distinction; rigid designators
Noonan, Harold 6
Northoff, see Heinzel and Northoff

Oderberg, David S. 122 n. 26
office persons, see persisting officers
offices as designata 36
Okasha, Samir 60 n. 5

Oliver, Alex 70
Olmsted, J. M. D. and Olmsted, E. Harris 211
origins, essential 44
Orlando, Eleonora 52, 114

Page, Don 180, 205, 206
Pagin P. see Glüer, K.
pain, see Kripke; skeptical argument against psychophysical identities
Papineau, David 149, 150, 151, 154, 173 n. 1, 175 n. 9, 191, 192
Pargetter, see Jackson, Pargetter, and Prior
parsimony, see methodological principles
Patterson, Sarah 151, 154, 173 n. 2, 180, 192
Perry, John 215 n. 7
persisting officers 27–8, 35–6, 188–9, 192
Peterson, Philip L. 21 n. 16, 84 n. 7, 85 n. 1
physicalism, see materialism
Plantinga, Alvin 4, 18 n. 9, 48, 62 n. 11, 63 n. 12, 107, 139, 140, 144 n. 2, 172, 217 n. 15, 218 n. 16
Polcyn, Karol 154
Polger, Thomas 145 n. 6, 154, 173 n. 1
possible-world semantics, see meanings, properties
pragmatics 40 n. 8, 126, 127, 145 n. 9; see also two-dimensionalism
predicative use of 'is' 69, 70–1, 73, 75, 76, 78–9, 86–7 n. 20, 87 n. 21
    vis-à-vis 'exemplifies' 78–9, 86 n. 19, 87 n. 21
predicative terms, see general terms
Prez, see persisting officers
Prien, Bernd 61 n. 9
Prior, see Jackson, Pargetter, and Prior
privileged insider's perspective 164–70, 175 n. 6, 177–9, 183–5
problematic theoretical identity statements, see theoretical identity statements—problematic
properties:
    allegedly distinct from kinds 1, 7, 17 n. 8
    fine-grained and coarse-grained 41 n. 10, 107, 120 n. 18, 194–5, 214 n. 4, 216 n. 10
    see also eliminativism; neutrality; property designators
property designators:
    distinguished from predicates 86 n. 15, 86–7 n. 20
    dual function as general terms and singular terms 87 n. 21; see also this entry—uniformly singular treatments
    dualistic treatment of property designators according to which it is either exclusively singular or exclusively predicative 64–5, 68–74, 79, 82, 87–8 n. 22, 89–90
predicables, see general terms

uniformly predicative treatments 21 n. 15, 82, 83 n. 4, 83–4 n. 5, 89–123
uniformly singular treatments of 20 n. 13, 64–88, 89, 118 n. 3
    as first-order terms 74–82
    as higher-order terms 74–5, 78–82, 86–7 n. 20, 87 n. 21, 117 n. 2; *see also* type theory
    see also Carnap; formalization; general terms; identification statements; properties; rigid designators; rigid–nonrigid distinction; singular terms
propositions, as opposed to statements, *see* pragmatics
psychophysical identities, *see* eliminativism; evidential gaps; functionalism; induction; Kripke; multiple realizability; rationalism; scientific necessitarianism; skeptical argument against psychophysical identities; supervenience; theoretical identity statements—problematic; token materialism; two-dimensionalism
Putnam, Hilary 5, 10, 17 n. 6, 39 n. 4, 49, 50, 51, 52, 53, 60 n. 7, 128, 141, 172, 198, 202, 218 n. 17

Quine, W. V. 72, 84 n. 6, 84 n. 8, 85 n. 11, 86 n. 15, 100, 121 n. 19, 121 n. 20

Randall, Lisa 205
rationalism 150, 171–2, 211–12; *see also* scientific necessitarianism
Rea, Michael 162
Read, Rupert and Sharrock, Wes 57
realism:
    about pains, *see* privileged insider's perspective
    about properties, *see* neutrality
recognitional theories 190–2, 214–15 n. 6
Redhead, Michael 204, 206, 207
Rees, Martin 205, 207
reference, *see* compositionality; descriptivism; designation; direct reference; name-like terms; recognitional theories; reference fixing
reference fixing 21 n. 16, 136, 139
Richard, Mark 54
relativity theory, general and special, *see* explanation
rigid application, *see* essential application
rigid designators:
    for concrete objects not controversial 15 n. 1, 44, 56
    de facto 61 n. 9, 65–6, 133, 135, 137–39, 145 n. 9
    de jure 61 n. 9, 66, 133, 135, 137, 139–41, 145–46 n. 9

obstinately rigid, strongly rigid, etc. 3–4, 16 n. 2, 58 n. 1, 59 n. 3, 83 n. 3, 119 n. 7, 122 n. 24
    for properties:
        controversial 1
        left unsettled by Kripke 15 n. 1
        as contrasted with nonrigid designators for properties 13, 23, 72–3, 75, 91, 94–101, 103, 108
    rigid readings of apparently nonrigid descriptions 41 n. 9; *see also* shadowing
    see also essential-property attributing statements; persisting officers; rigid–nonrigid distinction
rigid–nonrigid distinction:
    bearing for theoretical identity statements 11, 13–15, 45–6, 96–8, 109–10, 114, 120 n. 18, 214 n. 1
    central roles for 42, 52–3, 57–8, 97, 103, 111, 114, 124; *see also* this entry—for property designators; essence
    for designators in general 2–4, 82–3 n. 1, 144 n. 3
    for predicates as opposed to property designators 86 n. 15 and n. 17, 117 n. 2, 118 n. 3; *see also* identification statements
    for property designators:
        a genuine distinction 13, 21 n. 16, 22–41, 58, 85 n. 11
        genuinely rigid–nonrigid by virtue of roles executed 13–14, 38, 42–63
    for merely predicative property designators 14, 82, 118 n. 2
    neutral with respect to metaphysical and other questions, *see* neutrality
    see also artificial-; descriptions; property designators; shadowing; trivialization
    significant for what it is necessary for and for what it is sufficient for 45, 101
    whether threatened by a Russellian treatment of descriptions 65–8, 82
    uniform treatments of the distinction vis-à-vis dualist treatments 14, 64–5, 89, 98–100; *see also* property designators
    see also descriptions; essential application; general terms; necessity; rigid designators; singular terms
rigidification, *see* descriptions—world-indexed descriptions
Roberts, John 132
Robertson, Teresa 54, 117 n. 2, 146 n. 10
role, assigned to rigidity as its essential work, *see* descriptivism; rigid–nonrigid distinction
Ross, Don and Spurrett, David 157
Rubin, Michael 117 n. 2, 199 n. 9
Russell, Bertrand 5, 6, 16 n. 3, 17 n. 6, 17 n. 7, 55, 65, 67, 83 n. 2, 83 n. 4, 99, 146 n. 9

Sainsbury, Mark 45
Salmon, Nathan 4, 5, 13, 18 n. 10, 38 n. 1,
    53, 56, 62 n. 12, 74, 76, 85 n. 11, n. 13,
    86 n. 15, 87 n. 20, n. 21, 87–8 n. 22, 91,
    117 n. 2, 118 n. 6, 129, 133, 137, 138,
    141–2, 144 n. 3, 146 n. 10, n. 11, 215 n. 6
schm-entities 197–9, 216 n. 11, n. 12, 217 n. 15
Schnieder, Benjamin 18 n. 10, 70, 85 n. 12,
    87 n. 21, 117 n. 2, 118 n. 2
Schramm, David 204
Schrenk, Markus 204, 217 n. 15
Schwartz, Steven P. 4, 11, 23, 27, 36, 38 n. 3,
    39 n. 4, 39 n. 5, 42–3, 50, 51, 52, 59 n. 4,
    60 n. 5, 60 n. 7, 61 n. 9, 90, 91, 117 n. 1,
    117 n. 2, 119 n. 9, 146 n. 10
scientific necessitarianism 152, 168, 169,
    173 n. 1, 176, 193–213, 214 n. 3; *see also*
    laws; rationalism; schm-entities
Searle, John 209, 211
second-order languages, *see* formalization;
    property designators
Seddon, George 199
Sellars, W. 91, 108, 121 n. 20
semantic extension, *see* extensions
semantics, *see* grammar; metasemantics;
    pragmatics; two-dimensionalism
Senderowicz, Yaron 179
shadowing problem 25–36, 39 n. 3, 39–40 n. 5
Sharrock, W., *see* Read, R.
Shoemaker, Sydney 60 n. 5, 161, 193, 194, 196
Sidelle, Alan 27, 28, 60 n. 5, 62 n. 11, 84 n. 8,
    118 n. 2, 140, 155, 197, 212
Simchen, O. 144 n. 2
simplicity, *see* methodological principles
singular terms:
    first order vs. second order, *see* property
        designators
    genuinely-, by placement in identity
        statements 20–1 n. 15, 58, 65, 69, 72, 93
    grammatically 12–13, 21 n. 15, 58, 64, 69, 89
    property designators as, on best-case
        scenario 12–14, 74, 89, 90
    property designators as, on Kripke's
        understanding 12, 20–1 n. 15
    and Russellian treatment of definite
        descriptions, *see* descriptions; rigid–
        nonrigid distinction—whether
    see also descriptions; designation; extension;
        general terms; Mill, necessity—of
        identity statements—on account of
        rigidity; property designators; rigid–
        nonrigid distinction
skeptical argument against psychophysical
    identities 9–11, 19–20 n. 12, 96–7, 98,
    110, 120 n. 18, 123 n. 28, 145 n. 6,
    148–218; *see also* eliminativism; evidential
    gaps; functionalism; induction; Kripke;
    multiple realizability; rationalism;
    scientific necessitarianism; supervenience;
    token materialism; two-dimensionalism
Smith, Quentin 216, n. 13
Soames, Scott 5, 16 n. 4, 17 n. 8, 21 n. 15,
    38–9 n. 3, 39 n. 5, 43, 47, 59 n. 5,
    62 n. 12, 64, 68, 74, 84 n. 7, 85 n. 12,
    86 n. 15, 86 n. 17, 86 n. 19, 91, 101–2,
    111, 117–18 n. 2, 119 n. 10, 112 n.
    24, 128, 129, 131, 144 n. 3, 172, 215 n. 7
Sosa, David 45, 55, 61 n. 9, 62 n. 11
spatio–temporal-path sharing, *see* correlation
species terms, *see* Brontosaurus
Sprevak, Mark 165
Spurrett, David 157
Stalnaker, Robert C. 172, 193
Stamos, David N. 90
Stanford, P. Kyle and Kitcher, Philip 190
Stanley, Jason 4, 40 n. 8, 51, 60 n. 7, 61 n. 9,
    139, 140, 215 n. 6
Stanley and Szabó 40 n. 8
statements, as opposed to propositions,
    see pragmatics
Sterelny, Kim 62 n. 12, 172, 190, 191
Steward, Helen 60 n. 5, 133, 134, 142,
    146 n. 10
stipulation, *see* English-like refined languages;
    Kripke
Stjernfelt, *see* Emmeche, Køppe, and Stjernfelt
strong necessity, *see* rigid designators—
    obstinately rigid
strong rigidity, *see* rigid designators—obstinately
    rigid
subject terms of theoretical identity statements,
    see name-like terms
substances, *see* chemicals
Sullivan, Arthur 36, 39 n. 5, 120 n. 17, 129
supervenience 154–5, 157–61
Swinburne, Richard 41 n. 9
Swoyer, Chris 17 n. 8, 70, 80, 84 n. 8, 84 n. 9,
    85 n. 13, 107, 120 n. 18
syntax, *see grammar*
Szabó, Zoltán, *see* Stanley and Szabó

Ter Meulen, Alice 64
theoretical expressions:
    as compositional 61 n. 10, 139–41; *see also*
        compositionality
    as descriptions 132
    informative 126–7, 136–7, 139
    as opposed to name-like terms 8, 96, 98
    see also theoretical identity statements
theoretical identity statements:
    characterized in relation to essence 8, 132,
        134, 136–7, 139, 144 n. 4
    about concrete objects 8, 19 n. 11
    problematic or unconfirmable 181–90,
        195–213, 214 n. 3, 216 n. 10; *see also*
        de jure; mediating

realizer functionalists' recognition of 174–5 n. 6
subject terms in, *see* name-like terms
see also essentialism; evidential gaps; multiple realizability; skeptical argument against psychophysical identities; rigid–nonrigid distinction; supervenience; theoretical expressions; token materialism
theory of everything, *see* final theory
T'Hooft, Gerard et al. 205
Thomason, Richmond H. 107
Tobin, *see* Bird and Tobin
token materialism 123 n. 28, n. 29, 154–5, 157–8, 160–3
triplestatestuff, *see* theoretical identity statements—problematic
trivialization problems 93
 allegedly attending my predicative account of rigidity 100, 103–6
 allegedly attending rigidity in general 125–6
 see also artificial-property designators; rigid–nonrigid distinction; shadowing
two-dimensionalism 170–1, 175 n. 9
Tye, Michael 18 n. 10, 21 n. 16, 85 n. 12, 156, 191
type identity, *see* multiple realizability; supervenience; token materialism
type theory 80–1, 87 n. 21
Twain, Mark, *see* correlation

uniform treatments, *see* designation; formalization; property designators; rigid–nonrigid distinction

Van Brakel, J. 50
Vander Laan, David A. 41 n. 10
Van Gulick, Robert 153
Van Inwagen, Peter 217 n. 15
Venus' origins 6–7, 8
verbs 76–7
vitalism 209–11

Wald, David J. 86 n. 15
warrant, *see* theoretical identity statements—problematic
weak necessity, *see* rigid designators—obstinately rigid
weak rigidity, *see* rigid designators—obstinately rigid
Webb, *see* Barrow and Webb
Weinberg, Steven 205, 207
Weisberg, Josh 153
Wheeler, L. R. 211
Wiggins, David 69, 78, 86 n. 15
Wilson, Jessica 201
Witmer, D. Gene 126
Wöhler, Friedrich 209
Wolf, Michael P. 57, 129
Wolter, Lynsey 129
Wolterstorff, Nicholas 70
world indexing, *see* descriptions—world-indexed descriptions
Wright, Crispin 64, 69, 78, 80, 84 n. 8

Zalta, Edward N. 60 n. 5